The number *seven* is the basis of all these mysteries. We have already seen how the holy Church came to introduce the season of Septuagesima into her calendar. Let us now meditate on the doctrine hidden under the symbols of her liturgy. And first, let us listen to St. Augustine, who thus gives us the clue to the whole of our season's mysteries. 'There are two times,' says the holy Doctor: 'one which is *now*, and is spent in the temptations and tribulations of this life; the other which shall be *then*, and shall be spent in eternal security and joy. In figure of these, we celebrate two periods: the time before Easter, and the time after Easter. That which is before Easter signifies the sorrow of this present life; that which is after Easter, the blessedness of our future state. . . . Hence it is that we spend the first in fasting and prayer; and in the second we give up our fasting, and give ourselves to praise.'[1]

The Church, the interpreter of the sacred Scriptures, often speaks to us of two places, which correspond with these two times of St. Augustine. These two places are Babylon and Jerusalem. Babylon is the image of this world of sin, in the midst whereof the Christian has to spend his years of probation; Jerusalem is the heavenly country, where he is to repose after all his trials. The people of Israel, whose whole history is but one great type of the human race, was banished from Jerusalem and kept in bondage in Babylon.

Now, this captivity, which kept the Israelites exiles from Sion, lasted seventy years; and it is to express this mystery, as Alcuin, Amalarius, Ivo of Chartres, and all the great liturgists tell us, that the Church fixed the number of seventy for the days of expiation. It is true, there are but sixty-three days between Septuagesima and Easter; but the

[1] Enarrations; Ps. cxlviii.

Church, according to the style so continually used
in the sacred Scriptures, uses the round number
instead of the literal and precise one.

The duration of the world itself, according to the
ancient Christian tradition, is divided into seven
ages. The human race must pass through seven
ages before the dawning of the day of eternal life.
The first age included the time from the creation of
Adam to Noah; the second begins with Noah and
the renovation of the earth by the deluge, and ends
with the vocation of Abraham; the third opens
with this first formation of God's chosen people,
and continues as far as Moses, through whom God
gave the Law; the fourth consists of the period
between Moses and David, in whom the house of
Juda received the kingly power; the fifth is formed
of the years which passed between David's reign
and the captivity of Babylon, inclusively; the sixth
dates from the return of the Jews to Jerusalem, and
takes us on as far as the birth of our Saviour.
Then, finally, comes the seventh age; it starts with
the rising of this merciful Redeemer, the Sun of
justice, and is to continue till the dread coming of
the Judge of the living and the dead. These are
the seven great divisions of time; after which,
eternity.

In order to console us in the midst of the combats,
which so thickly beset our path, the Church, like a
beacon shining amidst the darkness of this our
earthly abode, shows us another seven, which is to
succeed the one we are now preparing to pass
through. After the Septuagesima of mourning, we
shall have the bright Easter with its seven weeks
of gladness, foreshadowing the happiness and bliss
of heaven. After having fasted with our Jesus, and
suffered with Him, the day will come when we shall
rise together with Him, and our hearts shall follow
Him to the highest heavens; and then after a brief

interval, we shall feel the Holy Ghost descending
upon us, with His seven Gifts. The celebration of
all these wondrous joys will take us seven weeks,
as the great liturgists observe in their interpretation of the rites of the Church. The seven joyous
weeks from Easter to Pentecost will not be too long
for the future glad mysteries, which, after all, will
be but figures of a still gladder future, the future of
eternity.

Having heard these sweet whisperings of hope,
let us now bravely face the realities brought before
us by our dear mother the Church. We are
sojourners upon this earth ; we are exiles and captives in Babylon, that city which plots our ruin.
If we love our country, if we long to return to it,
we must be proof against the lying allurements of
this strange land, and refuse the cup she proffers
us, and with which she maddens so many of our
fellow captives. She invites us to join in her feasts
and her songs ; but we must unstring our harps,
and hang them on the willows that grow on her
river's bank, till the signal be given for our return
to Jerusalem.[1] She will ask us to sing to her the
melodies of our dear Sion : but how shall we, who
are so far from home, have heart to ' sing the song
of the Lord in a strange land '?[2] No, there must
be no sign that we are content to be in bondage, or
we shall deserve to be slaves for ever.

These are the sentiments wherewith the Church
would inspire us during the penitential season
which we are now beginning. She wishes us to
reflect on the dangers that beset us; dangers which
arise from ourselves and from creatures. During
the rest of the year she loves to hear us chant the
song of heaven, the sweet *Alleluia;* but now, she
bids us close our lips to this word of joy, because
we are in Babylon. We are pilgrims absent from

[1] Ps. cxxv.   [2] Ps. cxxxvi.

our Lord':[1] let us keep our glad hymn for the day
of His return. We are sinners, and have but too
often held fellowship with the world of God's
enemies ; let us become purified by repentance, for
it is written that 'praise is unseemly in the mouth
of a sinner.'[2]

The leading feature, then, of Septuagesima, is the
total suspension of the *Alleluia*, which is not to be
again heard upon the earth until the arrival of that
happy day, when, having suffered death with our
Jesus, and having been buried together with Him,
we shall rise again with Him to a new life.[3]

The sweet hymn of the angels, *Gloria in excelsis
Deo*, which we have sung every Sunday since the
birth of our Saviour in Bethlehem, is also taken
from us; it is only on the feasts of the saints which
may be kept during the week that we shall be
allowed to repeat it. The night Office of the Sunday
is to lose also, from now till Easter, its magnificent
Ambrosian hymn, the *Te Deum;* and at the end of
the holy Sacrifice, the deacon will no longer dismiss the faithful with his solemn *Ite, Missa est,* but
will simply invite them to continue their prayers in
silence, and *bless the Lord,* the God of mercy, who
bears with us, notwithstanding all our sins.

After the Gradual of the Mass, instead of the
thrice repeated *Alleluia*, which prepared our hearts
to listen to the voice of God in the holy Gospel, we
shall hear but a mournful and protracted chant,
called, on that account, the Tract.

That the eye, too, may teach us that the season
we are entering on is one of mourning, the Church
will vest her ministers (both on Sundays and on
the days during the week which are not feasts of
saints) in the sombre purple. Until Ash Wednesday, however, she permits the deacon to wear his
dalmatic, and the subdeacon his tunic ; but from

[1] 2 Cor. v. 6.   [2] Ecclus. xv. 9.   [3] Col. ii. 12.

that day forward, they must lay aside these vestments of joy, for Lent will then have begun, and our holy mother will inspire us with the deep spirit of penance, by suppressing everything of that glad pomp, which she loves, at other seasons, to bring into the sanctuary of her God.

CHAPTER THE THIRD

PRACTICE DURING SEPTUAGESIMA

THE joys of Christmastide seem to have fled far from us. The forty days of gladness brought us by the birth of our Emmanuel are gone. The atmosphere of holy Church has grown overcast, and we are warned that the gloom is still to thicken. Have we, then, for ever lost Him whom we so anxiously and longingly sighed after during the four slow weeks of our Advent? Has our divine Sun of justice, that rose so brightly in Bethlehem, now stopped His course, and left our guilty earth?

Not so. The Son of God, the Child of Mary, has not left us. The Word was made Flesh in order that He might dwell among us. A glory far greater than that of His birth, when angels sang their hymns, awaits Him, and we are to share it with Him. Only, He must win this new and greater glory by strange, countless sufferings; He must purchase it by a most cruel and ignominious death: and we, if we would have our share in the triumph of His Resurrection, must follow Him in the way of the cross, all wet with the tears and the Blood He shed for us.

The grave, maternal voice of the Church will soon be heard, inviting us to the lenten penance; but she wishes us to prepare for this ' laborious baptism,' by employing these three weeks in con-

sidering the deep wounds caused in our souls by
sin. True, the beauty and loveliness of the little
Child born to us in Bethlehem, are great beyond
measure; but our souls are so needy that they
require other lessons than those He gave us of
humility and simplicity. Our Jesus is the Victim
of the divine justice, and He has now attained the
fullness of His age; the altar, on which He has to
be slain, is ready: and since it is for us that He is
to be sacrificed, we should at once set ourselves to
consider what are the debts we have contracted
towards that infinite justice, which is about to
punish the innocent One instead of us the guilty.

The mystery of a God becoming Incarnate for
the love of His creature, has opened to us the path
of the *illuminative way;* but we have not yet seen
the brightest of its light. Let not our hearts be
troubled; the divine wonders we witnessed at
Bethlehem are to be surpassed by those that are
to grace the day of our Jesus' triumph: but,
that our eye may contemplate these future mysteries, it must be purified by courageously looking
into the deep abyss of our own personal miseries.
God will grant us His divine light for the discovery;
and if we come to know ourselves, to understand
the grievousness of original sin, to see the malice
of our own sins, and to comprehend, at least in
some degree, the infinite mercy of God towards us,
we shall be prepared for the holy expiations of
Lent, and for the ineffable joys of Easter.

The season, then, of Septuagesima is one of most
serious thought. Perhaps we could not better show
the sentiments, wherewith the Church would have
her children to be filled at this period of her year,
than by quoting a few words from the eloquent ex-
hortation, given to his people, at the beginning of
Septuagesima, by the celebrated Ivo of Chartres.
He spoke thus to the faithful of the eleventh cen-

tury:[1] ' "We know," says the apostle, "that every
creature groaneth, and travaileth in pain even till
now: and not only it, but ourselves, also, who
have the first-fruits of the Spirit, even we ourselves
groan within ourselves, waiting for the adoption of
the sons of God, the redemption of our body."[2]
The creature here spoken of is the soul, that has
been regenerated from the corruption of sin unto
the likeness of God: she groaneth within herself,
at seeing herself made subject to vanity; she, like
one that travaileth, is filled with pain, and is
devoured by an anxious longing to be in that
country, which is still so far off. It was this
travail and pain that the psalmist was suffering,
when he exclaimed: "Woe is me, that my sojourn-
ing is prolonged!"[3] Nay, that apostle, who was
one of the first members of the Church, and had
received the holy Spirit, longed to have, in all its
reality, that adoption of the sons of God, which he
already had in hope; and he, too, thus exclaimed
in his pain: "I desire to be dissolved and to be with
Christ."[4] . . . During these days, therefore, we
must do what we do at all seasons of the year, only
we must do it more earnestly and fervently: we
must sigh and weep after our country, from which
we were exiled in consequence of having indulged
in sinful pleasures; we must redouble our efforts
in order to regain it by compunction and weeping
of heart. . . . Let us now shed tears in the way,
that we may afterwards be glad in our country.
Let us now so run the race of this present life, that
we may make sure of "the prize of the supernal
vocation."[5] Let us not be like imprudent way-
farers, forgetting our country, and preferring our
banishment to our home. Let us not become like
those senseless invalids, who feel not their ailments,

---

[1] Twelfth Sermon for Septuagesima. [2] Rom. viii. 22, 23.
[3] Ps. cxix.   [4] Phil. i. 23.   [5] *Ibid.*, iii. 14.

and seek no remedy.   We despair of a sick man
who will not be persuaded that he is in danger.
No: let us run to our Lord, the physician of eternal
salvation.   Let us show Him our wounds, and cry
out to Him with all our earnestness: "Have mercy
on me, O Lord, for I am weak : heal me, for my
bones are troubled."[1]   Then will He forgive us our
iniquities, heal us of our infirmities, and satisfy our
desire with good things.'[2]

From all this it is evident that the Christian,
who would spend Septuagesima according to the
spirit of the Church, must make war upon that
false security, that self-satisfaction, which are so
common to effeminate and tepid souls, and produce
spiritual barrenness.   It is well for them, if these
delusions do not insensibly lead them to the
absolute loss of the true Christian spirit.   He that
thinks himself dispensed from that continual watch-
fulness, which is so strongly inculcated by our
divine Master,[3] is already in the enemy's' power.
He that feels no need of combat and of struggle in
order to persevere and make progress in virtue
(unless he have been honoured with a privilege,
which is both rare and dangerous), should fear that
he is not even on the road to that kingdom of God,
which is only to be won by violence.[4]   He that
forgets the sins which God's mercy has forgiven
him, should fear lest he be the victim of a dangerous
delusion.[5]   Let us, during these days which we are
going to devote to the honest unflinching contemplation of our miseries, give glory to our God, and
derive from the knowledge of ourselves fresh
motives of confidence in Him, who, in spite of all
our wretchedness and sin, humbled Himself so low
as to become one of us, in order that He might
exalt us even to union with Himself.

[1] Ps. vi. 3.   [2] Ps. cii. 3, 5.   [3] St. Mark xiii. 37.
[4] St. Matt. xi. 12.   [5] Ecclus. v. 5.

CHAPTER THE FOURTH

MORNING AND NIGHT PRAYERS FOR SEPTUAGESIMA

DURING the season of Septuagesima, the Christian, on awaking in the morning, should unite himself with the Church, who, at the first dawn of day, begins her Psalms of Lauds with these words of the royal prophet:

Miserere mei Deus, secundum magnam misericordiam tuam.	Have mercy on me, O God, according to thy great mercy.

He should, after this, profoundly adore that great God, before whom the sinner should tremble, but whom he fears not to offend, as though deserving neither reverence nor love. It is with this deep sentiment of holy fear, that he must perform the first acts of religion, both interior and exterior, wherewith he begins each day of this present season. The time for morning prayer being come, he may use the following method, which is formed upon the very prayers of the Church:

MORNING PRAYERS

First, praise and adoration of the most holy Trinity:

V. Benedicamus Patrem et Filium, cum Sancto Spiritu:	*V.* Let us bless the Father and the Son, and the Holy Ghost.
R. Laudemus et superexaltemus eum in sæcula.	*R.* Let us praise him and extol him above all, for ever.
V. Gloria Patri et Filio, et Spiritui Sancto;	*V.* Glory be to the Father, and to the Son, and to the Holy Ghost.
R. Sicut erat in principio, et nunc et semper, et in sæcula sæculorum. Amen.	*R.* As it was in the beginning, is now and ever shall be, world without end. Amen.

Then, praise to our Lord and Saviour, Jesus Christ:

V. Adoramus te, Christe, et benedicimus tibi.

R. Quia per sanctam crucem tuam redemisti mundum.

V. We adore thee, O Christ, and we bless thee.

R. Because by thy holy cross thou hast redeemed the world.

Thirdly, invocation of the Holy Ghost:

Veni, Sancte Spiritus, reple tuorum corda fidelium, et tui amoris in eis ignem accende.

Come, O Holy Spirit, fill the hearts of thy faithful, and enkindle within them the fire of thy love.

After these fundamental acts of religion, recite the Lord's Prayer, begging your heavenly Father to be mindful of His infinite mercy and goodness; to forgive you your trespasses; to come to your assistance in the temptations and dangers which so thickly beset the path of this life; and finally, to deliver you from evil, by removing from you every remnant of sin, which is the great evil, the evil that offends God, and entails the sovereign evil of man himself.

THE LORD'S PRAYER

Pater noster, qui es in cœlis, sanctificetur nomen tuum : adveniat regnum tuum : fiat voluntas tua sicut in cœlo, et in terra. Panem nostrum quotidianum da nobis hodie : et dimitte nobis debita nostra, sicut et nos dimittimus debitoribus nostris : et ne nos inducas in tentationem : sed libera nos a malo. Amen.

Our Father, who art in heaven, hallowed be thy name: thy kingdom come: thy will be done on earth as it is in heaven. Give us this day our daily bread; and *forgive us our trespasses*, as we forgive them that trespass against us : and lead us not into temptation: but deliver us from evil. Amen.

Then address our blessed Lady, using the words of the angelical salutation. Pray to her with confidence and love, for she is the refuge of sinners.

THE ANGELICAL SALUTATION

Ave Maria, gratia plena, Dominus tecum; benedicta tu in mulieribus, et benedictus fructus ventris tui, Jesus.

Sancta Maria, Mater Dei, ora pro nobis peccatoribus, nunc et in hora mortis nostræ. Amen.

Hail Mary, full of grace: the Lord is with thee; blessed art thou among women, and blessed is the fruit of thy womb, Jesus.

Holy Mary, Mother of God, *pray for us sinners*, now and at the hour of our death. Amen.

After this you should recite the Creed, that is, the Symbol of faith. It contains the dogmas we are to believe; and during this season you should dwell with loving attention on that article, which is so full of hope, *the forgiveness of sins*. Let us do our utmost to merit, by our sincere conversion and amendment of our lives, that our Saviour, after the coming penitential forty days are over, may say to each of us those words which are so sweet to a penitent sinner: ' Go, thy sins are forgiven!'

THE APOSTLES' CREED

Credo in Deum Patrem omnipotentem, creatorem cœli et terræ. Et in Jesum Christum Filium ejus unicum, Dominum nostrum: qui conceptus est de Spiritu Sancto, natus ex Maria Virgine, passus sub Pontio Pilato, crucifixus, mortuus, et sepultus: descendit ad inferos, tertia die resurrexit a mortuis: ascendit ad cœlos, sedet ad dexteram Dei Patris omnipotentis: inde venturus est judicare vivos et mortuos.

Credo in Spiritum Sanctum, sanctam Ecclesiam Catholicam, sanctorum com-

I believe in God the Father almighty, Creator of heaven and earth. And in Jesus Christ, his only Son our Lord, who was conceived by the Holy Ghost, born of the Virgin Mary; suffered under Pontius Pilate, was crucified, dead, and buried; he descended into hell, the third day he rose again from the dead; he ascended into heaven, sitteth at the right hand of God the Father almighty; from thence he shall come to judge the living and the dead.

I believe in the Holy Ghost; the holy Catholic Church; the communion of saints, the *for-*

2

munionem, remissionem peccatorum, carnis resurrectionem, vitam æternam. Amen.

giveness of sins, the resurrection of the body, and life everlasting. Amen.

After having thus made the profession of your faith, endeavour to excite yourself to sorrow for the sins you have committed. For this purpose, recite one of the Penitential Psalms; the first on Sunday, the second on Monday, and so on with the rest. These admirable psalms, whereby David expressed his grief after he had fallen into sin, are most appropriate for the season of Septuagesima. The reader will find them at the end of this volume.

Then make a humble confession of your sins, reciting the general formula made use of by the Church.

THE CONFESSION OF SINS

Confiteor Deo omnipotenti, beatæ Mariæ semper Virgini, beato Michaeli archangelo, beato Joanni Baptistæ, sanctis apostolis Petro et Paulo, et omnibus sanctis, quia peccavi nimis cogitatione, verbo, et opere : mea culpa, mea culpa, mea maxima culpa. Ideo precor beatam Mariam semper Virginem, beatum Michaelem archangelum, beatum Joannem Baptistam, sanctos apostolos Petrum et Paulum, et omnes sanctos, orare pro me ad Dominum Deum nostrum.

Misereatur nostri omnipotens Deus, et dimissis peccatis nostris, perducat nos ad vitam æternam. Amen.

Indulgentiam, absolutionem, et remissionem pecca-

I confess to almighty God, to blessed Mary ever Virgin, to blessed Michael the archangel, to blessed John the Baptist, to the holy apostles Peter and Paul, and to all the saints, that I have sinned exceedingly in thought, word, and deed; through my fault, through my fault, through my most grievous fault. Therefore I beseech the blessed Mary ever Virgin, blessed Michael the archangel, blessed John the Baptist, the holy apostles Peter and Paul, and all the saints, to pray to the Lord our God for me.

May almighty God have mercy on us, and, our sins being forgiven, bring us to life everlasting. Amen.

May the almighty and merciful Lord grant us pardon,

torum nostrorum tribuat
nobis omnipotens et misericors Dominus.   Amen.

absolution, and remission of our
sins.   Amen.

This is the proper time for making your meditation, as no doubt you practise this holy exercise.
During Septuagesima, the subject of our meditation
ought mainly to be the evils brought on man by
original sin; the necessity of an untiring resistance
against our corrupt nature, whose tendencies and
inclinations would lead us to destruction ; the
grievousness of actual sin, how it robs us of countless blessings, and exposes us to punishments both
here and hereafter; the ineffable goodness of God,
who comes Himself to offer reconciliation to the
sinner, and who, after the salutary mournfulness
and the works of penance of the weeks of Septuagesima and Lent, will give all the joy, peace, and
blessing of a new life in our risen Jesus.

The next part of your morning prayer must be
to ask of God, by the following prayers, grace to
avoid every kind of sin during the day you are just
beginning.   Say, then, with the Church, whose
prayers must always be preferred to all others :

V. Domine, exaudi ora-
tionem meam.

R. Et clamor meus ad te
veniat.

V. O Lord, hear my prayer,

R. And let my cry come
unto thee.

OREMUS.

Domine, Deus omnipotens,
qui ad principium hujus diei
nos pervenire fecisti, tua nos
hodie salva virtute, ut in hac
die ad nullum declinemus
peccatum, sed semper ad
tuam justitiam faciendam
nostra procedant eloquia,
dirigantur cogitationes et
opera.   Per Dominum no-

LET US PRAY.

Almighty Lord and God,
who hast brought us to the
beginning of this day, let thy
powerful grace so conduct us
through it, that we may not fall
into any sin, but that all our
thoughts, words, and actions
may be regulated according to
the rules of thy heavenly justice, and tend to the observance

strum Jesum Christum Fi-
lium tuum, qui tecum vivit
et regnat in unitate Spiritus
Sancti Deus, per omnia sæcula sæculorum. Amen.

of thy holy law. Through
Jesus Christ our Lord. Amen.

Then beg the divine assistance for the actions
of the day, that you may do them well; and say
thrice :

V. Deus, in adjutorium
meum intende.
R. Domine, ad adjuvan-
dum me festina.
V. Deus, in adjutorium
meum intende.
R. Domine, ad adjuvan-
dum me festina.
V. Deus, in adjutorium
meum intende.
R. Domine, ad adjuvan-
dum me festina.

V. Incline unto my aid,
O God.
R. O Lord, make haste to
help me.
V. Incline unto my aid,
O God.
R. O Lord, make haste to
help me.
V. Incline unto my aid,
O God.
R. O Lord, make haste to
help me.

OREMUS.

Dirigere et sanctificare,
regere et gubernare dignare,
Domine Deus, Rex cœli et
terræ, hodie corda et corpora
nostra, sensus, sermones, et
actus nostros in lege tua,
et in operibus mandatorum
tuorum, ut hic et in æternum
te auxiliante, salvi et liberi
esse mereamur, Salvator
mundi. Qui vivis et regnas
in sæcula sæculorum. Amen.

LET US PRAY.

Lord God, and King of
heaven and earth, vouchsafe
this day to rule and sanctify, to
direct and govern our souls and
bodies, our senses, words, and
actions, in conformity to thy
law, and strict obedience to thy
commands : that by the help of
thy grace, O Saviour of the
world! we may be fenced and
freed from all evils. Who livest
and reignest for ever and ever.
Amen.

During the day, you will do well to use the instructions and prayers, which you will find in this
volume, for each day of the season, both for the
Proper of the time, and the Proper of the saints.
In the evening, you may use the following prayers.

NIGHT PRAYERS

After having made the sign of the cross, let us adore that sovereign Lord, who has so mercifully preserved us during this day, and blessed us, every hour, with His grace and protection. For this end, let us recite the following hymn, which the Church sings in her Vespers of Saturday.

HYMN

Jam sol recedit igneus :
Tu lux perennis, Unitas,
Nostris, beata Trinitas,
Infunde lumen cordibus.

Te mane laudum carmine,
Te deprecamur vespere :
Digneris, ut te supplices
Laudemus inter cœlites.

Patri simulque Filio,
Tibique, Sancte Spiritus,
Sicut fuit, sit jugiter
Sæculum per omne gloria.
Amen.

V. Vespertina oratio ascendat ad te, Domine.

R. Et descendat super nos misericordia tua.

The radiant sun hath set : do thou, O light unfading, O Unity and Trinity divine, pour thy rays into our hearts.

Our morning hymns give thee praise ; our evensong implores thy mercy : Oh! grant us to be one day companions with the blessed in heaven, to give thee ceaseless praise.

To thee, O Father, Son, and Holy Ghost! may glory be, as it hath ever been, for ever and for endless ages.
Amen.

V. May our evening prayer ascend to thee, O Lord.

R. And may thy mercy descend upon us.

After this hymn, say the Our Father, Hail Mary, and Apostles' Creed, as in the morning.

Then make the examination of conscience, going over in your mind all the faults you have committed during the day. Think how great is the obstacle put by sin to the merciful designs your God would work in you ; and make a firm resolution to avoid it for the time to come, to do penance for it, and to shun the occasions which might again lead you into it.

The examination of conscience concluded, recite the *Confiteor* (or 'I confess ') with heartfelt contrition, and then give expression to your sorrow by the following act which we have taken from the venerable Cardinal Bellarmine's catechism :

ACT OF CONTRITION

O my God, I am exceedingly grieved for having offended thee, and with my whole heart I repent of the sins I have committed : I hate and abhor them above every other evil, not only because, by so sinning, I have lost heaven and deserved hell, but still more because I have offended thee, O infinite Goodness, who art worthy to be loved above all things. I most firmly resolve, by the assistance of thy grace, never more to offend thee for the time to come, and to avoid those occasions which might lead me into sin.

You may then add the acts of faith, hope, and charity, to the recitation of which Pope Benedict XIV. has granted an indulgence of seven years and seven quarantines for each time.

ACT OF FAITH

O my God, I firmly believe whatsoever the holy Catholic apostolic Roman Church requires me to believe : I believe it, because thou hast revealed it to her, thou who art the very truth.

ACT OF HOPE

O my God, knowing thy almighty power, and thy infinite goodness and mercy, I hope in thee that, by the merits of the Passion and death of our Saviour Jesus Christ, thou wilt grant me eternal life, which thou hast promised to all such as shall do the works of a good Christian ; and these I resolve to do by the help of thy grace

ACT OF CHARITY

O my God, I love thee with my whole heart and above all things, because thou art the sovereign Good : I would rather lose all things than offend thee. For thy love also, I love and desire to love my neighbour as myself.

Then say to our blessed Lady the following anthem, which the Church uses from the feast of the Purification to Easter :

ANTHEM OF THE BLESSED VIRGIN

Ave Regina cœlorum,
Ave Domina angelorum :
Salve radix, salve porta,
Ex qua mundo lux est orta;
Gaude, Virgo gloriosa,
Super omnes speciosa :
Vale, O valde decora,
Et pro nobis Christum exora.

V. Dignare me laudare te, Virgo sacrata.

R. Da mihi virtutem contra hostes tuos.

Hail Queen of heaven! Hail Lady of the angels! Hail blessed root and gate, from which came light upon the world! Rejoice, O glorious Virgin, that surpassest all in beauty! Hail, most lovely Queen! and pray to Christ for us.

V. Vouchsafe, O holy Virgin, that I may praise thee.

R. Give me power against thine enemies.

OREMUS.

Concede, misericors Deus, fragilitati nostræ præsidium : ut, qui sanctæ Dei Genitricis memoriam agimus, intercessionis ejus auxilio a nostris iniquitatibus resurgamus. Per eumdem Christum Dominum nostrum. Amen.

LET US PRAY.

Grant, O merciful God, thy protection to us in our weakness; that we who celebrate the memory of the holy Mother of God, may, through the aid of her intercession, rise again from our sins. Through the same Christ our Lord. Amen.

You would do well to add the litany of our Lady. An indulgence of three hundred days, for each time it is recited, has been granted by the Church.

THE LITANY OF THE BLESSED VIRGIN

Kyrie, eleison.
Christe, eleison.
Kyrie, eleison.
Christe, audi nos.
Christe, exaudi nos.
Pater de cœlis, Deus, miserere nobis,
Fili, Redemptor mundi, Deus, miserere nobis.
Spiritus Sancte, Deus, miserere nobis.
Sancta Trinitas, unus Deus, miserere nobis.
Sancta Maria, ora pro nobis.
Sancta Dei Genitrix,

Lord, have mercy on us.
Christ, have mercy on us.
Lord, have mercy on us.
Christ, hear us.
Christ, graciously hear us.
God the Father of heaven, have mercy on us.
God the Son, Redeemer of the world, have mercy on us.
God the Holy Ghost, have mercy on us.
Holy Trinity, one God, have mercy on us.
Holy Mary, pray for us.
Holy Mother of God,

Sancta Virgo virginum,	Holy Virgin of virgins,
Mater Christi,	Mother of Christ,
Mater divinæ gratiæ,	Mother of divine grace,
Mater purissima,	Mother most pure,
Mater castissima,	Mother most chaste,
Mater inviolata,	Mother inviolate,
Mater intemerata,	Mother undefiled,
Mater amabilis,	Mother most amiable,
Mater admirabilis,	Mother most admirable,
Mater boni consilii,	Mother of good counsel,
Mater Creatoris,	Mother of our Creator,
Mater Salvatoris,	Mother of our Redeemer,
Virgo prudentissima,	Virgin most prudent,
Virgo veneranda,	Virgin most venerable,
Virgo prædicanda,	Virgin most renowned,
Virgo potens,	Virgin most powerful,
Virgo clemens,	Virgin most merciful,
Virgo fidelis,	Virgin most faithful,
Speculum justitiæ,	Mirror of justice,
Sedes sapientiæ,	Seat of wisdom,
Causa nostræ lætitiæ,	Cause of our joy,
Vas spirituale,	Spiritual vessel,
Vas honorabile,	Vessel of honour,
Vas insigne devotionis,	Singular vessel of devotion,
Rosa mystica,	Mystical rose,
Turris Davidica,	Tower of David,
Turris eburnea,	Tower of ivory,
Domus aurea,	House of gold,
Fœderis arca,	Ark of the covenant,
Janua cœli,	Gate of heaven,
Stella matutina,	Morning star,
Salus infirmorum,	Health of the weak,
Refugium peccatorum,	Refuge of sinners,
Consolatrix afflictorum,	Comforter of the afflicted,
Auxilium Christianorum,	Help of Christians,
Regina Angelorum,	Queen of Angels,
Regina Patriarcharum,	Queen of Patriarchs,
Regina Prophetarum,	Queen of Prophets,
Regina Apostolorum,	Queen of Apostles,
Regina Martyrum,	Queen of Martyrs,
Regina Confessorum,	Queen of Confessors,
Regina Virginum,	Queen of Virgins,
Regina Sanctorum omnium,	Queen of all Saints,
Regina sine labe originali concepta,	Queen conceived without original sin,
Regina sacratissimi rosarii.	Queen of the most holy rosary.
Regina pacis,	Queen of peace,

Agnus Dei, qui tollis peccata mundi, parce nobis, Domine.

Lamb of God, who takest away the sins of the world, spare us, O Lord.

Agnus Dei, qui tollis peccata mundi, exaudi nos, Domine.

Lamb of God, who takest away the sins of the world, graciously hear us, O Lord.

Agnus Dei, qui tollis peccata mundi, miserere nobis.

Lamb of God, who takest away the sins of the world, have mercy on us.

Christe, audi nos.

Christ, hear us.

Christe, exaudi nos.

Christ, graciously hear us.

V. Ora pro nobis, sancta Dei Genitrix.

V. Pray for us, O holy Mother of God.

R. Ut digni efficiamur promissionibus Christi.

R. That we may be made worthy of the promises of Christ.

OREMUS.

LET US PRAY.

Concede nos famulos tuos quæsumus, Domine Deus, perpetua mentis et corporis sanitate gaudere : et gloriosa beatæ Mariæ semper Virginis intercessione, a præsenti liberari tristitia, et æterna perfrui lætitia. Per Christum Dominum nostrum. Amen.

Grant, O Lord, we beseech thee, that we thy servants may enjoy constant health of body and mind ; and by the glorious intercession of blessed Mary, ever a Virgin, be delivered from all present affliction, and come to that joy which is eternal. Through Christ our Lord. Amen.

Here invoke the holy angels, whose protection is, indeed, always so much needed by us, but never so much as during the hours of night. Say with the Church :

Sancti angeli, custodes nostri, defendite nos in prælio, ut non pereamus in tremendo judicio.

Holy angels, our loving guardians, defend us in the hour of battle, that we may not be lost at the dreadful judgment.

V. Angelis suis Deus mandavit de te.

V. God hath given his angels charge of thee.

R. Ut custodiant te in omnibus viis tuis.

R. That they may guard thee in all thy ways.

OREMUS.

LET US PRAY.

Deus, qui ineffabili providentia sanctos angelos tuos ad nostram custodiam mit-

O God, who in thy wonderful providence, hast been pleased to appoint thy holy angels for

tere dignaris : largire supplicibus tuis, et eorum semper protectione defendi, et
æterna societate gaudere.
Per Christum Dominum no-
strum.   Amen.

our guardians : mercifully hear
our prayers, and grant we may
rest secure under their protection, and enjoy their fellowship
in heaven for ever.   Through
Christ our Lord.   Amen.

Then beg the assistance of the saints by the following antiphon and prayer of the Church :

ANT. Sancti Dei omnes,
intercedere dignemini pro
nostra omniumque salute.

ANT. All ye saints of God,
vouchsafe to intercede for us
and for all men, that we may
be saved.

V. Lætamini in Domino
et exsultate, justi.
R. Et gloriamini omnes
recti corde.

V. Rejoice in the Lord, ye
just, and be glad.
R. And glory, all ye right of
heart.

OREMUS.

LET US PRAY.

Protege, Domine, popu-
lum tuum, et apostolorum
tuorum Petri et Pauli, et
aliorum apostolorum patro-
cinio confidentem, perpetua
defensione conserva.

Protect, O Lord, thy people ;
and because we have confidence
in the intercession of blessed
Peter and Paul and thy other
apostles, ever defend and preserve us.

Omnes sancti tui, quæsu-
mus, Domine, nos ubique
adjuvent : ut dum eorum
merita recolimus, patroci-
nia sentiamus : et pacem
tuam nostris concede tem-
poribus, et ab Ecclesia tua
cunctam repelle nequitiam :
iter, actus, et voluntates nostras, et omnium famulorum
tuorum, in salutis tuæ pro-
speritate dispone : benefactoribus nostris sempiterna
bona retribue : et omnibus
fidelibus defunctis requiem
æternam concede. Per Christum Dominum nostrum.
Amen.

May all thy saints ever help
us, we beseech thee, O Lord !
and grant that, whilst we
honour their merits, we may
experience their intercession.
Grant thy holy peace unto these
our days, and drive all iniquity
from thy Church.   Direct and
prosper unto salvation every
step, and action, and desire, of
us and of all thy servants.
Repay our benefactors with
everlasting blessings ; and grant
eternal rest to all the faithful
departed.   Through Christ our
Lord.   Amen.

And here you may add a special mention of the saints to whom you bear a particular devotion, either as your patrons or otherwise; as also of those whose feast is kept in the Church that day, or who have been at least commemorated in the Divine Office.

This done, remember the necessities of the Church suffering, and beg of God that He will give to the souls in purgatory a place of refreshment, light, and peace. For this intention recite the usual prayers.

PSALM 129

De profundis clamavi ad te, Domine : Domine, exaudi vocem meam.

Fiant aures tuæ intendentes : in vocem deprecationis meæ.

Si iniquitates observaveris, Domine : Domine, quis sustinebit ?

Quia apud te propitiatio est : et propter legem tuam sustinui te, Domine.

Sustinuit anima mea in verbo ejus : speravit anima mea in Domino.

A custodia matutina usque ad noctem : speret Israel in Domino.

Quia apud Dominum misericordia : et copiosa apud eum redemptio.

Et ipse redimet Israel : ex omnibus iniquitatibus ejus.

Requiem æternam dona eis, Domine.

Et lux perpetua luceat eis.

V. A porta inferi.

R. Erue, Domine, animas eorum.

From the depths I have cried to thee, O Lord ; Lord, hear my voice.

Let thine ears be attentive to the voice of my supplication.

If thou wilt observe iniquities, O Lord, Lord, who shall endure it ?

For with thee there is merciful forgiveness ; and by reason of thy law I have waited for thee, O Lord.

My soul hath relied on his word ; my soul hath hoped in the Lord.

From the morning watch even until night, let Israel hope in the Lord.

Because with the Lord there is mercy, and with him plentiful redemption.

And he shall redeem Israel from all his iniquities.

Eternal rest give to them, O Lord.

And let perpetual light shine upon them.

V. From the gate of hell.

R. Deliver their souls, O Lord.

V. Requiescant in pace.
R. Amen.
V. Domine, exaudi orationem meam.
R. Et clamor meus ad te veniat.

V. May they rest in peace.
R. Amen.
V. O Lord, hear my prayer.
R. And let my cry come unto thee.

OREMUS.

Fidelium Deus omnium Conditor et Redemptor, animabus famulorum famularumque tuarum remissionem cunctorum tribue peccatorum ; ut indulgentiam, quam semper optaverunt, piis supplicationibus consequantur. Qui vivis et regnas in sæcula sæculorum. Amen.

LET US PRAY.

O God, the Creator and Redeemer of all the faithful, give to the souls of thy servants departed the remission of all their sins : that through the help of pious supplications, they may obtain the pardon they have always desired. Who livest and reignest for ever and ever. Amen.

Here make a special memento of such of the faithful departed as have a particular claim upon your charity ; after which, ask of God to give you His assistance, whereby you may pass the night free from danger. Say, then, still keeping to the words of the Church :

ANT. Salva nos, Domine, vigilantes, custodi nos dormientes : ut vigilemus cum Christo, et requiescamus in pace.
V. Dignare, Domine, nocte ista.
R. Sine peccato nos custodire.
V. Miserere nostri, Domine.
R. Miserere nostri.
V. Fiat misericordia tua, Domine, super nos.
R. Quemadmodum speravimus in te.
V. Domine, exaudi orationem meam.
R. Et clamor meus ad te veniat.

ANT. Save us, O Lord, while awake, and watch us as we sleep; that we may watch with Christ, and rest in peace.
V. Vouchsafe, O Lord, this night.
R. To keep us without sin.
V. Have mercy on us, O Lord.
R. Have mercy on us.
V. Let thy mercy, O Lord, be upon us.
R. As we have hoped in thee.
V. O Lord, hear my prayer.
R. And let my cry come unto thee.

OREMUS.

Visita, quæsumus, Domine, habitationem istam, et omnes insidias inimici ab ea longe repelle : angeli tui sancti habitent in ea, qui nos in pace custodiant, et benedictio tua sit super nos semper. Per Dominum nostrum Jesum Christum, Filium tuum, qui tecum vivit et regnat in unitate Spiritus Sancti Deus, per omnia sæcula sæculorum. Amen.

LET US PRAY.

Visit, we beseech thee, O Lord, this house and family, and drive from it all snares of the enemy : let thy holy angels dwell herein, who may keep us in peace, and may thy blessing be always upon us. Through Jesus Christ our Lord, thy Son, who liveth and reigneth with thee, in the unity of the Holy Ghost, God, world without end. Amen.

And that you may end the day in the same sentiments wherewith you began it, say once more to your God these words of the royal prophet :

Miserere mei, Deus, secundum magnam misericordiam tuam

Have mercy on me, O God, according to thy great mercy.

CHAPTER THE FIFTH

ON HEARING MASS DURING THE SEASON OF SEPTUAGESIMA

THE Christian who enters into the spirit of the Church during the season of Septuagesima, will find an increase in his soul of that holy fear of God, which the psalmist tells us is the beginning of wisdom.[1] The consideration of what original sin has brought upon him, the recollection of his own sins, and the dread of God's judgments, all combine to arouse him from the indifference which so easily fastens on the soul. He has need, therefore, of some refuge, some powerful and saving help, which may re-enkindle within his heart that Christian hope, without which he cannot be in the

[1] Ps. cx. 10.

grace of God. Nay more: he has need of a victim of propitiation, which may appease the divine anger; he has need of a sacrifice, whereby to stay the arm of God, which he knows is raised to punish his sins.

This Victim is ready; this infinitely efficacious Sacrifice is prepared for us. 'The Lamb of God, that taketh away the sins of the world,' is still on our earth. His birth has filled us with consolation; the joy we experienced as we stood near His crib, but which has suddenly given place to thoughts the very opposite of joy, will return to us, and be greater than when we had it at Christmas, on the Easter day of His Resurrection: but in the interval, while awaiting the dawn of that bright day which is to lead us to our Jesus purified from our sins and vigorous with our new life, we may and must trust that His merits will effect the regeneration of our souls. When, therefore, we would offer to our God the sacrifice of 'a contrite and humble heart,' let us ensure its acceptance by going to the altar, and supplicating the Victim, who there offers Himself for our sake, that He join His infinite merits with our feeble works. When we leave the house of God, the weight of our sins will be lessened, our confidence in divine mercy will be increased, and our love, renewed by compunction, will be firmer and truer.

We will now endeavour to embody these sentiments in our explanation of the mysteries of the holy Mass, and initiate the faithful into these divine secrets; not, indeed, by indiscreetly presuming to translate the sacred formulæ, but by suggesting such acts as will enable those who hear Mass to enter into the ceremonies and the spirit of the Church and of the priest.

On the three Sundays, of Septuagesima, Sexagesima, and Quinquagesima, the Mass is always celebrated according to the rite of the penitential season we are now keeping. These Sundays take precedence of all feasts, except Doubles of the First Class. Ash Wednesday does not admit of even that exception; the Mass of that feria is never omitted. But when a saint's feast (and there are many such during the time of Septuagesima) falls on any other day than the four just mentioned, the Church then lays aside her purple vestments, and celebrates the holy Sacrifice in memory of the saint.

On the Sundays, if the Mass at which the faithful assist be the Parochial, or, as it is often called, the public Mass, two solemn rites precede it, and they are full of instruction and blessing: the *Asperges*, or sprinkling of the holy water, and the procession.

During the *Asperges*, let us ask with David, whose words are used by the Church in this ceremony, that our souls may be purified by the *hyssop* of humility, and become *whiter than snow*.

ANTIPHON OF THE ASPERGES

Asperges me, Domine, hyssopo, et mundabor; lavabis me, et super nivem dealbabor.

Ps. Miserere mei, Deus, secundum magnam misericordiam tuam.

V. Gloria Patri, etc.

ANT. Asperges me, etc.

V. Ostende nobis, Domine, misericordiam tuam.

R. Et salutare tuum da nobis.

V. Domine, exaudi orationem meam.

Thou shalt sprinkle me with hyssop, O Lord, and I shall be cleansed; thou shalt wash me, and I shall be made whiter than snow.

Ps. Have mercy on me, O God, according to thy great mercy.

V. Glory, etc.

ANT. Sprinkle me, etc.

V. Show us, O Lord, thy mercy.

R. And grant us thy salvation.

V. O Lord, hear my prayer.

R. Et clamor meus ad te veniat.

V. Dominus vobiscum.

R. Et cum spiritu tuo.

R. And let my cry come unto thee.

V. The Lord be with you.

R. And with thy spirit.

OREMUS.

Exaudi nos, Domine sancte, Pater omnipotens, æterne Deus : et mittere digneris sanctum angelum tuum de cœlis, qui custodiat, foveat, protegat, visitet atque defendat omnes habitantes in hoc habitaculo. Per Christum Dominum nostrum.

R. Amen.

LET US PRAY.

Graciously hear us, O holy Lord, Father almighty, eternal God : and vouchsafe to send thy holy angel from heaven, who may keep, cherish, protect, visit, and defend all who are assembled in this place. Through Christ our Lord.

R. Amen.

The procession, which immediately precedes the Mass, shows us the ardour wherewith the Church advances towards her God. Let us imitate her fervour, for it is written : 'The Lord is good to them that hope in Him, to the soul that seeketh Him.'[1]

But see, Christians ! the Sacrifice begins ! The priest is at the foot of the altar ; God is attentive, the angels are in adoration, the whole Church is united with the priest, whose priesthood and action are those of the great High Priest, Jesus Christ. Let us make the sign of the cross with him.

THE ORDINARY OF THE MASS

In nomine Patris, et Filii, et Spiritus Sancti. Amen.

V. Introibo ad altare Dei.

R. Ad Deum qui lætificat juventutem meam.

In the name of the Father, and of the Son, and of the Holy Ghost. Amen.

I unite myself, O my God, with thy Church, whose heart is filled with the hope of soon seeing, and in all the splendour of his Resurrection, Jesus Christ thy Son, who is the true altar.

---

[1] Lam. iii. 25.

Judica me, Deus, et discerne causam meam de gente non sancta : ab homine iniquo et doloso erue me

Quia tu es, Deus, fortitudo mea : quare me repulisti ? et quare tristis incedo, dum affligit me inimicus ?

Emitte lucem tuam et veritatem tuam : ipsa me deduxerunt et adduxerunt in montem sanctum tuum, et in tabernacula tua.

Et introibo ad altare Dei : ad Deum qui lætificat juventutem meam.

Confitebor tibi in cithara Deus, Deus meus : quare tristis es anima mea ? et quare conturbas me ?

Spera in Deo, quoniam adhuc confitebor illi : salutare vultus mei, et Deus meus.

Gloria Patri, et Filio, et Spiritui Sancto.

Sicut erat in principio, et nunc et semper, et in sæcula sæculorum. Amen.

V. Introibo ad altare Dei.
R. Ad Deum qui lætificat juventutem meam.

V. Adjutorium nostrum in nomine Domini.
R. Qui fecit cœlum et terram.

Like her, I beseech thee to defend me against the malice of the enemies of my salva tion.

It is in thee that I have put my hope ; yet do I feel sad and troubled at being in the midst of the snares which are set for me.

Send me, then, him who is light and truth : it is he who will open to us the way to thy holy mount, to thy heavenly tabernacle.

He is the Mediator, and the living altar ; I will draw nigh to him, and be filled with joy.

When he shall have come, I will sing in my gladness. Be not sad, O my soul! Why wouldst thou be troubled ?

Hope in thy Jesus, who will soon show himself to thee as the conqueror of that death which he will have suffered in thy stead ; and thou wilt rise again together with him.

Glory be to the Father, and to the Son, and to the Holy Ghost.

As it was in the beginning, is now, and ever shall be, world without end. Amen.

I am to go to the altar of God, and feel the presence of him who desires to give me a new life !

This my hope comes not to me as thinking that I have any merits, but from the all-powerful help of my Creator.

The thought of being about to appear before his God, excites in the soul of the priest a lively sentiment of compunction. He cannot go further in the holy Sacrifice without confessing, and

publicly, that he is a sinner, and deserves not the
grace he is about to receive. Listen with respect
to this confession of God's minister, and earnestly
ask our Lord to show mercy to him; for the priest
is your father; he is answerable for your salvation,
for which he every day risks his own. When he
has finished, unite with the servers, or the sacred
ministers, in this prayer:

Misereatur tui omnipotens Deus, et dimissis peccatis tuis, perducat te ad vitam æternam.

May almighty God have mercy on thee, and, forgiving thy sins, bring thee to everlasting life.

The priest having answered *Amen*, make your
confession, saying with a contrite spirit:

Confiteor Deo omnipotenti, beatæ Mariæ semper Virgini, beato Michaeli archangelo, beato Joanni Baptistæ, sanctis apostolis Petro et Paulo, omnibus sanctis, et tibi, pater: quia peccavi nimis cogitatione, verbo, et opere: mea culpa, mea culpa, mea maxima culpa. Ideo precor beatam Mariam semper Virginem, beatum Michaelem archangelum, beatum Joannem Baptistam, sanctos apostolos Petrum et Paulum, omnes sanctos, et te, pater, orare pro me ad Dominum Deum nostrum.

I confess to almighty God, to blessed Mary ever Virgin, to blessed Michael the archangel, to blessed John the Baptist, to the holy apostles Peter and Paul, to all the saints, and to thee, father, that I have sinned exceedingly in thought, word, and deed; through my fault, through my fault, through my most grievous fault. Therefore I beseech blessed Mary ever Virgin, blessed Michael the archangel, blessed John the Baptist, the holy apostles Peter and Paul, and all the saints, and thee, father, to pray to the Lord our God for me.

Receive with gratitude the paternal wish of the
priest, who says to you:

Misereatur vestri omnipotens Deus, et dimissis peccatis vestris, perducat vos ad vitam æternam.
R. Amen.

May almighty God be merciful to you, and, forgiving your sins, bring you to everlasting life.
R. Amen.

Indulgentiam, absolutionem, et remissionem peccatorum nostrorum, tribuat nobis omnipotens et misericors Dominus.

R. Amen.

May the almighty and merciful Lord grant us pardon, absolution, and remission of our sins.

R. Amen.

Invoke the divine assistance, that you may approach to Jesus Christ.

V. Deus, tu conversus vivificabis nos.
R. Et plebs tua lætabitur in te.
V. Ostende nobis, Domine, misericordiam tuam.
R. Et salutare tuum da nobis.

V. Domine, exaudi orationem meam.
R. Et clamor meus ad te veniat.

V. O God, it needs but one look of thine to give us life.
R. And thy people shall rejoice in thee.
V. Show us, O Lord, thy mercy.
R. And give us to know and love the Saviour whom thou hast sent unto us.
V. O Lord, hear my prayer.

R. And let my cry come unto thee.

The priest here leaves you to ascend to the altar; but first he salutes you:

V. Dominus vobiscum.

V. The Lord be with you.

Answer him with reverence:

R. Et cum spiritu tuo.

R. And with thy spirit.

 OREMUS.

LET US PRAY.

He ascends the steps, and comes to the Holy of holies. Ask, both for him and for yourself, deliverance from sin:

Aufer a nobis quæsumus, Domine, iniquitates nostras; ut ad Sancta sanctorum puris mereamur mentibus introire. Per Christum Dominum nostrum. Amen.

Take from our hearts, O Lord, all those sins, which make us unworthy to appear in thy presence; we ask this of thee by thy divine Son, our Lord.

When the priest kisses the altar, out of reverence for the relics of the martyrs which are there, say :

Oramus te Domine, per merita sanctorum tuorum, quorum reliquiæ hic sunt, et omnium sanctorum : ut indulgere digneris omnia peccata mea. Amen.

Generous soldiers of Jesus Christ, who have mingled your own blood with his, intercede for us that our sins may be forgiven : that so we may, like you, approach unto God.

If it be a High Mass at which you are assisting, the priest here blesses the incense, saying :

Ab illo benedicaris, in cujus honore cremaberis. Amen.

Mayst thou be blessed by him, in whose honour thou art to be burned. Amen.

He then censes the altar in a most solemn manner. This white cloud, which you see ascending from every part of the altar, signifies the prayer of the Church, who addresses herself to Jesus Christ; while the divine mediator causes that prayer to ascend, united with His own, to the throne of the majesty of His Father.

The priest then says the Introit. It is a solemn opening-anthem, in which the Church, at the very commencement of the holy Sacrifice, gives expression to the sentiments which fill her heart.

It is followed by nine exclamations, which are even more earnest, for they ask for mercy. In addressing them to God, the Church unites herself with the nine choirs of angels, who are standing round the altar of heaven, one and the same as this before which you are kneeling.

To the Father :

Kyrie eleison.
Kyrie eleison.
Kyrie eleison.

Lord, have mercy on us !
Lord, have mercy on us !
Lord, have mercy on us !

To the Son:

Christe eleison.	Christ, have mercy on us!
Christe eleison.	Christ, have mercy on us!
Christe eleison.	Christ, have mercy on us!

To the Holy Ghost:

Kyrie eleison.	Lord, have mercy on us!
Kyrie eleison.	Lord, have mercy on us!
Kyrie eleison.	Lord, have mercy on us!

As we have already mentioned, the Church abstains, during the season of Septuagesima, from the heavenly hymn which the angels sang over the crib of the divine Babe. But, if she be keeping the feast of a saint, she recites this beautiful canticle on that day. The beginning of the *Angelic Hymn* seems more suitable for heavenly than for earthly voices; but the second part is in no way out of keeping with the sinner's wants and fears, for we there remind the Son of the eternal Father that He is the *Lamb*, who came down from heaven that He might *take away the sins of the world.* We beseech Him to *have mercy on us,* and *receive our humble prayer.* Let us foster these sentiments within us, for they are so appropriate to the present season.

THE ANGELIC HYMN

Gloria in excelsis Deo, et in terra pax hominibus bonæ voluntatis.

Laudamus te: benedicimus te: adoramus te: glorificamus te: gratias agimus tibi propter magnam gloriam tuam.

Domine Deus, Rex cœlestis, Deus Pater omnipotens.

Domine, Fili unigenite, Jesu Christe.

Glory be to God on high, and on earth peace to men of good will.

We praise thee: we bless thee: we adore thee: we glorify thee: we give thee thanks for thy great glory.

O Lord God, heavenly King, God the Father almighty.

O Lord Jesus Christ, the only-begotten Son.

Domine Deus, Agnus Dei, Filius Patris.	O Lord God, Lamb of God, Son of the Father.
Qui tollis peccata mundi, miserere nobis.	Who takest away the sins of the world, have mercy on us.
Qui tollis peccata mundi, suscipe deprecationem nostram.	Who takest away the sins of the world, receive our humble prayer.
Qui sedes ad dexteram Patris, miserere nobis.	Who sittest at the right hand of the Father, have mercy on us.
Quoniam tu solus sanctus, tu solus Dominus, tu solus altissimus, Jesu Christe, cum Sancto Spiritu, in gloria Dei Patris. Amen.	For thou alone art holy, thou alone art Lord, thou alone, O Jesus Christ, together with the Holy Ghost, art most high, in the glory of God the Father. Amen.

The priest then turns towards the people, and again salutes them, as it were to make sure of their pious attention to the sublime act, for which all this is but the preparation.

Then follows the Collect or Prayer, in which the Church formally expresses to the divine Majesty the special intentions she has in the Mass which is being celebrated. You may unite in this prayer, by reciting with the priest the Collects, which you will find in their proper places; but on no account omit to join with the server of the Mass in answering *Amen.*

After this, comes the Epistle, which is generally a portion of one or other of the Epistles of the apostles, or a passage from some Book of the old Testament. While it is being read, ask of God that you may profit by the instructions it conveys.

The Gradual is an intermediate formula of prayer between the Epistle and the Gospel. It again brings to us the sentiments already expressed in the Introit. Read it with devotion, that so you may enter more and more into the spirit of the mystery proposed to you by the Church.

During every other portion of her year, the

Church here repeats her joyous *Alleluia;* but now
she denies herself this demonstration of gladness,
until such time as her divine Spouse has passed
through that sea of bitterness, into which our sins
have plunged Him.   Instead of the *Alleluia*, then,
she sings in a plaintive tone some verses from the
Psalms, appropriate to the rest of that day's Office.
This is the Tract, of which we have already spoken.

If it be a High Mass, the deacon, meanwhile,
prepares to fulfil his noble office—that of announc-
ing the good tidings of salvation.   He prays God
to cleanse his heart and lips.   Then kneeling before
the priest, he asks a blessing; and, having received
it, goes to the place where he is to sing the Gospel.

As a preparation for hearing it worthily, you
may thus pray, together with both priest and
deacon :

Munda cor meum, ac la-
bia mea, omnipotens Deus,
qui labia Isaiæ prophetæ
calculo mundasti ignito : ita
me tua grata miseratione
dignare mundare, ut san-
ctum Evangelium tuum di-
gne valeam nuntiare.   Per
Christum Dominum no-
strum.   Amen.

Alas! these ears of mine are
but too often defiled with the
world's vain words: cleanse
them, O Lord, that so I may
hear the words of eternal life,
and treasure them in my heart.
Through our Lord Jesus Christ.
Amen.

Dominus sit in corde meo,
et in labiis meis : ut digne
et competenter annuntiem
Evangelium suum : In no-
mine Patris, et Filii, et Spiritus Sancti.   Amen.

Grant to thy ministers thy
grace, that they may faithfully
explain thy law; that so all,
both pastors and flock, may be
united to thee for ever.   Amen.

You will stand during the Gospel, as though you
were waiting for the orders of your Lord ; at the
commencement make the sign of the cross on your
forehead, lips, and breast ; and then listen to every
word of the priest or deacon.   Let your heart be
ready and obedient.   ' While my beloved was speaking,' says the bride in the Canticle, ' my soul

melted within me.'[1] If you have not such love as this, have at least the humble submission of Samuel, and say: 'Speak, Lord! thy servant heareth.'[2]

After the Gospel, if the priest says the Symbol of faith, the *Credo*, you will say it with him. Faith is that gift of God, without which we cannot please Him. It is faith that makes us see 'the light which shineth in darkness,' and which the darkness of unbelief 'did not comprehend.' It is faith alone that teaches us what we are, whence we come, and the end for which we are made. It alone can point out to us the path whereby we may return to our God, when once we have separated ourselves from Him. Let us love this admirable faith, which, if we but make it fruitful by good works, will save us. Let us, then, say with the Catholic Church, our mother:

THE NICENE CREED

Credo in unum Deum, Patrem omnipotentem, factorem cœli et terræ, visibilium omnium et invisibilium.

Et in unum Dominum Jesum Christum, Filium Dei unigenitum. Et ex Patre natum ante omnia sæcula; Deum de Deo, lumen de lumine, Deum verum de Deo vero. Genitum non factum, consubstantialem Patri, per quem omnia facta sunt. Qui propter nos homines, et propter nostram salutem, descendit de cœlis. Et incarnatus est de Spiritu Sancto, ex Maria Virgine; ET HOMO FACTUS EST. Crucifixus eti-

I believe in one God, the Father almighty, maker of heaven and earth, and of all things visible and invisible.

And in one Lord Jesus Christ, the only-begotten Son of God. And born of the Father before all ages; God of God, light of light; true God of true God. Begotten, not made; consubstantial with the Father, by whom all things were made. Who for us men, and for our salvation, came down from heaven. And became incarnate by the Holy Ghost of the Virgin Mary; AND WAS MADE MAN. He was crucified also for us,

---

[1] Cant. v. 6.   [2] 1 Kings iii. 10.

am pro nobis sub Pontio Pilato, passus et sepultus est. Et resurrexit tertia die, secundum Scripturas. Et ascendit in cœlum; sedet ad dexteram Patris. Et iterum venturus est cum gloria judicare vivos et mortuos; cujus regni non erit finis.

under Pontius Pilate, suffered, and was buried. And the third day he rose again, according to the Scriptures. And ascended into heaven, sitteth at the right hand of the Father. And he is to come again with glory, to judge the living and the dead; of whose kingdom there shall be no end.

Et in Spiritum Sanctum, Dominum et vivificantem, qui ex Patre Filioque procedit. Qui cum Patre et Filio simul adoratur, et conglorificatur; qui locutus est per prophetas. Et unam sanctam Catholicam et apostolicam Ecclesiam. Confiteor unum Baptisma in remissionem peccatorum. Et expecto resurrectionem mortuorum, et vitam venturi sæculi. Amen.

And in the Holy Ghost, the Lord and giver of life, who proceedeth from the Father and the Son. Who together with the Father and the Son, is adored and glorified; who spoke by the prophets. And one, holy, Catholic, and apostolic Church. I confess one Baptism for the remission of sins. And I expect the resurrection of the dead, and the life of the world to come. Amen.

The priest and the people should, by this time, have their hearts ready: it is time to prepare the offering itself. And here we come to the second part of the holy Mass; it is called the *Oblation*, and immediately follows that which was named the *Mass of Catechumens*, on account of its being formerly the only part at which the candidates for Baptism had a right to be present.

See, then, dear Christians! bread and wine are about to be offered to God, as being the noblest of inanimate creatures, since they are made for the nourishment of man; and even that is only a poor material image of what they are destined to become in our Christian Sacrifice. Their substance will soon give place to God Himself, and of themselves nothing will remain but the appearances. Happy creatures, thus to yield up their own being, that

God may take its place! We, too, are to undergo
a like transformation, when, as the apostle expresses it, that which is mortal shall put on
immortality.[1]   Until that happy change shall be
realized, let us offer ourselves to God, as often as
we see the bread and wine presented to Him in the
holy Sacrifice; and let us glorify Him, who, by
assuming our human nature, has made us 'partakers of the divine nature.'[2]

The priest again turns to the people with the
usual salutation, as though he would warn them to
redouble their attention.   Let us read the Offertory
with him, and when he offers the Host to God, let
us unite with him in saying:

Suscipe, sancte Pater,
omnipotens æterne Deus,
hanc immaculatam hostiam,
quam ego indignus famulus
tuus offero tibi Deo meo
vivo et vero, pro innumera-
bilibus peccatis et offensio-
nibus et negligentiis meis,
et pro omnibus circumstan-
tibus, sed et pro omnibus
fidelibus christianis vivis
atque defunctis; ut mihi
et illis proficiat ad salutem
in vitam æternam. Amen.

All that we have, O Lord,
comes from thee, and belongs
to thee; it is just, therefore,
that we return it unto thee.
But how wonderful art thou
in the inventions of thy
immense love! This bread
which we are offering to thee,
is to give place, in a few
moments, to the sacred Body
of Jesus. We beseech thee,
receive, together with this
oblation, our hearts which
long to live by thee, and to
cease to live their own life of
self.

When the priest puts the wine into the chalice,
and then mingles with it a drop of water, let your
thoughts turn to the divine mystery of the Incarnation, which is the source of our hope and our salvation; and say:

Deus, qui humanæ sub-
stantiæ dignitatem mirabiliter condidisti, et mirabi-

O Lord Jesus, who art the
true vine, and whose Blood,
like a generous wine, has

---

[1] 1 Cor. xv. 53.   [2] 2 St. Pet. i. 4.

lius reformasti : da nobis per hujus aquæ et vini myste-rium, ejus divinitatis esse consortes, qui humanitatis nostræ fieri dignatus est particeps, Jesus Christus Filius tuus Dominus noster : qui tecum vivit et regnat in unitate Spiritus Sancti Deus, per omnia sæcula sæculorum. Amen.

been poured forth under the pressure of the cross! thou hast deigned to unite thy divine nature to our weak humanity, which is signified by this drop of water. Oh, come and make us partakers of thy divinity, by showing thyself to us in thy sweet and wondrous visit.

The priest then offers the mixture of wine and water, beseeching God graciously to accept this oblation, which is so soon to be changed into the reality, of which it is now but the figure. Meanwhile, say, in union with the priest :

Offerimus tibi, Domine, calicem salutaris, tuam de-precantes clementiam : ut in conspectu divinæ Majestatis tuæ, pro nostra et totius mundi salute, cum odore suavitatis ascendat. Amen.

Graciously accept these gifts, O sovereign Creator of all things. Let them be fitted for the divine transformation, which will make them, from being mere offerings of created things, the instrument of the world's salvation.

After having thus held up the sacred gifts towards heaven, the priest bows down ; let us, also, humble ourselves, and say :

In spiritu humilitatis, et in animo contrito suscipia-mur a te, Domine : et sic fiat sacrificium nostrum in con-spectu tuo hodie, ut placeat tibi, Domine Deus.

Though daring, as we do, to approach thy altar, O Lord, we cannot forget that we are sinners. Have mercy on us, and delay not to send us thy Son, who is our saving Host.

Let us next invoke the Holy Ghost, whose opera-tion is about to produce on the altar the presence of the Son of God, as it did in the womb of the blessed Virgin Mary, in the divine mystery of the Incarnation :

Veni Sanctificator, omni-potens æterne Deus, et be-

Come, O divine Spirit, make fruitful the offering

nedic hoc sacrificium tuo sancto nomini præparatum.

which is upon the altar, and produce in our hearts him whom they desire.

If it be a High Mass, the priest, before proceeding further with the sacrifice, takes the thurible a second time, after blessing the incense in these words :

Per intercessionem beati Michaelis archangeli, stantis a dextris altaris incensi, et omnium electorum suorum, incensum istud dignetur Dominus benedicere, et in odorem suavitatis accipere. Per Christum Dominum nostrum. Amen.

Through the intercession of blessed Michael the archangel, standing at the right hand of the altar of incense, and of all his elect, may our Lord deign to bless this incense, and to receive it for an odour of sweetness. Through Christ our Lord. Amen.

He then censes first the bread and wine, which have just been offered, and then the altar itself ; hereby inviting the faithful to make their prayer, which is signified by the fragrant incense, more and more fervent, the nearer the solemn moment approaches. St. John tells us that the incense he beheld burning on the altar in heaven is made up of the ' prayers of the saints '; let us take a share in those prayers, and with all the ardour of holy desires, let us say with the priest :

Incensum istud, a te benedictum, ascendat ad te, Domine, et descendat super nos misericordia tua.

Dirigatur, Domine, oratio mea sicut incensum in conspectu tuo: elevatio manuum mearum sacrificium vespertinum. Pone, Domine, custodiam ori meo, et ostium circumstantiæ labiis meis; ut non declinet cor meum in verba malitiæ, ad excusandas excusationes in peccatis.

May this incense, blessed by thee, ascend to thee, O Lord, and may thy mercy descend upon us.

Let my prayer, O Lord, be directed like incense in thy sight : the lifting up of my hands as an evening sacrifice. Set a watch, O Lord, before my mouth, and a door round about my lips; that my heart may not incline to evil words, to make excuses in sins.

Giving back the thurible to the deacon, the priest says :

Accendat in nobis Dominus ignem sui amoris, et flammam æternæ charitatis. Amen.	May the Lord enkindle in us the fire of his love and the flame of eternal charity. Amen.

But the thought of his own unworthiness becomes more intense than ever in the heart of the priest. The public confession which he made at the foot of the altar is not enough; he would now at the altar itself express to the people, in the language of a solemn rite, how far he knows himself to be from that spotless sanctity, wherewith he should approach to God. He washes his hands. Our hands signify our works ; and the priest, though by his priesthood he bear the office of Jesus Christ, is, by his works, but man. Seeing your father thus humble himself, do you also make an act of humility, and say with him these verses of the Psalm.

PSALM 25

Lavabo inter innocentes manus meas : et circumdabo altare tuum, Domine.

Ut audiam vocem laudis : et enarrem universa mirabilia tua.

Domine, dilexi decorem domus tuæ, et locum habitationis gloriæ tuæ.

Ne perdas cum impiis, Deus, animam meam, et cum viris sanguinum vitam meam.

In quorum manibus iniquitates sunt: dextera eorum repleta est muneribus.

Ego autem in innocentia mea ingressus sum : redime me, et miserere mei.

I, too, would wash my hands, O Lord, and become like unto those who are innocent, that so I may be worthy to come near thy altar, and hear thy sacred canticles, and then go and proclaim to the world the wonders of thy goodness. I love the beauty of thy house, which thou art about to make the dwelling-place of thy glory. Leave me not, O God, in the midst of them that are enemies both to thee and me. Thy mercy having separated me from them, I entered on the path of innocence, and was restored to thy grace ; but have pity on

Pes meus stetit in directo : in ecclesiis benedicam te, Domine.

Gloria Patri, et Filio, et Spiritui Sancto.

Sicut erat in principio, et nunc, et semper, et in sæcula sæculorum. Amen.

my weakness still ; redeem me yet more, thou who hast so mercifully brought me back to the right path. In the midst of these thy faithful people, I give thee thanks. Glory be to the Father, and to the Son, and to the Holy Ghost; as it was in the beginning, is now, and ever shall be, world without end. Amen.

The priest, taking encouragement from the act of humility he has just made, returns to the middle of the altar, and bows down full of respectful awe, begging of God to receive graciously the Sacrifice which is about to be offered to Him, and expresses the intentions for which it is offered. Let us do the same.

Suscipe, sancta Trinitas, hanc oblationem, quam tibi offerimus ob memoriam Passionis, Resurrectionis, et Ascensionis Jesu Christi Domini nostri: et in honorem beatæ Mariæ semper Virginis, et beati Joannis Baptistæ, et sanctorum apostolorum Petri et Pauli, et istorum, et omnium sanctorum : ut illis proficiat ad honorem, nobis autem ad salutem : et illi pro nobis intercedere dignentur in cœlis, quorum memoriam agimus in terris. Per eumdem Christum Dominum nostrum. Amen.

O holy Trinity, graciously accept the Sacrifice we have begun. We offer it in remembrance of the Passion, Resurrection, and Ascension of our Lord Jesus Christ. Permit thy Church to join with this intention that of honouring the ever glorious Virgin Mary, the blessed Baptist John, the holy apostles Peter and Paul, the martyrs whose relics lie here under our altar awaiting their resurrection, and the saints whose memory we this day celebrate. Increase the glory they are enjoying, and receive the prayers they address to thee for us.

The priest again turns to the people ; it is for the last time before the sacred mysteries are accomplished. He feels anxious to excite the fervour of the people. Neither does the thought of his own unworthiness leave him ; and before entering the

cloud with the Lord, he seeks support in the
prayers of his brethren who are present.   He says
to them :

Orate, fratres : ut meum ac vestrum sacrificium acceptabile fiat apud Deum Patrem omnipotentem.	Brethren, pray that my Sacrifice, which is yours also, may be acceptable to God, our almighty Father.

This request made, he turns again to the altar,
and you will see his face no more until our Lord
Himself shall have come down from heaven upon
that same altar.   Assure the priest that he has
your prayers, and say to him :

Suscipiat Dominus sacrificium de manibus tuis, ad laudem et gloriam nominis sui, ad utilitatem quoque nostram totiusque Ecclesiæ suæ sanctæ.	May our Lord accept this Sacrifice at thy hands, to the praise and glory of his name, and for our benefit and that of his holy Church throughout the world.

Here the priest recites the prayers called the
Secrets, in which he presents the petition of the
whole Church for God's acceptance of the Sacrifice,
and then immediately begins to fulfil that great
duty of religion—thanksgiving.   So far he has
adored God, and has sued for mercy ; he has still
to give thanks for the blessings bestowed on us by
the bounty of our heavenly Father, and expressly
for that chiefest of all His gifts, the Messias.   We
are on the point of receiving a new visit of this Son
of God ; the priest, in the name of the Church, is
about to give expression to the gratitude of all
mankind.   In order to excite the faithful to that
intensity of gratitude which is due to God for all
His gifts, he interrupts his own and their silent
prayer by terminating it aloud, saying :

Per omnia sæcula sæculorum !	For ever and ever !

In the same feeling, answer your *Amen*. Then he continues:

V. Dominus vobiscum.	*V*. The Lord be with you.
R. Et cum spiritu tuo.	*R*. And with thy spirit,
V. Sursum corda !	*V*. Lift up your hearts !

Let your response be sincere:

R. Habemus ad Dominum.	*R*. We have them fixed on God.

And when he adds:

V. Gratias agamus Domino Deo nostro.	*V*. Let us give thanks to the Lord our God.

Answer him with all the earnestness of your soul:

R. Dignum et justum est.	*R*. It is meet and just.

Then the priest:

THE PREFACE

(*For the Sundays.*)

Vere dignum et justum est, æquum et salutare, nos tibi semper, et ubique gratias agere, Domine sancte, Pater omnipotens, æterne Deus. Qui cum unigenito Filio tuo et Spiritu Sancto unus es Deus, unus es Dominus: non in unius singularitate Personæ, sed in unius Trinitate substantiæ. Quod enim de tua gloria, revelante te, credimus, hoc de Filio tuo, hoc de Spiritu Sancto, sine differentiâ discretionis sentimus. Ut in confessione veræ, sempiternæque Deitatis, et in Personis proprietas, et in essentia unitas, et in Majestate

It is truly meet and just, right and available to salvation, that we should always and in all places give thanks to thee, O holy Lord, Father almighty, eternal God, who together with thy only-begotten Son and the Holy Ghost art one God, one Lord: not in the singleness of one Person, but in the Trinity of one substance. For what we believe of thy glory, as thou hast revealed, the same we believe of thy Son and of the Holy Ghost, without any difference or distinction. So that in the confession of the true and eternal Deity, we adore a distinction in the Persons, an

adoretur æqualitas. Quam laudant Angeli atque Archangeli, Cherubim quoque ac Seraphim ; qui non cessant clamare quotidie, una voce dicentes, Sanctus, etc.

unity in the essence, and an equality in the Majesty. Whom the Angels and Archangels, the Cherubim also and Seraphim praise ; who cease not daily to cry out with one voice, saying, Holy, etc.

THE PREFACE

(*For the Week-days.*)

Vere dignum et justum est, æquum et salutare, nos tibi semper et ubique gratias agere : Domine sancte, Pater omnipotens, æterne Deus, per Christum Dominum nostrum ; per quem majestatem tuam laudant Angeli, adorant Dominationes, tremunt Potestates ; Cœli, cœlorumque Virtutes, ac beata Seraphim, socia exsultatione concelebrant. Cum quibus et nostras voces, ut admitti jubeas deprecamur, supplici confessione, dicentes :

It is truly meet and just, right and available to salvation, that we should always and in all places give thanks to thee, O holy Lord, Father almighty, eternal God : through Christ our Lord ; by whom the Angels praise thy majesty, the Dominations adore it, the Powers tremble before it ; the Heavens and the heavenly Virtues, and the blessed Seraphim, with common jubilee, glorify it. Together with whom, we beseech thee that we may be admitted to join our humble voices, saying :

Here unite with the priest, who, on his part, unites himself with the blessed spirits, in giving thanks to God for the unspeakable gift ; bow down and say :

Sanctus, Sanctus, Sanctus, Dominus Deus sabaoth !
Pleni sunt cœli et terra gloria tua.
Hosanna in excelsis !
Benedictus qui venit in nomine Domini.

Hosanna in excelsis !

Holy, Holy, Holy, Lord God of hosts !

Heaven and earth are full of thy glory.
Hosanna in the highest !
Blessed be the Saviour who is coming to us in the name of the Lord who sends him.
Hosanna be to him in the highest !

After these words commences the *Canon*, that mysterious prayer, in the midst of which heaven bows down to earth, and God descends unto us. The voice of the priest is no longer heard; yea, even at the altar, all is silence. Let a profound respect stay all distractions, and keep our senses in submission to the soul. Let us fix our eyes on what the priest does in the holy place.

THE CANON OF THE MASS

In this mysterious colloquy with the great God of heaven and earth, the first prayer of the sacrificing priest is for the Catholic Church, his and our mother.

Te igitur, clementissime Pater, per Jesum Christum Filium tuum Dominum nostrum, supplices rogamus ac petimus, uti accepta habeas, et benedicas hæc dona, hæc munera, hæc sancta sacrificia illibata, in primis quæ tibi offerimus pro Ecclesia tua sancta Catholica: quam pacificare, custodire, adunare, et regere digneris toto orbe terrarum, una cum famulo tuo Papa nostro N., et Antistite nostro N., et omnibus orthodoxis, atque catholicæ et apostolicæ fidei cultoribus.

O God, who manifestest thyself unto us by means of the mysteries which thou hast entrusted to thy holy Church, our mother; we beseech thee, by the merits of this sacrifice, that thou wouldst remove all those hindrances which oppose her during her pilgrimage in this world. Give her peace and unity. Do thou thyself guide our holy Father the Pope, thy Vicar on earth. Direct thou our Bishop, who is our sacred link of unity; and watch over all the orthodox children of the Catholic apostolic Roman Church.

Here pray, together with the priest, for those whose interests should be dearest to you.

Memento, Domine, famulorum famularumque tuarum N. et N., et omnium circumstantium, quorum tibi fides cognita est, et nota devotio: pro quibus tibi

Permit me, O God, to intercede with thee in more earnest prayer for those, for whom thou knowest that I have a special obligation to pray: * * * Pour down thy bless-

offerimus, **vel** qui tibi offe- ings upon them. **Let them**
runt hoc sacrificium laudis, **partake of the fruits of this**
pro se, suisque omnibus, pro **divine** Sacrifice, which is
redemptione animarum sua- offered unto thee in the name
rum, pro spe salutis et in- of all mankind. Visit them
columitatis suæ ; tibique by thy grace, **pardon them**
reddunt vota sua æterno **their sins, grant them the**
Deo, vivo et vero. blessings of this present life
and of that which is eternal.

Here let us commemorate the saints : they are
that portion of the Body of Jesus Christ, which is
called the Church triumphant.

Communicantes, et me- But the offering of this Sa-
moriam venerantes, in pri- crifice, O my God, does not
mis gloriosæ semper Virgi- unite us with those only of our
nis Mariæ, Genitricis Dei et brethren who are still in this
Domini nostri Jesu Christi : transient life of trial : it brings
sed et beatorum apostolo- us closer to those also, who
rum ac martyrum tuorum, are already in possession of
Petri et Pauli, Andreæ, Ja- heaven. Therefore it is that
cobi, Joannis, Thomæ, Ja- we wish to honour by it the
cobi, Philippi, Bartholomæi, memory of the glorious and
Matthæi, Simonis, et Thad- ever Virgin Mary, of whom
dæi : Lini, Cleti, Clementis, Jesus was born to us; of the
Xysti, Cornelii, Cypriani, apostles, confessors, virgins,
Laurentii, Chrysogoni, Joan- and of all the saints; that so
nis et Pauli, Cosmæ et Da- they may assist us, by their
miani, et omnium sanctorum powerful intercession, to be-
tuorum, quorum meritis come worthy to contemplate
precibusque concedas, ut in thee, as they now do, in the
omnibus protectionis tuæ mansion of thy glory.
muniamur auxilio. Per
eumdem Christum Domi-
num nostrum. Amen.

The priest, who up to this time has been praying
with his hands extended, now joins them, and
holds them over the bread and wine, as the high
priest of the old Law did over the figurative
victim ; he thus expresses his intention of bringing
these gifts more closely under the notice of the
divine Majesty, and of marking them as the
material offering whereby we profess our depend-

ence, and which is, in a few instants, to yield its place to the living Host, upon whom all our iniquities are to be laid.

Hanc igitur oblationem servitutis nostræ, sed et cunctæ familiæ tuæ, quæsumus Domine, ut placatus accipias : diesque nostros in tua pace disponas, atque ab æterna damnatione nos eripi, et in electorum tuorum jubeas grege numerari. Per Christum Dominum nostrum. Amen.

Quam oblationem tu Deus in omnibus, quæsumus, benedictam, adscriptam, ratam, rationabilem, acceptabilemque facere digneris ; ut nobis Corpus et Sanguis fiat dilectissimi Filii tui Domini nostri Jesu Christi.

Vouchsafe, O God, to accept this offering which this thy assembled family presents to thee as the homage of its most happy servitude. In return, give us peace, save us from thy wrath, and number us among thy elect, through him who is coming to us—thy Son our Saviour.

Yea, Lord, this is the moment when this bread is to become his sacred Body, which is our food ; and this wine is to be changed into his Blood, which is our drink. Ah ! delay no longer, but send to us this divine Son our Saviour !

And here the priest ceases to act as man ; he now becomes more than a mere minister of the Church. His word becomes that of Jesus Christ, with all its power and efficacy. Prostrate yourself in profound adoration : for God Himself is about to descend upon our altar, coming down from heaven.

Qui pridie quam pateretur, accepit panem in sanctas ac venerabiles manus suas : et elevatis oculis in cœlum, ad te Deum Patrem suum omnipotentem, tibi gratias agens, benedixit, fregit, deditque discipulis suis, dicens : Accipite, et manducate ex hoc omnes. Hoc est enim Corpus meum.

What, O God of heaven and earth, my Jesus, the long-expected Messias, what else can I do at this solemn moment but adore thee, in silence, as my sovereign Master, and open my whole heart to thee, as to its dearest King ? Come, then, Lord Jesus, come !

The divine Lamb is now lying on our altar! Glory and love be to Him for ever! But He is come, that He may be immolated. Hence, the priest, who is the minister of the will of the Most High, immediately pronounces over the chalice those sacred words, which will produce the great mystical immolation, by the separation of the Victim's Body and Blood. The substances of bread and wine have ceased to exist: the species alone are left, veiling, as it were, the Body and Blood, lest fear should keep us from a mystery, which God gives us in order to give us confidence. Let us associate ourselves to the angels, who tremblingly look upon this deepest wonder.

Simili modo postquam cœnatum est, accipiens et hunc præclarum calicem in sanctas ac venerabiles manus suas : item tibi gratias agens, benedixit, deditque discipulis suis, dicens : Accipite et bibite ex eo omnes. HIC EST ENIM CALIX SANGUINIS MEI, NOVI ET ÆTERNI TESTAMENTI : MYSTERIUM FIDEI : QUI PRO VOBIS ET PRO MULTIS EFFUNDETUR IN REMISSIONEM PECCATORUM. Hæc quotiescumque feceritis, in mei memoriam facietis.

O precious Blood! thou price of my salvation! I adore thee! Wash away my sins, and give me a purity above the whiteness of snow. Lamb ever slain, yet ever living, thou comest to take away the sins of the world! Come also and reign in me by thy power and by thy love.

The priest is now face to face with God. He again raises his hands towards heaven, and tells our heavenly Father, that the oblation now on the altar is no longer an earthly offering, but the Body and Blood, the whole Person, of His divine Son.

Unde et memores, Domine, nos servi tui, sed et plebs tua sancta, ejusdem Christi Filii tui Domini

Father of infinite holiness, the Host so long expected is here before thee! Behold this thy eternal Son, who suf-

nostri tam beatæ Passionis,
necnon et ab inferis Resurrectionis, sed et in cœlos
gloriosæ Ascensionis : offerimus præclaræ majestati tuæ
de tuis donis ac datis Hostiam puram, Hostiam san-
ctam, Hostiam immacula-
tam : Panem sanctum vitæ
æternæ, et Calicem salutis
perpetuæ.

Supra quæ propitio ac
sereno vultu respicere digneris : et accepta habere,
sicuti accepta habere dignatus es munera pueri tui justi
Abel, et sacrificium patriarchæ nostri Abrahæ, et
quod tibi obtulit summus
sacerdos tuus Melchisedech,
sanctum sacrificium, immaculatam hostiam.

fered a bitter passion, rose
again with glory from the
grave, and ascended triumphantly into heaven. He is
thy Son ; but he is also our
Host, Host pure and spotless,
our meat and drink of everlasting life.

Heretofore thou didst accept
the sacrifice of the innocent
lambs offered to thee by Abel ;
and the sacrifice which Abraham made thee of his son
Isaac, who, though immolated,
yet lived ; and, lastly, the
sacrifice, which Melchisedech
presented thee, of bread and
wine. Receive our Sacrifice,
which is above all those others
It is the Lamb, of whom all
others could be but figures : it
is the undying Victim : it is
the Body of thy Son, who is
the Bread of life, and his
Blood, which, whilst a drink
of immortality for us, is a
tribute adequate to thy glory.

**The priest bows down to the altar, and kisses it
as the throne of love on which is seated the Saviour
of men.**

Supplices te rogamus, om-
nipotens Deus : jube hæc
perferri per manus sancti
angeli tui in sublime altare
tuum, in conspectu divinæ
Majestatis tuæ : ut quotquot
ex hac altaris participatione,
sacrosanctum Filii tui Corpus et Sanguinem sumpseri-
mus, omni benedictione cœlesti et gratia repleamur.

But, O God of infinite
power, these sacred gifts are
not only on this altar here below ; they are also on that sublime altar of heaven, which is
before the throne of thy divine Majesty. These two altars are but one and the same,
on which is accomplished the
great mystery of thy glory and
our salvation. Vouchsafe to

Per cumdem Christum Dominum nostrum. Amen.

make us partakers of the Body and Blood of the august Victim, from whom flow every grace and blessing.

Nor is the moment less favourable for making supplication for the Church suffering. Let us, therefore, ask the divine Liberator, who has come down among us, that He mercifully visit, by a ray of His consoling light, the dark abode of purgatory, and permit His Blood to flow, as a stream of mercy's dew, from this our altar, and refresh the panting captives there. Let us pray expressly for those among them who have a claim on our suffrages.

Memento etiam, Domine, famulorum famularumque tuarum N. et N., qui nos præcesserunt cum signo fidei, et dormiunt in somno pacis. Ipsis Domine, et omnibus in Christo quiescentibus, locum refrigerii, lucis et pacis, ut indulgeas, deprecamur. Per eumdem Christum Dominum nostrum. Amen.

Dear Jesus! let the happiness of this thy visit extend to every portion of thy Church. Thy face gladdens the elect in the holy city ; even our mortal eyes can see beneath the veil of our delighted faith ; ah! hide not thyself from those brethren of ours, who are imprisoned in the place of expiation. Be thou refreshment to them in their flames, light in their darkness, and peace in their agonies of torment.

This duty of charity fulfilled, let us pray for ourselves, sinners, alas! who profit so little by the visit which our Saviour pays us. Let us, together with the priest, strike our breast, saying :

Nobis quoque peccatoribus famulis tuis, de multitudine miserationum tuarum sperantibus, partem aliquam et societatem donare digneris cum tuis sanctis apostolis et martyribus : cum Joanne, Stephano, Matthia, Barnaba, Ignatio,

Alas! we are poor sinners, O God of all sanctity! yet do we hope that thy infinite mercy will grant us to share thy kingdom, not, indeed, by reason of our works, which deserve little else than punishment, but because of the merits of this Sacrifice, which

Alexandro, Marcellino, Petro, Felicitate, Perpetua, Agatha, Lucia, Agnete, Cæcilia, Anastasia, et omnibus sanctis tuis ; intra quorum nos consortium, non æstimator meriti, sed veniæ, quæsumus, largitor admitte. Per Christum Dominum nostrum. Per quem hæc omnia, Domine, semper bona creas, sanctificas, vivificas, benedicis, et præstas nobis : per ipsum, et cum ipso, et in ipso, est tibi Deo Patri omnipotenti, in unitate Spiritus Sancti, omnis honor et gloria.

we are offering unto thee. Remember, too, the merits of thy holy apostles, of thy holy martyrs, of thy holy virgins, and of all thy saints. Grant us, by their intercession, grace in this world, and glory eternal in the next : which we ask of thee, in the name of our Lord Jesus Christ, thy Son. It is by him thou bestowest upon us thy blessings of life and sanctification ; and by him also, with him, and in him, in the unity of the Holy Ghost, may honour and glory be to thee!

While saying these last few words, the priest has taken up the sacred 'Host, which was on the altar ; he has held it over the chalice, thus reuniting the Body and Blood of the divine Victim, in order to show that He is now immortal. Then raising up both Chalice and Host, he offers to God the most noble and perfect homage which the divine Majesty could receive.

This solemn and mysterious rite ends the Canon. The silence of the mysteries is broken. The priest concludes his long prayers, by saying aloud, and so giving the faithful the opportunity of expressing their desire that his supplications be granted :

Per omnia sæcula sæculorum.

For ever and ever.

Answer him with faith, and in a sentiment of union with your holy mother the Church :

Amen.

Amen ! I believe the mystery which has just been accomplished. I unite myself to the offering which has been made, and to the petitions of the Church.

It is time to recite the **prayer** which our Saviour Himself has taught us. Let it ascend to heaven together with the sacrifice of the Body and Blood of Jesus Christ. How could it be otherwise than heard, when He Himself who made it for us, is in our very hands now while we say it? As this prayer belongs in common to all God's children, the priest recites it aloud, and begins by inviting us all to join in it.

OREMUS.

LET US PRAY.

Præceptis salutaribus moniti, et divina institutione formati, audemus dicere:

Having been taught by a saving precept, and following the form given us by a divine instruction, we thus presume to speak:

THE LORD'S PRAYER

Pater noster, qui es in cœlis, sanctificetur nomen tuum: adveniat regnum tuum: fiat voluntas tua sicut in cœlo, et in terra. Panem nostrum quotidianum da nobis hodie: et dimitte nobis debita nostra, sicut et nos dimittimus debitoribus nostris: et ne nos inducas in tentationem.

Our Father, who art in heaven, hallowed be thy name: thy kingdom come: thy will be done on earth as it is in heaven. Give us this day our daily bread; and *forgive us our trespasses*, as we forgive them that trespass against us: and lead us not into temptation.

Let us answer, with a deep feeling of our misery:

Sed libera nos a malo.

But deliver us from evil.

The priest falls once more into the silence of the holy mysteries. His first word is an affectionate *Amen* to your last petition—*deliver us from evil*—on which he forms his own next prayer: and could he pray for anything more needed? Evil surrounds us everywhere, and the Lamb on our altar has been sent to expiate it and to deliver us from it.

Libera nos, quæsumus, Domine, ab omnibus malis, præteritis, præsentibus et futuris : et, intercedente beata et gloriosa semper Virgine Dei Genitrice Maria, cum beatis apostolis tuis Petro et Paulo, atque Andrea, et omnibus sanctis, da propitius pacem in diebus nostris : ut ope misericordiæ tuæ adjuti, et a peccato simus semper liberi, et ab omni perturbatione securi. Per eumdem Dominum nostrum Jesum Christum Filium tuum, qui tecum vivit et regnat in unitate Spiritus Sancti Deus.

How many, O Lord, are the evils which beset us! Evils past, which are the wounds left on our soul by our sins, and which strengthen her wicked propensities. Evils present, that is, the sins now at this very time upon our soul; the weakness of this poor soul, and the temptations which molest her. There are, also, future evils, that is the chastisement which our sins deserve from the hand of thy justice. In presence of this Host of our salvation, we beseech thee, O Lord, to deliver us from all these evils, and to accept in our favour the intercession of Mary the Mother of Jesus, of thy holy apostles Peter and Paul and Andrew. Liberate us, break our chains, give us peace : through Jesus Christ, thy Son, who with thee liveth and reigneth God.

The priest is anxious to announce the peace, which he has asked and obtained ; he therefore finishes his prayer aloud, saying :

Per omnia sæcula sæculorum.

R. Amen.

World without end.

R. Amen.

Then he says :

Pax Domini sit semper vobiscum.

May the peace of our Lord be ever with you.

To this paternal wish, reply :

R. Et cum spiritu tuo.

R. And with thy spirit.

The mystery is drawing to a close : God is about to be united with man, and man with God, by means of Communion. But first, an imposing and sublime rite takes place at the altar. So far the priest has announced the death of Jesus; it is time to proclaim His Resurrection. To this end, he reverently breaks the sacred Host; and having divided it into three parts, he puts one into the chalice, thus reuniting the Body and Blood of the immortal Victim. Do you adore and say:

Hæc commixtio et conse-cratio Corporis et Sanguinis Domini nostri Jesu Christi, fiat accipientibus nobis in vitam æternam. Amen.	Glory be to thee, O Saviour of the world, who didst, in thy Passion, permit thy precious Blood to be separated from thy sacred Body, afterwards uniting them again together by thy divine power.

Offer now your prayer to the ever-living Lamb, whom St. John saw on the altar of heaven, standing as though slain:[1] say to this your Lord and King, who has taken upon Himself all our iniquities in order to wash them away by His Blood:

Agnus Dei, qui tollis pec-cata mundi, miserere nobis.	Lamb of God, who takest away the sins of the world, have mercy on us.
Agnus Dei, qui tollis pec-cata mundi, miserere nobis.	Lamb of God, who takest away the sins of the world, have mercy on us.
Agnus Dei, qui tollis pec-cata mundi, dona nobis pa-cem.	Lamb of God, who takest away the sins of the world, give us peace.

Peace is the grand object of our Saviour's coming into the world: He is the Prince of peace. The divine Sacrament of the Eucharist ought therefore to be the mystery of peace, and the bond of Catholic unity; for, as the apostle says, all we who partake of one Bread, are all one bread and one body.[2] It is on this account that the priest, now that he is on the point of receiving, in Communion, the sacred Host, prays that fraternal peace may be preserved in the Church, and more especially in this portion

[1] Apoc. v. 6.   [2] 1 Cor. x. 17.

of it which is assembled round the altar. Pray with him, and for the same blessing:

Domine Jesu Christe, qui dixisti apostolis tuis: Pacem relinquo vobis, pacem meam do vobis : ne respicias peccata mea, sed fidem Ecclesiæ tuæ : eamque secundum voluntatem tuam pacificare, et coadunare digneris. Qui vivis et regnas Deus, per omnia sæcula sæculorum. Amen.

Lord Jesus Christ, who saidst to thy apostles, 'My peace I leave with you, my peace I give unto you:' regard not my sins, but the faith of thy Church, and grant her that peace and unity which is according to thy will. Who livest and reignest God for ever and ever. Amen.

If it be a High Mass, the priest here gives the kiss of peace to the deacon, who gives it to the subdeacon, and he to the choir. During this ceremony, you should excite within yourself feelings of Christian charity, and pardon your enemies, if you have any. Then continue to pray with the priest:

Domine Jesu Christe, Fili Dei vivi, qui ex voluntate Patris, cooperante Spiritu Sancto, per mortem tuam mundum vivificasti: libera me per hoc sacrosanctum Corpus, et Sanguinem tuum, ab omnibus iniquitatibus meis, et universis malis, et fac me tuis semper inhærere mandatis, et a te nunquam separari permittas. Qui cum eodem Deo Patre et Spiritu Sancto vivis et regnas Deus in sæcula sæculorum. Amen.

Lord Jesus Christ, Son of the living God, who, according to the will of the Father, through the co-operation of the Holy Ghost, hast by thy death given life to the world; deliver me by this thy most sacred Body and Blood from all my iniquities, and from all evils; and make me always adhere to thy commandments, and never suffer me to be separated from thee, who with the same God the Father and the Holy Ghost, livest and reignest God for ever and ever. Amen.

If you are going to Communion at this Mass, say the following prayer; otherwise prepare yourself to make a spiritual Communion:

Perceptio Corporis tui, Domine Jesu Christe, quod ego indignus sumere præsumo, non mihi proveniat in judicium et condemnationem : sed pro tua pietate prosit mihi ad tutamentum mentis et corporis, et ad medelam percipiendam. Qui vivis et regnas cum Deo Patre in unitate Spiritus Sancti Deus, per omnia sæcula sæculorum. Amen.

Let not the participation of thy Body, O Lord Jesus Christ, which I, though unworthy, presume to receive, turn to my judgment and condemnation ; but through thy mercy may it be a safeguard and remedy both to my soul and body. Who with God the Father, in the unity of the Holy Ghost, livest and reignest God for ever and ever. Amen.

When the priest takes the Host into his hands, in order to receive it in Communion, say :

Panem cœlestem accipiam, et nomen Domini invocabo.

Come, my dear Jesus, come !

When he strikes his breast, confessing his unworthiness, say thrice with him these words, and in the same disposition as the centurion of the Gospel, who first used them :

Domine, non sum dignus, ut intres sub tectum meum : sed tantum dic verbo, et sanabitur anima mea.

Lord, I am not worthy that thou shouldst enter under my roof ; say it only with one word of thine, and my soul shall be healed.

Whilst the priest receives the sacred Host, if you also are to communicate, adore profoundly your God, who is ready to take up His abode within you, and again say to Him with the bride : ' Come, Lord Jesus, come !'

But should you not be going to receive sacramentally, make a spiritual Communion. Adore Jesus Christ who thus visits your soul by His grace, and say to Him :

Corpus Domini nostri Jesu Christi, custodiat animam meam in vitam æternam. Amen.

I give thee, O Jesus, this heart of mine, that thou mayst dwell in it, and do with me what thou wilt.

Then the priest takes the chalice, in thanksgiving, and says:

Quid retribuam Domino pro omnibus, quæ retribuit mihi? Calicem salutaris accipiam, et nomen Domini invocabo. Laudans invocabo Dominum, et ab inimicis meis salvus ero.

What return shall I make to the Lord for all he hath given to me? I will take the chalice of salvation, and will call upon the name of the Lord. Praising I will call upon the Lord, and I shall be saved from mine enemies.

But if you are to make a sacramental Communion, you should, at this moment of the priest's receiving the precious Blood, again adore the God who is coming to you, and keep to your prayer: 'Come, Lord Jesus, come!'

If, on the contrary, you are going to communicate only spiritually, again adore your divine Master, and say to Him:

Sanguis Domini nostri Jesu Christi custodiat animam meam in vitam æternam. Amen.

I unite myself to thee, my beloved Jesus! do thou unite thyself to me! and never let us be separated.

It is here that you must approach to the altar, if you are going to Communion. The dispositions suitable for holy Communion, during this season of Septuagesima, are given in the next chapter.

The Communion being finished, and while the priest is purifying the chalice the first time, say:

Quod ore sumpsimus, Domine, pura mente capiamus: et de munere temporali fiat nobis remedium sempiternum.

Thou hast visited me, O God, in these days of my pilgrimage; give me grace to treasure up the fruits of this visit for my future eternity.

While the priest is purifying the chalice the second time, say:

Corpus tuum, Domine, quod sumpsi, et Sanguis quem potavi, adhæreat vis-

Be thou for ever blessed, O my Saviour, for having admitted me to the sacred mys-

ceribus meis : et præsta ut in me non remaneat scelerum macula, quem pura et sancta refecerunt Sacramenta. Qui vivis et regnas in sæcula sæculorum. Amen.

tery of thy Body and Blood. May my heart and senses preserve, by thy grace, the purity which thou hast imparted to them; and may I be thus rendered less unworthy of thy divine visit.

The priest, having read the antiphon called the Communion, which is the first part of his thanksgiving for the favour just received from God, whereby He has renewed His divine presence among us, turns to the people with the usual salutation; after which he recites the prayers, called the Postcommunion, which are the completion of the thanksgiving. You will join him here also, thanking God for the unspeakable gift He has just lavished on you, and asking Him, with most earnest entreaty, that He will bestow upon you a lasting spirit of compunction.

These prayers having been recited, the priest again turns to the people, and full of joy for the immense favour he and they have been receiving, he says :

Dominus vobiscum.   The Lord be with you.

Answer him :

Et cum spiritu tuo.   And with thy spirit.
Benedicamus Domino.   Let us bless the Lord.
R. Deo gratias.   *R.* Thanks be to God.

The priest makes a last prayer, before giving you his blessing ; pray with him :

Placeat tibi, sancta Trinitas, obsequium servitutis meæ, et præsta ut sacrificium quod oculis tuæ majestatis indignus obtuli, tibi sit acceptabile, mihique, et omnibus, pro quibus illud obtuli, sit, te miserante,

Eternal thanks be to thee, O adorable Trinity, for the mercy thou hast shown to me, in permitting me to assist at this divine Sacrifice. Pardon me the negligence and coldness wherewith I have received so great a favour, and

propitiabile. Per Christum Dominum nostrum. Amen.

deign to confirm the blessing, which thy minister is about to give me in thy name.

The priest raises his hand, and thus blesses you :

Benedicat vos omnipotens Deus, Pater, et Filius, et Spiritus Sanctus.

R. Amen.

May the almighty God, Father, Son, and Holy Ghost, bless you !

R. Amen.

He then concludes the Mass, by reading the first fourteen verses of the Gospel according to St. John, which tell us of the eternity of the Word, and of the mercy which led Him to take upon Himself our *flesh*, and to *dwell among us*. Pray that you may be of the number of those, who, now that He has come *unto His own*, *receive Him*, and are made *the sons of God*.

V. Dominus vobiscum.

R. Et cum spiritu tuo.

V. The Lord be with you.

R. And with thy spirit.

THE LAST GOSPEL

Initium sancti Evangelii secundum Joannem.

The beginning of the holy Gospel according to John.

Cap. 1.

In principio erat Verbum, et Verbum erat apud Deum, et Deus erat Verbum. Hoc erat in principio apud Deum. Omnia per ipsum facta sunt ; et sine ipso factum est nihil quod factum est. In ipso vita erat, et vita erat lux hominum : et lux in tenebris lucet, et tenebræ eam non comprehenderunt. Fuit homo missus a Deo, cui nomen erat Joannes. Hic venit in testimonium, ut testimonium perhiberet de lumine, ut omnes crederent

Ch. 1.

In the beginning was the Word, and the Word was with God, and the Word was God. The same was in the beginning with God. All things were made by him, and without him was made nothing that was made. In him was life, and the life was the light of men ; and the light shineth in the darkness, and the darkness did not comprehend it. There was a man sent from God, whose name was John. This man came for a witness, to give testimony of the light

per illum. Non erat ille lux, sed ut testimonium perhiberet de lumine. Erat lux vera, quæ illuminat omnem hominem venientem in hunc mundum. In mundo erat, et mundus per ipsum factus est, et mundus eum non cognovit. In propria venit, et sui eum non receperunt. Quotquot autem receperunt eum, dedit eis potestatem filios Dei fieri, his qui credunt in nomine ejus : qui non ex sanguinibus, neque ex voluntate carnis, neque ex voluntate viri, sed ex Deo nati sunt. ET VERBUM CARO FACTUM EST, et habitavit in nobis : et vidimus gloriam ejus, gloriam quasi Unigeniti a Patre, plenum gratiæ et veritatis.

R. Deo gratias.

that all men might believe through him. He was not the light, but was to give testimony of the light. That was the true light which enlighteneth every man that cometh into this world. He was in the world, and the world was made by him, and the world knew him not. He came unto his own, and his own received him not. But as many as received him, to them he gave power to be made the sons of God ; to them that believe in his name, who are born, not of blood, nor of the will of the flesh, nor of the will of man, but of God. AND THE WORD WAS MADE FLESH, and dwelt among us ; and we saw his glory, as it were the glory of the Only-Begotten of the Father, full of grace and truth.

R. Thanks be to God.

CHAPTER THE SIXTH

ON HOLY COMMUNION DURING SEPTUAGESIMA

WE have already said that the Christian who, by the meditations suitable to the spirit of Septuagesima, has come to a clearer knowledge, not only of the sad consequences of original sin, but also of the malice of his own personal faults, should be all the more eager to assist at the holy Sacrifice, wherein is offered the Victim of man's salvation. But now that his own unworthiness is more than ever evident to him, ought he to abstain from partaking, by holy Communion, of this life-giving and purifying Host? Such is not our Saviour's will. He came down from heaven, not to judge,

but to save us.[1]   He knows how long and rugged
is the road we have to traverse, before we reach
that happy day, on which we shall rest with Him,
in the joy of His Resurrection. He has compassion
on us ; He fears lest we faint in the way ;[2] and He,
therefore, offers us the divine food, which gives
life and strength to our souls, and refreshes them
in their toil. We feel that our hearts are not yet
pure enough ; let us, then, with a humble and
contrite heart, go to Him who has come that He
may restore to our souls their original beauty.
Let us, at all times, remember the solemn injunction, which this Saviour so graciously deigned
to give us : 'Except ye eat the Flesh of the Son
of Man, ye shall not have life in you.'[3]

If, therefore, sin has no longer dominion over
us ; if we have destroyed it by true sorrow and
sincere confession, made efficacious by the absolution of God's priest : let us not deprive ourselves
of the Bread of life,[4] no matter how great soever
our infirmities may seem ; for it is for us that our
Jesus has prepared the feast. If we feel that the
chains of sin are still upon us ; if by self-examina-
tion, made with the light of the truth that is now
granted to us, we discover in our souls certain
stains, which the false principles of the world and
too easy a conscience have hitherto made us over-
look ; let us lose no time, let us make a good
confession : and when we have made our peace with
the God of mercy, let us approach the holy Table,
and receive the pledge of our reconciliation.

Yes, let us go to holy Communion, during this
season of Septuagesima, with a most heart-felt
conviction of our unworthiness. It may be that
hitherto we have sometimes gone with too much
familiarity, on account of our not sufficiently

---

[1] St. John iii. 17.   [2] St. Matt. xv. 32.
[3] St. John vi. 54.   [4] *Ibid.*, 35.

understanding our nothingness, our misery, and the infinite holiness of the God who thus unites Himself with His sinful creatures.   Henceforth, our heart shall be more truthful; blending together the two sentiments of humility and confidence, we will say, with an honest conviction, those words of the centurion of the Gospel, which the Church puts upon our lips, when she is distributing to us the Bread of life: 'Lord, I am not worthy that thou shouldst enter under my roof; say but the word, and my soul shall be healed.'[1]

We will here give, as in the two preceding seasons, acts, which may serve as a preparation for holy Communion during these weeks of Septuagesima.   There are souls that feel the want of some such assistance as this ; and, for the same reason, we will add a form of thanksgiving for after Communion.

BEFORE COMMUNION

ACT OF FAITH

The signal grace which thou, O my God, hast granted to me, that I should know the wounds of my soul, has revealed to me the greatness of my misery.   I have been taught how deep was the darkness that covered me, and how much I needed thy divine light.   But whilst the torch of faith has thus shown me the abyss of my own poor nature, it has also taught me how wonderful are the works, which thy love of thy ungrateful creature has made thee undertake, in order that thou mightest raise him up and save him.   It was for me thou didst assume my human nature, and wast born at Bethlehem ; it is for me that thou art soon to shed thy Blood on the cross.   Thou commandest me to believe these miracles of thy love.   I do believe them, O my God, humbly and gratefully.   I also believe, and with an equally lively faith, that in a few moments thou art to give thyself to me in this ineffable mystery of holy Communion.   Thou sayest to me : 'This is my Body, this is my Blood':—thy word is enough; in spite of my unworthiness seeming to forbid the possibility

---

[1] St. Matt. viii. 8.

of such Communion, I believe, I consent, I bow down before
thine infinite truth. Oh! can there be Communion between
the God of all holiness and a sinner such as I? And yet
thou assurest me that thou art verily coming to me! I
tremble, O eternal Truth, but I believe. I confess that thy
love of me is infinite, and that, having resolved to give thyself to thy poor and sinful creature, thou wilt suffer no
obstacle to stand in thy way!

ACT OF HUMILITY

During the season just past, I have often contemplated, O
my Jesus, thy coming from thy high throne into the bosom
of Mary, thy uniting thy divine Person to our weak mortal
nature, and thy being born in the crib of a poor stable. And
when I thought on these humiliations of my God, they
taught me not only to love thee tenderly, but also to know
my own nothingness, for I saw more clearly what an infinite
distance there is between the creature and his Creator; and
seeing these prodigies of thy immense love, I gladly confessed
my own vileness. But now, dearest Saviour, I am led to
consider something far more humiliating than the lowliness
of my nature. That nothingness should be but nothingness,
is not a sin. No; it is my sins that appal me. Sin has so
long tyrannized over me; its consequences are still upon me;
it has given me such dangerous tendencies; and I am so
weak in resisting its bidding. When my first parent sinned,
he hid himself, lest he should meet thee; and thou biddest
me come unto thee, not to sentence me to the punishment I
deserve, but to give me, oh! such a mark of love—union with
thyself! Can this be? Art thou not the infinitely holy God? I
must needs yield, and come, for thou art my sovereign Master;
and who is there that dares resist thy will? I come, then,
humbling myself, even to my very nothingness, before thee,
and beseeching thee to pardon my coming, for I come because
thou wilt have it so.

ACT OF CONTRITION

And shall I, O my Jesus, confess thus the grievousness
and multitude of my sins, without promising thee to sin no
more? Thou wishest this sinner to be reconciled with thee,
thou desirest to press him to thy sacred Heart: and could he,
whilst thanking thee for this thy wonderful condescension,
still love the accursed cause which made him thine enemy?
No, my infinitely merciful God, no! I will not, like my first

parent, seek to escape thy justice, but, like the prodigal son, I will arise and go to my Father ; like Magdalene, I will take courage and enter the banquet-hall ; and, though trembling at the sight of my sins, I will comply with thy loving invitation. My heart has no further attachment to sin, which I hate and detest as the enemy of thy honour and of my own happiness. I am resolved to shun it from this time forward, and to spare no pains to free myself from its tyranny. There shall be no more of that easy life which chilled my love, nor of that studied indifference which dulled my conscience, nor of those dangerous habits which led me to stray from my loyalty to thee. Despise not, O God, this my humble and contrite heart.

ACT OF LOVE

Such is thy love for us in this world, O my Jesus, that, as thou thyself sayest, thou art come not to judge, but to save. I should not satisfy thee, in this happy Communion hour, were I to offer thee but this salutary fear, which has led me to thy sacred feet, and this shame-stricken conscience, which makes me tremble in thy holy presence. The visit thou art about to pay me is a visit of love. The Sacrament, which is going to unite me to thee, is the Sacrament of thy love. Thou, my good Shepherd, hast said, that he loves most, who has been forgiven most. My heart then must dare to love thee ; it must love thee with all its warmth ; the very recollection of its past disloyalty must make its loving thee doubly needed and doubly fervent. Ah ! sweet Lord ! See this poor heart of mine ; strengthen it, console it, drive away its fears, make it feel that thou art its Jesus ! It has come back to thee, because it feared thee ; if it love thee, it will never again leave thee.

And thou, O Mary, refuge of sinners, help me to love him, who is thy Son, and our Brother. Holy angels ! ye who live eternally on that love, which has never ceased to glow in your mighty spirits, remember, I reverently pray you, that this God created me, as he did you, that I might love him. All ye holy saints of God ! I beseech you, by the love wherewith ye are inebriated in heaven, graciously give me a thought, and prepare now my heart to be united with him. Amen.

AFTER COMMUNION

ACT OF ADORATION

Thou art here within me, great God of heaven! Thou art, at this moment, residing in a sinner's heart! I, yea, I, am thy temple, thy throne, thy resting-place! How shall I worthily adore thee, who hast deigned to come down into this abyss of my lowliness and misery? The angels veil their faces in thy presence; thy saints lay their crowns at thy feet; and I, that am but a sinful mortal, how shall I sufficiently honour thee, O infinite Power, infinite Wisdom, infinite Goodness? This soul, wherein thou art now dwelling, has presumed so many times to set thee at defiance, and boldly disobey and break thy commands. And thou canst come to me after all this, and bring all thy beauty and greatness with thee! What else can I do, but give thee the homage of a heart, that knows not how to bear the immensity of the honour thou art now lavishing on me? Yes, my own wonderful and loving God, I adore thee; I acknowledge thee to be the sovereign Being, the Creator and preserver of all creatures, and the undisputed Master of everything that belongs to me. I delightedly confess my dependence on thee, and offer thee, with all my heart, my humble service.

ACT OF THANKSGIVING

Thy greatness, O my God, is infinite; but thy goodness to me is incomprehensible. Thy being now present within this breast of mine is, I know, a proof of that immense power, which shows itself where and when it wills; but it is also a mark of thy love for me. Thou art come to my soul, that thou mayst be closely united with her, comfort her, give her a new life, and bring her all good things. Oh! who will teach me how to value this grace, and thank thee for it in a becoming way? But how shall I hope to value it as I ought, when I am not able to understand either the love that brings thee thus within me, or my own need of having thee? And when I think of my inability to make thee a suitable return of thanks, I feel as though I can give thee nothing but my speechless gratitude. Yet thou willest that this my heart, poor as it is, should give thee its thanks; thou takest delight in receiving its worthless homage. Take it, then, my loving Jesus! I give it thee with all possible joy, and beseech thee to reveal unto me the immensity of thy gift, and to enrich me more that I may give thee more.

ACT OF LOVE

But nothing will satisfy thee, O my infinite Treasure, unless I give thee my love. Thou hast ever loved me, and thou art still loving me; I must love thee in return! Thou hast borne with me; thou hast forgiven me; thou art, at this moment, overpowering me with honour and riches; and all this out of love for me! The return thou askest of me, is my love! Gratitude will not content thee, thou wilt have my love! But, Jesus, my dear Jesus!—my past life—the long years I have spent in offending thee—rise up before me, and tell me to hide myself from thee! And yet, whither could I go without carrying thee within me, for thou hast taken up thine abode in my inmost soul? No, I will not run from thee! I will summon all the energies of my heart to tell thee that I love thee; that thy love for me has emboldened me; that I belong to thee; that I love thee above all else that I love; and that, henceforth, all my joy and happiness shall be in pleasing thee, and doing whatsoever thou askest of me.

ACT OF OBLATION

I know, dear Jesus, that what thou askest of me is not the passing sentiment of a heart excited by the thought of thy goodness towards it. Thou hast loved me from eternity; thou lovedst me, even when I was doing nothing for thee; thou hast given me light to know my miseries; thou hast shielded me against thine own angry justice; thou hast mercifully pardoned me a countless number of times; thou art even now embracing me with tenderest love; and all these works of thy almighty hand have been but for one end—to make me give myself to thee, and live, at last, for thee. It is this thou wouldst obtain of me, by granting me this precious earnest of thy love, which I have just received. Thou hast said, speaking of this ineffable gift: ' As I live by the Father; so he that eateth me, the same also shall live by me.'[1] Henceforth, O Bread, which came down from heaven![2] thou art the source of my life. Now, more than ever, my life belongs to thee. I give it unto thee. I dedicate unto thee my soul, my body, my faculties, my whole being. Do thou direct and govern me. I resign myself entirely into thy hands. I am blind, but thy light will guide me; I am weak, but thy power will uphold me; I am inconstant, but thy unchangeableness will give me stability. I trust unreservedly in thy mercy, which never abandons them that hope in thee.

---

[1] St. John vi. 58.   [2] *Ibid.*, 51.

O Mary! pray for me, that I lose not the fruit of this visit.
Holy angels! watch over this dwelling-place of your Lord,
which he has so mercifully chosen: let nothing defile it.
O all ye saints of God! pray for the sinner, unto whom he
has given this pledge of his divine pardon.

CHAPTER THE SEVENTH

ON THE OFFICE OF VESPERS FOR SUNDAYS AND FEASTS DURING SEPTUAGESIMA

The Office of Vespers, or Evensong, consists firstly
of the five following psalms and antiphons. According to our custom, we preface each psalm with
a short explanation, in order to draw attention to
what is most in harmony with the spirit of Septuagesima.

After the *Pater* and *Ave* have been said in secret,
the Church commences this Hour with her favourite
supplication :

V. Deus in adjutorium meum intende.

R. Domine, ad adjuvandum me festina.

Gloria Patri, et Filio, et Spiritui Sancto:

Sicut erat in principio et nunc et semper, et in sæcula sæculorum. Amen.

Laus tibi, Domine, Rex æternæ gloriæ.

ANT. Dixit Dominus.

V. Incline unto my aid, O God.

R. O Lord, make haste to help me.

Glory be to the Father, and to the Son, and to the Holy Ghost.

As it was in the beginning, is now, and ever shall be, world without end. Amen.

Praise be to thee, O Lord, King of eternal glory.

ANT. The Lord said.

The first psalm is a prophecy of the future glory
of the Messias. It shows us His triumph; after
His humiliations and His cross, the Man-God
shall sit on the *right hand* of His Father. Moreover, He is to come again into this world, to *judge*

it, and to *crush* the proud *heads* of sinners. Whilst thus celebrating His glory, let us not forget His justice.

PSALM 109

Dixit Dominus Domino meo : * Sede a dextris meis.

Donec ponam inimicos tuos : * scabellum pedum tuorum.

Virgam virtutis tuæ emittet Dominus ex Sion : * dominare in medio inimicorum tuorum.

Tecum principium in die virtutis tuæ in splendoribus sanctorum : * ex utero ante luciferum genui te.

Juravit Dominus, et non pœnitebit eum : * Tu es Sacerdos in æternum secundum ordinem Melchisedech.

Dominus a dextris tuis : * confregit in die iræ suæ reges.

Judicabit in nationibus, implebit ruinas : * conquassabit capita in terra multorum.

De torrente in via bibet : * propterea exaltabit caput.

ANT. Dixit Dominus Domino meo, sede a dextris meis.

ANT. Magna opera Domini.

The Lord said to my Lord, *his Son :* Sit thou at my right hand, *and reign with me.*

Until, *on the day of thy last coming,* I make thy enemies thy footstool.

O Christ ! the Lord *thy Father,* will send forth the sceptre of thy power out of Sion : *from thence* rule thou in the midst of thy enemies.

With thee is the principality in the day of thy strength, in the brightness of the saints : *For the Father hath said to thee :* From the womb, before the day-star, I begot thee.

The Lord hath sworn, and he will not repent : *he hath said, speaking of thee, the God-Man :* Thou art a priest for ever, according to the order of Melchisedech.

Therefore, O Father, the Lord *thy Son* is at thy right hand : he hath broken kings in the day of his wrath.

He shall *also* judge among nations : *in that terrible coming,* he shall fill the ruins *of the world :* he shall crush the heads in the land of many.

He cometh now in humility : he shall drink, in the way, of the torrent *of sufferings :* therefore, shall he lift up the head.

ANT. The Lord said to my Lord, sit thou at my right hand.

ANT. Great are the works of the Lord.

The following psalm commemorates the mercies of God to His *people*, the promised *Covenant*, the *Redemption*, His *fidelity* to His word. But it also tells us that the *name* of the Lord is *terrible* because it is *holy;* and concludes by telling us, that *the fear of the Lord is the beginning of wisdom.*

PSALM 110

Confitebor tibi, Domine, in toto corde meo : * in consilio justorum et congregatione.

I will praise thee, O Lord, with my whole heart : in the counsel of the just, and in the congregation.

Magna opera Domini : * exquisita in omnes voluntates ejus.

Great are the works of the Lord : sought out according to all his wills.

Confessio et magnificentia opus ejus : * et justitia ejus manet in sæculum sæculi.

His work is praise and magnificence : and his justice continueth for ever and ever.

Memoriam fecit mirabilium suorum, misericors et miserator Dominus : * escam dedit timentibus se.

He hath made a remembrance of his wonderful works, being a merciful and gracious Lord : he hath given food to them that fear him.

Memor erit in sæculum testamenti sui : * virtutem operum suorum annuntiabit populo suo.

He will be mindful for ever of his covenant *with men :* he will show forth to his people the power of his works.

Ut det illis hæreditatem Gentium : * opera manuum ejus veritas et judicium.

That· he may give them, *his Church*, the inheritance of the Gentiles : the works of his hands are truth and judgment.

Fidelia omnia mandata ejus, confirmata in sæculum sæculi : * facta in veritate et æquitate.

All his commandments are faithful, confirmed for ever and ever : made in truth and equity.

Redemptionem misit populo suo : * mandavit in æternum testamentum suum.

He hath sent redemption to his people ; he hath *thereby* commanded his covenant for ever.

Sanctum et terribile nomen ejus : * initium sapientiæ timor Domini.

Holy and terrible is his name : the fear of the Lord is the beginning of wisdom.

Intellectus bonus omnibus facientibus eum : * laudatio ejus manet in sæculum sæculi.

A good understanding to all that do it : his praise continueth for ever and ever.

ANT. Magna opera Do-
mini: exquisita in omnes
voluntates ejus,
ANT. Qui timet Do-
minum.

ANT. Great are the works of
the Lord: sought out according to all his wills.
ANT. He that feareth the
Lord.

The next psalm sings the happiness of the *just
man*, and his hopes on the day of his Lord's coming.
It tells us, likewise, of the confusion and despair
which will torment the *sinner*, who, during life, was
insensible to his own interests, and deaf to the
invitations made him by the Church.

PSALM 111

Beatus vir, qui timet Do-
minum: * in mandatis ejus
volet nimis.

Blessed is the man that
feareth the Lord: he shall
delight exceedingly in his
commandments.

Potens in terra erit semen
ejus : * generatio rectorum
benedicetur.

His seed shall be mighty
upon earth: the generation
of the righteous shall be
blessed.

Gloria, et divitiæ in domo
ejus : * et justitia ejus manet
in sæculum sæculi.

Glory and wealth shall be
in his house : and his justice
remaineth for ever and ever.

Exortum est in tenebris
lumen rectis : * misericors,
et miserator, et justus.

To the righteous a light is
risen up in darkness : he is
merciful, and compassionate,
and just.

Jucundus homo, qui mise-
retur et commodat, disponet
sermones suos in judicio : *
quia in æternum non com-
movebitur.

Acceptable is the man that
showeth mercy and lendeth ;
he shall order his words with
judgment : because he shall
not be moved for ever.

In memoria æterna erit
justus : * ab auditione mala
non timebit.

The just shall be in everlasting remembrance : he shall
not fear the evil hearing.

Paratum cor ejus sperare
in Domino, confirmatum est
cor ejus : * non commovebi-
tur donec despiciat inimicos
suos.

His heart is ready to hope
in the Lord ; his heart is
strengthened ; he shall not
be moved until he look over
his enemies.

Dispersit, dedit pauperi-
bus, justitia ejus manet in

He hath distributed, he hath
given to the poor ; his justice

sæculum sæculi : * cornu ejus exaltabitur in gloria.

remaineth for ever and ever : his horn shall be exalted in glory.

Peccator videbit, et irasce- tur, dentibus suis fremet et tabescet : * desiderium pec- catorum peribit.

The wicked shall see, and shall be angry ; he shall gnash with his teeth, and pine away ; the desire of the wicked shall perish.

ANT. Qui timet Domi- num, in mandatis ejus cupit nimis.

ANT. He that feareth the Lord, in his commandments he hath delighted exceedingly.

ANT. Sit nomen Domini.

ANT. May the name of the Lord.

The psalm, *Laudate pueri,* is a canticle of praise to the Lord, who, from His high heaven, has taken pity on the fallen human race, and facilitated its return to its Maker.

PSALM 112

Laudate, pueri, Domi- num : * laudate nomen Do- mini.

Praise the Lord, ye chil- dren ; praise ye the name of the Lord.

Sit nomen Domini bene- dictum : * ex hoc nunc et usque in sæculum.

Blessed be the name of the Lord : from henceforth now and for ever.

A solis ortu usque ad oc- casum : * laudabile nomen Domini.

From the rising of the sun unto the going down of the same, the name of the Lord is worthy of praise.

Excelsus super omnes gentes Dominus : * et super cœlos gloria ejus.

The Lord is high above all nations : and his glory above the heavens.

Quis sicut Dominus Deus noster qui in altis habitat : * et humilia respicit in cœlo et in terra ?

Who is as the Lord our God, who dwelleth on high : and looketh down on the low things in heaven and in earth ?

Suscitans a terra inopem :* et de stercore erigens pau- perem.

Raising up the needy from the earth : and lifting up the poor out of the dunghill.

Ut collocet eum cum prin- cipibus : * cum principibus populi sui.

That he may place him with princes : with the princes of his people.

Qui habitare facit sterilem in domo : * matrem filiorum lætantem.

Who maketh a barren wo- man to dwell in a house, the joyful mother of children.

Ant. Sit nomen Domini benedictum in sæcula.
Ant. Deus autem noster.

Ant. May the name of the Lord be for ever blessed.
Ant. But our God.

The fifth psalm, *In exitu*, recounts the prodigies witnessed under the ancient Covenant: they were figures, whose realities are to be accomplished in us, if we will but return to the Lord our God. He will deliver *Israel* from Egypt, emancipate the *Gentiles* from their idolatry, and pour out a *blessing* on every man who will consent to fear and love the Lord.

PSALM 113

In exitu Israël de Ægypto: * domus Jacob de populo barbaro.

Facta est Judæa sanctificatio ejus: * Israël potestas ejus.

Mare vidit, et fugit: * Jordanis conversus est retrorsum.

Montes exsultaverunt ut arietes: * et colles sicut agni ovium.

Quid est tibi, mare, quod fugisti: * et tu Jordanis, quia conversus es retrorsum?

Montes exsultastis sicut arietes: * et colles sicut agni ovium?

A facie Domini mota est terra: * a facie Dei Jacob.

Qui convertit petram in stagna aquarum: * et rupem in fontes aquarum.

Non nobis, Domine, non nobis: * sed nomini tuo da gloriam.

Super misericordia tua, et veritate tua: * nequando

When Israel went out of Egypt, the house of Jacob from a barbarous people.

Judea was made his sanctuary, Israel his dominion.

The sea saw and fled; Jordan was turned back.

The mountains skipped like rams: and the hills like the lambs of the flock.

What ailed thee, O thou sea, that thou didst flee: and thou, O Jordan, that thou wast turned back?

Ye mountains that ye skipped like rams: and ye hills like lambs of the flock?

At the presence of the Lord the earth was moved, at the presence of the God of Jacob.

Who turned the rock into pools of water, and the stony hills into fountains of water.

Not to us, O Lord, not to us: but to thy name give glory.

For thy mercy, and for thy truth's sake: lest the Gentiles

dicant Gentes : Ubi est Deus eorum ?

Deus autem noster in cœlo : * omnia quæcumque voluit, fecit.

Simulacra Gentium argentum et aurum : * opera manuum hominum.

Os habent, et non loquentur : * oculos habent, et non videbunt.

Aures habent, et non audient : * nares habent et non odorabunt.

Manus habent, et non palpabunt, pedes habent et non ambulabunt : * non clamabunt in gutture suo.

Similes illis fiant qui faciunt ea : * et omnes qui confidunt in eis.

Domus Israël speravit in Domino : * adjutor eorum, et protector eorum est.

Domus Aaron speravit in Domino : * adjutor eorum, et protector eorum est.

Qui timent Dominum, speraverunt in Domino : * adjutor eorum, et protector eorum est.

Dominus memor fuit nostri : * et benedixit nobis.

Benedixit domui Israël : * benedixit domui Aaron.

Benedixit omnibus qui timent Dominum : * pusillis cum majoribus.

Adjiciat Dominus super vos : * super vos, et super filios vestros.

Benedicti vos a Domino : * qui fecit cœlum et terram.

Cœlum cœli Domino : * terram autem dedit filiis hominum.

should say : Where is their God ?

But our God is in heaven : he hath done all things whatsoever he would.

The idols of the Gentiles are silver and gold : the works of the hands of men.

They have mouths, and speak not : they have eyes, and see not.

They have ears, and hear not : they have noses, and smell not.

They have hands, and feel not : they have feet, and walk not : neither shall they cry out through their throat.

Let them that make them become like unto them : and all such as trust in them.

The house of Israel hath hoped in the Lord : he is their helper and their protector.

The house of Aaron hath hoped in the Lord : he is their helper and their protector.

They that feared the Lord have hoped in the Lord : he is their helper and their protector.

The Lord hath been mindful of us, and hath blessed us.

He hath blessed the house of Israel : he hath blessed the house of Aaron.

He hath blessed all that fear the Lord, both little and great.

May the Lord add blessings upon you : upon you, and upon your children.

Blessed be you of the Lord, who made heaven and earth.

The heaven of heaven is the Lord's : but the earth he has given to the children of men.

Non mortui laudabunt te, Domine : * neque omnes qui descendunt in infernum.

Sed nos qui vivimus, benedicimus Domino : * èx hoc nunc et usque in sæculum.

ANT. Deus autem noster in cœlo : omnia quæcumque voluit, fecit.

The dead shall not praise thee O Lord : nor any of them that go down to hell.

But we that live bless the Lord : from this time now and for ever.

ANT. But our God is in heaven : he hath done all things whatsoever he would.

After these five psalms, a short lesson from the holy Scriptures is read. It is called *Capitulum*, because it is always very short. The one for each Sunday is given in the *Proper*.

After the capitulum, follows the hymn, *Lucis Creator*. It was written by St. Gregory the Great. It sings of creation, and celebrates the praises of that portion of it which was called forth on this first day—the *light*. The saint teaches us to ask that our soul may be roused, may be loosed from the spells of this life, and may turn all her energies to eternal things.

HYMN *

Lucis Creator optime, Lucem dierum proferens : Primordiis lucis novæ, Mundi parans originem.

O infinitely good Creator of the light ! by thee was produced the light of day, providing thus the world's beginning with the beginning of the new-made light.

---

* According to the monastic rite, it is as follows :—

R. breve. Quam magnificata sunt, * Opera tua Domine. Quam. V. Omnia in sapientia fecisti. * Opera. Gloria Patri, etc. Quam.

Lucis Creator optime, Lucem dierum proferens ; Primordiis lucis novæ, Mundi parans originem.

Qui mane junctum vesperi Diem vocari præcipis, Tetrum chaos illabitur, Audi preces cum fletibus.

Ne mens gravata crimine, Vitæ sit exsul munere, Dum nil perenne cogitat, Seseque culpis illigat.

Cœlorum pulset intimum, Vitale tollat præmium : Vitemus omne noxium, Purgemus omne pessimum.

Præsta, Pater piissime, Patrique compar Unice, Cum Spiritu Paraclito Regnans per omne sæculum. Amen.

Qui mane junctum vesperi
Diem vocari præcipis,
Illabitur tetrum chaos.
Audi preces cum fletibus.

Ne mens gravata crimine,
Vitæ sit exsul munere,
Dum nil perenne cogitat.
Seseque culpis illigat.

Cœleste pulset ostium
Vitale tollat præmium :
Vitemus omne noxium,
Purgemus omne pessimum.

Præsta, Pater piissime,
Patrique compar Unice,
Cum Spiritu Paraclito
Regnans per omne sæculum.
Amen.
V. Dirigatur, Domine,
oratio mea,
R. Sicut incensum in
conspectu tuo.

Thou biddest us call the
time from morn till eve, *day;*
this *day* is over ; dark night
comes on—oh ! hear our tear-
ful prayers.

Let not our soul, weighed
down by crime mis-spend thy
gift of life, and, forgetting
what is eternal, be earth-tied
by her sins.

Oh ! may we strive to enter
our heavenly home, and bear
away the prize of life : may
we shun what would injure us,
and cleanse our soul from her
defilements.

Most merciful Father ! and
thou, his only-begotten Son,
coequal with him, reigning for
ever with the holy Paraclete !
grant this our prayer. Amen.
V. May my prayer, O Lord,
ascend,
R. Like incense in thy sight.

Then is said the *Magnificat* antiphon, which is
to be found in the proper. After this, the Church
sings the canticle of Mary, the *Magnificat*, in which
are celebrated the divine maternity and all its con-
sequent blessings. This exquisite canticle is an
essential part of the Vespers throughout the year.
Let us unite with *all generations,* and *call* her
' *blessed* '; but let us, also, enter into those sentiments of humility, which she recommends to us
both by her words and her example. Her inspired
lips speak to us this promise: If the great God,
whose triumph is to gladden us on the glorious day
of Easter, find us humble and submissive, He will
exalt us, yea, raise us up even to Himself ; if we
confess our misery and *poverty* to Him, He will
enrich us, even to the *full*, with every blessing.

OUR LADY'S CANTICLE

(*St. Luke* i.)

Magnificat : * anima mea Dominum.

My soul doth magnify the Lord.

Et exsultavit spiritus meus : * in Deo salutari meo.

And my spirit hath rejoiced in God my Saviour.

Quia respexit humilitatem ancillæ suæ : * ecce enim ex hoc beatam me dicent omnes generationes.

Because he hath regarded the humility of his handmaid : for, behold from henceforth all generations shall call me blessed.

Quia fecit mihi magna qui potens est : * et sanctum nomen ejus.

Because he that is mighty hath done great things to me : and holy is his name.

Et misericordia ejus a progenie in progenies : * timentibus eum.

And his mercy is from generation unto generation, to them that fear him.

Fecit potentiam in brachio suo : * dispersit superbos mente cordis sui.

He hath showed might in his arm : he hath scattered the proud in the conceit of their heart.

Deposuit potentes de sede : * et exaltavit humiles.

He hath put down the mighty from their seat : and hath exalted the humble.

Esurientes implevit bonis : * et divites dimisit inanes.

He hath filled the hungry with good things : and the rich he hath sent empty away.

Suscepit Israel puerum suum : * recordatus misericordiæ suæ.

He hath received Israel his servant, being mindful of his mercy.

Sicut locutus est ad patres nostros : * Abraham et semini ejus in sæcula.

As he spake to our fathers, to Abraham and to his seed for ever.

The *Magnificat* antiphon is then repeated. The prayer, or Collect, will be found in the proper of each Sunday.

The Vespers end with the following versicles :

V. Benedicamus Domino.

R. Deo gratias.

V. Fidelium animæ per misericordiam Dei requiescant in pace.

R. Amen.

V. Let us bless the Lord.

R. Thanks be to God.

V. May the souls of the faithful departed, through the mercy of God, rest in peace.

R. Amen.

CHAPTER THE EIGHTH

ON THE OFFICE OF COMPLINE DURING SEPTUAGESIMA

THIS Office, which concludes the day, commences by a warning of the dangers of the night: then immediately follows the public confession of our sins, as a powerful means of propitiating the divine justice, and obtaining God's help, now that we are going to spend so many hours in the unconscious and therefore dangerous state of sleep, which is also such an image of death.

The lector, addressing the priest, says to him:

V. Jube, domne, benedicere.

Pray, father, give me thy blessing.

The priest answers:

Noctem quietam, et finem perfectum concedat nobis Dominus omnipotens.
R. Amen.

May the almighty Lord grant us a quiet night and a perfect end.
R. Amen.

The lector then reads these words, from the first Epistle of St. Peter:

Fratres: Sobrii estote, et vigilate: quia adversarius vester diabolus, tamquam leo rugiens circuit quærens quem devoret: cui resistite fortes in fide. Tu autem, Domine, miserere nobis.

Brethren, be sober and watch: because your adversary the devil, as a roaring lion, goeth about, seeking whom he may devour: whom resist ye, strong in faith. But thou, O Lord, have mercy on us.

The choir answers:

R. Deo gratias.

R. Thanks be to God.

Then, the priest:

V. Adjutorium nostrum in nomine Domini.

V. Our help is in the name of the Lord.

The choir:

R. Qui fecit cœlum et terram.

R. Who hath made heaven and earth.

Then the Lord's Prayer is recited in secret; after which the priest says the *Confiteor;* and, when he has finished, the choir says:

Misereatur tui omnipotens Deus, et dimissis peccatis tuis, perducat te ad vitam æternam.

May almighty God have mercy on thee, and, forgiving thy sins, bring thee to everlasting life.

The priest having answered *Amen,* the choir repeats the *Confiteor,* thus:

Confiteor Deo omnipotenti, beatæ Mariæ semper Virgini, beato Michaeli archangelo, beato Joanni Baptistæ, sanctis apostolis Petro et Paulo, omnibus sanctis, et tibi, pater: quia peccavi nimis cogitatione, verbo, et opere: mea culpa, mea culpa, mea maxima culpa. Ideo precor beatam Mariam semper Virginem, beatum Michaelem archangelum, beatum Joannem Baptistam, sanctos apostolos Petrum et Paulum, omnes sanctos, et te, pater, orare pro me ad Dominum Deum nostrum.

I confess to almighty God, to blessed Mary ever Virgin, to blessed Michael the archangel, to blessed John the Baptist, to the holy apostles Peter and Paul, to all the saints, and to thee, father, that I have sinned exceedingly in thought, word, and deed; through my fault, through my fault, through my most grievous fault. Therefore I beseech blessed Mary ever Virgin, blessed Michael the archangel, blessed John the Baptist, the holy apostles Peter and Paul, and all the saints, and thee, father, to pray to the Lord our God for me.

The priest then says:

Misereatur vestri omnipotens Deus, et dimissis peccatis vestris, perducat vos ad vitam æternam.

R. Amen.

Indulgentiam, absolutionem, et remissionem peccatorum nostrorum, tribuat nobis omnipotens et misericors Dominus.

R. Amen.

V. Converte nos, Deus, Salutaris noster.

R. Et averte iram tuam a nobis.

V. Deus, in adjutorium meum intende.

R. Domine, ad adjuvandum me festina.

Gloria Patri, etc.

Laus tibi, Domine, Rex æternæ gloriæ.

ANT. Miserere.

May almighty God be merciful to you, and, forgiving your sins, bring you to everlasting life.

R. Amen.

May the almighty and merciful Lord grant us pardon, absolution, and remission of our sins.

R. Amen.

V. Convert us, O God, our Saviour.

R. And turn away thy anger from us.

V. Incline unto my aid, O God.

R. O Lord, make haste to help me.

Glory, etc.

Praise be to thee, O Lord, King of eternal glory.

ANT. Have mercy.

The first psalm expresses the confidence with which the just man *sleeps in peace*; but it also rebukes those tepid Christians, whose *dull hearts* are but too often enslaved to *vanity* and *lies*, and exhorts them to examine, at the close of the day, the thoughts of their *hearts*, and be *sorry for them* at that time of stillness and repose.

PSALM 4

Cum invocarem exaudivit me Deus justitiæ meæ: * in tribulatione dilatasti mihi.

When I called upon him, the God of my justice heard me: when I was in distress, thou hast enlarged me.

Miserere mei: * et exaudi orationem meam.

Filii hominum, usquequo gravi corde: * ut quid diligitis vanitatem, et quæritis mendacium?

Et scitote quoniam mirificavit Dominus sanctum suum: * Dominus exaudiet me, cum clamavero ad eum.

Irascimini, et nolite peccare: * quæ dicitis in cordibus vestris, in cubilibus vestris compungimini.

Sacrificate sacrificium justitiæ, et sperate in Domino: * multi dicunt: Quis ostendit nobis bona?

Signatum est super nos lumen vultus tui Domine: * dedisti lætitiam in corde meo.

A fructu frumenti, vini et olei sui: * multiplicati sunt.

In pace in idipsum: * dormiam et requiescam.

Quoniam tu, Domine, singulariter in spe: * constituisti me.

Have mercy on me: and hear my prayer.

O ye sons of men, how long will you be dull of heart? why do you love vanity, and seek after lying?

Know ye also that the Lord hath made his holy One wonderful: the Lord will hear me, when I cry unto him.

Be ye angry, and sin not: the things you say in your hearts, be sorry for them upon your beds.

Offer up the sacrifice of justice, and trust in the Lord: many say, who showeth us good things?

The light of thy countenance, O Lord, is signed upon us: thou hast given gladness in my heart.

By the fruit of their corn, their wine, and oil, they are multiplied.

In peace, in the self-same, I will sleep, and I will rest.

For thou, O Lord, singularly hast settled me in hope.

The second psalm gives the motives of the just man's confidence, even during the dangers of the night. The description here given of peace of mind should make the sinner long for a reconciliation with his God, that so he, too, may enjoy that divine protection, without which there can be no security or happiness in this life of peril and misery.

PSALM 90

Qui habitat in adjutorio Altissimi : * in protectione Dei cœli commorabitur.

Dicet Domino : Susceptor meus es tu, et refugium meum : * Deus meus, sperabo in eum.

Quoniam ipse liberavit me de laqueo venantium : * et a verbo aspero.

Scapulis suis obumbrabit tibi : * et sub pennis ejus sperabis.

Scuto circumdabit te veritas ejus : * non timebis a more nocturno.

A sagitta volante in die, a negotio perambulante in tenebris : * ab incursu, et dæmonio meridiano.

Cadent a latere tuo mille, et decem millia a dextris tuis : * ad te autem non appropinquabit.

Verumtamen oculis tuis considerabis : * et retributionem peccatorum videbis.

Quoniam tu es, Domine, spes mea : * Altissimum posuisti refugium tuum.

Non accedet ad te malum : * et flagellum non appropinquabit tabernaculo tuo.

Quoniam angelis suis mandavit de te : * ut custodiant te in omnibus viis tuis.

He that dwelleth in the aid of the Most High, shall abide under the protection of the God of heaven.

He shall say to the Lord : Thou art my protector, and my refuge : my God, in him will I trust.

For he hath delivered me from the snare of the hunters : and from the sharp word.

He will overshadow thee with his shoulders : and under his wings thou shalt trust.

His truth shall compass thee with a shield : thou shalt not be afraid of the terror of the night.

Of the arrow that flieth in the day : of the business that walketh about in the dark : of invasion, or of the noonday devil.

A thousand shall fall at thy side, and ten thousand at thy right hand : but it shall not come nigh thee.

But thou shalt consider with thy eyes : and shalt see the reward of the wicked.

Because *thou hast said :* Thou, O Lord, art my hope : thou hast made the Most High thy refuge.

There shall no evil come to thee, nor shall the scourge come near thy dwelling.

For he hath given his angels charge over thee : to keep thee in all thy ways.

In manibus portabunt te: * ne forte offendas ad lapidem pedem tuum.

In their hands they shall bear thee up: lest thou dash thy foot against a stone.

Super aspidem et basiliscum ambulabis. * et conculcabis leonem et draconem.

Thou shalt walk upon the asp and the basilisk: and thou shalt trample under foot the lion and the dragon.

Quoniam in me speravit, liberabo eum : * protegam eum, quoniam cognovit nomen meum.

God will say of thee : Because he hoped in me, I will deliver him : I will protect him, because he hath known my name.

Clamabit ad me, et ego exaudiam eum : * cum ipso sum in tribulatione, eripiam eum, et glorificabo eum.

He will cry to me, and I will hear him : I am with him in tribulation, I will deliver him, and I will glorify him.

Longitudine dierum replebo eum : * et ostendam illi salutare meum.

I will fill him with length of days : and I will show him my salvation.

The third psalm invites the *servants* of God to persevere, with fervour, in the prayers they offer during the *night*. The faithful should say this psalm in a spirit of gratitude to God, for raising up, in the Church, adorers of His holy name, whose grand vocation is to *lift up their hands*, day and night, for the safety of Israel. On such prayers depend the happiness and the destinies of the world.

PSALM 133

Ecce nunc benedicite Dominum : * omnes servi Domini.

Behold now bless ye the Lord, all ye servants of the Lord.

Qui statis in domo Domini : * in atriis domus Dei nostri.

Who stand in the house of the Lord, in the courts of the house of our God.

In noctibus extollite manus vestras in sancta : * et benedicite Dominum.

Benedicat te Dominus ex Sion : * qui fecit cœlum et terram.

ANT. Miserere mihi, Domine, et exaudi orationem meam.

In the nights lift up your hands to the holy places, and bless ye the Lord.

Say to Israel : May the Lord out of Sion bless thee, he that made heaven and earth.

ANT. Have mercy on me, O Lord, and hear my prayer.

HYMN[1]

Te lucis ante terminum,
Rerum Creator, poscimus,
Ut pro tua clementia
Sis præsul et custodia.

Procul recedant somnia,
Et noctium phantasmata ;
Hostemque nostrum comprime,
Ne polluantur corpora.

Præsta, Pater piissime,
Patrique compar Unice,
Cum Spiritu Paraclito
Regnans per omne sæculum.
Amen.

Before the closing of the light, we beseech thee, Creator of all things ! that in thy clemency, thou be our protector and our guard.

May the dreams and phantoms of night depart far from us ; and do thou repress our enemy, lest our bodies be profaned.

Most merciful Father ! and thou, his only-begotten Son, co-equal with him, reigning for ever with the holy Paraclete, grant this our prayer !
Amen.

CAPITULUM
(*Jeremias* xiv.)

Tu autem in nobis es, Domine, et nomen sanctum

But thou art in us, O Lord, and thy holy name has been

---

[1] According to the monastic rite, as follows :

Te lucis ante terminum,
Rerum Creator, poscimus,
Ut solita clementia
Sis præsul ad custodiam.

Procul recedant somnia
Et noctium phantasmata ;

Hostemque nostrum comprime
Ne polluantur corpora.

Præsta, Pater omnipotens,
Per Jesum Christum Dominum,
Qui tecum in perpetuum
Regnat cum sancto Spiritu.

tuum invocatum est super nos; ne derelinquas nos, Domine Deus noster.

R. In manus tuas, Domine: * Commendo spiritum meum. In manus tuas.

V. Redemisti nos, Domine Deus veritatis. * Commendo.

Gloria. In manus tuas.

V. Custodi nos, Domine, ut pupillam oculi.

R. Sub umbra alarum tuarum protege nos.

ANT. Salva nos.

invoked upon us. forsake us not, O Lord our God.

R. Into thy hands, O Lord : * I commend my spirit. Into thy hands.

V. Thou hast redeemed us, O Lord God of truth. * I commend.

Glory. Into thy hands.

V. Preserve us, O Lord, as the apple of thine eye.

R. Protect us under the shadow of thy wings.

ANT. Save us.

The canticle of the venerable Simeon—who, whilst holding the divine Infant in his arms, proclaimed Him to be the *light of the Gentiles,* and then slept the sleep of the just—admirably expresses the repose of heart which the soul that is in the grace of God will experience in her Jesus ; for, as the apostle says, we may live together with Jesus, whether we are awake or asleep. [1]

CANTICLE OF SIMEON

(*St. Luke* ii.)

Nunc dimittis servum tuum Domine : * secundum verbum tuum in pace.

Quia viderunt oculi mei : * salutare tuum.

Quod parasti : * ante faciem omnium populorum.

, Lumen ad revelationem Gentium : * et gloriam plebis tuæ Israel.

Gloria Patri, et Filio, etc.

ANT. Salva nos, Domine, vigilantes, custodi nos dormientes : ut vigilemus cum Christo, et requiescamus in pace.

Now dost thou dismiss thy servant, O Lord, according to thy word in peace.

Because my eyes have seen thy salvation.

Which thou hast prepared before the face of all peoples.

A light to the revelation of the Gentiles, and the glory of thy people Israel.

Glory, etc.

ANT. Save us, O Lord, while awake, and watch us as we sleep; that we may watch with Christ, and rest in peace.

[1] 1 Thess. v. 10.

PRAYERS

Kyrie eleison.
Lord have mercy on us.

Christe eleison.
Christ have mercy on us.

Kyrie eleison.
Lord have mercy on us.

Pater noster.
Our Father.

V. Et ne nos inducas in tentationem.
V. And lead us not into temptation.

R. Sed libera nos a malo.
R. But deliver us from evil.

Credo in Deum, etc.
I believe in God, etc.

V. Carnis resurrectionem.
V. The resurrection of the body.

R. Vitam æternam. Amen.
R. And life everlasting. Amen.

V. Benedictus es, Domine Deus patrum nostrorum.
V. Blessed art thou, O Lord God of our fathers.

R. Et laudabilis et gloriosus in sæcula.
R. And praiseworthy and glorious for ever.

V. Benedicamus Patrem et Filium cum sancto Spiritu.
V. Let us bless the Father and the Son, with the Holy Ghost.

R. Laudemus, et superexaltemus eum in sæcula.
R. Let us praise and magnify him for ever.

V. Benedictus es, Domine, in firmamento cœli.
V. Thou art blessed, O Lord, in the firmament of heaven.

R. Et laudabilis, et gloriosus, et superexaltatus in sæcula.
R. And praiseworthy, and glorious, and magnified for ever.

V. Benedicat et custodiat nos omnipotens et misericors Dominus. *R.* Amen.
V. May the almighty and merciful Lord bless us and keep us. *R.* Amen.

V. Dignare, Domine, nocte ista,
V. Vouchsafe, O Lord, this night,

R. Sine peccato nos custodire.
R. To keep us without sin.

V. Miserere nostri, Domine.
V. Have mercy on us, O Lord.

R. Miserere nostri.
R. Have mercy on us.

V. Fiat misericordia tua, Domine, super nos,
V. Let thy mercy be upon us, O Lord,

R. Quemadmodum speravimus in te.
R. As we have hoped in thee.

V. Domine, exaudi orationem meam.
V. O Lord, hear my prayer.

R. Et clamor meus ad te veniat.
R. And let my cry come unto thee.

After these *prayers* (which are omitted if the Office be of a double rite), the priest says :

V. Dominus vobiscum
R. Et cum spiritu tuo.

V. The Lord be with you.
R. And with thy spirit.

OREMUS.

Visita, quæsumus, Domine, habitationem istam, et omnes insidias inimici ab ea longe repelle : angeli tui sancti habitent in ea, qui nos in pace custodiant, et benedictio tua sit super nos semper. Per Dominum nostrum Jesum Christum, Filium tuum, qui tecum vivit et regnat in unitate Spiritus sancti Deus, per omnia sæcula sæculorum. Amen.

V. Dominus vobiscum.
R. Et cum spiritu tuo.
V. Benedicamus Domino.
R. Deo gratias.

Benedicat et custodiat nos omnipotens et misericors Dominus, Pater, et Filius, et Spiritus sanctus.
R. Amen.

LET US PRAY.

Visit, we beseech thee, O Lord, this house and family, and drive from it all snares of the enemy : let thy holy angels dwell herein, who may keep us in peace, and may thy blessing be always upon us. Through Jesus Christ our Lord, thy Son, who liveth and reigneth with thee, in the unity of the Holy Ghost, God, world without end. Amen.

V. The Lord be with you.
R. And with thy spirit.
V. Let us bless the Lord.
R. Thanks be to God.

May the almighty and merciful Lord, Father, Son, and Holy Ghost, bless and preserve us.
R. Amen.

ANTHEM TO THE BLESSED VIRGIN

Ave Regina cœlorum,
Ave Domina angelorum :
Salve radix, salve porta,
Ex qua mundo lux est orta ;
Gaude, Virgo gloriosa,
Super omnes speciosa :
Vale, O valde decora,
Et pro nobis Christum exora.

V. Dignare me laudare te, Virgo sacrata.
R. Da mihi virtutem contra hostes tuos.

Hail Queen of heaven ! Hail Lady of the angels ! Hail blessed root and gate, from which came light upon the world ! Rejoice, O glorious Virgin, that surpassest all in beauty ! Hail, most lovely Queen ! and pray to Christ for us.

V. Vouchsafe, O holy Virgin, that I may praise thee.
R. Give me power against thine enemies.

OREMUS.

Concede, misericors Deus, fragilitati nostræ præsidium : ut, qui sanctæ Dei Genitricis memoriam agimus, intercessionis ejus auxilio, a nostris iniquitatibus resurgamus. Per eumdem Christum Dominum nostrum. Amen.

V. Divinum auxilium maneat semper nobiscum.

R. Amen.[1]

LET US PRAY.

Grant, O merciful God, thy protection to us in our weakness; that we who celebrate the memory of the holy Mother of God, may, through the aid of her intercession, rise again from our sins. Through the same Christ our Lord. Amen.

V. May the divine assistance remain always with us.

R. Amen.[1]

Then, in secret, *Pater, Ave,* and *Credo ;* page 16.

[1] In the monastic rite, this response is as follows :

R. Et cum fratribus nostris absentibus. Amen.

R. And with our absent brethren. Amen.

PROPER OF THE TIME

SOME of the Sundays after the Epiphany have to be omitted, when Easter comes early in the year. But when that great solemnity comes late, the Sundays before Septuagesima may be as many as six. We have given the first four in our second Christmas volume; we now give the remaining two.

During this brief period, the Church no longer dwells on the mysteries of our Lord's infancy. She listens to His teachings and admires His miracles, but she selects no special circumstances of His life. The colour of the vestments she uses on these Sundays is green; we have elsewhere explained its symbolism.

We give the Mass and Vespers of these two Sundays without anything further than our usual commentary, inasmuch as they rarely have to be said. We omit the week-days altogether, since they offer no particular mystery for meditation: and their omission may be supplied by perusing the instructions, etc., given for the saints' feasts, which have to be celebrated on those days.

THE FIFTH SUNDAY AFTER THE EPIPHANY

MASS

INTROIT

Adorate Deum omnes angeli ejus : audivit et lætata est Sion : et exsultaverunt filiæ Judæ.

Ps. Dominus regnavit : exsultet terra, lætentur insulæ multæ. *V.* Gloria Patri. Adorate.

Adore God, all ye his angels : Sion heard and was glad, and the daughters of Juda rejoiced.

Ps. The Lord hath reigned : let the earth rejoice, let many islands be glad. *V.* Glory, etc. Adore.

COLLECT

Familiam tuam, quæsumus Domine, continua pietate custodi : ut quæ in sola spe gratiæ cœlestis innititur, tua semper protectione muniatur. Per Dominum.

Preserve, we beseech thee, O Lord, thy family by thy constant mercy ; that, as it leans solely on the hope of heavenly grace, it may always be defended by thy protection. Through, etc.

SECOND COLLECT

A cunctis nos, quæsumus Domine, mentis et corporis defende periculis : et intercedente beata et gloriosa semper Virgine Dei Genitrice Maria, cum beato Joseph, beatis apostolis tuis Petro et Paulo atque beato N. et omnibus sanctis, salutem nobis tribue benignus et pacem ; ut destructis adversitatibus et erroribus universis, Ecclesia tua secura tibi serviat libertate.

Preserve us, O Lord, we beseech thee, from all dangers of soul and body : and by the intercession of the glorious and blessed Mary, the ever Virgin Mother of God, of blessed Joseph, of thy blessed apostles, Peter and Paul, of blessed N. (*here is mentioned the titular saint of the church*), and of all the saints, grant us in thy mercy, health and peace ; that all adversities and errors being removed, thy Church may serve thee with undisturbed liberty.

A third Collect is added, at the choice of the priest.

EPISTLE

Lectio Epistolæ beati Pauli Apostoli ad Colossenses.

Lesson of the Epistle of St. Paul the Apostle to the Colossians.

Cap. iii.

Fratres, induite vos, sicut electi Dei, sancti, et dilecti, viscera misericordiæ, benignitatem, humilitatem, modestiam, patientiam, supportantes invicem, et donantes vobismetipsis, si quis adversus aliquem habet querelam : sicut et Dominus donavit vobis, ita et vos. Super omnia autem hæc, charitatem habete, quod est vinculum perfectionis : et pax Christi exsultet in cordibus vestris, in qua et vocati estis in uno corpore : et grati estote. Verbum Christi habitet in vobis abundanter, in omni sapientia, docentes, et commonentes vosmetipsos, psalmis, hymnis, et canticis spiritualibus, in gratia cantantes in cordibus vestris Deo. Omne quodcumque facitis, in verbo aut in opere, omnia in nomine Domini nostri Jesu Christi, gratias agentes Deo et Patri per Jesum Christum Dominum nostrum.

Ch. iii.

Brethren, put ye on therefore as the elect of God, holy, and beloved, the bowels of mercy, benignity, humility, modesty, patience ; bearing with one another, and forgiving one another, if any have a complaint against another ; even as the Lord hath forgiven you, so do you also. But above all these things have charity, which is the bond of perfection ; and let the peace of Christ rejoice in your hearts, wherein also you are called in one body ; and be ye thankful. Let the word of Christ dwell in you abundantly in all wisdom, teaching and admonishing one another in psalms, hymns, and spiritual canticles, singing in grace in your hearts to God. All whatsoever you do in word, or in work, all things do ye in the name of the Lord Jesus Christ, giving thanks to God and the Father, through Jesus Christ our Lord.

The Christian, trained as he has been in the school of the Man-God who deigned to dwell upon this earth, should ever show mercy towards his fellow-men. This world which has been purified by the presence of the Incarnate Word, would become an abode of *peace*, if we were but to live in such

manner as to merit the titles, given us by the
apostle, of *elect of God, holy, and beloved.* The
peace here spoken of should, first of all, fill the
heart of every Christian, and give it an uninterrupted joy, which would be ever pouring itself
forth in *singing* the praises of God. But it is
mainly on the Sundays, that the faithful, by taking
part with the Church in her *psalms, hymns, and
spiritual canticles,* fulfil this duty so dear to their
hearts. Let us, moreover, in our every-day life,
practise the advice given us by the apostle, of doing
all things in the name of our Lord Jesus Christ, in
order that we may, in all things, find favour with
our heavenly Father.

GRADUAL

Timebunt gentes nomen
tuum, Domine, et omnes
reges terræ gloriam tuam.
V. Quoniam   ædificavit
Dominus Sion, et videbitur
in majestate sua.
Alleluia, alleluia.
V. Dominus regnavit, exsultet terra : lætentur insulæ
multæ. Alleluia.

The Gentiles shall fear thy
name, O Lord, and all the
kings of the earth thy glory.
V. For the Lord hath built
up Sion, and he shall be seen
in his glory.
Alleluia, alleluia.
V. The Lord hath reigned,
let the earth rejoice : let many
islands be glad. Alleluia.

GOSPEL

Sequentia sancti Evangelii
secundum Matthæum.

Cap. xiii.

In illo tempore : Dixit Jesus turbis parabolam hanc :
Simile factum est regnum
cœlorum homini, qui semi-
navit bonum semen in agro
suo. Cum autem dormirent
homines,   venit   inimicus
ejus, et superseminavit zizania in medio tritici, et

Sequel of the holy Gospel
according to Matthew.

Ch. xiii.

At that time : Jesus spoke
this parable to the multitude,
saying : The kingdom of heaven is likened to a man that
sowed good seed in his field.
But while men were asleep,
his enemy came and over-
sowed cockle among the wheat
and went his way. And when

abiit. Cum autem crevisset herba, et fructum fecisset, tunc apparuerunt et zizania. Accedentes autem servi pa trisfamilias, dixerunt ei : Domine, nonne bonum semen seminasti in agro tuo ? Unde ergo habet zizania ? Et ait illis : Inimicus homo hoc fecit. Servi autem dixerunt ei : Vis, imus, et colligimus ea ? Et ait : Non ; ne forte colligentes zizania, eradicetis simul cum eis et triticum. Sinite utraque crescere usque ad messem, et in tempore messis dicam messoribus : Colligite primum zizania, et alligate ea in fasciculos ad comburendum, triticum autem congregate in horreum meum.

the blade was sprung up, and had brought forth fruit, then appeared also the cockle. Then the servants of the goodman of the house, coming said unto him : Sir, didst thou not sow good seed in thy field ? whence then hath it cockle ? And he said to them : An enemy hath done this. And the servants said to him : Wilt thou that we go and gather it up ? And he said : No, lest perhaps gathering up the cockle, you root up the wheat also together with it. Suffer both to grow until the harvest, and in the time of harvest I will say to the reapers : Gather up first the cockle, and bind it into bundles to burn, but the wheat gather ye into my barn.

The *kingdom of heaven*, here spoken of by our Lord, is the Church militant, the society of them that believe in Him. And yet, the *field* He has tilled with so much care is *oversown* with *cockle ;* heresies have crept in, scandals have abounded ; are we, on that account, to have misgivings about the foresight of the Master, who knows all things, and without whose permission nothing happens ? Far from us be such a thought ! He Himself tells us that these things must needs be. Man has been gifted with free-will ; it is for him to choose between good and evil ; but God will turn all to His own greater glory. Heresies, then, like weeds in a field, may spring up in the Church ; but the day must come when they will be uprooted ; some of them will wither on the parent stems, but the whole *cockle* shall be *gathered into bundles to burn.* Where are now the heresies that sprang up in the first ages of the Church ? And in another hundred years, what will have become of the heresy, which, under the pretentious name of 'the reformation,' has caused incalculable evil ? It is the same with the scandals which rise up within the pale of the Church : they are a hard trial; but trials must come. The divine Husbandman wills not that this *cockle* be torn up, lest the *wheat* should suffer injury. First of all, the mixture of good and bad is an advantage ; it teaches the good not to put their hopes in man, but in God. Then, too, the mercy of our Lord is so great, that at times the very *cockle* is converted, by divine grace, into *wheat*. We must therefore have patience. But, whereas it is *while the men are asleep that the enemy oversows* the field with *cockle,* it behoves us to pray for pastors, and ask their divine Master to bless them with that vigilance, which is the primary condition of the flock being safe, and is so essential a quality in every bishop, that his very name is 'one who watches.'

OFFERTORY

Dextera Domini fecit virtutem, dextera Domini exaltavit me : non moriar, sed vivam, et narrabo opera Domini.

The right hand of the Lord hath wrought strength, the right hand of the Lord hath exalted me : I shall not die, but live, and shall declare the works of the Lord.

SECRET

Hostias tibi, Domine, placationis offerimus, ut et delicta nostra miseratus absolvas, et nutantia corda tu dirigas. Per Dominum.

We offer thee, O Lord, this sacrifice of propitiation, that thou wouldst mercifully forgive us our sins, and guide our faltering hearts. Through, etc.

SECOND SECRET

Exaudi nos, Deus salutaris noster, ut per hujus Sacramenti virtutem, a cunctis nos mentis et corporis

Graciously grant us, O God our Saviour, that by virtue of this Sacrament, thou mayst defend us from all enemies,

hostibus tuearis, gratiam tribuens in præsenti, et gloriam in futuro.

both of soul and body; giving us grace in this life, and glory in the next.

A third Secret, at the choice of the priest, is added.

COMMUNION

Mirabantur omnes de his, quæ procedebant de ore Dei.

All wondered at the words that came from the mouth of God.

POSTCOMMUNION

Quæsumus, omnipotens Deus, ut illius salutaris capiamus effectum, cujus per hæc mysteria pignus accepimus. Per Dominum.

We beseech thee, O almighty God, that we may one day receive the effects of that salvation, of which we have received the pledge in these mysteries. Through, etc.

SECOND POSTCOMMUNION

Mundet et muniat nos, quæsumus, Domine, divini Sacramenti munus oblatum: et intercedente beata Virgine Dei genitrice Maria, cum beato Joseph, beatis apostolis tuis Petro et Paulo, atque beato N. et omnibus sanctis, a cunctis nos reddat et perversitatibus expiatos, et adversitatibus expeditos.

May the oblation of this divine Sacrament, we beseech thee, O Lord, both cleanse and defend us; and, by the intercession of blessed Mary, the Virgin-Mother of God, of blessed Joseph, of thy blessed apostles, Peter and Paul, of blessed N. and of all the saints, free us from all sin, and deliver us from all adversity.

The third Postcommunion is at the choice of the priest.

VESPERS

The psalms and antiphons as on page 72.

CAPITULUM

(2 Cor. i.)

Benedictus Deus et Pater Domini nostri Jesu Christi, Pater misericordiarum et

Blessed be the God and Father of our Lord Jesus Christ, the Father of mercies,

Deus totius consolationis, qui consolatur nos in omni tribulatione nostra.

and the God of all consolation, who comforteth us in all our tribulations.

The hymn and versicle, page 79.

ANTIPHON OF THE 'MAGNIFICAT'

Colligite primum zizania, et alligate ea in fasciculos ad comburendum : triticum autem congregate in horreum meum, dicit Dominus.

Gather up first the cockle, and bind it into bundles to burn : but gather the wheat into my barn, saith the Lord.

OREMUS.

Familiam tuam, quæsumus Domine, continua pietate custodi : ut quæ in sola spe gratiæ cœlestis innititur, tua semper protectione muniatur.　Per Dominum.

LET US PRAY.

Preserve, we beseech thee, O Lord, thy family by thy constant mercy ; that, as it leans solely on the hope of heavenly grace, it may always be defended by thy protection. Through, etc.

THE SIXTH SUNDAY AFTER THE EPIPHANY

MASS

INTROIT

Adorate Deum omnes angeli ejus : audivit et lætata est Sion : et exsultaverunt filiæ Judæ.
Ps. Dominus regnavit : exsultet terra, lætentur insulæ multæ.　*V.* Gloria Patri.　Adorate.

Adore God, all ye his angels : Sion heard and was glad, and the daughters of Juda rejoiced.
Ps. The Lord hath reigned : let the earth rejoice, let many islands be glad.　*V.* Glory, etc. Adore.

COLLECT

Præsta quæsumus omnipotens Deus : ut semper rationabilia meditantes, quæ tibi sunt placita et dictis

Grant, we beseech thee, O almighty God, that, ever meditating on such things as are reasonable, we may, both in

exsequamur et factis. Per Dominum.

word and deed, carry out the things which are pleasing unto thee. Through, etc.

For the other Collects, see page 94.

EPISTLE

Lectio Epistolæ beati Pauli Apostoli ad Thessalonicenses.

Lesson of the Epistle of St. Paul the Apostle to the Thessalonians.

1 *Cap.* i.

1 *Ch.* i.

Fratres, gratias agimus Deo semper pro omnibus vobis, memoriam vestri facientes in orationibus nostris sine intermissione, memores operis fidei vestræ, et laboris, et charitatis, et sustinentiæ spei Domini nostri Jesu Christi, ante Deum et Patrem nostrum: scientes, fratres dilecti a Deo, electionem vestram: quia Evangelium nostrum non fuit ad vos in sermone tantum, sed et in virtute, et in Spiritu sancto, et in plenitudine multa, sicut scitis quales fuerimus in vobis propter vos. Et vos imitatores nostri facti estis et Domini, excipientes verbum in tribulatione multa, cum gaudio Spiritus sancti: ita ut facti sitis forma omnibus credentibus in Macedonia, et in Achaïa. A vobis enim diffamatus est sermo Domini, non solum in Macedonia, et in Achaïa, sed et in omni loco fides vestra, quæ est ad Deum, profecta est, ita ut non sit nobis necesse quidquam loqui. Ipsi enim de nobis annuntiant qualem

Brethren, we give thanks to God always for you all: making a remembrance of you in our prayers without ceasing: being mindful of the work of your faith, and labour, and charity, and of the enduring of the hope of our Lord Jesus Christ, before God and our Father; knowing, brethren beloved of God, your election. For our Gospel hath not been to you in word only, but in power also, and in the Holy Ghost, and in much fullness, as you know what manner of men we have been among you for your sakes. And you became followers of us, and of the Lord, receiving the word in much tribulation, with joy of the Holy Ghost; so that you were made a pattern to all that believe, in Macedonia and in Achaia. For from you was spread abroad the word of the Lord, not only in Macedonia and in Achaia, but also in every place your faith, which is towards God, is gone forth, so that we need not to speak anything. For they themselves relate of us, what manner of entering in we had unto you; and how you turned

introitum habuerimus ad vos: et quomodo conversi estis ad Deum a simulacris, servire Deo vivo, et vero, et exspectare Filium ejus de cœlis (quem suscitavit ex mortuis) Jesum, qui eripuit nos ab ira ventura.

to God from idols, to serve the living and true God, and to wait for his Son from heaven (whom he raised up from the dead) Jesus, who hath delivered us from the wrath to come.

The praise which the apostle here gives to the Thessalonians for their fervour in the faith they had embraced, conveys a reproach to the Christians of our own times. These neophytes of Thessalonica, who, a short time before, were worshippers of idols, had become so earnest in the practice of the Christian religion, that even the apostle is filled with admiration. We are the descendants of countless Christian ancestors; we received our regeneration by Baptism at our first coming into the world; we were taught the doctrine of Jesus Christ from our earliest childhood: and yet, our faith is not so strong, or our lives so holy, as were those of the early Christians. Their main occupation was *serving the living and true God*, and *waiting* for the coming of their Saviour. Our hope is precisely the same as that which made their hearts so fervent; how comes it that our faith is not like theirs in its generosity? We love this present life, as though we had not the firm conviction that it is to pass away.

As far as depends upon us, we are handing down to future generations a Christianity very different from that which our Saviour established, which the apostles preached, and which the pagans of the first ages thought they were bound to purchase at any price or sacrifice.

GRADUAL

Timebunt gentes nomen tuum, Domine, et omnes reges terræ gloriam tuam.

The Gentiles shall fear thy name, O Lord, and all the kings of the earth thy glory.

V. Quoniam ædificavit Dominus Sion, et videbitur in majestate sua.

Alleluia, alleluia.

V. Dominus regnavit, exsultet terra : lætentur insulæ multæ. Alleluia.

V. For the Lord hath built up Sion, and he shall be seen in his glory.

Alleluia, alleluia.

V. The Lord hath reigned, let the earth rejoice : let many islands be glad. Alleluia.

GOSPEL

Sequentia sancti Evangelii secundum Matthæum.

Cap. xiii.

In illo tempore : Dixit Jesus turbis parabolam hanc : Simile est regnum cœlorum grano sinapis, quod accipiens homo seminavit in agro suo, quod minimum quidem est omnibus seminibus : cum autem creverit, majus est omnibus oleribus, et fit arbor, ita ut volucres cœli veniant, et habitent in ramis ejus. Aliam parabolam locutus est eis. Simile est regnum cœlorum fermento, quod acceptum mulier abscondit in farinæ satis tribus, donec fermentatum est totum. Hæc omnia locutus est Jesus in parabolis ad turbas : et sine parabolis non loquebatur eis : ut impleretur quod dictum erat per prophetam dicentem : Aperiam in parabolis os meum, eructabo abscondita a constitutione mundi.

Sequel of the holy Gospel according to Matthew.

Ch. xiii.

At that time : Jesus spoke to the multitude this parable : The kingdom of heaven is like to a grain of mustard-seed, which a man took and sowed in his field. Which indeed is the least of all seeds ; but when it is grown up, it is greater than all herbs, and becometh a tree, so that the birds of the air come and dwell in the branches thereof. Another parable he spoke to them : The kingdom of heaven is like to leaven, which a woman took and hid in three measures of meal, until the whole was leavened. All these things Jesus spoke in parables to the multitudes, and without parables he did not speak to them ; that the word might be fulfilled which was spoken by the prophet, saying : I will open my mouth in parables, I will utter things hidden from the foundation of the world.

Our Lord here teaches us, under the symbolism of two parables, what we are to believe concerning His Church, which is His *kingdom,* a kingdom that rises indeed here on the earth, but is to be perfected in *heaven.* What is this *grain of mustard-seed,* which is hidden under ground, is unseen by man's eye, then appears as the *least* of herbs, but, finally, becomes a *tree?* It is the Word of God, at first hidden in Judea, trampled on by man's malice even so as to be buried in a tomb, but, at length, rising triumphantly and reaching rapidly to every part of the world. Scarcely had a hundred years elapsed since Jesus was put to death, when His Church was vigorous even far beyond the limits of the Roman empire. During the past nineteen centuries, every possible effort has been made to uproot the *tree* of God; persecution, diplomacy, human wisdom, all have tried, and all have but wasted their time. True, they succeeded, from time to time, in severing a branch; but another grew in its place, for the sap of the *tree* is vigorous beyond measure. The *birds* that *come and dwell* upon it, are, as the holy fathers interpret it, the souls of men aspiring to the eternal goods of the better world. If we are worthy of our name of Christians, we shall love this *tree,* and find our rest and safety nowhere but beneath its shade. The *woman,* of whom the second parable speaks, is the Church, our mother. It was she that, from the commencement of Christianity, took the teaching of her divine Master, and *hid* it in the very hearts of men, making it the *leaven* of their salvation. The *three measures of meal* which she *leavened* into bread, are the three great families of mankind, the three that came from the children of Noah, who are the three fathers of the whole human race. Let us love this mother; and let us bless that heavenly *leaven,* which made us become children of God, by making us children of the Church.

OFFERTORY

Dextera Domini fecit vir-
tutem, dextera Domini ex-

The right hand of the Lord
hath wrought strength, the

altavit me : non moriar, sed vivam, et narrabo opera Domini.

right hand of the Lord hath exalted me : I shall not die, but live, and shall declare the works of the Lord.

SECRET

Hæc nos oblatio, Deus, mundet, quæsumus, et renovet, gubernet, et protegat. Per Dominum.

May this oblation, O God, we beseech thee, cleanse, renew, govern, and protect us. Through, etc.

The other Secrets are given on page 98.

COMMUNION

Mirabantur omnes de his, quæ procedebant de ore Dei.

All wondered at the words that came from the mouth of God.

POSTCOMMUNION

Cœlestibus, Domine, pasti deliciis, quæsumus, ut semper eadem, per quæ veraciter vivimus, appetamus. Per Dominum.

Being fed, O Lord, with heavenly dainties, we beseech thee, that we may always hunger after them, for by them we have true life. Through, etc.

The other Postcommunions are given on page 99.

VESPERS

The psalms and antiphons as on page 72.

CAPITULUM

(2 Cor. i.)

Benedictus Deus et Pater Domini nostri Jesu Christi, Pater misericordiarum et Deus totius consolationis, qui consolatur nos in omni tribulatione nostra.

Blessed be the God and Father of our Lord Jesus Christ, the Father of mercies, and the God of all consolation, who comforteth us in all our tribulations.

The hymn and versicle, page 79.

ANTIPHON OF THE 'MAGNIFICAT'

Simile est regnum cœlorum fermento, quod acceptum mulier abscondit in farinæ satis tribus, donec fermentatum est totum.

The kingdom of heaven is like to leaven, which a woman took and hid in three measures of meal, until the whole was leavened.

OREMUS.

Præsta, quæsumus omnipotens Deus : ut semper rationabilia meditantes, quæ tibi sunt placita, et dictis exsequamur, et factis. Per Dominum.

LET US PRAY.

Grant, we beseech thee, O almighty God, that ever meditating on such things as are reasonable, we may, both in word and deed, carry out the things which are pleasing unto thee. Through, etc.

SATURDAY BEFORE SEPTUAGESIMA SUNDAY

SUSPENSION OF THE 'ALLELUIA'

THE calendar of the liturgical year will soon bring us to the commemoration of the Passion and Resurrection of our Redeemer; we are but nine weeks from these great solemnities. It is time for the Christian to be preparing his soul for a fresh visit from his Saviour; a visit even more sacred and more important than that He so mercifully paid us at His Birth.

Our holy mother the Church knows how necessary it is for her to rouse our hearts from their lethargy, and give them an active tendency towards the things of God. On this day, the eve of Septuagesima, she uses a powerful means for infusing her own spirit into the minds of her children. She takes the song of heaven away from us : she forbids our further uttering that *Alleluia*, which is so dear to us, as giving us a fellowship with the choirs of angels, who are for ever repeating it. How is it that we poor mortals, sinners,

and exiles on earth, have dared to become so
familiar with this hymn of a better land? It is
true, our Emmanuel, who established peace between
God and men, brought it us from heaven on the
glad night of His Birth; and we have had the
courage to repeat it after the angels, and shall
chant it with renewed enthusiasm when we reach
our Easter. But to sing the *Alleluia* worthily, we
must have our hearts set on the country whence it
came. It is not a mere word, nor a profane un-
meaning melody; it is the song that recalls the land
we are banished from, it is the sweet sigh of the
soul longing to be at home.

The word *Alleluia* signifies *praise God:* but it
says much more than this, and says it as no other
word or words could. The Church is not going to
interrupt her giving praise to God during these
nine weeks. She will replace this heaven-lent word
by a formula also expressive of praise: *Laus tibi,
Domine, Rex æternæ gloriæ!* Praise be to Thee, O
Lord, King of eternal glory! But this is the language of earth; whereas *Alleluia* was sent us from
heaven. '*Alleluia*,' says the devout Abbot Rupert,
'is like a stranger amidst our other words. Its
mysterious beauty is as though a drop of heaven's
overflowing joy had fallen down on our earth. The
patriarchs and prophets relished it, and then the
Holy Ghost put it on the lips of the apostles, from
whom it flowed even to us. It signifies the eternal
feast of the angels and saints, which consists in
their endless praise of God, and in ceaselessly
singing their ever new admiration of the beauty of
the God on whose Face they are to gaze for everlasting ages. This mortal life of ours can in no
wise attain such bliss as this. But, to know where
it is to be found, and to have a foretaste of it by
the happiness of hope, and to hunger and thirst for
what we thus taste, this is the perfection of saints

here below. For this reason, the word *Alleluia* has not been translated; it has been left in its original Hebrew, as a stranger to tell us that there is a joy in his native land, which could not dwell in ours: he has come among us to signify, rather than to express that joy.'[1]

During this season of Septuagesima, we have to gain a clear knowledge of the miseries of our banishment, under pain of being left for ever in this tyrant Babylon. It was, therefore, necessary that we should be put on our guard against the allurements of our place of exile. It is with this view that the Church, taking pity on our blindness and our dangers, gives us this solemn warning. By taking from us our *Alleluia*, she virtually tells us that our lips must first be cleansed, before they again be permitted to utter this word of angels and saints; and that our hearts, defiled as they are by sin and attachment to earthly things, must be purified by repentance. She is going to put before our eyes the sad spectacle of the fall of our first parents, that dire event whence came all our woes, and our need of Redemption. This tender mother weeps over us, and would have us weep with her.

Let us, then, comply with the law she thus imposes upon us. If spiritual joy is thus taken away from us, what are we to think of the frivolous amusements of the world? And if vanities and follies are insults to the spirit of Septuagesima, would not sin be an intolerable outrage on that same spirit? We have been too long the slaves of this tyrant. Our Saviour is soon to appear, bearing His cross; and His sacrifice is to restore fallen man to all his rights. Surely, we can never allow that precious Blood to fall uselessly on our souls, as the morning dew that rains on the parched sands of a desert! Let us with humble hearts

---

[1] *De divinis Officiis*, lib. i., cap. xxxv.

confess that we are sinners, and, like the publican of the Gospel, who dared not so much as to raise up his eyes, let us acknowledge that it is only right that we should be forbidden, at least for a few weeks, those divine songs of joy, with which our guilty lips had become too familiar; and that we should interrupt those sentiments of presumptuous confidence which prevented our hearts from having the holy fear of God.

That indifference for the liturgy of the Church, which is the strongest indication of a weak faith, and which now reigns so universally in the world, is the reason why so many, even practical Catholics, can witness this yearly suspension of the *Alleluia*, without profiting by the lesson it conveys. A passing remark, or a chance thought, is the most they give to it, for they care for no other devotions but such as are private; the spirit of the Church, in her various seasons, is quite beneath their notice. If these lines should meet their eye, we would beg of them to reflect for a moment that the Church is their mother; that her authority is the highest on earth; that her wisdom enables her to know what is best for her children. Why, then, keep aloof from her spirit, as though there were some other to be found, that could better lead them to their God? Why be indifferent in this present instance? Why deem of no interest to piety this suspension of the *Alleluia*, which she, the Church, considers as one of the principal and most solemn incidents in her liturgical year? Perhaps we shall be doing them a service, by showing them how keenly this interruption of the word of heavenly joy was felt by the Christians of those ages, when faith was the grand ruling principle, not only with society at large, but with each individual.

The farewell to *Alleluia*, in the Middle Ages, varied in the different Churches. Here, it was an

affectionate enthusiasm, speaking the beauty of the
celestial word; there, it was a heart-felt regret at
the departure of the much-loved companion of all
their prayers.

We begin with two antiphons, which would seem
to be of Roman origin. We find them in the *Anti-
phonarium* of Saint Cornelius of Compiègne, pub-
lished by Dom Denys de Sainte Marthe. They are
a farewell to *Alleluia* made by our Catholic forefathers in the ninth century; they express, too, the
hope of its coming back, as soon as the Resurrection of Jesus shall have brightened up the firmament of the Church.

Ant. Angelus Domini
bonus comitetur tecum, Alleluia, et bene disponat itineri tuo, ut iterum cum
gaudio revertaris ad nos,
Alleluia, Alleluia.

Ant. Alleluia, mane apud
nos hodie, et crastina pro-
ficisceris, Alleluia; et dum
ortus fuerit dies, ambulabis
vias tuas, Alleluia, Alleluia,
Alleluia.

Ant. May the good angel
of the Lord accompany thee,
Alleluia, and give thee a good
journey, that thou mayst come
back to us in joy, Alleluia,
Alleluia.

Ant. Alleluia, abide with
us to-day, and to-morrow thou
shalt set forth, Alleluia; and
when the day shall have risen,
thou shalt proceed on thy way,
Alleluia, Alleluia, Alleluia.

The Gothic Church of Spain thus saluted the
Alleluia, on the eve of its interruption. We merely
make a selection from what is almost a complete
Office.

HYMN

Alleluia piis edite laudi-
bus,
Cives ætherei, psallite
unanimiter
Alleluia perenne.
Hinc vos perpetui luminis
accolæ,
Ad summum resonate hym-
niferis choris
Alleluia perenne.

Citizens of heaven! give
forth Alleluia in your holy
canticles; sing with one voice
your eternal Alleluia.

Inhabitants of light everlasting! make heaven resound,
as ye sing to the great God,
in your hymning choirs, the
eternal Alleluia.

Vos urbs eximia suscipiet
Dei,
Quæ lætis resonans canti-
bus, excitat
Alleluia perenne.
Almum sidereæ jam pa-
triæ decus
Victores capite, quo canere
possitis
Alleluia perenne.
Illic Regis honor vocibus
inclytis
Jocundum reboat carmine
perpetim
Alleluia perenne.
Hoc fessis requies, hoc
cibus, hoc potus
Oblectans reduces, hausti-
bus affluens
Alleluia perenne.

Te suavisonis Conditor
affatim
Rerum carminibus, laude-
que pangimus
Alleluia perenne.
Te Christe celebrat gloria
vocibus
Nostris, omnipotens, ac tibi
dicimus
Alleluia perenne :
Alleluia perenne. Amen.
Felici reditu gaudia su-
mite,
Reddentes Domino glorifi-
cum melos,
Alleluia perenne.

The glorious city of God
will receive you, the city
which echoes with songs of
joy, and awakens the eternal
Alleluia.
Ye have conquered ; go, take
the fair beauty of the starry
land, wherein ye may chant
the eternal Alleluia.

'Tis there the glory of the
King is proclaimed with sweetest voices singing ever their
joyous, their eternal Alleluia.

This is the rest to the wearied ; this is the food and
drink giving delight to exiles
reaching home ; and this is
their cup of overflowing nec-
tar : the eternal Alleluia.
We, too, O God, Creator of
all things ! in sweetest hymns
we praise thee, singing our
eternal Alleluia.

To thee, Jesus almighty !
our voices give glory : to thee
we say : Eternal Alleluia !
Eternal Alleluia ! Amen.

Be glad on the day of its
happy return ; and return to
your Lord with your melody
of glory, the eternal Alleluia.

CAPITULUM

Alleluia in cœlo, et in
terra : in cœlo perpetuatur,
et in terra cantatur. Ibi
sonat jugiter : hic fideliter.
Illic perenniter, hic suaviter. Illic feliciter, hic con-
corditer : illic ineffabiliter,

Alleluia is in heaven and on
earth : it is eternal in heaven,
and is even sung on earth.
There, unceasingly ; here,
faithfully. There, everlasting-
ly ; here, sweetly. There,
happily ; here, concordantly.

hic instanter. Illic sine syllabis : hic modulis. Illic ab angelis, hic a populis, quam Christo Domino nascente in laude et confessione nimis ejus, non solum in cœlo, sed et in terra cœlicolæ cecinerunt : dum gloriam in excelsis Deo, et pacem in terra bonæ voluntatis hominibus nuntiaverunt. Quæsumus ergo, Domine, ut quorum ministeria nitimur imitari laudando, eorum mereamur consortium beatæ vitæ vivendo.

There, ineffably ; here, heartily. There, it needs no syllables ; here, it needs our melodies. There, it has angels for its chanters ; here, it has men. When Christ our Lord was born, the heavenly host gave him exceeding praise and honour, singing Alleluia both in heaven and on earth, and proclaiming glory to God in the highest, and peace on earth to men of good - will. Therefore do we beseech thee, O Lord, that as we strive to imitate the angels in their ministry of praise, we may live in such manner as to deserve to be their companions in eternal life.

ANTHEM

Ibis, Alleluia. Prosperum iter habebis Alleluia ; et iterum cum gaudio revertaris ad nos, Alleluia. In manibus enim suis portabunt te : ne unquam offendas ad lapidem pedem tuum. Et iterum cum gaudio revertaris ad nos, Alleluia.

Thou shalt go, Alleluia ; thy journey shall be prosperous, Alleluia ; and again come back to us with joy, Alleluia. For they shall bear thee up in their hands, lest at any time thou dash thy foot against a stone. And again come back to us with joy, Alleluia.

BENEDICTION

Alleluia, nomen pium, atque jocundum, dilatetur ad laudem Dei in ora omnium populorum.
    R̷. Amen.
Sit in vocibus credentium clara, quæ in angelorum ostenditur concentibus gloriosa.

R̷. Amen.

May Alleluia, that sacred and joyful word, resound to God's praise from the lips of all people.
    R̷. Amen.
May this word, which expresses glory as chanted by the choirs of angels, be sweet as sung by the voices of believers.
    R̷. Amen.

Et, quæ in æternis civibus sine sonorum strepitu enitet, in vestris cordibus effectu planiore fructificet.

And may that which noiselessly gleams in the citizens of heaven, yield fruit in your hearts by ever growing love.

R. Amen.

R. Amen.

Angelus Domini bonus comitetur tecum, Alleluia; et omnia bona præparet itineri tuo. Et iterum cum gaudio revertaris ad nos. Alleluia.

May the Lord's good angel go with thee, Alleluia; and prepare all good things for thy journey. And again come back to us with joy, Alleluia.

The Churches of Germany, in the Middle Ages, expressed their farewell to the *Alleluia* in the following fine sequence, which is to be found in all their missals up to the fifteenth century.

SEQUENCE

Cantemus cuncti melodum nunc Alleluia.

Let us all now sing the melodious Alleluia.

In laudibus æterni regis, hæc plebs resultet Alleluia.

In praise of the eternal King, let this assembly give forth Alleluia.

Hoc denique cœlestes chori cantent in altum Alleluia.

And let the heavenly choirs loudly chant Alleluia.

Hoc beatorum per prata Paradisiaca psallat concentus Alleluia.

Let the choir of the blessed sing in the land of paradise, Alleluia.

Quin et astrorum micantia luminaria jubilent altum Alleluia.

Nay, let the bright stars hymn one loud Alleluia.

Nubium cursus, ventorum volatus, fulgurum coruscatio et tonitruum sonitus, dulce consonent simul Alleluia.

Fleet clouds, swift winds, flashing lightning, and pealing thunder, let all unite in a sweet Alleluia.

Fluctus et undæ, imber et procellæ, tempestas et serenitas, cauma, gelu, nix, pruinæ, saltus, nemora, pangant Alleluia.

Waves and billows, showers and storms, tempest and calm, heat, cold, snow, frost, woods and groves, let them tell their Alleluia.

Hinc variæ volucres Creatorem laudibus concinite cum Alleluia.

And ye countless birds, sing the praises of your Maker with an Alleluia.

8

Ast illic respondeant voces altæ diversarum bestiarum Alleluia.

Istinc montium celsi vertices sonent Alleluia.

Hinc vallium profunditates saltent Alleluia.

Tu quoque maris jubilans abysse, dic Alleluia.

Necnon terrarum molis immensitates : Alleluia.

Nunc omne genus humanum laudans exsultet Alleluia.

Et Creatori grates frequentans consonet Alleluia.

Hoc denique nomen audire jugiter delectatur Alleluia.

Hoc etiam carmen cœleste comprobat ipse Christus Alleluia.

Nunc vos socii cantate lætantes : Alleluia.

Et vos pueruli respondete semper : Alleluia.

Nunc omnes canite simul, Alleluia Domino, Alleluia Christo, Pneumatique Alleluia.

Laus Trinitati æternæ in baptismo Domini quæ clarificatur : hinc canamus Alleluia.

To which let the loud-voiced beasts respond another Alleluia.

Let the high mountain-tops ring with Alleluia.

And the deep valleys echo Alleluia.

Thou, too, deep jubilant sea, say Alleluia ;

And thou, boundless earth, Alleluia !

Now let the whole race of men say its praiseful Alleluia,

And oft to its Creator give this canticle of thanks, Alleluia !

He loves to hear this word eternally repeated, Alleluia ;

And Jesus too applauds the song, the heavenly Alleluia.

Do you, then, brethren, be glad, and sing : Alleluia !

And you, little children, never fail to respond : Alleluia !

Let all, then, sing together : Alleluia to the Lord ; Alleluia to Christ ; and to the Holy Ghost, Alleluia !

Praise be to the eternal Trinity, whose glory was declared at the baptism of our Lord ! Sing we, then, Alleluia !

The Churches of France, in the thirteenth century, and long even after that, used to sing at Vespers of the Saturday before Septuagesima the following beautiful hymn :

HYMN

Alleluia dulce carmen,
　Vox perennis gaudii,

The sweet Alleluia-song, the word of endless joy, is the

Alleluia laus suavis
  Est choris cœlestibus,
Quam canunt Dei ma-
  nentes
  In domo per sæcula.
Alleluia læta mater
  Concivis Jerusalem :
Alleluia vox tuorum
  Civium gaudentium :
Exsules nos flere cogunt
  Babylonis flumina.
Alleluia non meremur
  In perenne psallere ;
Alleluia vox reatus
  Cogit intermittere ;
Tempus instat quo peracta
  Lugeamus crimina.
Unde laudando precamur
  Te beata Trinitas,
Ut tuum nobis videre
  Pascha des in æthere,
Quo tibi læti canamus
  Alleluia perpetim.
    Amen.

melody of heaven's choir, chanted by them that dwell for ever in the house of God.

O joyful mother, O Jerusalem our city, Alleluia is the language of thy happy citizens. The rivers of Babylon, where we poor exiles live, force us to weep.

We are unworthy to sing a ceaseless Alleluia. Our sins bid us interrupt our Alleluia. The time is at hand when it behoves us to bewail our crimes.

We, therefore, beseech thee whilst we praise thee, O blessed Trinity! that thou grant us to come to that Easter of heaven, where we shall sing to thee our joyful everlasting Alleluia. Amen.

In the present form of the liturgy, the farewell to *Alleluia* is more simple. The Church, at the conclusion of to-day's Vespers, repeats the mysterious word four times :

Benedicamus Domino, Alleluia, Alleluia.
  Deo gratias, Alleluia, Alleluia.

Let us bless the Lord, Alleluia, Alleluia.
  Thanks be to God, Alleluia, Alleluia.

This song of heaven, then, is taken from us. It will return, when the triumph of Jesus' Resurrection is proclaimed upon our earth.

SEPTUAGESIMA SUNDAY

THE holy Church calls us together to-day in order that we may hear from her lips the sad history of the fall of our first parents. This awful event implies the Passion and cruel Death of the Son of God made Man, who has mercifully taken upon Himself to expiate this and every subsequent sin committed by Adam and us his children. It is of the utmost importance that we should understand the greatness of the remedy; we must, therefore, consider the grievousness of the wound inflicted. For this purpose, we will spend the present week in meditating on the nature and consequences of the sin of our first parents.

Formerly, the Church used to read in her Matins of to-day that passage of the Book of Genesis, where Moses relates to all future generations, but in words of most impressive and sublime simplicity, how the first sin was brought into the world. In the present form of the liturgy, the reading of this history of the fall is deferred till Wednesday, and the preceding days give us the account of the six days of creation. We will anticipate the great instruction, and begin it at once, inasmuch as it forms the basis of the whole week's teaching.

De Libro Genesis.

Cap. iii.

Sed et serpens erat callidior cunctis animantibus terræ, quæ fecerat Dominus Deus. Qui dixit ad mulierem : Cur præcepit vobis Deus ut non comederetis de omni ligno paradisi? Cui respondit mulier : De fructu lignorum quæ sunt in pa-

From the Book of Genesis.

Ch. iii.

Now the serpent was more subtle than any of the beasts of the earth, which the Lord God had made. And he said to the woman : Why hath God commanded you, that you should not eat of every tree of paradise? And the woman answered him, saying : Of the

radiso vescimur: de fructu vero ligni, quod est in medio paradisi, præcepit nobis Deus ne comederemus, et ne tangeremus illud, ne forte moriamur. Dixit autem serpens ad mulierem: Nequaquam morte moriemini; scit enim Deus quod in quocumque die comederitis ex eo, aperientur oculi vestri, et critis sicut dii, scientes bonum et malum. Vidit igitur mulier, quod bonum esset lignum ad vescendum, et pulchrum oculis, aspectuque delectabile: et tulit de fructu illius, et comedit: deditque viro suo, qui comedit. Et aperti sunt oculi amborum.

Cumque cognovissent se esse nudos, consuerunt folia ficus, et fecerunt sibi perizomata. Et cum audissent vocem Domini Dei deambulantis in paradiso, ad auram post meridiem, abscondit se Adam et uxor ejus a facie Domini Dei, in medio ligni paradisi. Vocavitque Dominus Deus Adam, et dixit ei: Ubi es? Qui ait: Vocem tuam audivi in paradiso, et timui, eo quod nudus essem et abscondi me. Cui dixit: Quis enim indicavit tibi quod nudus esses, nisi quod ex ligno de quo præceperam tibi ne comederes, comedisti? Dixitque Adam: Mulier, quam dedisti mihi sociam dedit mihi de ligno, et comedi. Et dixit Dominus Deus ad

fruit of the trees that are in paradise we do eat; but of the fruit of the tree which is in the midst of paradise, God hath commanded us that we should not eat, and that we should not touch it, lest perhaps we die. And the serpent said to the woman: No, you shall not die the death; for God doth know, that in what day soever you shall eat thereof, your eyes shall be opened, and you shall be as gods, knowing good and evil. And the woman saw that the tree was good to eat, and fair to the eyes, and delightful to behold: and she took of the fruit thereof, and did eat: and gave to her husband, who did eat. And the eyes of them both were opened.

And when they perceived themselves to be naked, they sewed together fig-leaves, and made themselves aprons. And when they heard the voice of the Lord God walking in paradise, at the afternoon air, Adam and his wife hid themselves from the face of the Lord God, amidst the trees of paradise. And the Lord God called Adam, and said to him: Where art thou? And he said: I heard thy voice in paradise, and I was afraid, because I was naked, and I hid myself. And he said to him: And who hath told thee that thou wast naked, but that thou hast eaten of the tree whereof I commanded thee that thou shouldst not eat? And Adam said: The woman, whom thou gavest me, to be my compan-

mulierem : Quare hoc fe-
cisti ? Quæ respondit : Serpens decepit me, et comedi.

Et ait Dominus Deus ad
serpentem : Quia fecisti hoc,
maledictus es inter omnia
animantia, et bestias terræ :
super pectus tuum gradieris,
et terram comedes cunctis
diebus vitæ tuæ. Inimicitias
ponam inter te et mulierem,
et semen tuum et semen illius ; ipsa conteret caput tuum, et tu insidiaberis calca-
neo ejus. Mulieri quoque dixit : Multiplicabo ærumnas
tuas, et conceptus tuos : in
dolore paries filios, et sub
viri potestate eris, et ipse
dominabitur tui. Adæ vero
dixit : Quia audisti vocem
uxoris tuæ, et comedisti de
ligno, ex quo præceperam
tibi ne comederes, maledicta
terra in opere tuo : in laboribus comedes ex ea cunctis
diebus vitæ tuæ. Spinas et
tribulos germinabit tibi, et
comedes herbam terræ. In
sudore vultus tui vesceris
pane, donec revertaris in terram, de qua sumptus es :
quia pulvis es, et in pulverem reverteris.

ion, gave me of the tree, and
I did eat. And the Lord God
said to the woman : Why hast
thou done this ? And she answered : The serpent deceived
me, and I did eat.

And the Lord God said to
the serpent : Because thou
hast done this thing, thou art
cursed among all cattle, and
beasts of the earth : upon thy
breast shalt thou go, and earth
shalt thou eat all the days of
thy life. I will put enmities
between thee and the woman,
and thy seed and her seed ;
she shall crush thy head, and
thou shalt lie in wait for her
heel. To the woman, also, he
said : I will multiply thy sorrows, and thy conceptions :
in sorrow shalt thou bring
forth children, and thou shalt
be under thy husband's power,
and he shall have dominion
over thee. And to Adam he
said : Because thou hast hearkened to the voice of thy wife,
and hast eaten of the tree,
whereof I commanded thee
that thou shouldst not eat,
cursed is the earth in thy
work : with labour and toil
shalt thou eat thereof all the
days of thy life. Thorns and
thistles shall it bring forth to
thee, and thou shalt eat the
herbs of the earth. In the
sweat of thy face shalt thou
eat bread, till thou return to
the earth, out of which thou
was taken : for dust thou art,
and into dust thou shalt return.

Oh ! terrible page of man's history ! It alone
explains to us our present position on the earth.

It tells us what we are in the eyes of God, and how humbly we should comport ourselves before His divine Majesty. We will make it the subject of this week's meditation. And now, let us prepare to profit by the liturgy of this Sunday, which we call *Septuagesima*.

In the Greek Church, it is called *Prophoné* (Proclamation), because on this day they announce to the people the coming fast of Lent, and the precise day of Easter. It is also called the Sunday of the prodigal son, because that parable is read in their liturgy for this Sunday, as an invitation to sinners to draw nigh to the God of mercy. But it is the last day of the week *Prophoné*, which, by a strange custom, begins with the preceding Monday, as do also the two following weeks.

MASS

The Station, at Rome, is in the church of Saint Lawrence *outside the walls*. The ancient liturgists observe the relation between the just Abel (whose being murdered by Cain is the subject of one of the responsories of to-day's Matins), and the courageous martyr, over whose tomb the Church of Rome commences her Septuagesima.

The Introit describes the fears of *death*, wherewith Adam and his whole posterity are tormented, in consequence of sin. But in the midst of all this misery there is heard a cry of hope, for man is still permitted to ask mercy from his God. God gave man a promise, on the very day of his condemnation: the sinner needs but to confess his miseries, and the very Lord against whom he sinned will become his *deliverer*.

INTROIT

Circumdederunt me gemitus mortis, dolores infer-

The groans of death surrounded me, and the sorrows

ni circumdederunt me : et in tribulatione mea invocavi Dominum, et exaudivit de templo sancto suo vocem meam.

Ps. Diligam te, Domine, fortitudo mea : Dominus firmamentum meum, et refugium meum, et liberator meus. *V.* Gloria Patri. Circumdederunt.

of hell encompassed me ; and in my affliction I called upon the Lord, and he heard my voice from his holy temple.

Ps. I will love thee, O Lord, my strength : the Lord is my firmament, my refuge, and my deliverer. *V.* Glory. The groans.

In the Collect, the Church acknowledges that her children justly suffer the chastisements which are the consequences of sin ; but she beseeches her divine Lord to send them that mercy which will deliver them.

COLLECT

Preces populi tui, quæsumus, Domine, clementer exaudi : ut qui juste pro peccatis nostris affligimur, pro tui nominis gloria misericorditer liberemur. Per Dominum.

Mercifully hear, we beseech thee, O Lord, the prayers of thy people ; that we who are justly afflicted for our sins, may be mercifully delivered for the glory of thy name. Through, etc.

SECOND COLLECT

A cunctis nos, quæsumus, Domine, mentis et corporis defende periculis : et intercedente beata et gloriosa semperque Virgine Dei Genitrice Maria, cum beato Joseph, beatis apostolis tuis Petro et Paulo, atque beato N., et omnibus sanctis, salutem nobis tribue benignus et pacem : ut destructis adversitatibus et erroribus universis, Ecclesia tua secura tibi serviat libertate.

Preserve us, O Lord, we beseech thee, from all dangers of soul and body : and by the intercession of the glorious and blessed Mary, the ever Virgin Mother of God, of blessed Joseph, of thy blessed apostles, Peter and Paul, of blessed N. (*here is mentioned the titular saint of the church*), and of all the saints, grant us, in thy mercy, health and peace ; that, all adversities and errors being removed, thy Church may serve thee with undisturbed liberty.

The priest adds a third Collect, which is left to his own choice.

Lectio Epistolæ beati Pauli Apostoli ad Corinthios.

Lesson of the Epistle of St. Paul the Apostle to the Corinthians.

1 *Cap* ix., x.

1 *Ch.* ix., x.

Fratres, nescitis quod ii qui in stadio currunt, omnes quidem currunt, sed unus accipit bravium? Sic currite, ut comprehendatis. Omnis autem, qui in agone contendit, ab omnibus se abstinet: et illi quidem ut corruptibilem coronam accipiant, nos autem incorruptam. Ego igitur sic curro, non quasi in incertum: sic pugno, non quasi aerem verberans: sed castigo corpus meum et in servitutem redigo: ne forte cum aliis prædicaverim, ipse reprobus efficiar. Nolo enim vos ignorare, fratres, quoniam patres nostri omnes sub nube fuerunt, et omnes mare transierunt, et omnes in Moyse baptizati sunt, in nube et in mari; et omnes eamdem escam spiritalem manducaverunt, et omnes eumdem potum spiritalem biberunt (bibebant autem de spiritali, consequente eos petra; petra autem erat Christus). Sed non in pluribus eorum beneplacitum est Deo.

Brethren, know you not that they that run in the race, all run indeed, but one receiveth the prize? So run that you may obtain. And every one that striveth for the mastery, refraineth himself from all things; and they indeed that they may receive a corruptible crown, but we an incorruptible one. I therefore so run, not as at an uncertainty: I so fight, not as one beating the air: but I chastise my body and bring it into subjection: lest, perhaps, when I have preached to others, I myself should become a castaway. For I would not have you ignorant, brethren, that our fathers were all under the cloud, and all passed through the sea, and all in Moses were baptized in the cloud, and in the sea: and did all eat the same spiritual food; and all drank the same spiritual drink (and they drank of the spiritual rock that followed them, and the rock was Christ). But with the most of them God was not well pleased.

These stirring words of the apostle deepen the sentiments already produced in us by the sad recollections of which we are this day reminded. He tells us that this world is *a race*, wherein all must run; but that they alone win *the prize*, who run well. Let us, therefore, rid ourselves of everything that could impede us, and make us lose our crown. Let us not deceive ourselves: we are never sure, until we reach the goal. Is our conversion more solid than was St. Paul's? Are our good works better done, or more meritorious, than were his? Yet he assures us that he was not without the fear that he might perhaps be lost; for which cause he chastised his body, and kept it in subjection to the spirit. Man, in his present state, has not the same will for all that is right and just, which Adam had before he sinned, and which, notwithstanding, he abused to his own ruin. We have a bias which inclines us to evil; so that our only means of keeping our ground is to sacrifice the flesh to the spirit. To many this is very harsh doctrine; hence, they are sure to fail; they never can win the *prize*. Like the Israelites spoken of by our apostle, they will be left behind to die in the desert, and so lose the promised land. Yet they saw the same miracles that Josue and Caleb saw! So true is it that nothing can make a salutary impression on a heart which is obstinately bent on fixing all its happiness in the things of this present life; and though it is forced, each day, to own that they are vain, yet each day it returns to them, vainly but determinedly loving them.

The heart, on the contrary, that puts its trust in God, and mans itself to energy by the thought of the divine assistance being abundantly given to him that asks it, will not flag or faint in the *race*, and will win the heavenly *prize*. God's eye is unceasingly on all them that toil and suffer. These are the truths expressed in the Gradual.

GRADUAL

Adjutor in opportunitatibus, in tribulatione : sperent in te qui noverunt te, quoniam non derelinquis quærentes te, Domine.

V. Quoniam non in finem oblivio erit pauperis ; patientia pauperum non peribit in æternum : exsurge, Domine, non prævaleat homo.

A helper in due time, in tribulation : let them trust in thee, who know thee, for thou dost not forsake them that seek thee, O Lord.

V. For the poor man shall not be forgotten to the end ; the patience of the poor man shall not perish for ever : arise, O Lord, let not man prevail.

The Tract sends forth our *cry* to God, and the *cry* is from the very *depths* of our misery. Man is humbled exceedingly by the fall; but he knows that God is full of *mercy*, and that, in His goodness, He punishes our *iniquities* less than they deserve : were it not so, none of us could hope for pardon.

TRACT

De profundis clamavi ad te, Domine : Domine, exaudi vocem meam.

V. Fiant aures tuæ intendentes in orationem servi tui.

V. Si iniquitates observaveris, Domine : Domine, quis sustinebit ?

V. Quia apud te propitiatio est, et propter legem tuam sustinui te, Domine.

From the depths I have cried to thee, O Lord : Lord, hear my voice.

V. Let thine ears be attentive to the prayer of thy servant.

V. If thou shalt observe iniquities, O Lord, Lord, who shall endure it ?

V. For with thee is propitiation, and by reason of thy law I have expected thee, O Lord.

GOSPEL

Sequentia sancti Evangelii secundum Matthæum.

Cap. xx.

In illo tempore, dixit Jesus discipulis suis parabolam hanc : Simile est regnum cælorum homini

Sequel of the holy Gospel according to Matthew.

Ch. xx.

At that time, Jesus spoke to his disciples this parable : The kingdom of heaven is like to a householder who went out

patrifamilias, qui exiit
primo mane conducere ope-
rarios in vineam suam. Con-
ventione autem facta cum
operariis ex denario diurno,
misit eos in vineam suam.
Et egressus circa horam
tertiam, vidit alios stantes
in foro otiosos, et dixit illis : Ite et vos in vineam
meam, et quod justum
fuerit, dabo vobis. Illi autem abierunt. Iterum autem
exiit circa sextam et nonam
horam, et fecit similiter.
Circa undecimam vero exiit;
et invenit alios stantes, et
dicit illis : Quid hic statis
tota die otiosi ? Dicunt ei :
Quia nemo nos conduxit.
Dicit illis : Ite et vos in
vineam meam. Cum sero
autem factum esset, dicit
dominus vineæ procuratori
suo : Voca operarios, et
redde illis mercedem, inci-
piens a novissimis usque ad
primos. Cum venissent ergo
qui circa undecimam horam
venerant, acceperunt singulos denarios. Venientes
autem et primi, arbitrati
sunt quod plus essent acce-
pturi : acceperunt autem et
ipsi singulos denarios. Et
accipientes murmurabant
adversus patremfamilias, dicentes : Hi novissimi una
hora fecerunt, et pares illos
nobis fecisti qui portavimus
pondus diei et æstus ? At
ille respondens uni eorum,
dixit : Amice, non facio tibi
injuriam ; nonne ex denario
convenisti mecum ? Tolle
quod tuum est, et vade :
volo autem et huic novis-

early in the morning to hire
labourers into his vineyard.
And having agreed with the
labourers for a penny a day, he
sent them into his vineyard.
And going out about the third
hour, he saw others standing
in the market-place idle. And
he said to them : Go you also
into my vineyard, and I will
give you what shall be just.
And they went their way.
And again he went out about
the sixth and the ninth hour,
and did in like manner. But
about the eleventh hour he
went out and found others
standing, and he saith to them :
Why stand you here all the
day idle ? They say to him :
Because no man hath hired us.
He saith to them : Go you also
into my vineyard. And when
evening was come, the lord of
the vineyard saith to his stew-
ard : Call the labourers and
pay them their hire, beginning
from the last even to the first.
When, therefore, they were
come that came about the
eleventh hour, they received
every man a penny. But when
the first also came, they
thought that they should receive more : and they also received every man a penny.
And receiving it they mur-
mured against the master of
the house, saying : These last
have worked but one hour,
and thou hast made them
equal to us that have borne
the burden of the day, and the
heats. But he answering said
to one of them : Friend, I do
thee no wrong : Didst thou not
agree with me for a penny ?

simo dare sicut et tibi. Aut non licet mihi quod volo facere? An oculus tuus nequam est, quia ego bonus sum? Sic erunt novissimi primi, et primi novissimi. Multi enim sunt vocati, pauci vero electi.

Take what is thine, and go thy way: I will also give to this last even as to thee. Or, is it not lawful for me to do what I will? Is thy eye evil, because I am good? So shall the last be first, and the first last. For many are called, but few chosen.

It is of importance that we should well understand this parable of the Gospel, and why the Church inserts it in to-day's liturgy. Firstly, then, let us recall to mind on what occasion our Saviour spoke this parable, and what instruction He intended to convey by it to the Jews. He wishes to warn them of the fast approach of the day when their Law is to give way to the Christian Law; and He would prepare their minds against the jealousy and prejudice which might arise in them, at the thought that God was about to form a Covenant with the Gentiles. The *vineyard* is the Church in its several periods, from the beginning of the world to the time when God Himself dwelt among men, and formed all true believers into one visible and permanent society. The *morning* is the time from Adam to Noah; the *third hour* begins with Noah and ends with Abraham; the *sixth hour* includes the period which elapsed between Abraham and Moses; and lastly, the *ninth hour* opens with the age of the prophets, and closes with the birth of the Saviour. The Messias came at the *eleventh hour*, when the world seemed to be at the decline of its day. Mercies unprecedented were reserved for this last period, during which salvation was to be given to the Gentiles by the preaching of the apostles. It is by this mystery of mercy that our Saviour rebukes the Jewish pride. By the selfish murmurings made against the *master of the house* by the early *labourers*, our Lord signifies the indignation which the scribes and pharisees would show at the Gentiles being adopted as God's children. Then He shows them how their jealousy would be chastised : Israel, that had laboured before us, shall be rejected for their obduracy of heart, and we Gentiles, the *last* comers, shall be made *first*, for we shall be made members of that Catholic Church, which is the bride of the Son of God.

This is the interpretation of our parable given by St. Augustine and St. Gregory the Great, and by the generality of the holy fathers. But it conveys a second instruction, as we are assured by the two holy doctors just named. It signifies the calling given by God to each of us individually, pressing us to labour, during this life, for the *kingdom* prepared for us. The *morning* is our childhood. The *third hour*, according to the division used by the ancients in counting their day, is sunrise ; it is our youth. The *sixth hour*, by which name they called our midday, is manhood. The *eleventh hour*, which immediately preceded sunset, is old age. The *Master of the house* calls His *labourers* at all these various *hours*. They must go that very hour. They that are called in the morning may not put off their starting for the vineyard, under pretext of going afterwards, when the Master shall call them later on. Who has told them that they shall live to the eleventh hour ? They that are called at the third hour may be dead at the sixth. God will call to the labours of the last hour such as shall be living when that hour comes ; but, if we should die at midday, that last call will not avail us. Besides, God has not promised us a second call, if we excuse ourselves from the first.

At the Offertory, the Church invites us to celebrate the praises of God. God has mercifully granted us, that the hymns we sing to the glory of His name should be our consolation in this vale of tears.

OFFERTORY

Bonum est confiteri Domino, et psallere nomini tuo, Altissime.

It is good to give praise to the Lord, and to sing to thy name, O Most High.

SECRET

Muneribus nostris, quæsumus, Domine, precibusque susceptis : et cœlestibus nos munda mysteriis, et clementer exaudi. Per Dominum.

Having received, O Lord, our offerings and prayers, cleanse us, we beseech thee, by these heavenly mysteries, and mercifully hear us. Through, etc.

SECOND SECRET

Exaudi nos, Deus salutaris noster : ut per hujus Sacramenti virtutem, a cunctis nos mentis et corporis hostibus tuearis, gratiam tribuens in præsenti, et gloriam in futuro.

Graciously grant us, O God, our Saviour, that by virtue of this Sacrament, thou mayst defend us from all enemies, both of soul and body ; giving us grace in this life, and glory in the next.

The third Secret is left to the priest's own choice.

In the Communion antiphon, the Church prays that man, having now been regenerated by the Bread of heaven, may regain that likeness to his God which Adam received at his creation. The greater our misery, the stronger should be our hope in Him, who descended to us that we might ascend to Him.

COMMUNION

Illumina faciem tuam super servum tuum, et salvum me fac in tua misericordia : Domine, non confundar, quoniam invocavi te.

Make thy face to shine upon thy servant; save me in thy mercy. Let me not be confounded, O Lord, for I have called upon thee.

POSTCOMMUNION

Fideles tui, Deus, per tua dona firmentur : ut eadem

May thy faithful, O God, be strengthened by thy gifts ;

et percipiendo requirant, et
quærendo sine fine perci-
piant. Per Dominum.

that by receiving them, they
may ever hunger after them,
and hungering after them,
they may have their desires
satisfied in the everlasting
possession of them. Through,
etc.

SECOND POSTCOMMUNION

Mundet et muniat nos,
quæsumus Domine, divini
Sacramenti munus oblatum,
et intercedente beata Virgine
Dei Genitrice Maria, cum
beato Joseph, beatis apostolis Petro et Paulo, atque
beato N. et omnibus sanctis,
a cunctis nos reddat et perversitatibus expiatos, et adversitatibus expeditos.

May the oblation of this
divine Sacrament, we beseech
thee, O Lord, both cleanse
and defend us ; and by the
intercession of blessed Mary,
the Virgin-Mother of God, of
blessed Joseph, of the blessed
apostles, Peter and Paul, of
blessed N., and of all the
saints, free us from all sin,
and deliver us from all adversity.

The third Postcommunion is left to the priest's
own choice.

VESPERS

The psalms and antiphons as on page 72.

CAPITULUM

1 *Cor.* ix.

Fratres, nescitis quod ii,
qui in stadio currunt, omnes quidem currunt, sed
unus accipit bravium ? Sic
currite, ut comprehendatis.

Brethren, know you not, that
they that run in the race, all
run indeed, but one receiveth
the prize ? So run, that you
may obtain.

The hymn and versicle, page 79.

ANTIPHON OF THE 'MAGNIFICAT'

Dixit paterfamilias operariis suis: Quid hic statis
tota die otiosi ? At illi re-
spondentes, dixerunt: Quia

The householder said to the
labourers : Why stand you here
all the day idle ? But they
answering said to him : Be-

nemo nos conduxit. Ite et vos in vineam meam: et quod justum fuerit, dabo vobis.

cause no man hath hired us. Go ye, also, into my vineyard, and I will give you what is just.

OREMUS.

Preces populi tui, quæsumus Domine, clementer exaudi, ut qui juste pro peccatis nostris affligimur, pro tui nominis gloria misericorditer liberemur. Per Dominum.

LET US PRAY.

Mercifully hear, we beseech thee, O Lord, the prayers of thy people; that we who are justly afflicted for our sins, may be mercifully delivered for the glory of thy name. Through, etc.

For each day of this week we select a few stanzas from the hymn, which the Greek liturgy uses in the Office for the Sunday preceding the fast of Lent. It is a lamentation over Adam's fall.

IN DOMINICA TYROPHAGI

Excidit e paradiso voluptatis Adamus, Domini præceptum, amaro cibo intemperanter degustato, transgressus, damnatusque fuit terræ unde desumptus fuerat colendæ, suoque pani per sudorem multum comedendo ; nos igitur temperantiam appetamus, ne velut ille extra paradisum ploremus, sed intus admittamur.

Because he broke the commandment of his Lord, and was led by intemperance to taste a food which was to be one of bitterness to him, Adam was banished from the paradise of delight, and condemned to till the earth whence he himself was taken, and to eat his bread in the sweat of his brow. Let us, therefore, covet temperance, lest, like him, we may have to weep out of paradise ; let us be temperate and enter heaven.

Conditor meus Dominus, pulvere e terra accepto, me vivifico spiritu animavit, atque visibilium omnium super terram dominatione, angelorumque consortio dignatus est; dolosus autem Satan, serpentis instrumento usus, esca decepit, et a Dei gloria procul amandavit,

God, my Creator, took dust from the earth, quickened me with a living soul, graciously made me the king of all visible things on earth, and gave me fellowship with the angels; but crafty Satan, making the serpent his instrument, allured me with food, banished me far from the glory

9

mortique in infimis terræ addixit : tu vero, utpote Dominus, atque benignus, ab exilio me revoca.

Stola divinitus texta spoliatus fui miser ego, divino præcepto tuo, Domine, ex inimici fraude violato, foliisque ficulneis et pelliceis tunicis modo circumdor ; panem laboris in sudore manducandi sententiam excepi, utque spinas et tribulos tellus mihi ferat, diris devota est ; sed qui postremis temporibus e Virgine incarnatus es, revocatum me in paradisum restitue.

Paradise, omni honore dignissime, pulcherrima species, tabernaculum divinitus structum, perenne gaudium et oblectamentum, gloria justorum, prophetarum lætitia, sanctorumque domicilium, foliorum tuorum sonitu Conditorem universorum deprecare, ut fores, quas prævaricatione clausi, mihi adaperiat, utque dignus efficiar ligni vitæ participatione, eoque gaudio quod dulcissime prius in temetipso degustavi.

of God, and made me a slave to death in the bowels of the earth : but thou, O God, art my Lord, and full of mercy : recall me from exile.

Being deceived by the craft of the enemy, I, miserable man, violated thy commandment, O Lord ; and being stripped of the garment which thy divine hand had woven for me, I am now clad with leaves of the fig-tree, and with a skin garment ; I am condemned to eat a bread for which I must toil with the sweat of my brow, and the earth is cursed, so that it may yield me thorns and thistles : but do thou, that in after-times tookest flesh from the Virgin, recall and restore me to paradise.

O paradise ! most worthy of all our reverence, beautiful beyond measure, tabernacle built by God, joy and delight without end, glory of the just, joy of the prophets, and dwelling of the saints ; may thy prayers, the sound of thy leaves, obtain for me from the Creator of all things, that thy gates, which my sin hath shut against me, may be thrown open to me, and that I may be made worthy to partake of the tree of life, and of that joy which I once so sweetly tasted in thy bosom.

MONDAY OF SEPTUAGESIMA WEEK

THE serpent said to the woman: ' Why hath God commanded you, that you should not eat of every tree of paradise?' [1] Thus opened the conversation, which our mother Eve so rashly consents to hold with God's enemy. She ought to refuse all intercourse with Satan; she does not; and thereby she imperils the salvation of the whole human race.

Let us recall to mind the events that have happened up to this fatal hour. God, in His omnipotence and love, has created two beings, upon whom He has lavished all the riches of His goodness. He has destined them for immortality; and this undying life is to have everything that can make it perfectly happy. The whole of nature is made subject to them. A countless posterity is to come from them, and love them with all the tenderness of grateful children. Nay, this God of goodness who has created them, deigns to be on terms of intimacy with them; and such is their simple innocence, that this adorable condescension does not seem strange to them. But there is something far beyond all this. He, whom they have hitherto known by favours of an inferior order, prepares for them a happiness which surpasses all they could picture with every effort of thought. They must first go through a trial; and if faithful, they will receive the great gift as a recompense they have merited. And this is the gift: God will give them to know Him in Himself, make them partakers of His own glory, and make their happiness infinite and eternal. Yes, this is what God has done, and is preparing to do for these two beings, who but a while ago were nothing.

[1] Gen. iii. 1.

In return for all these gratuitous and magnificent gifts, God asks of them but one thing : that they acknowledge His dominion over them. Nothing, surely, can be sweeter to them than to make such a return ; nothing could be more just. All they are, and all they have, and all the lovely creation around them, has been produced out of nothing by the lavish munificence of this God ; they must, then, live for Him, faithful, loving, and grateful. He asks them to give Him one only proof of this fidelity, love, and gratitude : He bids them not to eat of the fruit of one single tree. The only return He asks for all the favours He has bestowed upon them, is the observance of this easy commandment. His sovereign justice will be satisfied by this act of obedience. They ought to accept such terms with hearty readiness, and comply with them with a holy pride, as being not only the tie which will unite them with their God, but the sole means in their power of paying Him what He asks of them.

But there comes another voice, the voice of a creature, and it speaks to the woman : ' Why hath God commanded you, that you should not eat of every tree ?' And Eve dares, and has the heart, to listen to him that asks why her divine Benefactor has put a command upon her ! She can bear to hear the justice of God's will called in question ! Instead of protesting against the sacrilegious words, she tamely answers them ! Her God is blasphemed, and she is not indignant ! How dearly we shall have to pay for this ungrateful indifference, this indiscretion ! ' And the woman answered him, saying : Of the fruit of the trees that are in para-dise we do eat ; but of the fruit of the tree which is in the midst of paradise, God hath commanded us that we should not eat, and that we should not touch it, lest perhaps we die.'[1] Thus Eve not only

[1] Gen iii. 2, 3.

listens to the serpent's question, she answers him; she converses with the wicked spirit that tempts her. She exposes herself to danger; her fidelity to her Maker is compromised. True, the words she uses show that she has not forgotten His command; but they imply a certain hesitation, which savours of pride and ingratitude.

The spirit of evil finds that he has excited, in this heart, a love of independence; and that, if he can but persuade her that she will not suffer from her disobedience, she is his victim. He, therefore, further addresses her with these blasphemous and lying words: 'No, you shall not die the death; for God knoweth, that in what day soever you shall eat thereof, your eyes shall be opened, and you shall be as gods, knowing good and evil.'[1] What he proposes to Eve is open rebellion. He has enkindled within her that perfidious love of self which is man's worst evil, and which, if it be indulged, breaks the tie between him and his Creator. Thus the blessings God has bestowed, the obligation of gratitude, personal interest, all are to be disregarded and forgotten. Ungrateful man would become a god; he would imitate the rebel angels: he shall fall as they did.

IN DOMINICA TYROPHAGI

Adesdum anima mea infelix, actus tuos hodie defle, memoria recolens priorem in Eden nuditatem, propter quam deliciis et perenni gaudio excidisti.

Pro multa pietate atque miserationibus, Conditor creaturæ et factor universorum, me pulvere prius animatum una cum angelis

Come, my poor soul! bewail this day thy deeds. Think within thyself of that sin which made thee naked in Eden, and robbed thee of delight and joy eternal.

Creator of me and of all things! in thy great goodness and mercy, thou, having made me out of dust, and given me a soul, didst command me to

---

[1] Gen. iii. 4, 5.

tuis te collaudare præce-
pisti.

Propter bonitatis divi-
tias, plantas tu, Conditor
et Domine, paradisi delicias
in Eden, jubens me speciosis
jucundisque minimeque ca-
ducis fructibus oblectari.

Hei mihi! anima mea
misera, fruendarum Eden
voluptatum facultatem a
Deo acceperas, vetitumque
tibi ne scientiæ lignum
manducares : qua de causa
Dei legem violasti?

(Virgo Dei Genitrix, ut-
pote Adami ex genere filia,
per gratiam vero Christi
Dei Mater, nunc me revoca
ex Eden ejectum.)

Serpens dolosus honorem
meum quondam mihi in-
videns, in Evæ auribus dolum insusurravit, unde ego
deceptus, hei mihi! e vitæ
sede exsulavi.

Manu temere extensa,
scientiæ lignum degustavi,
quod ne contingerem mihi
Deus omnino præscripserat,
et cum acerbo doloris sensu
divinam gloriam exsul amisi.

Hei mihi! misera anima
mea, quomodo dolum non
nosti? Quomodo fraudem
et inimici invidiam minime
sensisti? Sed mente obte-
nebrata Conditoris tui man-
datum neglexisti.

(Spes et protectio mea,
O veneranda, quæ sola olim
lapsi Adami nuditatem co-
operuisti puerperio tuo, rursus, O pura, me incorru-
ptionis veste circumda.)

unite with the angels in praising
thee.

My Maker and Lord! in the
riches of thy goodness, thou
plantest a paradise of delights
in Eden, and biddest me feast
on its lovely, sweet, and incorruptible fruits.

Woe is me, O my wretched
soul! Thy God permitted thee
that thou shouldst enjoy the
Eden of delights, if thou
wouldst obey him and not eat
of the tree of knowledge.
Wherefore didst thou violate
his law?

(O Virgin-Mother of God!
Daughter of Adam by nature,
but Mother of Christ by grace!
recall me now the exile from
Eden.)

The crafty serpent envying
me such honour, whispered
his guile into Eve's ear ; and I,
alas! deceived by her, was
banished from the land of
life.

Rashly stretching forth my
hand, I tasted of the tree of
knowledge, which God forbade
me even to touch : and then,
with keen sense of grief, I, an
exile, lost the glory of God.

Alas, miserable man! How
came I not to know the snare?
How was it that I suspected
not the enemy's craft and
envy? My soul was darkened
and I set at nought my Creator's
command.

(O most venerable one! my
hope and refuge! who by giving birth to thy Jesus, didst
cover the nakedness of fallen
Adam, clothe me too, O Virgin, with this incorruptible
garb!)

TUESDAY OF SEPTUAGESIMA WEEK

THE serpent's promises had stifled, in Eve's heart,
every sentiment of love for the God that had
created her and loaded her with blessings : she is
ambitious to be God like Him! Her faith, too, is
wavering; she is not sure that God may not have
deceived her, by threatening her with death should
she disobey His command. Flushed by pride, she
looks up to the forbidden fruit; it seems good to
eat, and it is fair to her eyes.[1] So that her senses
too conspire against . God, and against her own
happiness. The sin is already committed in her
heart; it needs but a formal act to make it complete. She cares for nothing but self; God is no
more heeded than if He did not exist. She stretches
forth her daring hand; she plucks the fruit; she
puts it to her mouth, and eats!

God had said that if she broke His commandment she should die; she has eaten, she has sinned,
and yet she lives as before! Her pride exults at
this triumph, and, convinced that she is too strong
for God's anger to reach her, she resolves on
making Adam a partner in her victory. Boldly she
hands him the fruit, which she herself has eaten
without any evil coming to her. Whether he was
emboldened by the impunity of his wife's sin, or,
from a feeling of blind affection, wished to share
the lot of her who was the 'flesh of his flesh and
bone of his bones,' our first father, also, forgets all
he owes to his Creator, and, as though there had
never been aught of love between him and his God,
he basely does as Eve suggests : he eats of the fruit,
and by that act ruins himself and all his posterity.

No sooner have they broken the tie which united
them with God, than they sink into themselves.

[1] Gen. iii. 6.

As long as God dwells in the creature, whom He has raised to the supernatural state, his being is complete; but, let that creature drive his God away from himself by sin, and he finds himself in a state worse than nothing—the state of evil. That soul which, a moment before, was so beautiful and pure, is a hideous wreck. Thus is it with our first parents: they stand alone; creatures without God; and an intolerable shame seizes them. They thought to become gods, they aspired at infinite being; see them now:—sinners, the prey of concupiscence. Hitherto, their innocence was their all-sufficient garb; the world was obedient to them; they knew not how to blush, and there was nothing to make them fear; but now, they tremble at their nakedness, and must needs seek a place wherein to hide!

The same self-love that had worked their ruin, had made them forget the greatness and goodness of God, and despise His commandment. Now that they have committed the great sin, the same blindness prevents them from even thinking of confessing it, or asking the forgiveness of the Master they have offended. A sullen fear possesses them. They can think of nothing but how and where to hide!

IN DOMINICA TYROPHAGI

Miser ego, honore a te, Domine, in Eden affectus fui: hei mihi! quomodo in errorem inductus, et diabolica invidia appetitus, depulsus sum e facie tua?

Angelorum ordines, paradisi ornamenta, et plantarum quæ illic sunt decus, me fraude misera abductum et a Deo longius digressum lugete.

Unhappy me! thou hadst laden me, O Lord, with honours in Eden. But, alas! I was led into sin; I became a victim to the envy of the devil; I have been driven from thy face.

O ye choirs of angels! ye that give paradise such beauty, and to its flowers their loveliness; weep over me the dupe of wretched craft, now far from your God.

Pratum beatum, plantatæ a Deo arbores, paradisi deliciæ, e foliis velut ex oculis lacrymas nunc effundite super me, nudum et a Dei gloria abdicatum.

(Domina sancta, quæ fidelibus omnibus paradisi januas ab Adam per inobedientiam quondam clausas aperuisti, misericordiæ mihi fores expande.)

Invidens mihi olim inimicus, hominum osor, beatum paradisi domicilium me specie serpentis supplantavit, atque ab æterna gloria submovit.

Lugeo et animo discrucior, oculisque lacrymarum multitudinem adjungere exopto, respiciens et intelligens partam mihi ex transgressione nuditatem.

Dei manus me e terra plasmavit; at in terram rursus revertendi miser legem accepi; quisnam me ejectum a Deo, et inferos pro Eden assecutum, non defleat?

(Te, labis omnis expers Dei Genitrix, fideles universi mysticum gloriæ thalamum annunciamus, unde lapsum me, precor, o pura, 'aptum fac paradisi thalamum.)

O fair garden land! O ye trees, charm of paradise, planted by God's own hand, let your leaves be turned into eyes, and shed your tears over me, for I am a naked king, dethroned of God's glory.

(O holy Mother! thou that didst throw open to the faithful those gates of heaven that had been shut by Adam's disobedience, open now to me the gates of God's mercy.)

The enemy, the hater of mankind, envied me my blissful home in Eden; under the form of a serpent he supplanted me, and robbed me of eternal glory.

My soul weeps and is racked, and I fain would give floods of tears to mine eyes, when I see and understand the nakedness that has come to me by my transgression.

The hand of God formed me out of the earth; but I have miserably brought on myself the sentence: I must return into the earth. Who is there that will not weep over me, that have lost my God, and have given up Eden for hell?

(Sinless Mother of God! the faithful throughout the world proclaim thee to be the mystic throne of glory. I, then, that am fallen, beseech thee, spotless Virgin! prepare me for a throne in heaven!)

WEDNESDAY OF SEPTUAGESIMA WEEK

THE guilty pair appear before the great God, whom they have offended; and instead of acknowledging their guilt, they seek to palliate and excuse it. But divine justice pronounces their condemnation, and the sentence will be felt by their posterity, even to the last generation. The two beings, that had committed the heinous crime, had been enriched with every gift of nature and grace. It was not with them, as it is with us. Concupiscence which gives us an inclination for what is wrong; ignorance and forgetfulness which cloud the intellect of fallen man, these miseries had nothing whatever to do with the fall of our first parents. They sinned through sheer ingratitude. They began by weighing the proposal of revolt, when they ought to have spurned it with indignation and conquered by flight. Then, by degrees, the proposed crime seemed no great harm, because, though God would lose their obedience, they would gain by the disobedience! And at length, the love of God was made to give place to the love of self, and they declared their independence! Yet God had mercy on them, because of their posterity.

The angels were all created at one and the same instant, and each of them was subjected to the trial, which was to decide his eternal future. Each angel depended on his own act, on his own choice between fidelity to his Creator and rebellion against Him; so that they who rebelled drew on themselves the eternity of God's chastisement. The human race, on the contrary, existed not save as represented in its two first parents, and was plunged by and with them into the abyss of God's reprobation: therefore, God, who spared not the angels, mercifully spared the human race.

But let us listen to the three sentences pronounced by God after the fall of man. The first is against the serpent, and is the severest. The curse, which is already upon him, is deepened, and the pardon, which is about to be promised to the human race, is to be given in the form of an anathema against that wicked spirit, that has dared to war with God in the work of His hands.

'I will put enmities between thee and the woman; she shall crush thy head.'[1] Thus does God avenge Himself on His enemy. The victory won over the woman is made to turn against the proud conqueror, and become his humiliation and his defeat. In his fiendish craft, he had directed his first attack, not against the man, but against the woman. She, by nature, was weaker and more credulous; and if he conquered her, he hoped—too well, alas!—that Adam would be led to turn against his Creator, in order not to displease the creature. All happened as he willed it: but now, see how God uses the woman to foil and punish him. He enkindles in her heart an implacable hatred against His and our enemy. This cruel serpent may raise his proud head, and, here and there, find men that will adore him: the day will come, when a woman's foot shall crush this head, which refused to bend before God. This daughter of Eve, whom all generations are to call blessed,[2] shall be prefigured by other women: by Debbora, Judith, Esther, and others, all celebrated for their victories over the serpent. She shall be followed, until the end of time, by an uninterrupted succession of Christian virgins and matrons, who, with all their weakness, shall be powerful in co-operating with God's designs, and, as the apostle says, 'the unbelieving husband shall be sanctified by the believing wife.'[3]

Thus will God punish the serpent's pride. Before

[1] Gen. iii. 15.   [2] St. Luke i. 48.   [3] 1 Cor. vii. 14.

pronouncing upon our first parents the sentence they have deserved, He promises to bless their posterity, and pours into their own hearts a ray of hope.

IN DOMINICA TYROPHAGI.

Tunc sedit Adamus, ploravitque contra paradisi delicias, oculos manibus feriens, atque dicebat: Misericors. miserere mei lapsi.

Then did Adam look back on the Eden of delights, and sitting wept; he hid his face in his hands, and said: O merciful God! have mercy on me the fallen one!

Intuitus Adamus angelum impellentem claudentemque divini horti fores, ingenuit vehementer, dicebatque: Misericors, miserere mei lapsi.

He saw the angel that drove him from the garden of God; and as he beheld him shutting its gates against him, he heaved a deep sigh, and said: O merciful God! have mercy on me the fallen one!

Doleas vices, paradise, domini tui ad mendicitatem detrusi, foliorumque tuorum sonitu Conditorem deprecare ne te claudat. Misericors, miserere mei lapsi.

Weep, Eden, over thy master thus made poor! Let the rustling of thy leaves become a prayer, asking our Creator that he close thee not. O merciful God! have mercy on me the fallen one!

THURSDAY OF SEPTUAGESIMA WEEK

FORGIVENESS is promised; but atonement must be made. Divine justice must be satisfied, and future generations be taught that sin can never pass unpunished. Eve is the guiltier of the two, and her sentence follows that of the serpent. Destined by God to aid man in peopling the earth with happy and faithful children, formed by this God out of man's own substance 'flesh of his flesh, and bone of his bones,' woman was to be on an equality with man. But sin has subverted this order, and God's sentence is this: conjugal union, notwithstanding the humiliation of concupiscence now brought upon it, is to be, as before, holy and sacred ; but it is to be inferior in dignity, before both God and man, to the state of virginity, which disdains the ambitions of the flesh.

Secondly, woman shall be mother still, as she would have been in the state of innocence ; but her honour shall be a burden. Moreover, she shall give birth to her children amidst cruel pains, and sometimes even death must be the consequence of her infant's coming into the world. The sin of Eve shall thus be memorialized at every birth, and nature shall violently resist the first claims of him, whom sin has made her unwelcome lord.

Lastly, she who was at first created to enjoy equality of honour with man, is now to forfeit her independence. Man is to be her superior, and she must obey him. For long ages, this obedience will be no better than slavery; and this degradation shall continue till that Virgin comes, whom the world shall have expected for four thousand years, and whose humility shall crush the serpent's head. She shall restore her sex to its rightful position, and give to Christian woman that influence of gentle persuasiveness, which is compatible with the duty imposed upon her by divine justice, and which can never be remitted : the duty of submission.

IN DOMINICA TYROPHAGI.

Dominator sæculorum omnium Domine, qui me voluntate tua procreasti, dolosi draconis invidia quondam afflictum, teque, Salvator, ad iracundiam concitantem, ne despicias, Deus, sed revoca me.

Hei mihi! pro stola splendida, turpitudinis indumentis obvolutus, lugeo, Salva-

O Lord! King of all ages! who didst create me by thy love ; I have been injured by the envy of the crafty serpent, and have provoked thee, my Saviour, to anger : but despise me not, O God! Call me back to thee.

Alas! my bright robe has been changed into this garb of shame. I bewail my ruin, O

tor, exitium meum, et fide ad te clamo; ne despicias me bone Deus, sed revoca.

Serpentium ferarumque dominus effectus, quo pacto serpenti animabus exitiali familiariter congressus es, inimico veluti bono consiliario usus? O errorem tuum, miserrima anima mea!

(Canimus te, Maria, Dei gratia plena, lucidum divinæ incarnationis tabernaculum; quare me cupiditatibus fœde obtenebratum illumina, fons misericordiæ, spes eorum quos omnis spes dereliquit.)

Saviour, and to thee do I cry with confidence: My good God! Despise me not, but call me back to thee.

How, my soul, couldst thou, that wast made the lord of serpents and beasts, treat the soul-slaying serpent with familiarity, and use thine enemy as a trusty counsellor? Bewail, my wretched soul, thy fatal error!

(To thee do we sing, O Mary, full of divine grace! Hail bright tabernacle of the Incarnation! O fount of mercy, hope of them that are in despair, enlighten me that am dishonoured by the dark clouds of my passions.)

FRIDAY OF SEPTUAGESIMA WEEK

THE curse, which is henceforth to lie so heavily on every human being, has been expressed in the sentence pronounced against Eve; the curse, to which the earth itself is to be subjected, is Adam's sentence. 'Because thou hast hearkened to the voice of thy wife, and hast eaten of the tree, whereof I commanded thee that thou shouldst not eat, cursed is the earth in thy work (that is, on account of what thou hast done).'[1] Adam had excused his sin. God does not admit his excuse; yet He mercifully makes allowance for him, seeing that he sinned, not so much to gratify himself, as to please the frail creature that had been formed out of his own substance. He is not the originator of the disobedient act. God, therefore, sentences him to the personal humiliation of labour and toil, and of eat-

[1] Gen. iii. 17.

ing his bread in the sweat of his brow.[1] Outside
the garden of Eden, there lies the immense desert
of the earth. It is to be the valley of tears; and
there must Adam dwell in exile for upwards of nine
hundred years, with the sad recollection in his
heart of the few happy days spent in paradise!
This desert is barren: Adam must give it fruitfulness by his toil, and draw from it, by the sweat of
his brow, his own and his children's nourishment.
If, in after ages, some men shall live without toil,
they are the exception confirming the general law
and chastisement. They rest, because others have
laboured long and hard for them; neither will God
ratify their exceptional dispensation from labour,
except on the condition that they give encouragement, by their charity and other virtues, to their
fellow-men, in whom Adam's sentence is literally
carried out. Such is the necessity of toil, that if it
be refused, the earth will yield but thorns and
thistles;[2] such, too, the importance of this law
imposed on fallen man, that idleness shall not only
corrupt his heart, it shall also enervate his bodily
strength.

Before his sin, the trees of paradise bent down
their branches, and man fed on their delicious
fruits; but now he must till the earth and draw
from it, with anxiety and fatigue, the seed which is
to give him bread. Nothing could better express
the penal relation between him and the earth, from
which he was originally formed, and which is henceforth to be his tomb, than this law to which God
sentences him, of being indebted to the earth for
the nourishment which is to keep him in life. And
yet here also divine mercy shall show itself; for,
when God shall have been appeased, it shall be
granted to man to unite himself to his Creator by
eating the Bread of life, which is to come down

[1] Gen. iii. 17, 19. [2] *Ibid.*, 18.

from heaven, and whose efficacy for the nourishing
of our souls shall be greater than ever the fruit of
the tree of life could have been for the immortal-
izing of our bodily existence.

IN DOMINICA TYROPHAGI

Dulcis ad vescendum
fructus scientiæ in Eden
visus est mihi, amore capto;
at demum in bilem conver-
sus est. Hei mihi! misera
anima, quomodo intempe-
rantia te e paradisi laribus
exturbavit?

Deus universorum, mise-
ricordiæ Domine, ad humi-
litatem meam benigne re-
spice, nec a divino Eden
longe me ejicias, quo venu-
states unde excidi aspiciens,
fletibus rursus amissa bona
recipiam.

Fleo, ingemo, atque la-
mentor Cherubim ad para-
disi ingressum custodien-
dum igneo ense locata
conspiciens, transgressori-
bus omnibus, hei mihi!
inaccessum, nisi tu, Salvator, aditum mihi facilem
præstes.

Confido in multitudine
misericordiæ tuæ, Christe
salvator, ac divini lateris
tui sanguine, unde homi-
num naturam sanctificasti,
et colentibus te aperuisti, o
bone, paradisi portas antea
Adamo præclusas.

(Vitæ porta, impervia,
spiritualis, virgo Deipara,
innupta, pande mihi pre-
cibus tuis, paradisi clausas
olim fores, quo te meam

My desire blinded me; and
the fruit that grew on Eden's
tree of knowledge seemed to
me to be sweet to eat; but it
has been turned into bitterness.
Unhappy man, I have been
driven from my home of paradise by intemperance!

O God of the universe! O
merciful Lord! look with pity
upon my lowliness, and suffer
me to dwell near thy divine
Eden, that so my eyes may
turn towards the fair land I
have lost, and I, by my tears,
regain it.

I weep, and sigh, and am
afflicted, as I behold the Cherubim guarding, with a flaming
sword, the gate of paradise,
which is shut against all sinners.
Alas! how can I enter, unless
thou, my Saviour, grant me
admission?

O Christ, my Saviour, my
hope is in thy great mercy, and
in the Blood which flowed from
thy sacred Side, whereby thou
didst sanctify mankind, and
open, O good Jesus, to them
that serve thee, the gate of
paradise, which heretofore was
shut against Adam.

(O gate of life! Spiritual
gate, which God has kept for
himself! O Virgin-Mother of
God, espoused to none but him!
Open to me, by thy prayers,

post Deum auxiliatricem
firmumque refugium glori-
ficem.)

the once closed gate of heaven;
that so I may glorify thee, who,
after God, art my helper and
sure refuge !)

SATURDAY OF SEPTUAGESIMA WEEK

THE sentence pronounced by the Almighty upon
our first parents was to fall upon their children to
the end of time. We have been considering, during
this week of Septuagesima, the penalties of the
great sin; but the severest and most humiliating of
them all remains to be told. It is the transmission
to the whole human race of original sin. It is true
that the merits of the promised Redeemer will be
applied to each individual man, in the manner
established by God at various periods of time: still,
this spiritual regeneration, whilst cleansing us from
the leprosy which covered us, and restoring us to
the dignity of children of God, will not remove
every scar of the old wound. It will save us from
eternal death, and restore us to life; but, as long
as our pilgrimage lasts, we shall be weak and sickly.
Thus it is that ignorance makes us short-sighted in
those great truths, which should engross all our
thoughts; and this fills us with illusions, which,
by an unhappy inclination of our will, we cling to
and love. Concupiscence is ever striving to make
our soul a slave to the body; and in order to escape
this tyranny, our life has to be one continual
struggle. An unruly love for independence is unceasingly making us desire to be our own masters,
and forget that we were born to obey. We find
pleasure in sin, whereas virtue rewards us with
nothing, in this life, save the consciousness of our
having done our duty.

Knowing all this, we are filled with admiration
and love when we think of thee, O Mary! thou

10

purest of God's creatures. Thou art our sister in nature; thou art a daughter of Eve; but thou wast conceived without sin, and art therefore the honour of the human race. Thou art of the same flesh and blood as ourselves; and yet thou art immaculate. The divine decree, which condemned us to inherit the disgrace of original sin, could not include thy most pure conception; and the serpent felt, as thy foot crushed his haughty head, that thou hadst never been under his power. In thee, O Mary! we find our nature such as it was when our God first created it. Hail, then, spotless Mirror of justice!

O Mary! beautiful in thine unsullied holiness, pray for us who are weighed down by the consequences of that sin of our first parents, which God would not suffer to approach thee. Thou art the implacable enemy of the serpent; watch over us, lest his sting inflict death on our souls. We were conceived in sin, and born in sorrow; pray for us, that we may so live as to merit blessing. We are condemned to toil, to suffering, and to death; intercede for us, that our atonement may find acceptance with our Lord. We are exposed to the treachery of our evil inclinations; we are in love with this present life; we forget eternity; we are ever striving to deceive our own hearts: how could we escape hell, were the grace of thy divine Son not unceasingly offered to us, enabling us to triumph over all our enemies? Thou, O Immaculate Mother of Jesus, art the Mother of divine grace! Pray for us, that we, who glory in being thy kindred by nature, may be daily more and more enriched with this priceless gift.

Let us salute the blessed Mother of God in the words of the following sequence, taken from the ancient missal of Cluny. Catholic piety has consecrated to Mary the Saturday of each week.

SEQUENCE

Ad laudem Matris Dei
Modulemur licet rei,
    Poscentes remedia.

Hæc nostræ forma spei,
Spes mirandæ speciei,
    Quæ vernat in gloria.
Hæc virtutis nutrimen-
    tum,
Spes solaris, sola laris
    Terreni fiducia.

Stella maris quæ vocaris,
Passus rectos et directos,
    Da pacis suffragia.
Sicut sidus naufrago,
Fulgens dux in pelago,
    Tu præclara.

Mundi lux in tenebris,
Stella nitens celebris,
    Deo cara.

In sede cœlica
Residens, hæc mellica
Admitte cantica,
    Virgo pia.
Paventi psallere,
Trementi pro scelere
    Des ausus,
    Tu plausus,
    Veri vena.
Tu cœli regina,
Mundi medicina,
Munda scelus nostrum,
    Piissima.

In mortis ruina,
Nos ad vitam mina,
    Placans Deum,
    Tu benignissima.
Cara parens, O Maria,
Patris parens, Virgo pia,
Nos in umbræ mortis via
    Sedentes illumina !

Let us, though sinners, sing a hymn in praise of the Mother of God ; let us sing our prayer for help.

Oh ! how well may we hope in her, that beautiful Mother, whose glory is bright as spring !

It is she that trains us to virtue, and warms our earthly home with the sunny beam of hope.

Thou that art called Star of the sea, direct us, steer us, get us the calm of peace.

Thou brightly shinest on life's sea, guiding us, as does the friendly star which leads the shipwrecked into port.

Thou art a light to world-lings in their darkness, thou art the shining well-known star, so dear to God.

Seated on thy heavenly throne, receive, O Virgin-Mother, these our sweet canticles.

To the sinner who fears to sing, do thou, fount of truth, give courage and applause.

Thou art the Queen of heaven, thou art the solace of the world; may thy loving prayers cleanse us from our guilt.

We have merited death; but intercede for us to God, most merciful Queen ! and so lead us unto life.

O Mary, dear Mother ! Mother of thy Creator ! Virgin ever merciful ! enlighten us that are sitting in the shades of death.

Ut te nobis stella duce,
Tui Nati tuti cruce,
Mereamur cœli luce
    Per te frui, Domina.
    Amen.

That, guided by thee our star, and protected by the cross of thy Son, we may, through thy intercession, be brought to the enjoyment of light eternal. Amen.

SEXAGESIMA SUNDAY

The Church offers to our consideration, during this week of Sexagesima, the history of Noah and the deluge. Man has not profited by the warnings already given him. God is obliged to punish him once more, and by a terrible chastisement. There is found out of the whole human race one just man; God makes a covenant with him, and with us through him. But, before He draws up this new alliance, He would show that He is the sovereign Master, and that man, and the earth whereon he lives, subsist solely by His power and permission.

As the ground-work of this week's instructions, we give a short passage from the Book of Genesis: it is read in the Office of this Sunday's Matins.

De Libro Genesis.

From the Book of Genesis.

Cap. vi.

Ch. vi.

Videns autem Deus quod multa malitia hominum esset in terra, et cuncta cogitatio cordis intenta esset ad malum omni tempore, pœnituit eum quod hominem fecisset in terra. Et tactus dolore cordis intrinsecus: Delebo, inquit, hominem quem creavi, a facie terræ, ab homine usque ad animantia, a reptili usque ad volucres cœli. Pœnitet enim me fecisse eos. Noë

And God seeing that the wickedness of men was great on the earth, and that all the thought of their heart was bent upon evil at all times, it repented him that he had made man on the earth. And being touched inwardly with sorrow of heart, he said: I will destroy man, whom I have created, from the face of the earth, from man even to beasts, from the creeping thing even to the fowls of the air. For it repenteth

vero invenit gratiam coram Domino.

me that I have made them. But Noah found grace before the Lord.

Hæ sunt generationes Noë: Noë vir justus atque perfectus fuit in generationibus suis, cum Deo ambulavit. Et genuit tres filios, Sem, Cham, et Japheth. Corrupta est autem terra coram Deo, et repleta est iniquitate. Cumque vidisset Deus terram esse corruptam (omnis quippe caro corruperat viam suam super terram) dixit ad Noë: Finis universæ carnis venit coram me: repleta est terra iniquitate a facie eorum, et ego disperdam eos cum terra.

These are the generations of Noah: Noah was a just and perfect man in his generations: he walked with God. And he begot three sons: Sem, Cham, and Japheth. And the earth was corrupted before God, and was filled with iniquity. And when God had seen that the earth was corrupted (for all flesh had corrupted its way upon the earth), he said to Noah: The end of all flesh is come before me: the earth is filled with iniquity through them, and I will destroy them with the earth.

This awful chastisement of the human race by the deluge was a fresh consequence of sin. This time, however, there was found one just man; and it was through him and his family that the world was restored. Having once more mercifully renewed His covenant with His creatures, God allows the earth to be repeopled, and makes the three sons of Noah become the fathers of the three great families of the human race.

This is the mystery of the Divine Office during the week of Sexagesima. The mystery expressed in to-day's Mass is of still greater importance, and the former is but a figure of it. The earth is deluged by sin and heresy. But the word of God, the seed of life, is ever producing a new generation: a race of men, who, like Noah, fear God. It is the word of God that produces those happy children, of whom the beloved disciple speaks, saying: 'They are born not of blood, nor of the will of the flesh, nor of the will of man, but of

God.'[1] Let us endeavour to be of this family; or, if we are already numbered among its members, let us zealously maintain our glorious position. What we have to do, during these days of Septuagesima, is to escape from the deluge of worldliness, and take shelter in the Ark of salvation; we have to become that good soil, which yields a hundred-fold from the heavenly seed. Let us flee from the wrath to come, lest we perish with the enemies of God: let us hunger after that word of God, which converteth and giveth life to souls.[2]

With the Greeks, this is the seventh day of their week *Apocreos*, which begins on the Monday after our Septuagesima Sunday. They call this week *Apocreos*, because they then begin to abstain from flesh-meat, which abstinence is observed till Easter Sunday.

MASS

At Rome the Station is in the basilica of St. Paul outside the walls. It is around the tomb of the Doctor of the Gentiles, the zealous sower of the divine seed, the father by his preaching of so many nations, that the Roman Church assembles her children on this Sunday, whereon she is about to announce to them how God spared the earth on the condition that it should be peopled with true believers and with faithful adorers of His name.

The Introit, which is taken from the Psalms, cries out to our Lord for help. The human race, all but extinct after the deluge, is here represented as beseeching its Creator to bless and increase it. The Church adopts the same prayer, and asks her Saviour to multiply the children of the Word, as He did in former days.

[1] St. John i. 13.   [2] Ps. xviii.

INTROIT

Exsurge, quare obdormis, Domine? Exsurge, et ne repellas in finem; quare faciem tuam avertis, oblivisceris tribulationem nostram? Adhæsit in terra venter noster: exsurge, Domine, adjuva nos, et libera nos.

Ps. Deus, auribus nostris audivimus : patres nostri annuntiaverunt nobis. *V.* Gloria Patri. Exsurge.

Arise, why sleepest thou, O Lord? Arise, and cast us not off to the end. Why turnest thou thy face away? and forgettest our tribulation? Our belly cleaveth to the earth. Arise, O Lord, help us, and deliver us.

Ps. We have heard, O God, with our ears: our fathers have declared to us thy wonders. *V.* Glory. Arise.

In the Collect, the Church expresses the confidence she puts in the prayers of the great apostle St. Paul, that zealous sower of the divine seed, who laboured more than the other apostles in preaching the word to the Gentiles.

COLLECT

Deus, qui conspicis quia ex nulla nostra actione confidimus : concede propitius, ut contra adversa omnia, Doctoris Gentium protectione, muniamur. Per Dominum.

O God, who seest that we place no confidence in anything we do : mercifully grant that, by the protection of the Doctor of the Gentiles, we may be defended against all adversity. Through, etc.

Then are added two other Collects, as in the Mass of Septuagesima Sunday, page 120.

The Epistle is that admirable passage from one of St. Paul's Epistles, in which the great apostle, for the honour and interest of his sacred ministry, is necessitated to write his defence against the calumnies of his enemies. We learn from this his apology what labours the apostles had to go through, in order to sow the word of God in the barren soil of the Gentile world, and make it Christian.

EPISTLE

Lectio Epistolæ beati Pauli Apostoli ad Corinthios.

Lesson of the Epistle of Saint Paul the Apostle to the Corinthians.

2 *Cap.* xi.

Fratres, libenter suffertis insipientes, cum sitis ipsi sapientes. Sustinetis enim si quis vos in servitutem redigit, si quis devorat, si quis accipit, si quis extollitur, si quis in faciem vos cædit. Secundum ignobilitatem dico, quasi nos infirmi fuerimus in hac parte. In quo quis audet (in insipientia dico), audeo et ego. Hebræi sunt, et ego. Israelitæ sunt, et ego. Semen Abrahæ sunt, et ego. Ministri Christi sunt (ut minus sapiens dico), plus ego: in laboribus plurimis, in carceribus abundantius, in plagis supra modum, in mortibus frequenter. A Judæis quinquies quadragenas, una minus, accepi. Ter virgis cæsus sum, semel lapidatus sum, ter naufragium feci, nocte et die in profundo maris fui; in itineribus sæpe, periculis fluminum, periculis latronum, periculis ex genere, periculis ex gentibus, periculis in civitate, periculis in solitudine, periculis in mari, periculis in falsis fratribus; in labore et ærumna, in vigiliis multis, in fame et siti, in jejuniis multis, in frigore et nuditate. Præter illa, quæ extrinsecus sunt, instantia mea quotidiana, sollicitudo

2 *Ch.* xi.

Brethren, you gladly suffer the foolish, whereas yourselves are wise. For you suffer if a man bring you into bondage, if a man devour you, if a man take from you, if a man be lifted up, if a man strike you on the face. I speak according to dishonour, as if we had been weak in this part. Wherein if any man dare (I speak foolishly) I dare also. They are Hebrews: so am I. They are Israelites: so am I. They are the seed of Abraham: so am I. They are the ministers of Christ: (I speak as one less wise) I am more: in many more labours, in prisons more frequently, in stripes above measure, in deaths often. Of the Jews five times did I receive forty stripes, save one. Thrice was I beaten with rods, once I was stoned, thrice I suffered shipwreck; a night and a day I was in the depth of the sea. In journeying often, in perils of waters, in perils of robbers, in perils from my own nation, in perils from the Gentiles, in perils in the city, in perils in the wilderness, in perils in the sea, in perils from false brethren. In labour and painfulness, in much watchings, in hunger and thirst, in fastings often, in cold and nakedness. Besides those things which are without: my daily instance, the solicitude for all

omnium Ecclesiarum. Quis
infirmatur, et ego non in-
firmor? Quis scandalizatur,
et ego non uror ? Si gloriari
oportet, quæ infirmitatis
meæ sunt, gloriabor. Deus
et Pater Domini nostri Jesu
Christi, qui est benedictus
in sæcula, scit quod non
mentior. Damasci præposi-
tus gentis Aretæ regis, cus-
todiebat civitatem Damas-
cenorum, ut me compre-
henderet ; et per fenestram
in sporta dimissus sum per
murum, et sic effugi manus
ejus. Si gloriari oportet (non
expedit quidem), veniam
autem ad visiones et reve-
lationes Domini. Scio hominem in Christo ante annos
quatuordecim (sive in corpore nescio, sive extra corpus
nescio, Deus scit), raptum
hujusmodi usque ad tertium
cœlum. Et scio hujus-
modi hominem (sive in corpore, sive extra corpus
nescio, Deus scit), quoniam
raptus est in paradisum, et
audivit arcana verba quæ
non licet homini loqui. Pro
hujusmodi gloriabor ; pro
me autem nihil gloriabor,
nisi in infirmitatibus meis.
Nam, et si voluero gloriari,
non ero insipiens ; veritatem enim dicam : parco autem, ne quis me existimet
supra id quod videt in me,
aut aliquid audit ex me. Et
ne magnitudo revelationum
extollat me, datus est mihi
stimulus carnis meæ, angelus Satanæ, qui me colaphi-
zet. Propter quod ter Do-
minum rogavi ut discederet

the churches. Who is weak,
and I am not weak ? Who is
scandalized, and I am not on
fire ? If I must needs glory,
I will glory of the things that
concern my infirmity. The
God and Father of our Lord
Jesus Christ, who is blessed for
ever, knoweth that I lie not.
At Damascus the governor of
the nation under Aretas the
king, guarded the city of the
Damascenes, to apprehend me ;
and through a window in a
basket was I let down by the
wall, and so escaped his hands.
If I must glory (it is not expe-
dient indeed), but I will come
to the visions and revelations
of the Lord. I know a man in
Christ about fourteen years ago
(whether in the body, I know
not, or out of the body, I know
not, God knoweth), such an one
rapt even to the third heaven.
And I know such a man
(whether in the body, or out
of the body, I cannot tell, God
knoweth), that he was caught
up into paradise, and heard
secret words, which it is not
granted to man to utter. For
such an one I will glory ; but
for myself I will glory nothing,
but in my infirmities. For
though I should have a mind
to glory, I shall not be foolish :
for I will say the truth. But
I forbear, lest any man should
think of me above that which
he seeth in me, or anything he
heareth from me. And lest the
greatness of the revelations
should exalt me, there was
given me a sting of my flesh,
an angel of Satan to buffet me.
For which thing thrice I be-

a me: et dixit mihi: Sufficit tibi gratia mea; nam
virtus in infirmitate perfi-
citur. Libenter igitur gloriabor in infirmitatibus
meis, ut inhabitet in me
virtus Christi.

sought the Lord that it might
depart from me: and he said
to me: My grace is sufficient
for thee: for power is made
perfect in infirmity. Gladly,
therefore, will I glory in my
infirmities, that the power of
Christ may dwell in me.

In the Gradual, the Church beseeches her Lord
to give her strength against those who oppose the
mission He has entrusted to her, of gaining for Him
a new people, adorers of His sovereign Majesty.

GRADUAL

Sciant gentes, quoniam
nomen tibi Deus: tu solus
Altissimus super omnem
terram.

V. Deus meus, pone illos
ut rotam, et sicut stipulam
ante faciem venti.

Let the Gentiles know that
God is thy name: thou alone
art the Most High over all the
earth.

V. O my God, make them
like a wheel, and as stubble
before the wind.

Whilst the earth is being *moved*, and is suffering
those terrible revolutions which, deluge-like, come
first on one nation and then on another, the Church
prays for her faithful children, in order that they
may be spared, for they are the *elect*, and the hope
of the world. It is thus she prays in the following
Tract, which precedes the Gospel of the word.

TRACT

Commovisti, Domine, ter-
ram, et conturbasti eam.

V. Sana contritiones ejus,
quia mota est.

V. Ut fugiant a facie ar-
cus: ut liberentur electi tui.

Thou hast moved the earth,
O Lord, and hast troubled it.

V. Heal the breaches thereof, for it is moved.

V. That they may flee from
before the bow: that thy elect
may be delivered.

GOSPEL

Sequentia sancti Evangelii secundum Lucam.

Cap. viii.

In illo tempore, cum turba plurima convenirent, et de civitatibus properarent ad Jesum, dixit per similitudinem : Exiit, qui seminat, seminare semen suum : et dum seminat, aliud cecidit secus viam, et conculcatum est, et volucres cœli comederunt illud. Et aliud cecidit supra petram : et natum, aruit; quia non habebat humorem. Et aliud cecidit inter spinas, et simul exortæ spinæ suffocaverunt illud. Et aliud cecidit in terram bonam : et ortum fecit fructum centuplum. Hæc dicens clamabat : Qui habet aures audiendi, audiat. Interrogabant autem eum discipuli ejus, quæ esset hæc parabola. Quibus ipse dixit : Vobis datum est nosse mysterium regni Dei, cæteris autem in parabolis ; ut videntes non videant, et audientes non intelligant. Est autem hæc parabola. Semen est verbum Dei. Qui autem secus viam, hi sunt qui audiunt : deinde venit diabolus, et tollit verbum de corde eorum, ne credentes salvi fiant. Nam qui supra petram : qui cum audierint, cum gaudio suscipiunt verbum : et hi radices non habent : quia ad tempus credunt, et in tempore tentationis recedunt. Quod au-

Sequel of the holy Gospel according to Luke.

Ch. viii.

At that time, when a very great multitude was gathered together, and hastened out of the cities to meet Jesus, he spoke by a similitude. The sower went out to sow his seed; and as he sowed, some fell by the wayside, and it was trodden down, and the fowls of the air devoured it. And other some fell upon a rock : and as soon as it was sprung up, it withered away, because it had no moisture. And other some fell among thorns ; and the thorns growing up with it, choked it. And other some fell upon good ground, and being sprung up, yielded fruit a hundred-fold. Saying these things he cried out : He that hath ears to hear, let him hear. And his disciples asked him what this parable might be. To whom he said : To you it is given to know the mystery of the kingdom of God; but to the rest in parables : that seeing they may not see, and hearing they may not understand. Now the parable is this : The seed is the word of God. And they by the wayside are they that hear ; then the devil cometh, and taketh the word out of their heart, lest believing they should be saved. Now they upon the rock are they who, when they hear, receive the word with joy : and these have no roots ; for they believe for a while, and in time of

tem in spinas cecidit, hi sunt qui audierunt, et a sollicitudinibus, et divitiis, et voluptatibus vitæ, euntes, suffocantur, et non referunt fructum. Quod autem in bonam terram : hi sunt, qui in corde bono et optimo audientes verbum retinent, et fructum afferunt in patientia.

temptation fall away. And that which fell among thorns, are they who have heard, and going their way, are choked with the cares and riches and pleasures of this life, and yield no fruit. But that on the good ground, are they, who in a good and very good heart hearing the word, keep it, and bring forth fruit in patience.

St. Gregory the Great justly remarks, that this parable needs no explanation, since eternal Wisdom Himself has told us its meaning. All that we have to do, is to profit by this divine teaching, and become the good soil, wherein the heavenly seed may yield a rich harvest. How often have we, hitherto, allowed it to be trampled on by them that passed by, or to be torn up by the birds of the air! How often has it found our heart like a stone, that could give no moisture, or like a thorn plot, that could but choke! We listened to the word of God; we took pleasure in hearing it; and from this we argued well for ourselves. Nay, we have often received this *word* with joy and eagerness. Sometimes, even, it took root within us. But, alas! something always came to stop its growth. Henceforth, it must both grow and yield fruit. The *seed* given to us is of such quality, that the divine Sower has a right to expect a *hundred-fold.* If the soil, that is, our *heart*, be *good;* if we take the trouble to prepare it, by profiting by the means afforded us by the Church; we shall have an abundant harvest to show our Lord on that grand day, when, rising triumphant from His tomb, He will come to share with His faithful people the glory of His Resurrection.

Inspirited by this hope, and full of confidence in Him who has once more thrown this seed into this long ungrateful soil, let us sing with the Church, in her Offertory, these beautiful words of the royal psalmist : they are a prayer for holy resolution and perseverance.

OFFERTORY

Perfice gressus meos in semitis tuis, ut non moveantur vestigia mea : inclina aurem tuam et exaudi verba mea : mirifica misericordias tuas, qui salvos facis sperantes in te, Domine.

Perfect thou my goings in thy paths ; that my footsteps be not moved. O incline thy ear unto me and hear my words. Show forth thy wonderful mercies ; who savest them that hope in thee, O Lord.

SECRET

Oblatum tibi, Domine, sacrificium vivificet nos semper, et muniat. Per Dominum.

May the sacrifice we have offered to thee, O Lord, always quicken us and defend us. Through, etc.

To this are added the other Secrets, as on Septuagesima Sunday, page 127.

The visit, which our Lord makes to us in the Sacrament of His love, is the grand means whereby He gives fertility to our souls. Hence it is that the Church invites us, in the Communion antiphon, to draw nigh to the altar of our God ; there, our heart shall regain all the youthful fervour of its best days.

COMMUNION

Introibo ad altare Dei, ad Deum qui lætificat juventutem meam.

I will go up to the altar of God ; to God, who rejoiceth my youth.

POSTCOMMUNION

Supplices te rogamus, omnipotens Deus; ut quos tuis reficis sacramentis, tibi etiam placitis moribus dignanter deservire concedas. Per Dominum.

Grant, we humbly beseech thee, O almighty God, that those whom thou refreshest with thy sacraments, may, by a life well pleasing to thee, worthily serve thee. Through, etc.

Two other Postcommunions are said after this, as on Septuagesima Sunday, page 128.

VESPERS

The psalms and antiphons as on page 72.

CAPITULUM

(2 *Cor.* xi.)

Fratres, libenter suffertis insipientes, cum sitis ipsi sapientes. Sustinetis enim si quis vos in servitutem redigit, si quis devorat, si quis accipit, si quis extollitur, si quis in faciem vos cædit.

Brethren, you gladly suffer the foolish, whereas yourselves are wise. For you suffer if a man bring you into bondage, if a man devour you, if a man take from you, if a man be lifted up, if a man strike you on the face.

The hymn and versicle, page 79.

ANTIPHON OF THE 'MAGNIFICAT'

Vobis datum est nosse mysterium regni Dei, cæteris autem in parabolis, dixit Jesus discipulis suis.

To you it is given to know the mystery of the kingdom of God, but to the others in parables, said Jesus to his disciples.

OREMUS.

Deus, qui conspicis quia ex nulla nostra actione confidimus: concede propitius, ut contra adversa omnia, Doctoris Gentium protectione, muniamur. Per Dominum.

LET US PRAY.

O God, who seest that we place no confidence in anything we do: mercifully grant that by the protection of the Doctor of the Gentiles, we may be defended against all adversity. Through, etc.

We will end our Sunday by a hymn taken from the ancient breviaries of the Churches of France: it will help us to keep up in our souls the sentiments proper to the season of Septuagesima.

HYMN

Dies absoluti prætereunt;
Dies observabiles redeunt.
Tempus adest sobrium :
Quæramus puro corde Dominum.

Hymnis et in confessionibus
Judex complacabitur Dominus.
Non negabit hic veniam,
Qui vult ut homo quærat gratiam.
Post jugum servile Pharaonis,
Post catenas diræ Babylonis:
Liber homo patriam
Quærat cœlestem Hierosolymam.
Fugiamus de hoc exilio :
Habitemus cum Dei Filio :
Hoc decus est famuli
Si sit cohæres sui Domini.

Sis Christe nobis dux hujus vitæ :
Memento quod sumus oves tuæ,
Pro quibus ipse tuam
Pastor ponebas morte animam.
Gloria sit Patri et Filio :
Sancto simul honor Paraclito :
Sicut erat pariter
In principio et nunc et semper. Amen.

The days of ease are about to close ; the days of holy observance are returning ; the time of temperance is at hand ; let us seek our Lord in purity of heart.

Our sovereign Judge will be appeased by our hymns and praise. He who would have us sue for grace, will not refuse us pardon.

The slavish yoke of Pharaoh, and the fetters of cruel Babylon, have been borne too long : let man now claim his freedom, and seek his heavenly country, Jerusalem.

Let us quit this place of exile : let us dwell with the Son of God. Is it not the servant's glory, to be made co-heir with his Lord ?

O Jesus! be thou our guide through life. Remember that we are thy sheep, for whom thou, the Shepherd, didst lay down thine own life

Glory be to the Father, and to the Son ; honour too be to the holy Paraclete : as it was in the beginning, now is, and shall ever be. Amen.

MONDAY OF SEXAGESIMA WEEK

ALL flesh had corrupted its way upon the earth.[1]
The terrible lesson, then, which men had received,
by being driven out of paradise in the person of our
first parents, had been without effect.   Neither the
certainty of death, when they would have to stand
before the divine Judge, nor the humiliations which
attend man's first coming into this world, nor the
pains and fatigues and trials which beset the whole
path of life, had subdued men's hearts, or brought
them into submission to that sovereign Master
whose hand lay thus heavy upon them.   They had
the divine promise that a Saviour should be given
to them, and that this Redeemer (who was to be the
Son of her that was to crush the serpent's head),
would not only bring them salvation, but would
moreover reinstate them in all the happiness and
honours they had lost.   But even this was not
enough to make them rise above the base passions
of corrupt nature.   The example of Adam's nine
hundred years' penance, and the admonitions he
could so feelingly give who had received such proofs
of God's love and anger, began to lose their influence
upon his children; and when he at last descended
into the grave, his posterity grew more and more
heedless of what they owed to their Creator.   The
long life, which had been granted to man in this the
first age of the world, was made but a fresh means
of offending Him who gave it.   When, finally, the
sons of Seth took to themselves wives of the family
of Cain, the human race reached the height of
wickedness, rebelled against the Lord, and made
their own passions their god.

Yet, all this while, they had had granted to them
the power of resisting the evil propensities of their

[1] Gen vi. 12

hearts. God had offered them His grace, whereby they were enabled to conquer pride and concupiscence. The merits of the Redeemer to come were even then present to divine justice, and the Lamb, slain, as St. John tells us, from the beginning of the world,[1] applied the merits of His Blood to this as to every generation which existed before the great Sacrifice was really immolated. Each individual of the human family might have been just, as Noah was, and, like him, have found favour with the Most High; but the thought of their heart was bent upon evil, and not upon good, and the earth became peopled with enemies of God. Then it was that it repented God that He had made man,[2] as the sacred Scripture forcibly expresses it. He decreed that man's life on earth should be shortened, in order that the thought of death might be ever before us. He, moreover, resolved to destroy, by a universal deluge, the whole of this perverse generation, saving only one family. The world would thus be renewed, and man would learn from this awful chastisement to serve and love this his sovereign Lord and God.

We find the following liturgical formula in the Mozarabic missal. Nothing could be more appropriate to the season of Septuagesima.

MISSA

(Dominica ante carnes tollendas.)

Ecce jam in proximo sunt dies illi salutis, in quibus revoluto anni circulo, per salutaris abstinentiæ opus, remedia cupimus suscipere pravorum actuum nostro-

Behold, now are close at hand those days of salvation, which the cycle of the year brings round to us, and in which we desire, by the exercise of salutary abstinence, to

---

[1] Apoc. xiii. 8.   [2] Gen. vi. 6.

rum. Etenim sicut ait apostolus : Hoc est acceptabile tempus, et hi sunt dies salutis, in quibus spiritualis medela exquirenti adveniat animæ, et mala dulcia scrabra peccaminum evellantur a mente ; ut qui consuetudine noxia semper cogimur deorsum fluere, tandem divina nos erigente clementia, conemur sursum surgere, ut horum dierum votiva exhibentes susceptione, et malorum nostrorum levemur a crimine, et beatitudinis electorum mereamur compotes esse. Amen.

apply a remedy to our evil doings. For, as the apostle says : This is the acceptable time, and, these are the days of salvation, wherein a spiritual cure is given to the soul that seeks it, and the evil delights of sin are rooted from the mind. Hereby, we, whose evil habits are ever forcing us to a downward tendency, are by the uplifting mercy of God, encouraged to rise above this earth ; that thus, by the devout observance of what these days require, we may not only be delivered from the guilt of our sins, but may moreover deserve to be companions with the elect in eternal bliss. Amen.

TUESDAY OF SEXAGESIMA WEEK

WHEN we reflect upon the terrible events which happened in the first age of the world, we are lost in astonishment at the wickedness of man, and at the effrontery wherewith he sins against his God. How was it that the dread words of God, which were spoken against our first parents in Eden, could be so soon forgotten ? How could the children of Adam see their father suffering and doing such endless penance, without humbling themselves and imitating this model of repentance ? How was it that the promise of a Mediator, who was to reopen the gate of heaven for them, could be believed, and yet not awaken in their souls the desire of making themselves worthy to be His ancestors, and partakers of that grand regeneration, which He was to bring to mankind ? And yet, the years which followed the death of Adam were years of crime and scandal; nay, he himself lived to see one of his own children become the murderer of a brother. But why be thus surprised at the wickedness of these our first brethren? The earth is now six thousand years old in the continued reception of divine blessings and chastisements; and are men less dull of heart, less ungrateful, less rebellious towards their Maker? For the generality of men—we mean, of those who deign to believe in the fall and chastisement of our first parents, and in the destruction of the world by the deluge—what are these great truths? Mere historical facts, which have never once inspired them with a fear of God's justice. More favoured than these early generations of the human race, they know that the Messias has been sent, that God has come down upon the earth, that He has been made Man, that He has broken Satan's rule, that the way to heaven has been made easy by the graces embodied by the Redeemer in the Sacraments: and yet, sin reigns and triumphs in the midst of Christianity. Undoubtedly, the just are more numerous than they were in the days of Noah; but then, what riches of grace has our Redeemer poured out on our degenerate race by the ministry of His bride the Church! Yes, there are faithful Christians to be found upon the earth, and the number of the elect is every day being added to; but the multitude are living at enmity with God, and their actions are in contradiction to their faith.

When, therefore, the holy Church reminds us of those times, wherein all flesh had corrupted its way, she is urging us to think about our own conversion. Her motive in relating to us the history of the sins committed at the beginning of the world, is to induce us to examine our own consciences. Why, too, does she read to us those pages of sacred Writ,

which so vividly describe the flood-gates of heaven
opening and deluging the guilty earth, if not that
she would warn us against mocking that great God,
who thus chastised the sins of His rebellious
creatures? Last week we were called upon to
consider the sad consequences of Adam's sin, a sin
which we ourselves did not commit, but the effects
of which lie so heavy upon us. This week we must
reflect upon the sins we ourselves have committed.
Though God has loaded us with favours, guided us
by His light, redeemed us with His Blood, and
strengthened us against all our enemies by His
grace, yet have we corrupted our way, and caused
our God to repent of having created us. Let us
confess our wickedness, and humbly acknowledge
that we owe it to the mercies of the Lord, that we
have not been consumed.[1]

The Ambrosian missal contains the following
exhortation for this season of the year.

TRANSITORIUM

(*Dominica in Septuagesima.*)

Convertimini omnes simul ad Deum mundo corde et animo, in oratione, jejuniis, et vigiliis multis. Fundite preces vestras cum lacrymis; ut deleatis chirographa peccatorum vestrorum, priusquam vobis repentinus superveniat interitus; antequam vos profundum mortis absorbeat; et cum Creator noster advenerit, paratos nos inveniat.

Be converted to God, all ye people, in purity of heart and soul, in prayer, fasting, and much watching. Pour out your prayers with tears; that the hand-writing of your sins may be blotted out, before sudden destruction come upon you, and before the deep flood of death engulf you. When our Creator comes, let him find us ready.

---

[1] Lam. iii. 22.

WEDNESDAY OF SEXAGESIMA WEEK

O God of infinite justice! we have sinned; we have abused the life Thou hast given us : and when we read, in Thy Scriptures, how Thine anger chastised the sinners of former days, we are forced to acknowledge, that we have deserved to be treated in like manner. We have the happiness to be Christians and children of Thy Church; the light of faith, and the power of Thy grace, have brought us once more into Thy friendship; but how can we forget that we were once Thy enemies? And are we so deeply rooted in virtue, that we can promise ourselves perseverance in it to the end? Pierce, O Lord! pierce my flesh with Thy fear.[1] Man's heart is hard, and unless it fear Thy sovereign Majesty, it may again offend Thee.

We are penetrated with fear, when we remember that Thou didst bury the world and destroy mankind by the waters of the deluge; for we learn by this, how Thy patience and long-suffering may be changed into inexorable anger. Thou art just, O Lord! and who shall presume to take scandal, or to murmur, when Thy wrath is enkindled against sinners?

We have defied Thy justice, we have braved Thine anger; for, though Thou hast told us that Thou wilt never more destroy sinners by a deluge of water, yet we know that Thou hast created, in Thy hatred for sin, a fire, which shall eternally prey on them that depart this life without being first reconciled with Thy offended Majesty.

O wonderful dignity of our human nature! We cannot be indifferent towards that infinite Being that created us: we must be His friends or His

---

[1] Ps. cxviii. 120.

enemies! It could not have been otherwise. He gave us understanding and free-will: we know what is good and what is evil, and we must choose the one or the other: we cannot remain neutral. If we choose good, God turns towards us and loves us; if evil, we separate from Him, who is our sovereign Good. But, whereas He bears most tender mercy towards this frail creature whom He created out of pure love, and because He wills that all men should be saved, He waits with patience for the sinner to return to Him, and, in countless ways, draws his heart to repentance.

But woe to him that obeys not the divine call, when that call is the last! Then justice takes the place of mercy, and revelation tells us how fearful a thing it is to fall into the hands of the living God.[1] Let us, then, flee from the wrath to come,[2] by making our peace with the God we have offended. If we be already restored to grace, let us walk in His fear, until love shall have grown strong enough in our hearts to make us run the way of the commandments.[3]

The following prayer is from the Mozarabic breviary of the Gothic Church of Spain.

ORATIO

(*In capite jejunii.*)

Averte faciem tuam a peccatis nostris, Domine, et omnes iniquitates nostras dele; remove ab oculis tuis malarum nostrarum facinus voluptatum, nostræque confessioni clementer tuum appone auditum. Miserere, quæsumus, rogantibus nobis,

Turn away thy face from our sins, O Lord, and blot out all our iniquities. Take from thine eyes the guilt of our sinful pleasures, and mercifully incline thine ear to our confession. Have mercy, we beseech thee, upon us thy suppliants, O thou that lookest

---

[1] Heb. x. 31.   [2] St. Matt. iii. 7.   [3] Ps. cxviii. 32.

qui propitius respicis in adversis, et qui desperatis cor pœnitens tribuis ad confessionem gloriæ tuæ. Sed quia publicanus a longe stans et percutiens pectus suum, sola confessione purgatus est, similiter et nos peccatores exaudi; ut sicut illi meritos petitionis suæ fructus donasti, ita et nobis supplicantibus indignis servis tuis veniam digneris impendere peccatis. Amen.

with pity on them that are in affliction, and givest to the disconsolate a penitent heart, that so they may praise thy name. The publican who stood afar off and struck his breast, found forgiveness by this alone, that he confessed his sin; do thou, in like manner, mercifully hear us sinners · and as thou didst give to him the fruit his prayer deserved, so also vouchsafe to grant unto us, thy suppliant unworthy servants, the pardon of our sins. Amen.

THURSDAY OF SEXAGESIMA WEEK

God promised Noah that He would never more punish the earth with a deluge. But, in His justice, He has many times visited the sins of men with a scourge which, in more senses than one, bears a resemblance to a deluge: the invasion of enemies. We meet with these invasions in every age; and each time we see the hand of God. We can trace the crimes that each of them was sent to punish, and in each we find a manifest proof of the infinite justice wherewith God governs the world.

It is not requisite that we should here mention the long list of these revolutions, which we might almost say make up the history of mankind, for in its every page we read of conquests, extinction of races, destruction of nations, and violent amalgamations, which effaced the traditions and character of the several peoples that were thus forced into union. We will confine our considerations to the two great invasions, which the just anger of God has permitted to come upon the world since the commencement of the Christian era.

The Roman Empire had made itself as preeminent in crime as it was in power. It conquered the world, and then corrupted it. Idolatry and immorality were the civilization it gave to the nations which had come under its sway. Christianity could save individuals in the great empire, but the empire itself could not be made Christian. God let loose upon it the deluge of barbarians. The stream of the wild invasion rose to the very dome of the Capitol; the empire was engulfed. The ruthless ministers of divine justice were conscious of their being chosen for this mission of vengeance, and they gave themselves the name of 'God's scourge.'

When, later on, the Christian nations of the east had lost the faith which they themselves had transmitted to the western world; when they had disfigured the sacred symbol of faith by their blasphemous heresies; the anger of God sent upon them, from Arabia, the deluge of Mahometanism. It swept away the Christian Churches, that had existed from the very times of the apostles. Jerusalem, the favoured Jerusalem, on which Jesus had lavished His tenderest love, even she became a victim to the infidel hordes. Antioch and Alexandria, with their patriarchates, were plunged into the vilest slavery; and at length Constantinople, that had so obstinately provoked the divine indignation, was made the very capital of the Turkish empire.

And we, the western nations, if we return not to the Lord our God, shall we be spared? Shall the flood-gates of heaven's vengeance, the torrent of fresh Vandals, ever be menacing to burst upon us, yet never come? Where is the country of our own Europe, that has not corrupted its way, as in the days of Noah? that has not made conventions against the Lord and against His Christ?[1] that has

[1] Ps. ii. 2.

THURSDAY OF SEXAGESIMA WEEK

not clamoured out that old cry of revolt: Let us break their bonds asunder, let us cast away their yoke from us?[1]   Well may we fear lest the time is at hand, when, despite our haughty confidence in our means of defence, Christ our Lord, to whom all nations have been given by the Father, shall rule us with a rod of iron, and break us in pieces like a potter's vessel.[2]   Let us propitiate the anger of our offended God, and follow the inspired counsel of the royal prophet: Serve ye the Lord with fear; embrace the discipline of His Law; lest, at any time, the Lord be angry, and ye perish from the just way.[3]

We find the following beautiful words in the Ambrosian liturgy for Septuagesima. They occur in the missal.

TRANSITORIUM

(Dominica in Quinquagesima.)

Venite, convertimini ad me, dicit Dominus. Venite flentes, fundamus lacrymas ad Deum : quia nos neglexi- mus, et propter nos terra patitur. Nos iniquitatem fecimus, et propter nos fun- damenta commota sunt. Festinemus iram Dei ante- vertere, flentes, et dicentes : Qui tollis peccata mundi, miserere nobis.

Come, be converted unto me, saith the Lord. Let us come weeping, and pour out our tears before God, for we have been negligent, and because of us is the earth suffering. We have committed iniquity, and because of us are the founda- tions of the world moved. Let us hasten to avert the wrath of God ; let us weep, and say : O thou, that takest away the sins of the world, have mercy upon us !

---

[1] Ps. ii. 3.   [2] *Ibid.*, 9.   [3] *Ibid.*, 12.

FRIDAY OF SEXAGESIMA WEEK

GOD chastises the world by the deluge; but He is faithful to the promise made to our first parents, that the head of the serpent should be crushed. The human race has to be preserved, therefore, until the time shall come for the fulfilment of this promise. The Ark gives shelter to the just Noah, and to his family. The angry waters reach even to the tops of the highest mountains; but the frail yet safe vessel rides peacefully on the waves. When the day fixed by God shall come, they that dwell in this Ark shall once more tread the earth, purified as it then will be; and God will say to them, as heretofore to our first parents: 'Increase, and multiply, and fill the earth.'[1]

Mankind, then, owes its safety to the Ark. O saving Ark, that wast planned by God Himself, and didst sail unhurt amidst the universal wreck! But if we can thus bless this contemptible wood,[2] how fervently should we love that other Ark, of which Noah's was but the figure, and which, for now eighteen hundred years, has been saving and bringing men to their God! How fervently should we bless that Church, the bride of our Jesus, out of which there is no salvation, and in which we find that truth which delivers us from error and doubt,[3] that grace which purifies the heart, and that food which nourishes the soul and fits her for immortality!

O sacred Ark! thou art inhabited, not by one family alone, but by people of every nation under the sun. Ever since that glorious day, when our Lord launched thee in the sea of this world, thou hast been tossed by tempests, yet never wrecked.

[1] Gen. ix. 1.   [2] Wisd. x. 4.   [3] St. John viii. 32.

Thou wilt reach the eternal shore, witnessing, by thy unworn vigour and beauty, to the divine guidance of the Pilot, who loves thee, both for thine own sake, and for the work thou art doing for His glory. It is by thee that He peoples the world with His elect, and it is for them that He created the world.[1] When He is angry, He remembers mercy,[2] because of thee, for it is through thee that He has made His covenant with mankind.

O venerable Ark! be thou our refuge in the deluge. When Rome's great empire, that was drunk with the blood of the martyrs,[3] sank beneath the invasion of the barbarians, the Christians were safe, because sheltered by thee; the waters slowly subsided, and the race of men that had fled to thee for protection, though conquered according to the flesh, was victorious by the spirit. Kings, who till then had been haughty despots and barbarians, kissed reverently the hand of the slave, who was now their pastor and baptized them. New peoples sprang up, and, with the Gospel as their law, began their glorious career in those very countries which the Cæsars had degraded and forfeited.

When the Saracen invasion came sweeping into ruin the eastern world, and menacing the whole of Europe, which would have been lost had not the energy of thy sons repelled the infidel horde, was it not within thee, O Ark of salvation! that the few Christians took refuge, who had resisted schism and heresy, and who, whilst the rest of their brethren apostatized from the faith, still kept alive the holy flame? Under thy protection they are even now perpetuating, in their unfortunate countries, the traditions of faith, until the divine mercy shall bring happier times, and they be permitted to multiply, as did of old the sons of Sem, in that land once so glorious and holy.

[1] St. Matt. xxiv. 22.   [2] Hab. iii. 2.   [3] Apoc. xvii. 6.

Oh! happy we, dear Church of God! that are
sheltered within thee, and protected by thee against
that wild sea of anarchy, which the sins of men
have let loose on our earth! We beseech our Lord
to check the tempest with that word of His omnipotence: 'Thus far shalt thou come, and no further,
and here shalt thou break thy swelling waves.'[1]
But if His divine justice has decreed that it prevail
for a time, we know that it cannot reach such as
dwell in thee. Of this happy number are we. In
thy peaceful bosom, dear mother, we find those
true riches, the riches of the soul, of which no
violence can deprive us.[2] The life thou givest us
is the only real life. Our true fatherland is the
kingdom formed by thee. Keep us, O thou Ark of
our God! Keep us, and all that are dear to us,
and shelter us beneath thy roof, until the deluge of
iniquity be passed away.[3] When the earth, purified
by its chastisements, shall once more receive the
seed of the divine word which produces the children
of God, those among us, whom thou shalt not have
led to our eternal home, will then venture forth,
and preach to the world the principles of authority
and law, of family and social rights : those sacred
principles, which came from heaven, and which
thou, O holy Church, art commissioned to maintain
and teach, even to the end of time.

We borrow from the Mozarabic missal the following eloquent appeal to divine mercy.

PRAYER

(In Dominica V. post Epiphaniam.)

Exaudi nos Domine Deus
noster, et humanæ iniqui-
tatis oblitus, divinæ so-

Graciously hear, O Lord our
God, and forgetting man's
iniquity, remember only thine

---

[1] Job xxxviii. 11.   [2] St. Matt. vi. 20.   [3] Ps. lvi. 2.

lius misericordiæ recordare. Exaudi, quæsumus, dum peccare non pateris, dum umondaro non prœoipio, dum rogare permittis: dum patientia reditum quærendæ correctionis exspectat: dum justitia metum futuræ discussionis insinuat: dum misericordia locum evadendæ mortis ostentat. Inveniant ante oculos tuos sacrificia nostra gratiam: peccata veniam: vulnera medicinam: suspiria pietatem: flagella consolationem: lamenta temperiem: tempora quietem: officia dignitatem: vota mercedem. Mereatur petitio effectum, contritio solatium, consecratio Sacramentum. Oblatio sanctificatione pinguescat, trepidatio securitate discedat, benedictio salubritate proficiat; ut in omnibus multiplici pietatis tuæ gratia redundante, erigas plebem, dum lætificas sacerdotem. Amen.

own mercy. Graciously hear us, we beseech thee, O thou that forbiddest us to sin, that commandest us to repent, that permittest us to pray! Thy patience awaits our return to the needed repentance; thy justice inspires us with a fear of the future judgment; thy mercy shows us how we may avoid death. May our sacrifices find favour in thine eyes; our sins, pardon; our wounds, cure; our sighs, pity; our chastisements, consolation; our tears, joy; our days, peace; our duties, honour; our prayers, reward. May our petition produce its effect; our contrition, forgiveness; our consecration, the sacred mystery. May our oblation be rich unto sanctification, our fear be cast out by security, and our blessing be fruitful unto salvation; that thus in all things, by the manifold and overflowing grace of thy mercy, thou mayst bless the people, whilst thou givest joy to the priest. Amen.

SATURDAY OF SEXAGESIMA WEEK

On the Saturday of the preceding week, which was devoted to the consideration of the fall of our first parents both in its own malice and in its sad consequences upon us, we turned our thoughts towards our blessed Lady, who, though a daughter of Eve, was, by the special mercy of God, preserved from the stain of original sin. Let us end this week with a like act of veneration and love towards this Immaculate Queen of heaven. We, even the most saintly among us, have not only been stained with original sin; we have our actual sins to grieve over and do penance for. This should give us a higher appreciation of her, the one single member of the human family who never committed the slightest sin. Let us turn towards her, and give expression to our feelings.

We, O Mary! have corrupted our way; we have disobeyed our Lord; we have broken His law; we have preferred our own selfish gratifications to the service we owed Him: but thou wast ever filled with His holy love, and there passed not even a shadow of sin upon thy soul, O spotless mirror of justice and holiness! Virgin most faithful! the grace of thy Son ever triumphed in thy heart. Mystical rose! the fragrance of thy virtues unceasingly ascended to His throne, changing only in its daily increase of sweetness. Tower of ivory! fair beyond measure, without one spot to mar thy purity! House of gold! thou didst ever reflect the precious gifts of the Holy Ghost. Have pity, then, upon us, for we are sinners.

We have obliged our God to repent that He made us: but in thee, dear Mother, He has ever been well pleased. Thou art the good land, wherein His divine seed yielded its thousandfold of fruit: pray for us, that He give fresh fertility to our hearts, and root up from them the thorns, which choke the heavenly plant. We are defiled by sin; may He, through the merits of the tears thou didst shed at the foot of the cross, mercifully cleanse us. If thy divine Son have already pardoned us, there are the consequences of our sins, which still weaken and humble us, like the sores of wounds that have been cured: take us, sweet Mother of our Jesus, under the mantle of thy tender care. We have too little dread of sin; we are so often on the verge of offending our God; oh! obtain for these poor children of thine courage and firmness of resolution, and ambition for holiness of life. Thy intercession must win for us that precious devotedness to God's honour, which kills self-love, the root of sin. Oh! accursed self-love, which may lead us to hell, who are now perhaps in the grace of thy divine Son!

The deluge, brought on by our sins, is hurrying its vengeance against mankind; and we, O Mary! are resolved to seek our refuge in the Ark of the Church, the safe shelter created for us by thy Jesus. But we presume to pray to thee for our brethren throughout the world. Our God has given thee a power to stay His anger, and to win for guilty mortals an extension of mercy: show this power now, for our world is provoking its Master to destroy it. If the flood-gate of His just indignation burst upon the face of our earth, millions of souls that have been redeemed by the Blood of thy divine Son would be lost eternally. If the sweet dove of peace bring her olive-branch only when that terrible justice is appeased, it would be too late for thy loving heart. Come before the deluge, O beautiful rainbow of our Father's reconciliation! The love of a Mother, who is the very Queen of mercy, emboldens us to sue for universal mercy. Can the prayer of her, in whose purity and innocence the very God of holiness finds no blemish, be denied? Pray Him, then, to pardon us, and all sinners!

We select a few stanzas from the celebrated 'Complaint to Mary,' composed by the monk Euthymius. The Greek Church has inserted it in her liturgy.

CANON

Quomodo, O Domina, vitam meam impuram et immensorum peccatorum meorum multitudinem la-	O blessed Lady! how shall I worthily lament over my impure life, and the multitude of my grievous sins? I know

mentabor? Nescio quid dicam tibi, castissima, et male metuo; sed adjuva me.

Unde exordiar dicere ego miser de improbitate mea, et delictis nefandis? Ha! quid de me fiet? Verum age, Domina, et mei ante exitum ex hac luce miserere.

Omnem viam peccatorum cum ambulassem, immaculata Virgo, salutis semitam haudquaquam inveni. Sed ad bonitatem tuam confugio; ne me ex animo pœnitentem aspernare.

Mortis horam, O purissima, terribileque tribunal assidue cogito; sed peccandi consuetudine vehementer ad peccatum illicior. Fer mihi opem.

Bonorum exitiabilis inimicus cernens me nunc nudum, et patrono ac tutore destitutum, et a divinis virtutibus alienissimum, ad devorandum me irruit. Præveni, et averte illum, o Domina.

Proh dolor! imaginem Dei in me ego miser mentis arrogantia contaminavi. Quo in posterum me vertam? Festina, Virgo, ad auxilium.

Angelorum ordines et exercitus, Virtutes cœlorum, potentiam Filii tui contremiscunt, o castissima. Ego vero desperatus omni timore vaco.

not how to address thee, most chaste Virgin! I tremble with fear; but do thou help me.

I will speak of my wickedness and my hateful sins; but where shall I begin? Alas! what will become of me, a wretched sinner? Do thou, O blessed Lady, have compassion on me before my departure from this life.

I, having gone in every path that sinner ever trod, how shall I find now the way of salvation, O Immaculate Virgin? Yet have I recourse to thy goodness; despise me not, for I repent from my heart.

My thoughts are ever on the hour of death, and on the dread tribunal; and yet an evil habit violently tempts me to sin. O most pure Virgin, do thou help me.

The deadly enemy of all that is good, seeing me poor and naked, without patron or protector, and most destitute of heavenly virtue, rushes forward that he may devour me. O blessed Lady! forbid him, and drive him far from me.

Alas, unhappy man! in the arrogance of my soul, I have defiled the image of God that was in me. Whither shall I now turn? Hasten to my assistance, O Virgin ever holy!

The choirs and hosts of Angels, the heavenly Powers, tremble in the presence of thy all-powerful Son, O Immaculate Mother! and I, who have nothing wherein to hope, am so devoid of fear!

In fovea delictorum meorum suffocatum non me derelinquas, Domina. Improbissimus enim hostis me desperatione conflictantem videns, ridet; sed tu potenti manu tua me erige.

Formidabile est judicium, O misera et stolida anima mea, et pœna horribilis atque sempiterna. Nihilominus vel nunc ante Matrem judicis ac Dei tui, supplex procumbe. Cur enim te ipsam desperas?

O intaminata Virgo, ego ob multitudinem immensorum peccatorum meorum repletus sum tenebris, oculique animæ meæ, et mens mea immutata sunt. Quare tu luminis tui splendoribus ad dulcedinem in vacuitate passionum sitam celeriter me revoca.

Gemitus perennes mihi largire, Domina, fontemque lacrymarum, ut tam multa flagitia mea vulneraque inexplicabilia eluam, quo vitam æternam adipiscar.

En ego servus tuus, incorruptissima Virgo, multo cum timore et desiderio ad te accedo : gnarus quantum sæpenumero tua valuerit deprecatio. Valet sane plurimum, O benedictissima, apud Filium Matris supplicatio, et ejus viscera commovet.

Judicem misericordem et benignum exspecto Filium tuum, O linguis omnium prædicanda; ne me despicias, sed eum mihi redde

Suffer me not, O blessed Lady! to perish in the pit of my sins, into which I have fallen. The cruel enemy sees me struggling in despair, and mocks me. Do thou stretch forth thy hand, that can so well deliver me.

Awful is the judgment of God, unhappy senseless soul! and everlasting is the punishment. But turn thee, whilst yet there is time, and prostrate in prayer before the Mother of thy Judge and Lord. Why wouldst thou despair?

O Immaculate Virgin! the multitude of my grievous sins has set a thick darkness around me; the eyes of my soul, and my understanding, are blinded. Wherefore, I beseech thee, quickly lead me, by the brightness of thy light, to sweet freedom from my passions.

Grant me an unceasing sorrow, O blessed Lady, and a fount of tears, that I may wash away my countless sins and wounds, and gain eternal life.

Lo! I thy servant, most sinless Virgin! approach thee in deep reverence and love, for I know the power of thy prayer. Great, indeed, with her Son, is the power of the Mother's prayer, and his heart is moved when she asks, O most blessed Mother!

O Mother worthy of the whole world's praise! thy Son will be to me a merciful and compassionate Judge. Despise me not, but let me find

propitium, ut me tunc ad dexteram tribunalis sui incorrupti statuat : in te enim speravi.

favour in his sight, that he may set me on the right hand of his most just tribunal ; for in thee have I put my trust.

QUINQUAGESIMA SUNDAY

THE Church gives us to-day another subject for our meditation : it is the vocation of Abraham. When the waters of the deluge had subsided, and mankind had once more peopled the earth, the immorality, which had previously excited God's anger, again grew rife among men. Idolatry, too, into which the antediluvian race had not fallen, now showed itself, and human wickedness seemed thus to have reached the height of its malice. Foreseeing that the nations of the earth would fall into rebellion against Him, God resolved to select one people that should be peculiarly His, and among whom should be preserved those sacred truths, of which the Gentiles were to lose sight. This new people was to originate from one man, who would be the father and model of all future believers. This was Abraham. His faith and devotedness merited for him that he should be chosen to be the father of the children of God, and the head of that spiritual family, to which belong all the elect of both the old and the new Testament.

It is necessary, therefore, that we should know Abraham, our father and our model. This is his grand characteristic : fidelity to God, submissiveness to His commands, abandonment and sacrifice of everything in order to obey His holy will. Such ought to be the prominent virtues of every Christian. Let us, then, study the life of our great patriarch, and learn the lessons it teaches.

The following passage from the Book of Genesis,

which the Church gives us in her Matins of to-day, will serve as the text of our considerations.

De Libro Genesis.

Cap. xii.

Dixit autem Dominus ad Abram : Egredere de terra tua, et de cognatione tua, et de domo patris tui, et veni in terram quam monstrabo tibi. Faciamque te in gentem magnam, et benedicam tibi, et magnificabo nomen tuum, erisque benedictus. Benedicam benedicentibus tibi, et maledicam maledicentibus tibi; atque in te benedicentur universæ cognationes terræ. Egressus est itaque Abram sicut præceperat ei Dominus, et ivit cum eo Lot. Septuaginta quinque annorum erat Abram, cum egrederetur de Haran. Tulitque Saraï uxorem suam, et Lot filium fratris sui, universamque substantiam quam possederant, et animas quas fecerant in Haran : et egressi sunt ut irent in terram Chanaan. Cumque venissent in eam, pertransivit Abram terram usque ad locum Sichem, usque ad convallem illustrem : Chananæus autem tunc erat in terra. Apparuit autem Dominus Abram, et dixit ei : Semini tuo dabo terram hanc. Qui ædificavit ibi altare Domino, qui apparuerat ei. Et inde transgrediens ad montem, qui erat contra orientem Bethel tetendit ibi tabernaculum

From the Book of Genesis.

Ch. xii.

And the Lord said to Abram : Go forth out of thy country, and from thy kindred and out of thy father's house, and come into the land which I shall show thee. And I will make of thee a great nation, and I will bless thee, and magnify thy name, and thou shalt be blessed. I will bless them that bless thee, and curse them that curse thee; and in thee shall all the kindred of the earth be blessed. So Abram went out as the Lord had commanded him, and Lot went with him. Abram was seventy-five years old when he went forth from Haran. And he took Sarai his wife, and Lot, his brother's son, and all the substance which they had gatherde, and the souls which they had gotten in Haran : and they went out to go into the land of Chanaan. And when they were come into it, Abram passed through the country into the place of Sichem, as far as the noble vale : now the Chanaanite was at that time in the land. And the Lord appeared to Abram, and said to him : To thy seed will I give this land. And he built there an altar to the Lord, who had appeared to him. And passing on from thence to a mountain, that was on the east side of Bethel, he

suum, ab occidente habens Bethel, et ab oriente Haï. Ædificavit quoque ibi altare Domino, et invocavit nomen ejus.	there pitched his tent, having Bethel on the west, and Haï on the east. He built there, also, an altar to the Lord, and called upon his name.

Could the Christian have a finer model than this holy patriarch, whose docility and devotedness in following the call of his God are so perfect? We are forced to exclaim, with the holy fathers: 'O true Christian, even before Christ had come on the earth! He had the spirit of the Gospel, before the Gospel was preached! He was an apostolic man before the apostles existed!' God calls him: he leaves all things—his country, his kindred, his father's house—and he goes into an unknown land. God leads him, he is satisfied; he fears no difficulties; he never once looks back. Did the apostles themselves more? But see how grand is his reward! God says to him: 'In thee shall all the kindred of the earth be blessed.' This Chaldean is to give to the world Him that shall bless and save it. Death will, it is true, close his eyes ages before the dawning of that day, when one of his race, who is to be born of a Virgin and be united personally with the divine Word, shall redeem all generations, past, present, and to come. But meanwhile, till heaven shall be thrown open to receive this Redeemer and the countless just who have won the crown, Abraham shall be honoured, in the limbo of expectation, in a manner becoming his great virtue and merit. It is in his bosom,[1] that is, around him, that our first parents (having atoned for their sin by penance), Noah, Moses, David, and all the just, including poor Lazarus, received that rest and happiness, which were a foretaste of, and a preparation for, eternal bliss in heaven. Thus is

---

[1] St. Luke xvi. 22.

Abraham honoured; thus does God requite the love and fidelity of them that serve Him.

When the fullness of time came, the Son of God, who was also Son of Abraham, declared His eternal Father's power, by saying that He was about to raise up a new progeny of Abraham's children from the very stones, that is, from the Gentiles.[1] We Christians are this new generation. But are we worthy children of our father? Let us listen to the apostle of the Gentiles: 'By faith, Abraham, when called (by God), obeyed to go out into a place, which he was to receive for an inheritance: and he went out not knowing whither he went. By faith, he abode in the land, dwelling in tents, with Isaac and Jacob, the co-heirs of the same promise; for he looked for a city that hath foundations, whose builder and maker is God.'[2]

If, therefore, we be children of Abraham, we must, as the Church tells us during Septuagesima, look upon ourselves as exiles on the earth, and dwell by hope and desire in that true country of ours, from which we are now banished, but towards which we are each day drawing nigher, if, like Abraham, we are faithful in the various stations allotted us by our Lord. We are commanded to use this world as though we used it not;[3] to have an abiding conviction of our not having here a lasting city,[4] and of the misery and danger we incur when we forget that death is one day to separate us from everything we possess in this life.

How far from being true children of Abraham are those Christians who spend this and the two following days in intemperance and dissipation, because Lent is soon to be upon us! We can easily understand how the simple manners of our Catholic forefathers could keep a leave-taking of the ordinary

---

[1] St. Matt. iii. 9.
[2] Heb. xi. 8-10.
[3] 1 Cor. vii. 31.
[4] Heb. xiii. 14.

way of living, which Lent was to interrupt, and reconcile their innocent carnival with Christian gravity; just as we can understand how their rigorous observance of the laws of the Church for Lent would inspire certain festive customs at Easter. Even in our own times, a joyous shrovetide is not to be altogether reprobated, provided the Christian sentiment of the approaching holy season of Lent be strong enough to check the evil tendency of corrupt nature; otherwise the original intention of an innocent custom would be perverted, and the forethought of penance could in no sense be considered as the prompter of our joyous farewell to ease and comforts. While admitting all this, we would ask, what right or title have they to share in these shrovetide rejoicings, whose Lent will pass and find them out of the Church, because they will not have complied with the precept of Easter Communion? And they, too, who claim dispensations from abstinence and fasting during Lent, and, for one reason or another, evade every penitential exercise during the solemn forty days of penance, and will find themselves at Easter as weighed down by the guilt and debt of their sins as they were on Ash Wednesday—what meaning, we would ask, can there possibly be in their feast-making at shrovetide?

Oh! that Christians would stand on their guard against such delusions as these, and gain that holy liberty of children of God,[1] which consists in not being slaves to flesh and blood, and preserves man from moral degradation! Let them remember that we are now in that holy season, when the Church denies herself her songs of holy joy, in order the more forcibly to remind us that we are living in a Babylon of spiritual danger, and to excite us to regain that genuine Christian spirit, which everything in

[1] Rom. viii. 21.

the world around us is quietly undermining. If the disciples of Christ are necessitated, by the position they hold in society, to take part in the profane amusements of these few days before Lent, let it be with a heart deeply imbued with the maxims of the Gospel. If, for example, they are obliged to listen to the music of theatres and concerts, let them imitate St. Cecily, who thus sang, in her heart, in the midst of the excitement of worldly harmonies : 'May my heart, O God, be pure, and let me not be confounded !' Above all, let them not countenance certain dances, which the world is so eloquent in defending, because so evidently according to its own spirit ; and therefore they who encourage them will be severely judged by Him, who has already pronounced woe upon the world. Lastly, let those who must go, on these days, and mingle in the company of worldlings, be guided by St. Francis of Sales, who advises them to think, from time to time, on such considerations as these :—that while all these frivolous, and often dangerous, amusements are going on, there are countless souls being tormented in the fire of hell, on account of the sins they committed on similar occasions ; that, at that very hour of the night, there are many holy religious depriving themselves of sleep in order to sing the divine praises and implore God's mercy upon the world, and upon them that are wasting their time in its vanities ; that there are thousands in the agonies of death, while all that gaiety is going on ; that God and His angels are attentively looking upon this thoughtless group ; and finally, that life is passing away, and death so much nearer each moment.[1]

We grant that, on these three days immediately preceding the penitential season of Lent, some provision was necessary to be made for those countless

[1] 'Introduction to a Devout Life,' part iii., chapter xxxiii.

souls, who seem scarce able to live without some excitement. The Church supplies this want. She gives a substitute for frivolous amusements and dangerous pleasures; and those of her children upon whom faith has not lost its influence, will find, in what she offers them, a feast surpassing all earthly enjoyments, and a means whereby to make amends to God for the insults offered to His divine Majesty during these days of carnival. The Lamb, that taketh away the sins of the world, is exposed upon our altars. Here, on this His throne of mercy, He receives the homage of them who come to adore Him, and acknowledge Him for their King; He accepts the repentance of those who come to tell Him how grieved they are at having ever followed any other Master but Him; He offers Himself to His eternal Father for poor sinners, who not only treat His favours with indifference, but seem to have made a resolution to offend Him during these days more than at any other period of the year.

It was the pious Cardinal Gabriel Paleotti, archbishop of Bologna, who first originated the admirable devotion of the *Forty Hours*. He was a contemporary of St. Charles Borromeo, and, like him, was eminent for his pastoral zeal. His object in this solemn Exposition of the most blessed Sacrament was to offer to the divine Majesty some compensation for the sins of men, and, at the very time when the world was busiest in deserving His anger, to appease it by the sight of His own Son, the Mediator between heaven and earth. St. Charles immediately introduced the devotion into his own diocese and province. This was in the sixteenth century. Later on, that is, in the eighteenth century, Prosper Lambertini was archbishop of Bologna; he zealously continued the pious design of his ancient predecessor, Paleotti, by encouraging his flock to devotion towards the blessed Sacrament during the three days of carnival; and when he was made Pope, under the name of Benedict XIV., he granted many Indulgences to all who, during these days, should visit our Lord in this mystery of His love, and should pray for the pardon of sinners. This favour was, at first, restricted to the faithful of the Papal States; but in the year 1765 it was extended, by Pope Clement XIII., to the universal Church. Thus, the *Forty Hours' Devotion* has spread throughout the whole world, and become one of the most solemn expressions of Catholic piety. Let us, then, who have the opportunity, profit by it during these last three days of our preparation for Lent. Let us, like Abraham, retire from the distracting dangers of the world, and seek the Lord our God. Let us go apart, for at least one short hour, from the dissipation of earthly enjoyments, and, kneeling in the presence of our Jesus, merit the grace to keep our hearts innocent and detached, whilst sharing in those we cannot avoid.[1]

We will now resume our considerations upon the liturgy of Quinquagesima Sunday. The passage of the Gospel selected by the Church, is that wherein our Saviour foretells to His apostles the sufferings He was to undergo in Jerusalem. This solemn announcement prepares us for Passiontide. We ought to receive it with feeling and grateful hearts, and make it an additional motive for imitating the devoted Abraham, and giving our whole selves to our God. The ancient liturgists tell us that the blind man of Jericho spoken of in this same Gospel is a figure of those poor sinners, who, during these days, are blind to their Christian character, and rush into excesses, which even paganism would have coveted. The blind man recovered his sight, because he was aware of his wretched state, and

[1] The Litanies for the *Forty Hours* are given at the end of this volume.

desired to be cured and to see. The Church wishes us to have a like desire, and she promises us that it shall be granted.

In the Greek Church, this Sunday is called *Tyrophagos*, because it is the last day on which is allowed the use of white meats, or, as we call them, milk-meats. From to-morrow it is forbidden to eat them, for Lent then begins, and with all the severity wherewith the oriental Churches observe it.

MASS

The station is in the church of St. Peter, on the Vatican. The choice was suggested, as we learn from the Abbot Rupert's 'Treatise on the Divine Offices,' by the lesson of the Law given to Moses, which used then to be read in this Sunday's Office. Moses was looked upon, by the early Christians of Rome, as a type of St. Peter. The Church having, since that time, substituted the vocation of Abraham for the passage from Exodus (which is now deferred till Lent), the station for this Sunday is still in the basilica of the prince of the apostles, who was prefigured also by Abraham, the father of believers.

The Introit is the prayer of mankind, blind and wretched as the poor man of Jericho; it asks for pity from its Redeemer, and beseeches Him to *guide* and *feed* it.

INTROIT

Esto mihi in Deum protectorem, et in locum refugii, ut salvum me facias: quoniam firmamentum meum, et refugium meum es tu : et propter nomen tuum dux mihi eris et enutries me.

Ps. In te, Domine, speravi, non confundar in æter-

Be thou unto me a God, a protector, and a house of refuge, to save me; for thou art my strength, and my refuge ; and for thy name's sake thou wilt lead me, and nourish me.

Ps. In thee, O Lord, have I hoped, let me never be con-

num : in justitia tua libera me, et eripe me. *V.* Gloria Patri. Esto.

founded ; deliver me in thy justice, and rescue me. *V.* Glory. Be thou.

COLLECT

Preces nostras, quæsumus, Domine, clementer exaudi : atque a peccatorum vinculis absolutos, ab omni nos adversitate custodi. Per Dominum.

Mercifully hear our prayers O Lord, we beseech thee ; and delivering us from the bonds of sin, preserve us from all adversity. Through, etc.

Then are added two other Collects, as in the Mass of Septuagesima Sunday, page 120.

EPISTLE

Lectio Epistolæ beati Pauli Apostoli ad Corinthios.

Lesson of the Epistle of Saint Paul the Apostle to the Corinthians.

1 *Cap.* xiii.

1 *Ch.* xiii.

Fratres, si linguis hominum loquar, et angelorum, charitatem autem non habeam, factus sum velut æs sonans, aut cymbalum tinniens. Et si habuero prophetiam, et noverim mysteria omnia, et omnem scientiam : et si habuero omnem fidem, ita ut montes transferam, charitatem autem non habuero, nihil sum. Et si distribuero in cibos pauperum omnes facultates meas : et si tradidero corpus meum ita ut ardeam, charitatem autem non habuero, nihil mihi prodest. Charitas patiens est, benigna est : charitas non æmulatur, non agit peram, non inflatur, non est ambitiosa, non quærit

Brethren, if I speak with the tongues of men and of angels, and have not charity, I am become as sounding brass, or a tinkling cymbal. And if I should have prophecy, and should know all mysteries, and all knowledge, and if I should have all faith, so that I could remove mountains, and have not charity, I am nothing. And if I should distribute all my goods to feed the poor, and if I should deliver my body to be burned, and have not charity, it profiteth me nothing. Charity is patient, is kind, charity envieth not, dealeth not perversely ; is not puffed up, is not ambitious, seeketh not her own, is not provoked to anger, thinketh no evil, rejoiceth not in iniquity,

quæ sua sunt, non irritatur, non cogitat malum, non gaudet super iniquitate, congaudet autem veritati : omnia suffert, omnia credit, omnia sperat, omnia sustinet. Charitas nunquam excidit : sive prophetiæ evacuabuntur, sive linguæ cessabunt, sive scientia destruetur. Ex parte enim cognoscimus, et ex parte prophetamus. Cum autem venerit quod perfectum est, evacuabitur quod ex parte est. Cum essem parvulus, loquebar ut parvulus, sapiebam ut parvulus, cogitabam ut parvulus. Quando autem factus sum vir, evacuavi quæ erant parvuli. Videmus nunc per speculum in ænigmate : tunc autem facie ad faciem. Nunc cognosco ex parte : tunc autem cognoscam sicut et cognitus sum. Nunc autem manent fides, spes, charitas, tria hæc : major autem horum est charitas.

but rejoiceth with the truth ; beareth all things, believeth all things, hopeth all things, endureth all things. Charity never falleth away ; whether prophecies shall be made void, or tongues shall cease, or knowledge shall be destroyed. For we know in part, and we prophesy in part ; but when that which is perfect is come, that which is in part shall be done away. When I was a child, I spoke as a child, I understood as a child, I thought as a child ; but when I became a man,[1] I put away the things of a child. We see now through a glass in a dark manner ; but then, face to face. Now I know in part ; but then I shall know, even as I am known. And now there remain faith, hope, charity, these three : but the greater of these is charity.

How appropriate for this Sunday is the magnificent eulogy of *charity*, here given by our apostle ! This virtue, which comprises the love both of God and of our neighbour, is the light of our souls. Without charity we are in darkness, and all our works are profitless. The very power of working miracles cannot give hope of salvation, unless he who does them have charity. Unless we are in charity, the most heroic acts of other virtues are but one snare more for our souls. Let us beseech our Lord to give us this light. But let us not forget that, however richly He may bless us with it here below, the fullness of its brightness is reserved

for when we are in heaven; and that the sunniest day we can have in this world, is but darkness when compared with the splendour of our eternal charity. *Faith* will then give place, for we shall be face to face with all truth; *hope* will have no object, for we shall possess all good; *charity* alone will continue, and, for this reason, is greater than faith and hope, which must needs accompany her in this present life. This being the glorious destiny reserved for man when redeemed and enlightened by Jesus, is it to be wondered at that we should leave all things, in order to follow such a Master? What should surprise us, and what proves how degraded is our nature by sin, is to see Christians, who have been baptized in this faith and this hope, and have received the first-fruits of this love, indulging, during these days, in every sort of worldliness, which is only the more dangerous because it is fashionable. It would seem as though they were making it their occupation to extinguish within their souls the last ray of heavenly light, like men that had made a covenant with darkness. If there be charity within our souls, it will make us feel these offences that are committed against our God, and inspire us to pray to Him to have mercy on these poor blind sinners, for they are our brethren.

In the Gradual and Tract, the Church sings the praises of God's goodness towards His elect. He has set them free from the slavish yoke of the world, by enlightening them with His grace; they are His own children, the favoured *sheep of His pasture.*

GRADUAL

Tu es Deus qui facis mirabilia solus : notam fecisti in gentibus virtutem tuam.

V. Liberasti in brachio

Thou art God, who alone dost wonders : thou hast made thy power known among the nations.

V. Thou hast delivered thy

tuo populum tuum, filios Israel et Joseph.

people, the children of Israel and Joseph, by the strength of thine arm.

TRACT

Jubilate Deo omnis terra : servite Domino in lætitia.

V. Intrate in conspectu ejus, in exsultatione ; scitote quoniam Dominus ipse est Deus.

V. Ipse fecit nos, et non ipsi nos : nos autem populus ejus et oves pascuæ ejus.

Sing joyfully to God, all the earth : serve ye the Lord with gladness.

V. Come in before his presence with joy ; know ye that the Lord he is God.

V. He made us, and not we ourselves : and we are his people and the sheep of his pasture.

GOSPEL

Sequentia sancti Evangelii secundum Lucam.

Sequel of the holy Gospel according to Luke.

Cap. xviii.

Ch. xviii.

In illo tempore, assumpsit Jesus duodecim, et ait illis : Ecce ascendimus Jerosolymam, et consummabuntur omnia quæ scripta sunt per prophetas de Filio hominis. Tradetur enim gentibus, et illudetur, et flagellabitur, et conspuetur, et postquam flagellaverint, occident eum, et tertia die resurget. Et ipsi nihil horum intellexerunt, et erat verbum istud absconditum ab eis, et non intelligebant quæ dicebantur. Factum est autem, cum appropinquaret Jericho, cæcus quidam sedebat secus viam, mendicans. Et cum audiret turbam prætereuntem, interrogabat quid hoc esset. Dixerunt autem

At that time, Jesus took unto him the twelve, and said to them : Behold we go up to Jerusalem, and all things shall be accomplished which were written by the prophets concerning the Son of Man. For he shall be delivered to the Gentiles, and shall be mocked, and scourged, and spit upon ; and after they have scourged him, they will put him to death, and the third day he shall rise again. And they understood none of these things. And this word was hid from them, and they understood not the things that were said. Now it came to pass, when he drew nigh to Jericho, that a certain blind man sat by the wayside, begging. And when he heard

ei, quod Jesus Nazarenus transiret. Et clamavit dicens : Jesu, fili David, miserere mei Et qui præibant, increpabant eum ut taceret. Ipse vero multo magis clamabat : Fili David, miserere mei. Stans autem Jesus, jussit illum adduci ad se. Et cum appropinquasset, interrogavit illum dicens : Quid tibi vis faciam ? At ille dixit : Domine, ut videam. Et Jesus dixit illi : Respice, fides tua te salvum fecit. Et confestim vidit, et sequebatur illum, magnificans Deum. Et omnis plebs ut vidit, dedit laudem Deo.

the multitude passing by, he asked what this meant. And they told him that Jesus of Nazareth was passing by. And he cried out, saying : Jesus, Son of David, have mercy on me. And they that went before, rebuked him, that he should hold his peace. But he cried out much more : Son of David, have mercy on me. And Jesus standing, commanded him to be brought unto him. And when he was come near, he asked him, saying : What wilt thou that I do to thee ? But he said : Lord, that I may see. And Jesus said to him : Receive thy sight : thy faith hath made thee whole. And immediately he saw, and followed him, glorifying God. And all the people when they saw it gave praise to God.

Jesus tells His apostles, that His bitter Passion is at hand ; it is a mark of His confidence in them ; but they understand not what He says. They are as yet too carnal-minded to appreciate our Saviour's mission ; still, they do not abandon Him ; they love Him too much to think of separating from Him. Greater by far than this is the *blindness* of those false Christians, who, during these three days, not only do not think of the God who shed His Blood and died for them, but are striving to efface from their souls every trace of the divine image ! Let us adore that sweet mercy, which has drawn us, as it did Abraham, from the midst of a sinful people ; and let us, like the blind man of our Gospel, cry out to our Lord, beseeching Him to grant us an increase of His holy *light*. This was his prayer : *Lord ! that I may see !* God has given us His light ; but He gave it us in order to excite within us

SEPTUAGESIMA
also, *to see* the land of the living! But our first
Augustine has so beautifully expressed it, that we

In the Offertory, the Church prays that her

OFFERTORY

Benedictus es, Domine, doce me justificationes tuas: in labiis meis pronuntiavi omnia judicia oris tui.

Blessed art thou, O Lord teach me thy justifications: with my lips I have pronounced all the judgments of thy mouth.

SECRET

Hæc hostia, Domine, quæsumus, emundet nostra delicta; et ad sacrificium celebrandum, subditorum tibi corpora, mentesque sanctificet. Per Dominum.

May this offering, we beseech thee, O Lord, cleanse away our sins; and sanctify the bodies and souls of thy servants, to prepare them for worthily celebrating this sacrifice. Through, &c.

Then are added two other Secrets, as given in the Mass of Septuagesima Sunday, page 127.

The Communion antiphon commemorates the miracle of the manna, which fed in the desert the descendants of Abraham; and yet this food, though it came from heaven, did not preserve them from death. The living Bread, which we have had given to us from heaven, gives eternal life to the soul: and he who eats it worthily shall never die.

COMMUNION

Manducaverunt et satu-
rati sunt nimis, et desiderium eorum attulit eis Dominus : non sunt fraudati a
desiderio suo.

They did eat and were filled
exceedingly, and the Lord gave
them their desire : they were
not defrauded of that which
they craved.

POSTCOMMUNION

Quæsumus, omnipotens
Deus ; ut qui cœlestia alimenta percepimus, per hæc
contra omnia adversa mu-
niamur. Per Dominum.

We beseech thee, O almighty
God, that we who have taken
this heavenly food, may be defended by it from all adversity.
Through, etc.

Two other Postcommunions are said after this,
as on Septuagesima Sunday, page 128.

VESPERS

The psalms and antiphons as on page 72.

CAPITULUM

(1 *Cor.* xiii.)

Fratres, si linguis homi-
num loquar et angelorum,
charitatem autem non ha-
beam, factus sum velut æs
sonans, aut cymbalum tin-
niens.

Brethren, if I speak with
the tongues of men and of
angels, and have not charity,
I am become as sounding brass,
or a tinkling cymbal.

The hymn and versicle, page 79.

ANTIPHON OF THE 'MAGNIFICAT'

Stans autem Jesus, jussit
cæcum adduci ad se, et ait
illi : Quid vis ut faciam
tibi ? Domine, ut videam.
Et Jesus ait illi : Respice,
fides tua te salvum fecit.
Et confestim vidit, et sequebatur illum, magnificans
Deum.

But Jesus standing, ordered
the blind man to be brought,
and said to him : What wilt
thou, that I do for thee ? Lord,
that I may see. And Jesus
saith to him : See : thy faith
hath made thee whole. And
he immediately saw, and followed him, praising God.

13

OREMUS

LET US PRAY

Preces nostras, quæsumus, Domine, clementer exaudi : atque a peccatorum vinculis absolutos, ab omni nos adversitate custodi. Per Dominum.

Mercifully hear our prayers, we beseech thee, O Lord, and delivering us from the bonds of sin, preserve us from all adversity. Through, etc.

Before the day is over, we may recite the following stanzas of the hymn, in which the Greek Church proclaims the annual fast of Lent.

HYMN

(Feria II. Tyrophagi)

Advenit nunc, ver designans, præpurgatrix hebdomas hæc sacrorum jejuniorum, omnino veneranda, corporibus et animabus omnium lucem ministrans.

En reserata est pœnitentiæ janua, Dei amatores ; adeste igitur, alacriter ipsam ingrediamur, priusquam a Christo nobis velut indignis claudatur.

Puritatem, abstinentiam, et modestiam, et fortitudinem, ac prudentiam, orationes et lacrymas comparemus, fratres, per quæ patet nobis justitiæ semita.

Ne corpori saginando, neque ciborum deliciis incumbamus, mortales, imo vero parcimonia ipsum pinguefaciamus, quo semper in pugnis cum adversario, animæ junctum prævaleat.

Primum jejunium præviæ expiationis animarum et corporum nostrorum or-

The week, the harbinger of spring, is come ; the week that cleanses away sin by the sacred and ever venerable fast, which enlightens the body and soul of every man.

Lo! the gate of penance is thrown open, O ye that love God ! Come, then, let us joyously go in, before Christ shut it against us as being unworthy to enter.

Brethren, let us prepare, and bring with us purity, abstinence, and modesty, and fortitude, and prudence, and prayers, and tears ; for it is by these we enter on the path of justice.

Be not solicitous, O mortals ! about the body, how you may pamper it, nor seek delicacies in what you give it to eat ; give it, rather, fullness of vigour by abstinence ; that so it may aid the soul to conquer in the battle with the enemy.

This day, O ye that love God ! begins the fast, which is to prepare our souls and

tum est hodie, spargens in cordibus nostris, Dei amatores, sacræ et venerandæ Christi Passionis, luminis instar, largum splendorem.

Læto animo amplectamur jejunium, o populi : advenit siquidem spiritualium certaminum exordium : abjiciamus carnis mollitudinem, animæ charismata augeamus, compatiamur, ut servi Christi, quo tanquam filii Dei conglorificemur, animasque nostras Spiritus sanctus in nobis inhabitans illuminabit.

Alacriter excipiamus, fideles, divinitus inspiratum jejunii nuntium, ut olim Ninivitæ, itemque meretrices, et publicani ab Joanne pœnitentiæ prædicationem acceperunt. Præparemur per abstinentiam ad participationem Dominici in Sion sacrificii ; prius lacrymis quam divina ejus lotione purgemur, petamus typici ibi Paschatis consummationem, et veri demonstrationem intueri ; parati simus ad crucis et Resurrectionis Christi Dei adorationem, clamantes ad ipsum : Ne confundas nos ab exspectatione nostra, o philanthrope.

bodies by expiation, and infuse into our hearts the generous light of the sacred and venerable Passion of Christ.

Let us, O ye people ! enter on our fast with a glad heart ; for lo ! the spiritual combat begins. Let us throw off the effeminacy of the flesh, redouble the gifts of the spirit, and suffer with Christ, as it behoves them that are his servants ; that thus, we may rejoice together with him, and our souls be enlightened by the indwelling of the Holy Ghost within us.

Let us, O ye faithful ! cheerfully receive the divinely inspired messenger of our fast, as did the Ninivites ; and as the harlots and the publicans did, of old, receive John, when he preached penance unto them. Let us prepare, by abstinence, for a participation in the Sacrifice of our Lord on Sion. Let his divine laver be preceded by that of our tears. Let us beseech him to show unto us, when the time is come, the consummation of both Paschs, the figurative, and the true. Let us put ourselves in readiness to adore the cross and Resurrection of Christ ; saying unto him : Let me not be confounded in my expectation, O thou Lover of mankind.

MONDAY OF QUINQUAGESIMA WEEK

THE life of a faithful Christian, like that of the
patriarch Abraham, is neither more nor less than a
courageous journeying onwards to the place destined for him by his Creator. He must put aside
everything that could impede his progress, nor
must he look back. This is, undoubtedly, hard
doctrine; but if we reflect, for a moment, on the
dangers which surround fallen man during his
earthly pilgrimage, and on what our own sad experience has taught us, we shall not think it hard or
strange, that our Saviour has made the renouncing
and denying of ourselves an ·essential condition of
our salvation. But, independently of this, is it not
far better to put our life under God's guidance,
than to keep it in our own? Are we so wise or so
strong, as to be able to guide ourselves? We may
resist as we please, but God is our sovereign Lord
and Master; and by giving us free-will, whereby we
may either resist His will or follow it, He has not
abdicated His own infinite rights to His creatures'
obedience. Our refusal to obey would not make
Him less our Master.

Had Abraham, after receiving the divine call,
chosen to remain in Chaldea, and refused to break
up the home which God had bade him leave, God
would then have selected some other man to be the
patriarch of His chosen people, and father of that
very family, which was to have the Messias as one
of its children. This substitution of one for another
in the order of grace is frequently forced upon
divine justice; but what a terrible punishment it is
for him that caused the substitution! When a soul
refuses salvation, heaven does not therefore lose
one of its elect: God, finding that He is despised

by the one He called, offers the grace to another, until His call is followed.

The Christian life consists in this untiring, unreserved obedience to God. The first effect of this spirit of submission is, that it takes the soul from the region of sin and death, wherein she was wasting away her existence; it takes her from the dark Chaldea, and places her in the promised land of light. Lest she should faint on her way along the narrow path, and fall a victim to the dangers which never leave her because they are within herself, God asks her for sacrifices, and these brace her. Here, again, we have Abraham for our model. God loves him, and promises him the richest of blessings; He gives him a son, as pledge of the promise; and then, shortly after, tests the holy patriarch's devotedness, by commanding him to slay with his own hand this dear child, on whom he has been told to build his hopes!

Man's path on earth is sacrifice. We cannot *go out* from evil except by the way of self-resistance, nor keep our footing on good ground but by constant combating. Let us imitate Abraham: fix our eyes steadfastly on the eternal hills, and consider this world as a mere passing dwelling, a tent, put up for a few days. Our Jesus has said to us: 'I came not to send peace, but the sword; for I came to separate.'[1] Separation, then, and trials are sure to be sent us; but we are equally sure that they are for our good, since they are sent us by Him who so loved us, that He became one of ourselves. But this same Jesus has also said: 'Where thy treasure is, there too is thy heart.'[2] Christians! can our treasure be in this wretched world? No it must be in that fair land above. There, then, must we be, in desire and affection.

These are the thoughts the Church would have

---

[1] St. Matt. x. 34, 35.　　　　[2] *Ibid.*, vi. 21.

us meditate upon during these days, which immediately precede the forty of Lent. They will help
to purify our hearts and make them long to be
with their God. The noise of the world's sins and
scandals reaches our ears : let us pray, that the
kingdom of God may come to us and to those poor
sinners; for God's infinite mercy can change them,
if He will, into children of Abraham. Not a day
passes but He so changes many a sinner. He has,
perhaps, shown that miracle of His mercy to us,
and those words of the apostle may be applied to
us : 'You, who some time were afar off, are now
made nigh (to God) by the Blood of Christ.'[1]

Let us pray for ourselves and for all sinners, in
these beautiful words of the Mozarabic breviary.

PRAYER

Dum te, omnipotens
Deus, nostræ delinquentiæ
reddunt adversum, tua in-
spiratione, quæsumus, no-
stra te invocatio propitium
et confessio faciat esse placatum: ut, te miserante,
nec tribulatio sæcularis
nostram mentem dejiciat,
nec persuasio nociva possi-
deat, nec infidelitas tene-
brosa concludat ; sed vultus
tui super nos signato lumine
fulgeamus, semperque in
eodem splendore stabilitate
veræ fidei gradiamur.
Amen.

We beseech thee, O al-
mighty God ! that whereas
our sins have angered thee
against us, our prayers and
praise, which thou inspirest,
may propitiate and please
thee : that thus, by thy mercy,
the vexations of this world
may not cast down our soul,
nor hurtful delusion possess
her, nor the darkness of unbelief surround her; but may
we gleam with the light of thy
countenance, wherewith thou
hast signed us, and ever, by
firmness in the true faith, walk
in the brightness of the same.
Amen.

---

[1] Eph. ii. 13.

TUESDAY OF QUINQUAGESIMA WEEK

THE fundamental rule of Christian life is, as almost every page of the Gospel tells us, that we should live out of the world, separate ourselves from the world, hate the world. The world is that ungodly land which Abraham, our sublime model, is commanded by God to quit. It is that Babylon of our exile and captivity, where we are beset with dangers. The beloved disciple cries out to us : ' Love not the world, nor the things which are in the world. If any man love the world, the charity of the Father is not in him.'[1] Our most merciful Jesus, at the very time when He was about to offer Himself as a sacrifice for all men, spoke these awful words : ' I pray not for the world.'[2] When we were baptized, and were signed with the glorious and indelible character of Christians, the condition required of us, and accepted, was that we should renounce the works and pomps of the world (which we expressed under the name of Satan); and this solemn baptismal promise we have often renewed.

But what is the meaning of our promise to renounce the world ? Is it that we cannot be Christians, unless we flee into the desert and separate ourselves from our fellow-creatures ? Such cannot be God's will for all, since, in that same Scripture, wherein He commands us to flee from the world, He also tells us what are our duties to each other, and sanctions and blesses those ties which He Himself has willed should exist among us. His apostle, also, tells us to use this world as though we did not use it.[3] It is not, therefore, forbidden us to live in, and to use, the world. Then, what means this renouncing of the world ? Can there be contradiction

[1] St. John ii. 15.   [2] *Ibid.*, xvii. 9.   [3] 1 Cor. vii. 31.

in God's commandments? Is it possible that we are condemned to wander blindly on the brink of a precipice, into which we must at last inevitably fall?

There is neither contradiction nor snare. If by the world, we mean these visible things around us which God created in His power and goodness; if we mean this outward world, which He made for His own glory and our benefit; it is worthy of its divine Author, and to us, if we but use it aright, is a ladder whereby our souls may ascend to their God. Let us gratefully use this world; go through it, without making it the object of our hope; not waste upon it that love, which God alone deserves; and ever be mindful, that we are not made for this, but for another and a happier, world.

But the majority of men are not thus prudent in their use of the world. Their hearts are fixed upon it, and not upon heaven. Hence it was, that when the Creator deigned to come into this world, in order that He might save it, the world knew Him not.[1] Men were called after the name of the object of their love. They shut their eyes to the light; they became darkness; God calls them 'the world.'

In this sense, then, the world is everything that is opposed to our Lord Jesus Christ, that refuses to recognize Him, and that resists His divine guidance. Those false maxims which tend to weaken the love of God in our souls; which recommend the vanities that fasten our hearts to this present life; which cry down everything that can raise us above our weaknesses or vices; which decoy and gratify our corrupt nature by dangerous pleasures, which, far from helping us to the attainment of our last end, only mislead us—all these are 'the world.'

This world is everywhere, and holds a secret league within our very hearts. Sin has brought it into this exterior world created by God for Himself,

---

[1] St. John i. 10.

and has given it prominence. Now, we must conquer it, and trample upon it, or we shall perish with
it. There is no being neutral; we must be its
enemies, or its slaves. During these three days, its
triumphs are fearful; and thousands of those who,
at their Baptism, swore eternal enmity to it, are
enrolling themselves its votaries. Let us pray for
them; but let us also tremble for ourselves; and
that our courage may not fail us, let us ponder
those consoling words, which our Saviour, at His
last Supper, addressed to His eternal Father. He
is speaking of His disciples, and He says: 'Father!
I have given them Thy word, and the world hath
hated them, because they are not of the world, as
I also am not of the world. I pray not, that Thou
shouldst take them out of the world, but that Thou
shouldst keep them from evil.'[1]

As an appropriate conclusion of this day, we may
use this formula of the Ambrosian liturgy. It puts
two truths in contrast: the spiritual indifference of
worldlings, and the dread severity of God's future
judgment.

INGRESSA

(Dominica in Quinquagesima)

Jucunda est præsens vita, et transit: terribile est, Christe, judicium tuum, et permanet. Quapropter incertum amorem relinquamus, et de infinito timore cogitemus, clamantes: Christe, miserere nobis.

Sweet is this present life, but it passes away; terrible, O Christ, is thy judgment, and it endures for ever. Let us, therefore, cease to love what is unstable, and fix our thoughts on the fear of what is eternal; saying: Christ, have mercy upon us!

---

[1] St. John xvii. 14, 15.

ASH WEDNESDAY

Yesterday, the world was busy in its pleasures, and the very children of God were taking a joyous farewell to mirth: but this morning, all is changed. The solemn announcement, spoken of by the prophet, has been proclaimed in Sion:[1] the solemn fast of Lent, the season of expiation, the approach of the great anniversaries of our Redemption. Let us, then, rouse ourselves, and prepare for the spiritual combat.

But in this battling of the spirit against the flesh we need good armour. Our holy mother the Church knows how much we need it; and therefore does she summon us to enter into the house of God, that she may arm us for the holy contest. What this armour is we know from St. Paul, who thus describes it: 'Have your loins girt about with truth, and having on the breastplate of justice. And your feet shod with the preparation of the Gospel of peace. In all things, taking the shield of faith. Take unto you the helmet of salvation, and the sword of the Spirit, which is the word of God.'[2] The very prince of the apostles, too, addresses these solemn words to us: 'Christ having suffered in the flesh, be ye also armed with the same thought.'[3] We are entering, to-day, upon a long campaign of the warfare spoken of by the apostles: forty days of battle, forty days of penance. We shall not turn cowards, if our souls can but be impressed with the conviction, that the battle and the penance must be gone through. Let us listen to the eloquence of the solemn rite which opens our Lent. Let us go whither our mother leads us, that is, to the scene of the fall.

[1] See the Epistle of to-day's Mass.   [2] Eph. vi. 14-17.
[3] 1 St. Pet. iv. 1.

The enemies we have to fight with, are of two kinds: internal, and external. The first are our passions; the second are the devils. Both were brought on us by pride, and man's pride began when he refused to obey his God. God forgave him his sin, but He punished him. The punishment was death, and this was the form of the divine sentence: 'Thou art dust, and into dust thou shalt return.'[1] Oh that we had remembered this! The recollection of what we are and what we are to be, would have checked that haughty rebellion, which has so often led us to break the law of God. And if, for the time to come, we would persevere in loyalty to Him, we must humble ourselves, accept the sentence, and look on this present life as a path to the grave. The path may be long or short; but to the tomb it must lead us. Remembering this, we shall see all things in their true light. We shall love that God, who has deigned to set His heart on us notwithstanding our being creatures of death: we shall hate, with deepest contrition, the insolence and ingratitude, wherewith we have spent so many of our few days of life, that is, in sinning against our heavenly Father: and we shall be not only willing, but eager, to go through these days of penance, which He so mercifully gives us for making reparation to His offended justice.

This was the motive the Church had in enriching her liturgy with the solemn rite, at which we are to assist this morning. When, upwards of a thousand years ago, she decreed the anticipation of the lenten fast by the last four days of Quinquagesima week, she instituted this impressive ceremony of signing the forehead of her children with ashes, while saying to them those awful words, wherewith God sentenced us to death: 'Remember, O man, that thou art dust, and into dust thou shalt return!'

[1] Gen. iii. 19.

But the making use of ashes as a symbol of humiliation and penance, is of a much earlier date than
the institution to which we allude. We find frequent
mention of it in the Old Testament. Job, though a
Gentile, sprinkled his flesh with ashes, that, thus
humbled, he might propitiate the divine mercy:[1]
and this was two thousand years before the coming
of our Saviour. The royal prophet tells us of himself, that he mingled ashes with his bread, because
of the divine anger and indignation.[2] Many such
examples are to be met with in the sacred Scriptures;
but so obvious is the analogy between the sinner
who thus signifies his grief, and the object whereby
he signifies it, that we read such instances without
surprise. When fallen man would humble himself
before the divine justice, which has sentenced his
body to return to dust, how could he more aptly
express his contrite acceptance of the sentence,
than by sprinkling himself, or his food, with ashes,
which is the dust of wood consumed by fire? This
earnest acknowledgment of his being himself but
dust and ashes, is an act of humility, and humility
ever gives him confidence in that God, who resists
the proud and pardons the humble.

It is probable that, when this ceremony of the
Wednesday in Quinquagesima week was first instituted, it was not intended for all the faithful, but
only for such as had committed any of those crimes
for which the Church inflicted a public penance.
Before the Mass of the day began, they presented
themselves at the church, where the people were all
assembled. The priests received the confession of
their sins, and then clothed them in sackcloth, and
sprinkled ashes on their heads. After this ceremony, the clergy and the faithful prostrated, and
recited aloud the seven Penitential Psalms. A
procession, in which the penitents walked bare-

---

[1] Job xvi. 16.   [2] Ps. ci. 10, 11.

footed, then followed; and on its return, the bishop addressed these words to the penitents: 'Behold, we drive you from the doors of the church by reason of your sins and crimes, as Adam, the first man, was driven out of paradise because of his transgression.' The clergy then sang several responsories, taken from the Book of Genesis, in which mention was made of the sentence pronounced by God when He condemned man to eat his bread in the sweat of his brow, for that the earth was cursed on account of sin. The doors were then shut, and the penitents were not to pass the threshold until Maundy Thursday, when they were to come and receive absolution.

Dating from the eleventh century, the discipline of public penance began to fall into disuse, and the holy rite of putting ashes on the heads of all the faithful indiscriminately became so general that, at length, it was considered as forming an essential part of the Roman liturgy. Formerly, it was the practice to approach bare-footed to receive this solemn memento of our nothingness; and in the twelfth century, even the Pope himself, when passing from the church of St. Anastasia to that of St. Sabina, at which the station was held, went the whole distance bare-footed, as also did the Cardinals who accompanied him. The Church no longer requires this exterior penance; but she is as anxious as ever that the holy ceremony, at which we are about to assist, should produce in us the sentiments she intended to convey by it, when she first instituted it.

As we have just mentioned, the station in Rome is at St. Sabina, on the Aventine Hill. It is under the patronage of this holy martyr that we open the penitential season of Lent.

THE BLESSING OF THE ASHES

The function begins with the blessing of the ashes, which are to be put on our foreheads. These ashes are made from the palms, which were blessed the previous Palm Sunday. The blessing they are now to receive in this their new form, is given in order that they may be made more worthy of that mystery of contrition and humility which they are intended to symbolize.

The choir begins by chanting this antiphon, which is a prayer for mercy.

ANTIPHON

Exaudi nos, Domine, quoniam benigna est misericordia tua: secundum multitudinem miserationum tuarum, respice nos, Domine.

Ps. Salvum me fac, Deus: quoniam intraverunt aquæ usque ad animam meam. *V.* Gloria Patri. Exaudi nos.

Hear us, O Lord, for thy mercy is kind: look on us, O Lord, according to the multitude of thy mercies.

Ps. Save me, O God: for the waters have reached my soul. *V.* Glory, etc. Hear us, etc.

The priest, standing at the altar, and having the ashes near him, begs of God, by the following prayers, that He would make them an instrument of our sanctification.

V. Dominus vobiscum.
R. Et cum spiritu tuo.

V. The Lord be with you.
R. And with thy spirit.

OREMUS

Omnipotens sempiterne Deus, parce pœnitentibus; propitiare supplicantibus: et mittere digneris sanctum angelum tuum de cœlis, qui benedicat, et sanctificet hos cineres, ut sint remedium salubre omnibus nomen sanctum tuum humiliter im-

LET US PRAY

O almighty and eternal God, spare those that repent, show mercy to those that humbly entreat thee; and vouchsafe to send from heaven thy holy angel, to bless, and sanctify these ashes, that they may be a wholesome remedy to all who humbly call upon thy holy

plorantibus, ac semetipsos pro conscientia delictorum suorum accusantibus, ante conspectum divinæ clemen tiæ tuæ facinora sua deplorantibus, vel serenissimam pietatem tuam suppliciter obnixeque flagitantibus : et præsta, per invocationem sanctissimi nominis tui : ut quicumque per eos aspersi fuerint, pro redemptione peccatorum suorum, corporis sanitatem et animæ tutelam percipiant. Per Christum Dominum nostrum. *R.* Amen.

name, and conscious of their sins, accuse themselves, and deplore their crimes in sight of thy divine Majesty, or humbly and earnestly have recourse to thy sovereign bounty ; and grant, by our calling on thy most holy name, that whoever shall be touched by these ashes for the remission of their sins, may receive health of body and defence of soul. Through Christ our Lord. *R.* Amen.

OREMUS

Deus, qui non mortem sed pœnitentiam desideras peccatorum : fragilitatem conditionis humanæ benignissime respice : et hos cineres, quos causa proferendæ humilitatis, atque promerendæ veniæ, capitibus nostris imponi decernimus, benedicere pro tua pietate dignare : ut, qui nos cinerem esse, et ob pravitatis nostræ demeritum in pulverem reversuros cognoscimus, peccatorum omnium veniam, et præmia pœnitentibus repromissa, misericorditer consequi mereamur. Per Christum Dominum nostrum. *R.* Amen.

LET US PRAY

O God, who desirest the conversion, and not the death of sinners, graciously consider the weakness of human nature, and mercifully vouchsafe to bless these ashes, which we design to receive on our heads, in token of our humiliation, and to obtain forgiveness ; that we, who know that we are but ashes, and must return to dust because of our wickedness, may obtain through thy mercy, pardon of all our sins, and the recompense promised to penitents. Through Christ our Lord. *R.* Amen.

OREMUS

Deus qui humiliatione flecteris et satisfactione placaris : aurem tuæ pietatis inclina precibus nostris : et capitibus servorum tuorum, horum cinerum aspersione contactis, effunde propitius

LET US PRAY

O God, who art appeased by humiliation, and pacified by satisfaction, incline to our prayers the ears of thy mercy ; and pour upon the heads of thy servants, covered with these ashes, the grace of thy blessing,

gratiam tuæ benedictionis : ut eos et spiritu compunctionis repleas, et quæ juste postulaverint, efficaciter tribuas ; et concessa perpetuo stabilita et intacta manere decernas. Per Christum Dominum nostrum. *R*. Amen.

so as both to fill them with the spirit of compunction, and to grant them the effects of their just desires ; and, when granted, to remain stable and untouched for ever. Through Christ our Lord. *R*. Amen.

OREMUS

Omnipotens sempiterne Deus, qui Ninivitis in cinere et cilicio pœnitentibus indulgentiæ tuæ remedia præstitisti : concede propitius, ut sic eos imitemur habitu, quatenus veniæ prosequamur obtentu. Per Dominum. *R*. Amen.

LET US PRAY

O almighty and eternal God, who forgavest the Ninivites, when they did penance in sackcloth and ashes ; mercifully grant us so to imitate their penance, that we may obtain pardon of our sins. Through, etc. *R*. Amen.

Having said the last of these prayers, the priest sprinkles the ashes with holy water, and censes them. The first in order of the priests who are present, marks the celebrant's forehead with them. Then the ministers at the altar and the clergy receive them from the celebrant, who finally gives them to the faithful, saying :

Memento homo, quia pulvis es, et in pulverem reverteris.

Remember man, that thou art dust, and into dust thou shalt return.

When the priest puts the holy emblem of penance upon you, accept in a spirit of submission, the sentence of death, which God Himself pronounces against you : 'Remember, O man, that thou art dust, and into dust thou shalt return !' Humble yourself, and remember what it was that brought the punishment of death upon us : man wished to be as a god, and preferred his own will to that of his sovereign Master. Reflect, too, on that long list of sins, which you have added to the sin of your first parents, and adore the mercy of your God,

who asks only one death for all these your trans-
gressions.

During the time the priest is giving the ashes, the
choir sings the following antiphons and responsory.

ANTHEM

Immutemur habitu, in
cinere et cilicio : jejunemus
et ploremus ante Dominum,
quia multum misericors est
dimittere peccata nostra
Deus noster.

Let us change our dress for
ashes and sackcloth; let us fast
and weep in the presence of the
Lord ; for our God is very
merciful to forgive us our sins.

ANTHEM

Inter vestibulum et altare
plorabunt sacerdotes ministri Domini, et dicent :
Parce, Domine, parce populo
tuo : et ne claudas ora canen-
tium te, Domine.

The priests, the ministers of
the Lord, shall weep between
the porch and the altar, and
say : Spare, O Lord, spare thy
people, and shut not the mouths
of those who praise thee, O
Lord.

RESPONSORY

Emendemus in melius
quæ ignoranter peccavimus:
ne subito præoccupati die
mortis, quæramus spatium
pœnitentiæ, et invenire non
possimus. * Attende, Do-
mine, et miserere, quia peccavimus tibi.

Let us amend the sins we
have committed through ignorance : lest suddenly overtaken
by the day of our death, we
seek for time to do penance,
and be not able to find it. *
Look down on us, O Lord, and
take pity ; for we have sinned
against thee.

Ps. Adjuva nos Deus sa-
lutaris noster : et propter
honorem nominis tui Do-
mine, libera nos. * Attende.
V. Gloria Patri. * Attende.

Ps. Help us, O God our
Saviour : and deliver us for the
glory of thy name, O Lord. *
Look down, etc. *V.* Glory, etc.
Look down, etc.

As soon as all the faithful have received the
ashes, the priest sings the following prayer :

V. Dominus vobiscum.
R. Et cum spiritu tuo.

V. The Lord be with you.
R. And with thy spirit.

14

OREMUS

LET US PRAY

Concede nobis, Domine, præsidia militiæ christianæ sanctis inchoare jejuniis : ut contra spirituales nequitias pugnaturi, continentiæ muniamur auxiliis. Per Christum Dominum nostrum. *R.* Amen.

Grant us, O Lord, to begin with holy fasting our Christian warfare ; that being to fight against spiritual wickedness, we may be aided therein by temperance. Through Christ our Lord. *R.* Amen.

MASS

The soul has regained her confidence by the act of humility she has performed. She approaches the God of mercy, and reminds Him of the tender love He bears to His creature man, and of the patience wherewith He waits for his repentance. These are the sentiments expressed in the Introit, which is taken from the Book of Wisdom.

INTROIT

Misereris omnium, Domine, et nihil odisti eorum quæ fecisti, dissimulans peccata hominum propter pœnitentiam, et parcens illis : quia tu es Dominus Deus noster.

Thou, O Lord, hast mercy on all, and hatest none of those things which thou hast created ; thou overlookest the sins of men, to draw them to repentance, and thou pardonest them ; because thou art the Lord our God.

Ps. Miserere mei Deus, miserere mei ; quoniam in te confidit anima mea. *V.* Gloria Patri. Misereris.

Ps. Have mercy on me, O God, have mercy on me ; for my soul trusteth in thee. *V.* Glory, etc. Thou, O Lord, etc.

In the Collect, the Church prays that her children may have the two-fold grace of a fervent commencement and steady perseverance in the salutary fast of Lent.

COLLECT

Præsta, Domine, fidelibus tuis, ut jejuniorum veneranda solemnia, et congrua

Grant, O Lord, that thy faithful may enter on this solemn and venerable fast with suitable

pietate suscipiant, et secura devotione percurrant. Per Dominum.

piety, and go through it with unmolested devotion. Through, etc.

SECOND COLLECT

A cunctis nos, quæsumus, Domine, mentis et corporis defende periculis: et intercedente beata et gloriosa semperque Virgine Dei Genitrice Maria, cum beato Joseph, beatis apostolis tuis Petro et Paulo, atque beato N. et omnibus sanctis, salutem nobis tribue benignus et pacem: ut, destructis adversitatibus et erroribus universis, Ecclesia tua secura tibi serviat libertate.

Preserve us, O Lord, we beseech thee, from all dangers of soul and body: and by the intercession of the glorious and blessed Mary, the ever Virgin Mother of God, of blessed Joseph, of thy blessed apostles Peter and Paul, of blessed N. *(here is mentioned the titular saint of the church)*, and of all the saints, grant us, in thy mercy, health and peace; that all adversities and errors being removed, thy Church may serve thee with undisturbed liberty.

THIRD COLLECT

Omnipotens sempiterne Deus, qui vivorum dominaris simul et mortuorum, omniumque misereris, quos tuos fide et opere futuros esse prænoscis: te supplices exoramus; ut pro quibus effundere preces decrevimus quosque vel præsens sæculum adhuc in carne retinet, vel futurum jam exutos corpore suscepit, intercedentibus omnibus sanctis tuis, pietatis tuæ clementia, omnium delictorum suorum veniam consequantur. Per Dominum.

O almighty and eternal God, who hast dominion over the living and the dead, and art merciful to all whom thou knowest will be thine by faith and good works: we humbly beseech thee, that they, for whom we have proposed to offer our prayers, whether this world still retains them in the flesh, or the next world hath already received them divested of their bodies, may, by the clemency of thine own goodness, and the intercession of thy saints, obtain pardon and full remission of their sins. Through, etc.

Lectio Joelis Prophetæ.

Cap. ii.

Hæc dicit Dominus : Convertimini ad me in toto corde vestro, in jejunio, et in fletu, et in planctu. Et scindite corda vestra, et non vestimenta vestra, et convertimini ad Dominum Deum vestrum : quia benignus et misericors est, patiens et multæ misericordiæ, et præstabilis super malitia. Quis scit si convertatur et ignoscat, et relinquat post se benedictionem, sacrificium et libamen Domino Deo vestro ? Canite tuba in Sion, sanctificate jejunium, vocate cœtum, congregate populum, sanctificate Ecclesiam, coadunate senes, congregate parvulos et sugentes ubera : egrediatur sponsus de cubili suo, et sponsa de thalamo suo. Inter vestibulum et altare plorabunt sacerdotes ministri Domini, et dicent : Parce, Domine, parce populo tuo : et ne des hæreditatem tuam in opprobrium, ut dominentur eis nationes. Quare dicunt in populis : Ubi est Deus eorum ? Zelatus est Dominus terram suam, et pepercit populo suo. Et respondit Dominus, et dixit populo suo : Ecce ego mittam vobis frumentum, et vinum, et oleum, et replebimini eis : et non dabo vos ultra opprobrium in gentibus : dicit Dominus omnipotens.

Lesson from the Prophet Joel.

Ch.

Thus saith the Lord : Be converted to me with all your heart, in fasting, and in weeping, and in mourning. And rend your hearts, and not your garments, and turn to the Lord your God : for he is gracious and merciful, patient and rich in mercy, and ready to repent of the evil. Who knoweth but he will return, and forgive, and leave a blessing behind him ; sacrifice and libation to the Lord your God ? Blow the trumpet in Sion, sanctify a fast, call a solemn assembly, gather together the people, sanctify the Church, assemble the ancients, gather together the little ones, and them that suck at the breasts : let the bridegroom go forth from his bed, and the bride out of the bridechamber. Between the porch and the altar the priests, the Lord's ministers, shall weep, and shall say : Spare, O Lord, spare thy people ; and give not thine inheritance to reproach, that the heathens should rule over them. Why should they say among the nations : Where is their God ? The Lord hath been zealous for his land, and hath spared his people. And the Lord answered, and said to his people : Behold, I will send you corn, and wine, and oil ; you shall be filled with them, and I will no more make you a reproach among the nations, saith the Lord almighty.

We learn from this magnificent passage of the prophet Joel how acceptable to God is the expiation of fasting. When the penitent sinner inflicts corporal penance upon himself, God's justice is appeased. We have a proof of it in the Ninivites. If the Almighty pardoned an infidel city, as Ninive was, solely because its inhabitants sought for mercy under the garb of penance; what will He not do in favour of His own people, who offer Him the two-fold sacrifice, exterior works of mortification, and true contrition of heart? Let us, then, courageously enter on the path of penance. We are living in an age when, through want of faith and of fear of God, those practices which are as ancient as Christianity itself, and on which we might almost say it was founded, are falling into disuse; it behoves us to be on our guard, lest we, too, should imbibe the false principles, which have so fearfully weakened the Christian spirit. Let us never forget our own personal debt to the divine justice, which will remit neither our sins nor the punishment due to them, except inasmuch as we are ready to make satisfaction. We have just been told that these bodies, which we are so inclined to pamper, are but dust; and as to our souls, which we are so often tempted to sacrifice by indulging the flesh, they have claims upon the body, claims of both restitution and obedience.

In the Gradual, the Church again pours forth the expressions of her confidence in the God of all goodness, for she counts upon her children being faithful to the means she gives them of propitiating His justice.

The Tract is that beautiful prayer of the psalmist, which she repeats thrice during each week of Lent, and which she always uses in times of public calamity, in order to appease the anger of God.

GRADUAL

Miserere mei Deus, miserere mei: quoniam in te confidit anima mea.

V. Misit de cœlo, et liberavit me: dedit in opprobrium conculcantes me.

Have mercy on me, O God, have mercy on me; for my soul hath trusted in thee.

V. He hath sent from heaven, and delivered me; he hath made them a reproach that trod upon me.

TRACT

V. Domine non secundum peccata nostra, quæ fecimus nos, neque secundum iniquitates nostras retribuas nobis.

V. Domine, ne memineris iniquitatum nostrarum antiquarum: cito anticipent nos misericordiæ tuæ, quia pauperes facti sumus nimis.

V. Deal not with us, O Lord, according to our sins, which we have committed, nor punish us according to our iniquities.

V. Remember not, O Lord, our former iniquities; let thy mercies speedily prevent us, for we are become exceeding poor.

At this next verse the priest kneels down.

V. Adjuva nos, Deus Salutaris noster: et propter gloriam nominis tui, Domine, libera nos: et propitius esto peccatis nostris, propter nomen tuum.

V. Help us, O God, our Saviour, and for the glory of thy name, O Lord, deliver us and forgive us our sins for thy name's sake.

GOSPEL

Sequentia sancti Evangelii secundum Matthæum.

Sequel of the holy Gospel according to Matthew.

Cap. vi.

Ch. vi.

In illo tempore: Dixit Jesus discipulis suis: Cum jejunatis, nolite fieri sicut hypocritæ tristes. Exterminant enim facies suas, ut appareant hominibus jejunantes. Amen dico vobis, quia receperunt mercedem suam. Tu autem cum jeju-

At that time, Jesus said to his disciples: When you fast, be not as the hypocrites, sad. For they disfigure their faces, that they may appear unto men to fast. Amen, I say to you, they have received their reward. But thou, when thou fastest, anoint thy head, and

nas, unge caput tuum, et faciem tuam lava, ne videaris hominibus jejunans, sed Patri tuo, qui est in abscondito: et Pater tuus qui videt in abscondito, reddet tibi. Nolite thesaurizare vobis thesauros in terra, ubi ærugo et tinea demolitur, et ubi fures effodiunt, et furantur. Thesaurizate autem vobis thesauros in cœlo: ubi neque ærugo, neque tinea demolitur; et ubi fures non effodiunt, nec furantur. Ubi enim est thesaurus tuus, ibi est et cor tuum.

wash thy face, that thou appear not to men to fast, but to thy Father, who is in secret: and thy Father, who seeth in secret, will repay thee. Lay not up to yourselves treasures on earth, where the rust and moth consume, and where thieves break through and steal. But lay up to yourselves treasures up in heaven, where neither rust nor moth doth consume, and where thieves do not break through, nor steal. For where thy treasure is, there is thy heart also.

Our Redeemer would not have us receive the announcement of the great fast as one of sadness and melancholy. The Christian who understands what a dangerous thing it is to be behindhand with divine justice, welcomes the season of Lent with joy; it consoles him. He knows that if he be faithful in observing what the Church prescribes, his debt will be less heavy upon him. These penances, these *satisfactions* (which the indulgence of the Church has rendered so easy), being offered to God unitedly with those of our Saviour Himself, and being rendered fruitful by that holy fellowship which blends into one common propitiatory sacrifice the good works of all the members of the Church militant, will purify our souls, and make them worthy to partake in the grand Easter joy. Let us not, then, be *sad* because we are to *fast;* let us be *sad* only because we have sinned and made fasting a necessity. In this same Gospel, our Redeemer gives us a second counsel, which the Church will often bring before us during the whole course of Lent: it is that of joining almsdeeds with our fasting. He bids us to *lay up treasures in heaven.* For this, we need intercessors; let us seek them amidst the poor.

In the Offertory, the Church rejoices in her children being set free; she foresees that the wounds of our souls will be healed, for she has confidence in us that we shall persevere, and this fills her with gladness.

OFFERTORY

Exaltabo te, Domine, quoniam suscepisti me, nec delectasti inimicos meos super me : Domine, clamavi ad te, et sanasti me.

I will extol thee, O Lord, for thou hast upholden me, and hast not made my enemies to rejoice over me. O Lord, I have cried to thee, and thou hast healed me.

SECRET

Fac nos, quæsumus, Domine, his muneribus offerendis convenienter aptari; quibus ipsius venerabilis sacramenti celebramus exordium. Per Dominum.

Grant, O Lord, that we may be duly prepared to present these our offerings, by which we celebrate the institution of this venerable mystery. Through, etc.

SECOND SECRET

Exaudi nos, Deus Salutaris noster : ut per hujus Sacramenti virtutem, a cunctis nos mentis et corporis hostibus tuearis, gratiam tribuens in præsenti, et gloriam in futuro.

Graciously grant us, O God our Saviour, that by virtue of this Sacrament, thou mayst defend us from all enemies, both of soul and body; giving us grace in this life, and glory in the next.

THIRD SECRET

Deus, cui soli cognitus est numerus electorum in superna felicitate locandus; tribue quæsumus, ut intercedentibus omnibus sanctis tuis, universorum, quos in **oratione** commendatos sus-

O God, to whom alone is known the number of thine elect to be placed in eternal bliss: grant, we beseech thee, by the intercession of all thy saints, that the book of predestination may contain the

cepimus, et omnium fidelium nomina, beatæ prædestinationis liber adscripta retineat. Per Dominum.

names of all those for whom we have undertaken to pray, as well as those of all the faithful. Through, etc.

THE PREFACE

Vere dignum et justum est, æquum et salutare, nos tibi semper, et ubique gratias agere, Domine sancte, Pater omnipotens, æterne Deus. Qui corporali jejunio vitia comprimis, mentem elevas, virtutem largiris et præmia, per Christum Dominum nostrum. Per quem majestatem tuam laudant Angeli, adorant Dominationes, tremunt Potestates : Cœli, cœlorumque Virtutes, ac beata Seraphim, socia exsultatione concelebrant. Cum quibus et nostras voces, ut admitti jubeas deprecamur, supplici confessione, dicentes : Sanctus, Sanctus, Sanctus.

It is truly meet and just right and available to salvation, that we should always and in all places give thanks to thee, O holy Lord, Father almighty, eternal God. Who by this bodily fast extinguishest our vices, elevatest our understanding, bestowest on us virtue and its rewards, through Christ our Lord. By whom the Angels praise thy majesty, the Dominations adore it, the Powers tremble before it ; the Heavens and the heavenly Virtues, and the blessed Seraphim, with common jubilee, glorify it. Together with whom, we beseech thee that we may be admitted to join our humble voices, saying : Holy! Holy! Holy!

The words of the Church in the Communion antiphon contain an instruction of great importance to us. During this long career of penance, we shall stand in need of something to keep up our courage : let us *meditate on the law* and the mysteries of our *Lord*. If we relish the word of God as it is offered us by the Church on each day of this holy season, our hearts will receive an increase of light and love, and when our Lord shall rise from His tomb, the brightness of His Resurrection will shine upon us.

COMMUNION

Qui meditabitur in lege Domini die ac nocte, dabit

He that meditateth day and night on the law of the Lord,

fructum suum in tempore   shall yield his fruit in due
suo.   season.

POSTCOMMUNION

Percepta nobis, Domine   May the mysteries we have
præbeant Sacramenta subsi-   received, O Lord, afford us
dium: ut tibi grata sint   help, that our fasting may be
nostra jejunia, et nobis pro-   acceptable to thee, and become
ficiant ad medelam. Per Do-   a remedy to us.   Through, etc.
minum.

SECOND POSTCOMMUNION

Mundet et muniat nos,   May the oblation of this
quæsumus, Domine, divini   divine Sacrament, we beseech
Sacramenti munus oblatum :   thee, O Lord, both cleanse and
et intercedente beata Virgine   defend us : and by the inter-
Dei Genitrice Maria, cum   cession of blessed Mary, the
beato Joseph, beatis apostolis   Virgin Mother of God, of blessed
tuis Petro et Paulo, atque   Joseph, of thy blessed apos-
beato N. et omnibus sanctis,   tles, Peter and Paul, of blessed
a cunctis nos reddat et per-   N., and of all the saints, free us
versitatibus expiatos, et ad-   from all sin, and deliver us
versitatibus expeditos.   from all adversity.

THIRD POSTCOMMUNION

Purificent nos, quæsu-   May the mysteries we have
mus, omnipotens et miseri-   received, purify us, we beseech
cors Deus, Sacramenta quæ   thee, O almighty and merciful
sumpsimus : et interceden-   God; and grant by the inter-
tibus omnibus sanctis tuis,   cession of all thy saints, that
præsta ut hoc tuum Sacra-   this thy Sacrament may not
mentum non sit nobis rea-   increase our guilt to punish-
tus ad pœnam, sed inter-   ment, but be a means of ob-
cessio salutaris ad veniam :   taining pardon in order to
sit ablutio scelerum, sit for-   salvation.   May it wash away
titudo fragilium, sit contra   sin, strengthen our frailty,
omnia mundi pericula fir-   secure us against the dangers
mamentum : sit vivorum   of the world; and procure
atque mortuorum fidelium   forgiveness for all the faith-
remissio omnium delicto-   ful, both living and dead.
rum. Per Dominum.   Through, etc.

Every day during Lent, Sundays excepted, the
priest, before dismissing the faithful, here adds a

special prayer, which is preceded by these words of admonition :

OREMUS LET US PRAY

Humiliate capita vestra Deo.

Bow down your heads to God.

PRAYER

Inclinantes se, Domine, majestati tuæ, propitiatus intende : ut qui divino munere sunt refecti, cœlestibus semper nutriantur auxiliis. Per Dominum.

Mercifully look down upon us, O Lord, bowing down before thy divine Majesty, that they who have been refreshed with thy divine mysteries, may always be supported by thy heavenly aid. Through, etc.

THURSDAY AFTER ASH WEDNESDAY

ALTHOUGH the law of fasting began yesterday, yet Lent, properly so called, does not begin till the Vespers of Saturday next. In order to distinguish the rest of Lent from these four days which have been added to it, the Church continues to chant Vespers at the usual hour, and allows her ministers to break their fast before having said that Office. But, beginning with Saturday, the Vespers will be anticipated ; every day (Sundays excepted, which always exclude fasting), they will be said at such an early hour, that when the faithful take their full meal, the evening Office will be over. It is a remnant of the discipline of the primitive Church, which forbade the faithful to break their fast before sunset, in other words, before Vespers or Evensong.

The Church has given to these three days after Ash Wednesday a resemblance to the other ferias of her lenten season, by assigning to each of them a lesson from the Old Testament, and a Gospel, for

Mass. We, of course, insert them, adding a few reflections to each. We also give the Collects of these three days.

The station, in Rome, for the Thursday after Ash Wednesday, is in the church of St. George *in Velabro* (the veil of gold).

COLLECT

Deus, qui culpa offenderis, pœnitentia placaris : preces populi tui supplicantis propitius respice : et flagella tuæ iracundiæ, quæ pro peccatis nostris meremur, averte. Per Christum Dominum nostrum. Amen.

O God, who by sin art offended, and by penance pacified, mercifully regard the prayers of thy suppliant people : and turn away the scourges of thy wrath, which we deserve for our sins. Through Christ our Lord. Amen.

EPISTLE

Lectio Isaiæ Prophetæ.

Lesson from Isaias the Prophet.

Cap. xxxviii.

Ch. xxxviii.

In diebus illis, ægrotavit Ezechias usque ad mortem : et introivit ad eum Isaias filius Amos propheta, et dixit ei : Hæc dicit Dominus : Dispone domui tuæ, quia morieris tu, et non vives. Et convertit Ezechias faciem suam ad parietem, et oravit ad Dominum, et dixit : Obsecro, Domine, memento, quæso, quomodo ambulaverim coram te in veritate, et in corde perfecto, et quod bonum est in oculis tuis fecerim. Et flevit Ezechias fletu magno. Et factum est verbum Domini ad Isaiam dicens : Vade, et dic Ezechiæ : Hæc dicit Dominus Deus David patris tui : Au-

In those days, Ezechias was sick even to death, and Isaias the son of Amos the prophet came unto him, and said to him : Thus saith the Lord : Take order with thy house, for thou shalt die, and not live. And Ezechias turned his face towards the wall, and prayed to the Lord, and said : I beseech thee, O Lord, remember how I have walked before thee in truth, and with a perfect heart, and have done that which is good in thy sight. And Ezechias wept with great weeping. And the word of the Lord came to Isaias, saying : Go and say to Ezechias : Thus saith the Lord the God of David thy father :

divi orationem tuam, et vidi lacrymas tuas : ecce ego adjiciam super dies tuos quindecim annos : et de manu regis Assyriorum eruam te, et civitatem istam, et protegam eam, ait Dominus omnipotens.

I have heard thy prayer, and I have seen thy tears : behold I will add to thy days fifteen years: and I will deliver thee and this city out of the hands of the king of the Assyrians, and I will protect it, saith the Lord almighty.

Yesterday, the Church spoke to us upon the certainty of death. Die we must: we have not only God's infallible word for it, but no reasonable man could ever entertain the thought that he was to be an exception to the rule. But if the fact of our death be certain, the day on which we are to die is also fixed. God, in His wisdom, has concealed the day from us ; it becomes our duty not to be taken by surprise. This very night, it might be said to us, as it was to Ezechias : *Take order with thy house, for thou shalt die.* We ought to spend each day, as though it were to be our last. Were God even to grant us, as He did to the holy king of Juda, a prolongation of life, we must come, sooner or later, to that last hour, beyond which there is no time, and eternity begins. The Church's intention in thus reminding us of our mortality, is to put us on our guard against the allurements of this short life, and urge us to earnestness in the great work of regeneration, for which she has been preparing us during these last three weeks. How many there are of those who yesterday received the ashes, who will never see the joys of Easter, at least in this world ! To them, the ceremony has been a prediction of what is to happen to them, perhaps before the month is out. And yet the very same words that were pronounced over them, were said to us. May not we ourselves be of the number of those who are thus soon to be victims of death? In this uncertainty, let us gratefully accept the warning, which our Jesus came down from heaven to give us : 'Do penance ; for the kingdom of God is at hand.'[1]

GOSPEL

Sequentia sancti Evangelii secundum Matthæum.	Sequel of the holy Gospel according to Matthew.
Cap. viii.	*Ch.* viii.

In illo tempore : Cum introisset Jesus Capharnaum, accessit ad eum centurio, rogans eum et dicens : Domine, puer meus jacet in domo paralyticus, et male torquetur. Et ait illi Jesus : Ego veniam, et curabo eum. Et respondens centurio, ait : Domine, non sum dignus ut intres sub tectum meum ; sed tantum dic verbo, et sanabitur puer meus. Nam et ego homo sum sub potestate constitutus, habens sub me milites, et dico huic : Vade, et vadit ; et alii : Veni, et venit ; et servo meo : Fac hoc, et facit. Audiens autem Jesus miratus est, et sequentibus se dixit : Amen dico vobis, non inveni tantam fidem in Israel : Dico autem vobis, quod multi ab oriente et occidente venient, et recumbent cum Abraham, et Isaac, et Jacob in regno cœlorum ; filii autem regni ejicientur in tenebras exteriores : ibi erit fletus et stridor dentium. Et dixit Jesus centurioni : Vade, et sicut credidisti, fiat tibi. Et sanatus est puer in illa hora.

At that time : When Jesus had entered into Capharnaum, there came to him a centurion, beseeching him, and saying : Lord, my servant lieth at home sick of the palsy, and is grievously tormented. And Jesus saith to him : I will come and heal him. And the centurion making answer said : Lord, I am not worthy that thou shouldst enter under my roof ; but only say the word, and my servant shall be healed. For I also am a man under authority, having under me soldiers ; and I say to this, Go, and he goeth ; and to another, Come, and he cometh ; and to my servant, Do this, and he doth it. And Jesus hearing this, marvelled, and said to them that followed him : Amen, I say to you, I have not found so great faith in Israel. And I say to you, that many shall come from the east and the west, and shall sit down with Abraham, and Isaac, and Jacob, in the kingdom of heaven ; but the children of the kingdom shall be cast out into exterior darkness : there shall be weeping and gnashing of teeth. And Jesus said to the centurion : Go, and as thou hast believed, so be it done to thee. And the servant was healed at the same hour.

---

[1] St. Matt. iv. 17.

The sacred Scriptures, the fathers, and theologians, tell us that there are three eminent good works which are, at the same time, works of penance: prayer, fasting, and almsdeeds. In the lessons she gives us on these three days, which form as it were the threshold of Lent, the Church instructs us upon these works. To-day it is prayer she recommends to us. Look at this centurion, who comes to our Saviour, beseeching Him to heal his servant. His prayer is humble; in all the sincerity of his heart, he deems himself unworthy to receive Jesus under his roof. His prayer is full of faith; he doubts not for an instant that Jesus is able to grant him what he asks. And with what ardour he prays! The faith of this Gentile is greater than that of the children of Israel, and elicits praise from the Son of God. Such ought to be our prayer, when we solicit the cure of our souls. Let us acknowledge that we are not worthy to speak to God, and yet, let us have an unshaken confidence in the power and goodness of Him, who only commands us to pray that He may pour out His mercies upon us. The season we are now in is one of prayer; the Church redoubles her supplications; it is for us that she makes them; we must take our share in them. Let us, during this season of grace, cast off that languor which fastens on the soul at other times; let us remember that it is prayer which repairs the faults we have already committed, and preserves us from sin for the future.

Humiliate capita vestra Deo.

Bow down your heads to God.

Parce Domine, parce populo tuo, ut dignis flagellationibus castigatus, in tua miseratione respiret. Per Christum Dominum nostrum. Amen.

Spare, O Lord, spare thy people; that having been justly chastised, they may find comfort in thy mercy. Through Christ our Lord. Amen.

FRIDAY AFTER ASH WEDNESDAY

THE station for to-day is in the church of the holy martyrs, St. John and St. Paul.

COLLECT

Inchoata jejunia, quæsumus Domine, benigno favore prosequere : ut observantiam, quam corporaliter exhibemus, mentibus etiam sinceris exercere valeamus. Per Christum Dominum nostrum. Amen.

Graciously favour us, O Lord, we beseech thee, in the fast we have undertaken : that what we observe outwardly, we may perform with sincere minds. Through Christ our Lord. Amen.

EPISTLE

Lectio Isaiæ Prophetæ.

Lesson from Isaias the Prophet.

Cap. lviii.

Hæc dicit Dominus Deus : Clama, ne cesses ; quasi tuba exalta vocem tuam, et annuntia populo meo scelera eorum, et domui Jacob peccata eorum. Me etenim de die in diem quærunt, et scire vias meas volunt : quasi gens quæ justitiam fecerit, et judicium Dei sui non dereliquerit : rogant me judicia justitiæ : appropinquare Deo volunt. Quare jejunavimus et non aspexisti : humiliavimus animas nostras et nescisti ? Ecce in die jejunii vestri invenitur voluntas vestra, et omnes debitores vestros repetitis. Ecce ad lites et contentiones jejunatis, et percutitis pugno impie. Nolite jejunare sicut usque ad hanc diem, ut audiatur in excelso clamor vester. Num-

Ch. lviii.

Thus saith the Lord God : Cry, cease not, lift up thy voice like a trumpet, and show my people their wicked doings, and the house of Jacob their sins. For they seek me from day to day, and desire to know my ways, as a nation that hath done justice, and hath not forsaken the judgment of their God ; they ask of me the judgments of justice : they are willing to approach to God. Why have we fasted, and thou hast not regarded : why have we humbled our souls, and thou hast not taken notice ? Behold, in the day of your fast, your own will is found, and you exact of all your debtors. Behold you fast for debates and strife, and strike with the fist wickedly. Do not fast as you have done until this day, to make your

quid tale est jejunium, quod elegi, per diem affligere hominem animam suam? numquid contorquere quasi circulum caput suum, et saccum et cinerem sternere? numquid istum vocabis jejunium, et diem acceptabilem Domino? Nonne hoc est magis jejunium, quod elegi? dissolve colligationes impietatis, solve fasciculos deprimentes, dimitte eos qui confracti sunt liberos, et omne onus disrumpe. Frange esurienti panem tuum, et egenos vagosque induc in domum tuam : cum videris nudum, operi eum, et carnem tuam ne despexeris. Tunc erumpet quasi mane lumen tuum, et sanitas tua citius orietur, et anteibit faciem tuam justitia tua, et gloria Domini colliget te. Tunc invocabis, et Dominus exaudiet : clamabis, et dicet : Ecce adsum. Quia misericors sum, Dominus Deus tuus.

cry to be heard on high. Is this such a fast as I have chosen : for a man to afflict his soul for a day? Is this it, to wind his head about like a circle, and to spread sackcloth and ashes? wilt thou call this a fast, and a day acceptable to the Lord? Is not this rather the fast that I have chosen? loose the bands of wickedness, undo the bundles that oppress, let them that are broken go free, and break asunder every burden. Deal thy bread to the hungry, and bring the needy and the harbourless into thy house ; when thou shalt see one naked, cover him, and despise not thy own flesh. Then shall thy light break forth as the morning, and thy health shall speedily arise, and thy justice shall go before thy face, and the glory of the Lord shall gather thee up. Then shalt thou call, and the Lord shall hear : thou shalt cry, and he shall say : Here I am ; for I the Lord thy God am merciful.

We are told, in this lesson from the prophet Isaias, what are the dispositions which should accompany our fast. It is God Himself who here speaks to us—that God who had Himself commanded His people to fast. He tells us that the fasting from material food is a mere nothing in His eyes, unless they who practise it abstain also from sin. He demands the sacrifice of the body; but it is not acceptable to Him, unless that of the soul goes along with it. The living God can never consent to be treated as were the senseless gods of wood and stone, which the Gentiles adored, and which were incapable of receiving any other than a

15

mere external homage. Let, then, the heretic cease to find fault with the Church for her observance of practices, which he pretends to scorn as being material; it is he that grows material by his system of letting the body have every indulgence. The children of the Church fast, because fasting is recommended in almost every page of both the old and the new Testament, and because Jesus Christ Himself fasted for forty days; but they are fully aware that this practice, which is thus recommended and urged, is then alone meritorious, when it is ennobled and completed by the homage of a heart that is resolved to reform its vicious inclinations. And after all, it would be an injustice, if the body, which has been led into guilt solely through the malice of the soul, were to be made to suffer, and the soul herself be allowed to continue in her sinful course. Hence it is that they whose ill-health prevents them from observing the bodily austerities of Lent, are equally bound to impose on their soul that spiritual fast, which consists in the amendment of their life, in avoiding everything that is sinful, and in the zealous performance of every good work in their power.

GOSPEL

Sequentia sancti Evangelii secundum Matthæum.

Cap. v., vi.

In illo tempore: Dixit Jesus discipulis suis: Audistis quia dictum est: Diliges proximum tuum, et odio habebis inimicum tuum. Ego autem dico vobis: Diligite inimicos vestros, benefacite his qui oderunt vos: et orate pro persequentibus et calumniantibus vos: ut sitis filii Patris vestri, qui in

Sequel of the holy Gospel according to Matthew.

Ch. v., vi.

At that time: Jesus said to his disciples: You have heard that it hath been said: Thou shalt love thy neighbour, and hate thy enemy. But I say to you: love your enemies, do good to them that hate you, and pray for them that persecute and calumniate you; that you may be the children of your Father who is in heaven,

cœlis est, qui solem suum oriri facit super bonos et malos, et pluit super justos et injustos. Si enim diligitis eos qui vos diligunt, quam mercedem habebitis? Nonne et publicani hoc faciunt? Et si salutaveritis fratres vestros tantum : quid amplius facitis? Nonne et ethnici hoc faciunt? Estote ergo vos perfecti, sicut et Pater vester cœlestis perfectus est. Attendite ne justitiam vestram faciatis coram hominibus, ut videamini ab eis : alioquin mercedem non habebitis apud Patrem vestrum qui in cœlis est. Cum ergo facis eleemosynam, noli tuba canere ante te, sicut hypocritæ faciunt in synagogis, et in vicis, ut honorificentur ab hominibus. Amen dico vobis, receperunt mercedem suam. Te autem faciente eleemosynam, nesciat sinistra tua, quid faciat dextera tua : ut sit eleemosyna tua in abscondito, et Pater tuus qui videt in abscondito, reddet tibi.

who maketh his sun to rise upon the good and bad, and raineth upon the just and the unjust. For if you love them that love you, what reward shall you have? do not even the publicans this? And if you salute your brethren only, what do you do more? do not also the heathens this? Be you therefore perfect, as also your heavenly Father is perfect. Take heed that you do not your justice before men to be seen by them: otherwise you shall not have a reward of your Father who is in heaven. Therefore, when thou dost an almsdeed, sound not a trumpet before thee, as the hypocrites do in the synagogues and in the streets, that they may be honoured by men. Amen, I say to you, they have received their reward. But when thou dost alms, let not thy left hand know what thy right hand doth; that thy alms may be in secret, and thy Father, who seeth in secret, will repay thee.

Almsdeeds is the third of the great penitential works : it is the sister virtue of prayer and fasting. For this reason, the Church puts before us, to-day, the instructions given by our Saviour on the manner in which we ought to do works of mercy. He puts upon us the duty of loving our fellow-men, without distinction of friends or enemies. God, who has created them all, loves them Himself; this is motive enough to make us show mercy to all. If He bears with them even when they are His enemies by sin, and patiently waits for their conversion even to the

end of their lives, so that they who are lost are lost
through their own fault, what ought not we to do,
we who are sinners as they are, and their brethren,
and created like them out of nothing?　When,
therefore, we do an act of kindness or mercy towards
those who have God for their Father, we offer Him
a most acceptable homage.　Charity, the queen of
virtues, absolutely requires of us the love of our
neighbour, as being part of our love of God; and
this charity, at the same time that it is a sacred
obligation incumbent upon each member of the
family of mankind, is, in the acts it inspires us to do
towards each other, a work of penance, because it
imposes upon us certain privations, and requires us
to overcome every repugnance which nature stirs up
within us, when we have to show this charity to
certain individuals.　And finally, we must in our
almsdeeds follow the counsel our blessed Saviour
gives us; it is the one He recommended to us, when
He bade us fast: we must do it in secret, and shun
ostentation.　Penance loves humility and silence;
it has a dread of being noticed by men; the only
one whose applause it seeks, is He who *seeth in
secret.*

Humiliate capita vestra
Deo.

Tuere, Domine, populum
tuum, et ab omnibus peccatis clementer emunda : quia
nulla ei nocebit adversitas,
si nulla ei dominetur ini-
quitas. Per Christum Do-
minum nostrum.　Amen.

Bow down your heads to
God.

Defend, O Lord, thy people,
and mercifully cleanse them
from all their sins : for no mis-
fortune can hurt them, if no
wickedness rule over them.
Through Christ our Lord.
Amen.

SATURDAY AFTER ASH WEDNESDAY

THE station for to-day is, as noted in the missal, in the church of St. Trypho, martyr; but this church having been destroyed many centuries ago, the station is now in that of St. Augustine, which is built on the same site.

COLLECT

Adesto, Domine, supplicationibus nostris, et concede ut hoc solemne jejunium, quod animabus corporibusque curandis salubriter institutum est, devoto servitio celebremus. Per Christum Dominum nostrum. Amen.

Give ear, O Lord, to our prayers, and grant that we may, with true devotion, observe this solemn fast which was wholesomely instituted for the healing of both our soul and body. Through Christ our Lord. Amen.

EPISTLE

Lectio Isaiæ Prophetæ.

Lesson from Isaias the Prophet.

Cap. lviii.

Ch. lviii.

Hæc dicit Dominus Deus : Si abstuleris de medio tui catenam, et desieris extendere digitum et loqui quod non prodest ; cum effuderis esurienti animam tuam, et animam afflictam repleveris, orietur in tenebris lux tua, et tenebræ tuæ erunt sicut meridies. Et requiem tibi dabit Dominus semper, et implebit splendoribus animam tuam, et ossa tua liberabit, et eris quasi hortus irriguus et sicut fons aquarum, cujus non deficient

Thus saith the Lord God : If thou wilt take away the chain out of the midst of thee, and cease to stretch out the finger, and to speak that which profiteth not; when thou shalt pour out thy soul to the hungry, and shalt satisfy the afflicted soul, then shall thy light rise up in darkness, and thy darkness shall be as the noon-day. And the Lord will give thee rest continually, and will fill thy soul with brightness, and deliver thy bones, and thou shalt be like a watered garden,

aquæ. Et ædificabuntur in te deserta sæculorum : fundamenta generationis et generationis suscitabis : et vocaberis ædificator sepium, avertens semitas in quietem. Si averteris a Sabbato pedem tuum, facere voluntatem tuam in die sancto meo, et vocaveris Sabbatum delicatum, et sanctum Domini gloriosum, et glorificaveris eum dum non facis vias tuas, et non invenitur voluntas tua, ut loquaris sermonem : tunc delectaberis super Domino ; et sustollam te super altitudines terræ, et cibabo te hereditate Jacob patris tui : os enim Domini locutum est.

and like a fountain of water, whose waters shall not fail. And the places that have been desolate for ages, shall be built in thee ; thou shalt raise up the foundations of generation and generation : and thou shalt be called the repairer of the fences, turning the paths into rest. If thou turn away thy foot from the Sabbath, from doing thy own will in my holy day, and call the Sabbath delightful, and the holy of the Lord glorious, and glorify him, while thou dost not thy own ways, and thy own will is not found, to speak a word : then shalt thou be delighted in the Lord, and I will lift thee up above the high places of the earth, and will feed thee with the inheritance of Jacob thy father. For the mouth of the Lord hath spoken it.

Saturday is a day replete with mystery. It is the day of God's rest; it is a figure of the eternal peace, which awaits us in heaven after the toils of this life are over. The object of the Church in giving us, to-day, this lesson from Isaias, is to teach us how we are to merit our eternal *Sabbath*. We have scarcely entered on our campaign of penance, when this affectionate mother of ours comes to console us. If we abound in good works during this holy season, in which we have taken leave of the distracting vanities of the world, the *light* of grace *shall rise up* even in the *darkness* which now clouds our soul. This soul which has been so long obscured by sin and by the love of the world and self, shall become bright as the *noon-day ;* the glory of Jesus' Resurrection shall be ours too ; and, if we are faithful to grace, the Easter of time will lead us to the Easter of eternity. Let us, therefore, *build up the places that have been* so long *desolate;* let us *raise up the foundations, repair the fences, turn away our feet* from the violation of holy observances; *do not our own ways and our own will* in opposition to those of our divine Master; and then He will give us everlasting *rest,* and *fill* our *soul with* His own *brightness.*

GOSPEL

Sequentia sancti Evangelii secundum Marcum.	Sequel of the holy Gospel according to Mark.
Cap. vi.	*Ch.* vi.

In illo tempore : Cum sero esset, erat navis in medio mari, et Jesus solus in terra. Et videns discipulos suos laborantes in remigando (erat enim ventus contrarius eis), et circa quartam vigiliam noctis, venit ad eos ambulans supra mare : et volebat præterire eos. At illi, ut viderunt eum ambulantem supra mare, putaverunt phantasma esse, et exclamaverunt. Omnes enim viderunt eum, et conturbati sunt. Et statim locutus est cum eis, et dixit eis : Confidite, ego sum, nolite timere. Et ascendit ad illos in navim, et cessavit ventus. Et plus magis intra se stupebant : non enim intellexerunt de panibus : erat enim cor eorum obcæcatum. Et cum transfretassent, venerunt in terram Genesareth, et applicuerunt. Cumque egressi

At that time : When it was late, the ship was in the midst of the sea, and Jesus alone on the land. And seeing them labouring in rowing (for the wind was against them), and about the fourth watch of the night, he cometh to them, walking upon the sea, and he would have passed by them. But they seeing him walking upon the sea, thought it was an apparition, and they cried out. For they all saw him and were troubled. And immediately he spoke with them, and said to them : Have a good heart, it is I, fear ye not. And he went up to them into the ship, and the wind ceased. And they were far more astonished within themselves : for they understood not concerning the loaves : for their heart was blinded. And when they had passed over, they came into the land of Genesareth, and set to the shore. And when

essent de navi, continuo co-
gnoverunt eum: et percur-
rentes universam regionem
illam, cœperunt in grabatis
eos qui se male habebant
circumferre, ubi audiebant
eum esse. Et quocumque
introibat, in vicos, vel in vil-
las, aut civitates, in plateis
ponebant infirmos, et de-
precabantur eum, ut vel
fimbriam vestimenti ejus
tangerent: et quotquot tan-
gebant eum, salvi fiebant.

they were gone out of the ship
immediately they knew him;
and running through that whole
country, they began to carry
about in beds those that were
sick, where they heard he was.
And whithersoever he entered,
into towns, or into villages, or
cities, they laid the sick in
the streets, and besought him
that they might touch but
the hem of his garment: and
as many as touched him were
made whole.

The ship, the Church, has set sail; the voyage is
to last forty days. The disciples *labour in rowing,
for the wind is against them;* they begin to fear
lest they may not be able to gain the port. But
Jesus comes to them *on the sea; He goes up to them
in the ship;* the rest of the voyage is most prosperous. The ancient liturgists thus explain the
Church's intention in her choice of to-day's Gospel.
Forty days of penance are, it is true, little enough
for a long life that has been spent in everything
save God's service; and yet our cowardice would
sink under these forty days, unless we had Jesus
with us. Let us not fear; it is He; He prays with
us, fasts with us, and does all our works of mercy
with us. Was it not He that first began these
forty days of expiation? Let us keep our eyes
fixed on Him, and *be of good heart.* If we grow
tired, let us go to Him, as did the poor sick ones of
whom our Gospel speaks. The very touch of His
garments sufficed to restore health to such as had
lost it; let us go to Him in His adorable Sacrament;
and the divine life, whose germ is already within
us, will develop itself, and the energy, which was
beginning to droop in our hearts, will regain all its
vigour.

Humiliate capita vestra Deo.

Bow down you heads to God.

Fideles tui, Deus, per tua dona firmentur : ut eadem et percipiendo requirant, et quærendo sine fine percipiant.   Per Christum Dominum nostrum.   Amen.

May thy faithful, O God, be strengthened by thy gifts, that, by receiving them, they may ever hunger after them, and hungering after them, they may have their desires satisfied in the everlasting possession of them.   Through Christ our Lord.   Amen.

Let us close our Saturday with a prayer to Mary, the refuge of sinners.   Let us express the confidence we have in her, by the following devout sequence. It is taken from the German missals of the fourteenth century.

SEQUENCE

Tibi cordis in altari
Decet preces immolari,
  Virgo sacratissima.

It behoves us, O most holy Virgin, to offer thee, on the altar of our hearts, the offering of our prayers.

Nam cum in se sit inepta,
Tuo Nato sit accepta
  Per te precum victima.

For whereas the sacrifice of our prayers has no merit of its own, it may be made acceptable, through thee, to thy Son.

Pro peccatis immolato
Peccatorum præsentato
  Precum sacrificia.

Present to him, who was sacrificed for sin, the sacrifice of sinners' prayers.

Per te Deum adit reus,
Ad quem per te venit Deus :
  Amborum tu media.

It is through thee the sinner comes to God, for this God came to the sinner through thee, O thou the mediatrix between God and man !

Nec abhorre peccatores
Sine quibus nunquam fores
  Tanto digna Filio.

It was for the sake of sinners that thou wast made worthy of such a Son : canst thou, then, despise them ?

Si non essent redimendi,
Nulla tibi pariendi
  Redemptorem ratio.

It was because there were sinners to be redeemed, that thou wast made Mother of the Redeemer.

Sed nec Patris ad conses-
    sum
Habuisses huc accessum,
  Si non ex te genitum
  Esset ibi positum.

Neither wouldst thou be
seated nigh the Father's
throne, hadst thou not been
Mother of him who shares his
Father's throne.

Virgo, Virgo sic promota
Causa nostri, nostra vota
  Promovenda suscipe
  Coram summo Principe.
    Amen.

Take, then, O holy Virgin,
who for our sake hast been
thus exalted, take thou our
prayers, and present them to
our sovereign Lord. Amen.

PROPER OF THE SAINTS

FEBRUARY 3

SAINT BLASE, BISHOP AND MARTYR

Now that the Church has closed the joyous period of her forty days of Christmas, and is putting us through a course of meditations on subjects which are to excite a spirit of penance within us, each of the saints' feasts must produce an impression, which shall be in accordance with that spirit. From this day till Easter, we will study the saints, as they come to us, in this special light: how much they laboured and suffered during their pilgrimage of life, and what was the plan they took for conquering the world and the flesh. ' They went,' says the psalmist, ' and wept, casting their seeds: but coming they shall come with joyfulness, carrying their sheaves.'[1] It shall be the same with us; and at the end of our lenten labours, our risen Jesus will hail us as His living, regenerated children.

The calendar of this portion of the year abounds with martyrs; and, at the very outset, we meet with one of the most celebrated of these glorious champions of Christ. The scene of his pastoral virtues and of his martyrdom was Sebaste, a city of Armenia, the same that will give us forty martyred soldiers on a single day. The devotion to St. Blase is, even to this day, most fervently kept up in the east, especially in Armenia. The western Churches soon began to love and honour his memory, and so universally, that we might call him one of the most popular of our saints. His feast, however, with us

[1] Ps. cxxv. 6, 7.

is only a simple, and the Church of Rome has given only one lesson on his life.

Blasius, Sebaste in Armenia cum virtutum laude floreret, ejusdem civitatis episcopus eligitur. Qui quo tempore Diocletianus insatiabilem crudelitatem in Christianos exercebat, se in speluncam abdidit montis Argæi, ubi tamdiu latuit, dum ab Agricolai præsidis militibus venantibus deprehensus, et ad præsidem ductus, ejus jussu conjectus est in vincula. Quo in loco multos ægrotos sanavit, qui ad Blasium, ejus fama sanctitatis adducti, deferebantur. In illis puer fuit, qui, desperata a medicis salute, transversa spina faucibus inhærente, animam agebat. Productus autem ad præsidem Blasius semel et iterum, cum nec blanditiis, nec minis adduci posset ut diis sacrificaret, primum virgis cæsus, deinde in equuleo ferreis pectinibus dilaniatus est : postremo, dempto capite, illustre fidei testimonium Christo Domino dedit, tertio Nonas Februarii.

Blase, whose signal virtues made him dear to the people of Sebaste in Armenia, was chosen bishop of that city. When the emperor Diocletian waged his cruel persecution against the Christians, the saint hid himself in a cave on Mount Argeus, and there he remained some time concealed, but was at length discovered by some soldiers of the governor Agricolaus, while they were hunting. They led him to the governor, who gave orders that he should be put into prison. During his imprisonment, many sick people, attracted by the reputation of his sanctity, came to him, and he healed them. Among these was a boy, whose life was despaired of by the physicians, on account of his having swallowed a bone, which could not be extracted from his throat. The saint was twice brought before the governor, but neither fair promises nor threats could induce him to offer sacrifice to the gods. Whereupon, he was first beaten with rods, and then his flesh was torn with iron hooks while he lay stretched on the rack. At length he was beheaded, and nobly gave testimony to the faith of Christ our Lord, on the third of the Nones of February (February 3).

Accept, O glorious martyr, the praise which we, too, offer thee in union with that given thee by the whole Church. In return for this homage of our veneration, look down upon the Christian people, who are now preparing to enter on the season of penance, and to be converted to the Lord their God by holy compunction and tears. We ask it of thee by thine own combat: assist us in the one for which we are preparing. When duty required thee to undergo tortures and death, it found thee ready and brave ; our duty is expiation by penance, and thy prayers must get us courage. Our enemies are not more cruel than thine, but they are more treacherous, and if we spare them we are lost. Obtain for us that heavenly assistance, which enabled thee to conquer. We are children of the martyrs ; God forbid we should be degenerate ! Pray, too, O holy pontiff, for the country thou didst water with thy blood. Armenia lost the faith for which thou didst lay down thy life. Intercede for her, that she may be restored to the Church, and let her conversion bring consolation to the few that have remained orthodox and faithful.

FEBRUARY 4

SAINT ANDREW CORSINI, BISHOP AND CONFESSOR

THE saintly bishop, whose feast we keep to-day pressingly invites us, by his austere life and his burning zeal for the salvation of souls, to procure, at all costs, our own reconciliation with the divine justice. We are indebted for this feast to a member of the illustrious family of the Corsini, Pope Clement XII., who, however, was but the instrument used by divine Providence. The holy bishop of the little town of Fiesole ever sought to be unknown during his life, and God, who willed that he should be glorified by the whole Church, inspired the sovereign Pontiff to inscribe his name among the saints of the universal calendar. Andrew the saint was once a sinner; his example will encourage us in the work of our conversion.

Let us read the account of his virtues as given us by the Church.

Andream Florentiæ ex nobili Corsinorum familia natum parentes precibus a Deo impetrarunt, et beatæ Virgini spoponderunt. Qualis autem futurus esset, divino præsagio, antequam nasceretur, ostensum est : nam mater gravida sibi visa est per quietem lupum edidisse, qui, ad Carmelitarum ædem pergens, in ipso templi vestibulo statim in agnum conversus est. Adolescens pie et ingenue educatus, cum sensim ad vitia declinaret, sæpe a matre increpatus fuit. Ubi autem cognovit, se parentum voto Deiparæ Virgini dicatum fuisse, Dei amore succensus, deque visu matris admonitus, Carmelitarum institutum amplexus est, in quo variis tentationibus a dæmone vexatus, numquam tamen potuit a religionis proposito dimoveri. Mox Lutetiam missus, emenso studiorum curriculo, et laurea donatus in patriam revocatur, suique Ordinis regimini in Etruria præficitur.

Andrew was born at Florence, of the noble Corsini family. He was the fruit of his parents' prayers, and was consecrated by them to the blessed Virgin. His future was thus shown by God to the mother. She dreamt that she had given birth to a wolf, which went to the church of the Carmelites, and, as it crossed the threshold, was suddenly changed into a lamb. Though his early education was calculated to form him to piety, and to everything that suited his high birth, he, by degrees, fell into a vicious manner of life, notwithstanding the frequent reproaches made him by his mother. But as soon as he was told that he had been consecrated by his parents to the Virgin Mother of God, and heard of his mother's vision, he entered the Order of Carmelites. The devil ceased not to molest him, even then, with manifold temptations; but nothing could make him change his resolution of entering the religious life. Shortly after his profession, he was sent to Paris for a course of study; having completed it, and taken his degrees, he returned to Italy, and was made superior of his Order in the province of Tuscany.

Interea Fesulana Ecclesia suo viduata pastore eum sibi episcopum elegit : quo munere se indignum æstimans, diu latuit ignotus, donec pueri voce mirabiliter loquentis proditus, et extra urbem inventus, ne divinæ contradiceret voluntati episcopatum suscepit. Ea dignitate auctus, humilitate, quam semper coluerat, impensius incubuit et pastorali solicitudini, misericordiam in pauperes, liberalitatem, orationis assiduitatem, vigilias, aliasque virtutes adjunxit, et spiritu etiam prophetico clarus fuit, adeo ut ejus sanctitas ab omnibus celebraretur.

His permotus Urbanus quintus ad sedandas Bononiæ turbas Andream legatum misit : quo in munere multa perpessus, civium odia, quæ ad internecionem exarserant, summa prudentia restinxit ; tum restituta tranquillitate ad propria reversus est. Nec multo post assiduis laboribus, et voluntaria carnis maceratione confectus, obitus die a beata Virgine sibi prædicto, ad cœlestia regna migravit, anno Domini millesimo trecentesimo septuagesimo tertio, ætatis suæ septuagesimo

It happened about that time, that the Church of Fiesole lost its bishop, and Andrew was chosen as his successor. But looking on himself as unworthy of such a dignity, he hid himself so that no one knew where he was. But a child, who had not yet received the use of speech, miraculously revealed the place, outside the town, where he was : upon which the saint, fearing that further refusal would be a resistance to the divine will, was consecrated bishop. Thus exalted to so great a dignity, he applied himself more than ever to the practice of humility, which had always been his favourite virtue. To the zeal of a good pastor, he united tender compassion for the poor, abundant almsgiving, a life of prayer, long watchings, and other virtues ; all which, together with the gift of prophecy he had received, gained for him a great reputation for sanctity.

Pope Urban V., hearing of his great merits, sent him as his legate to Bologna, that he might quell a sedition that had arisen in that city. The fulfilment of this charge cost him much suffering ; but such was his prudence, that he succeeded in restoring peace among the citizens, and so preventing further bloodshed ; he then returned to Fiesole. Not long after this, being worn out by ceaseless labours and bodily mortifications, and having been told by the blessed Virgin of the precise day of his death, he passed from this life to the

primo. Quem Urbanus octavus multis magnisque miraculis clarum, sanctorum numero adscripsit. Ejus corpus Florentiæ in ecclesia sui Ordinis quiescit, et maxima civium veneratione colitur: quibus non semel in præsenti discrimine præsidio fuit.

kingdom of heaven, in the year of our Lord thirteen hundred and seventy three, and in the seventy-first year of his age. Great was the reputation of his name on account of the many and wonderful miracles wrought through his intercession, and at length he was canonized by Urban VIII. His body reposes in the church of his Order at Florence, where it is held in great veneration, the citizens having often experienced his protection in times of public calamity.

Hear, O holy pontiff, our prayer : we are sinners, and would learn from thee how we are to return to the God we have offended. His mercy was poured out upon thee; obtain the same for us. Have pity on Christians throughout the world, for the grace of repentance is now being offered to all; pray for us, that we may be filled with the spirit of compunction. We have sinned; we sue for pardon; intercession like thine can win it for us. From wolves, change us into lambs. Strengthen us against our enemies; obtain for us an increase of the virtue of humility, which thou hadst in such perfection; and intercede for us with our Lord, that He crown our efforts with perseverance, as He did thine; that thus we may be enabled to unite with thee in singing, for ever, the praises of our Redeemer.

FEBRUARY 5

SAINT AGATHA, VIRGIN AND MARTYR

SINCE the commencement of the ecclesiastical year, we have kept the feasts of two out of the four illustrious virgins whose names are daily honoured in the holy Sacrifice of the Lamb: the third comes to-day, lighting up the heaven of the Church with her bright soft rays. Lucy first, then Agnes, and now the gracious visit of Agatha. The fourth, Cecily, the immortal Cecily, is to be one of that magnificent constellation which gives such splendour to the closing of the year. To-day, then, let us keep a feast in honour of Agatha, the virgin daughter of that same fair Sicily which can boast of her Lucy. We must not allow the holy sadness of our present season to take aught from the devotion we owe to our saint. The joy wherewith we celebrate her merits will lead us to study her virtues. She will repay us by her prayers; she will encourage us to persevere in the path which is to bring us to the God she so nobly loved and served, and with whom she is now for ever united.

Let us begin by reading what the Church tells us of the virtues and combats of this glorious bride of Christ.

Agatha virgo, in Sicilia nobilibus parentibus nata, quam Panormitani et Catanenses civem suam esse dicunt, in persecutione Decii imperatoris Catanæ gloriosi martyrii coronam consecuta est. Nam cum pari pulchritudinis et castitatis laude commendaretur, Quintianus, Siciliæ prætor, ejus amore captus est. Sed cum, tentata modis omnibus ejus pudicitia, Agatham in suam sententiam perducere non posset, Christianæ superstitionis nomine comprehensam, Aphrodisiæ cuidam mulieri depravandam tradit. Quæ Aphrodisiæ consuetudine cum de constantia

The holy virgin Agatha was born in Sicily, of noble parents. The cities of Palermo and Catania both claim the honour of having been the place of her birth. She received the crown of a glorious martyrdom at Catania, under the persecution of the Emperor Decius. Her beauty, which was as great as her chaste and innocent life was praiseworthy, attracted the notice of Quintianus, the governor of Sicily. He spared no means whereby to compass his lustful designs upon the innocent virgin; but seeing that she scorned his offers, he had her apprehended as being guilty of the Christian superstition, and gave

16

242 SEPTUAGESIMA

colendæ Christianæ fidei, et servandæ virginitatis, removeri non posset, nuntiat illa Quintiano, se in Agatha operam perdere. Quare ille ad se virginem adduci jubet : et nonne, inquit, te pudet nobili genere natam humilem et servilem Christianorum vitam agere? Cui Agatha : Multo præstantior est Christiana humilitas et servitus, regum opibus, ac superbia.

Quamobrem iratus prætor hanc ei optionem dat, velitne potius venerari deos, an vim tormentorum subire. At illa constans in fide, primum colaphis cæsa mittitur in carcerem : unde postridie educta, cum in sententia permaneret, admotis candentibus laminis in equuleo torquetur : tum ei mamilla absciditur. Quo in vulnere Quintianum appellans virgo : Crudelis, inquit, tyranne, non te pudet, amputare in femina, quod ipse in matre suxisti ? Mox conjecta in vincula, sequenti nocte a sene quodam, qui se Christi apostolum esse dicebat, sanata est. Rursum evocata a prætore, et in Christi confessione perseverans, in acutis testulis, et

her in charge of a woman, named Aphrodisia, who was noted for her power of alluring to evil. But finding that her words and company had no effect on the holy maiden, and that she was immovable in her resolution to maintain both her faith and her virginity, Aphrodisia told Quintianus that she was but losing her time with Agatha. Whereupon, he ordered the virgin to be brought before him, and he said to her: 'Art not thou, that art so noble by birth, ashamed to lead the life of a base and slavish Christian ?' She replied : 'Better by far is the baseness and slavery of a Christian than the wealth and pride of kings.'

Angered by her words, the governor bids her choose one of these two : adoration of the gods, or sharp tortures. On her refusal to deny her faith, he ordered her to be buffeted, and cast into prison. On the following day, she was again led to trial. Finding that she was still firm in her purpose, they hoisted her on the rack, and laid hot iron plates on her flesh, and cut off her breast. While suffering this last torture, she thus spoke to Quintianus : 'Cruel tyrant, art thou not ashamed to cut a woman's breast, who wast thyself fed at the breast of thy mother ?' She was then sent back to prison, where, during the night, a venerable old man, who told her that

candentibus carbonibus ei subjectis volutatur.

he was the apostle of Christ, healed her. A third time she was summoned by the governor, and being still firm in confessing Christ, she was rolled upon sharp potsherds, and burning coals.

Quo tempore ingenti terræ motu urbs tota contremuit, ac duo parietes corruentes, Silvinum et Falconium intimos prætoris familiares oppresserunt. Quare vehementer commota civitate, veritus populi tumultum Quintianus, Agatham semimortuam clam reduci imperat in carcerem. Quæ sic Deum precata: Domine, qui me custodisti ab infantia, qui abstulisti a me amorem sæculi, qui me carnificum tormentis superiorem præstitisti, accipe animam meam. Ea in oratione migravit in cœlum Nonis Februarii: cujus corpus a Christianis sepelitur.

Suddenly, the whole city was shaken by a violent earthquake, and two of the governor's intimate friends were killed by the falling of two walls. The people were in such a state of excitement that the governor began to fear a sedition, and therefore ordered the almost lifeless Agatha to be secretly conveyed back to her prison. She thus prayed to our Lord: 'O God! who hast watched over me from my infancy, who hast separated me from the love of this world, and hast given me strength to bear the tortures of my executioners, receive my soul!' Her prayer being ended, her soul took its flight to heaven, on the Nones of February (February 5), and the Christians buried her body.

The ancient books of the liturgy abound with verses in honour of St. Agatha; but most of them are so poor in sentiment that we pass them over. The following beautiful hymn is the composition of Pope St. Damasus.

HYMN

Martyris ecce dies Agathæ
Virginis emicat eximiæ:
Christus eam sibi qua sociat,
Et diadema duplex decorat.

Lo! the bright festal day of the glorious martyr and virgin Agatha, when Christ took her to himself, and a double crown wreathed her brow.

Stirpe decens, elegans
  specie,
Sed magis actibus atque
  fide,
Terrea prospera nil repu-
  tans,
Jussa Dei sibi corde ligans.
  Fortior hæc trucibusque
    viris,
Exposuit sua membra fla-
  gris,
Pectore quam fuerit valido
Torta mamilla docet patulo.
  Deliciæ cui carcer erat,
Pastor ovem Petrus hanc re-
  creat:
Inde gavisa magisque fla-
  grans,
Cuncta flagella cucurrit
  ovans.
  Ethnica turba rogum fu-
    giens
Hujus et ipsa meretur opem;
Quos fidei titulus decorat,
His Venerem magis ipsa
  premat.
  Jam renitens quasi sponsa
    polo,
Pro miseris supplica Domi-
  no,
Sic tua festa coli faciat,
Te celebrantibus ut faveat.

  Gloria cum Patre sit Ge-
    nito,
Spirituique proinde sacro,
Qui Deus unus et omnipo-
  tens
Hanc nostri faciat memo-
  rem.
  Amen.

Though noble by birth and
blessed with beauty, her
grandest riches were her deeds
and her faith. Earthly prosperity was nothing in her
eyes, but her whole heart was
on the precepts of her God.

Her bravery tired out the
men that tortured her; she
flinched not as they lashed
her limbs: and her wounded
breast reveals a dauntless
heart.

Her prison was her para-
dise, where the pastor Peter
heals his bleeding lamb; and
thence once more she runs to
suffer, gladder and braver at
every wound.

A pagan city once in flames
was saved by Agatha's prayer.
The same can check, in Christian hearts, the threatening fire
of lust.

Now that thou art in heaven,
clad as a bride of Christ, intercede with him for us miserable sinners, that he grant us
so to spend thy feast, that our
celebration may draw down his
grace.

Glory be to the Son, to-
gether with the Father and
the Holy Ghost. May the
one almighty God grant that
this his saint be mindful of us.
Amen.

How lovely are thy palms, O Agatha! But how
long and cruel was thy combat for them! The day
was thine; thy faith and thy virginity triumphed,
but the battle-field streamed with thy blood, and

thy glorious wounds bear testimony to the angels how stern was the courage of thy fidelity to Jesus thy Spouse. When thine enemies left thee, it was to Him thou didst look up; and then thy soul flew to its rest, in the bosom of thy King and God. The whole Church keeps feast to-day, praising her Lord in thee, great martyr and virgin! She knows the love thou bearest her, and how, amidst the joys of heaven, her interests and her wants are the object of thy prayers. Thou art our sister; be, too, our mother, by interceding for us. Centuries have passed away since that day, whereon thy soul quitted the body thou hadst sanctified by purity and suffering; but the great battle between the spirit and the flesh is still waging here on earth, and will do so to the end of time. Assist us in the struggle; keep up within our hearts the holy fire, which the world and our passions are ever seeking to quench.

It is now the season when every Christian should renew his whole being by repentance and compunction. We know the power of thy prayer; let it procure us these gifts: the fear of God, which keeps down the workings of corrupt nature; the spirit of penance, which repairs the injuries caused by our sins; and a solid love for our dear Lord, which sweetens the yoke, and ensures perseverance. More than once a whole people has witnessed how a relic of thine, thy veil, has checked the stream of lava which rolled down the sides of Etna; we are threatened with a torrent of vice, which will drive the world back to pagan corruption, unless divine mercy stay its wild fury; and prayers such as thine can obtain it for us. Delay not, O Agatha! each day gives strength to the danger. Not a nation but is now infected with the poison of a literature that is infidel and immoral; by thy prayers keep the poisonous cup from them that have not tasted, neutralize its power in them that have drunk its venom of death. Oh! spare us the shame of seeing our Europe the slave of sensuality, and the dupe of hell.

FEBRUARY 6

SAINT DOROTHY, VIRGIN AND MARTYR

To-DAY again, it is one of the most amiable of Christ's brides that comes to console us by her presence; it is Dorothy, the simple and intrepid virgin, who strews the path of her martyrdom with prodigies of sweetest charity. The religion of Christ alone can produce in timid women, like the saint of to-day, an energy which at times surpasses that of the most valiant martyrs among men. Thus does our Lord glorify His infinite power, by crushing Satan's head with what is by nature so weak. The enmity put by God between the woman and the serpent,[1] is for ever showing itself in those sublime Acts of the Martyrs, where the rebel angel is defeated by an enemy whom he knew to be weak, and therefore scorned to fear; but that very weakness, which made her victory the grander, made his humiliation the bitterer. Surely, such history must have taught him how powerful an enemy he has in a Christian woman; and we, who can boast of having so many heroines among the ancestors of our holy faith, should cherish their memory, and confide in their protection, for their intercession is powerful with Him for whom they died. One of the noblest of these comes to us to-day; let us celebrate her victory, and merit her patronage.

The lessons given in the Dominican breviary are so much fuller than the legend of the Roman

[1] Gen. iii. 15.

liturgy that we have not hesitated to insert them here.

Dorothea virgo, in Cæsarea Cappadociæ, propter Christi confessionem, ab Apricio illius provinciæ præfecto comprehensa, Crystæ et Callistæ sororibus, quæ a fide defecerant, tradita est, ut eam a proposito removeret. Sed ipsa reduxit eas ad finem, propter quam in cupam missæ et incensæ sunt. Dorotheam vero jussit præses in catasta levari ; quæ dixit ad illum : Numquam in tota vita mea sic lætata sum sicut hodie. Tum ad ejus latera lampades ardentes apponi, dein faciem diutissime cædi, tandem caput gladio percuti præses imperat.

The holy virgin Dorothy, of Cesarea in Cappadocia, was apprehended by Apricius, the governor of that province, for professing the faith of Christ. She was put under the care of her two sisters, Chrysta and Callista, who had apostatized from the faith, and would be able to shake the resolute constancy of Dorothy. But she brought them back to the faith, for which they were burnt to death in a cauldron. The governor ordered Dorothy to be hoisted on the rack, and she said to him, as she lay upon it : 'Never in my whole life have I felt such joy, as I do to-day.' Then the governor ordered the executioners to burn her sides with lighted lamps, and beat her for a very long time on the face, and finally behead her with the sword.

Ea porro dum duceretur ad supplicium dicente : Gratias tibi, amator animarum, qui me ad paradisum tuum vocasti, Theophilus quidam præsidis advocatus irridens : Eia tu, inquit, sponsa Christi, mitte mihi de paradiso sponsi tui mala, aut rosas. Et Dorothea respondit : Et plane ita faciam. Cum ante ictum breviter precari permissa esset, pulchra specie puer ante eam apparuit, ferens in orario tria mala, et tres rosas. Cui illa ait : Obsecro ut feras ea Theophilo.

While she was being led to the place of execution, she said : 'I give thee thanks, O thou lover of our souls, that thou callest me to thy paradise !' Theophilus, one of the governor's officers, hearing her words, laughed, and said to her : 'Hear me, bride of Christ ! I ask thee to send me some apples and roses from this paradise of thy Spouse.' Dorothy replied : 'Well, and so I will.' Before she was beheaded, she was allowed a moment for prayer ; when lo ! a beautiful child

Et mox gladio percussa perrexit ad Christum.

Igitur cum Theophilus
irridens, promissionem sanctæ Dorotheæ sodalibus nar-
raret, ecce puer ante eum
cum orario, in quo ferens
tria mala magnifica, et tres
rosas elegantissimas, dixit
ei : En sicut petenti promisit
virgo sacratissima Doro-
thea, transmisit hæc tibi de
paradiso sponsi sui. Tum
Theophilus stupens, quod
esset Februarius, et gelu
cuncta rigerent, ea accepit,
atque exclamavit : Vere
Deus Christus est. Sicque
palam fidem Christi professus, gravissimum quoque
pro ea martyrium strenue
pertulit.

came to her, bringing with
him in a napkin three apples
and three roses. She said to
him : ' Take them, I pray thee,
to Theophilus.' Then the
executioner struck her head off
with his sword, and her soul
fled to Christ.

While Theophilus was jo-
cosely telling his fellows the
promise made him by Dorothy,
he sees a boy bringing him in
a napkin three fine apples, and
three most lovely roses, who,
as he gave them, said: 'Lo !
the most holy virgin Dorothy
sends thee, as she promised,
these gifts from the paradise
of her Spouse.' Theophilus
was beside himself with surprise, for it was February,
and the frost most sharp; but
taking the gifts he exclaimed :
' Christ is truly God !' He
openly professed the Christian
faith, and courageously suffered for the same a most
painful martyrdom.

The missals and breviaries of the Middle Ages
contain several pieces in honour of St. Dorothy.
The following is one that was used in Germany,
and is most appropriate for the season of Septuagesima.

SEQUENCE

Psallat concors sympho-
  nia,
Laudes pangat harmonia,
  Cum sonora melodia
Cordisque tripudio.

In hoc festo lætabundo
Dorotheæ, corde mundo,

Let tuneful instruments
breathe forth concordant
strains, and harmony sound
forth her praise, and we, with
joyous heart, sing sweet melodious hymns.

'Tis the pure-hearted Do-
rothy's happy feast ; let our

Sono plaudat vox jucundo
Neumatum præludio.

Generosa Christi verna
Labe carens, et lucerna
Mundo lucens, ac pincerna,
Vina donans mystica.

Paradisi tu colona,
Quæ pro malo reddis bona,
  Scribæ mittis cœli dona
Rosas, mala pistica.
Vitam ducens angelorum,
Dum in carne præter forum
  Carnis vivis, spernis to-
    rum
Viri propter Dominum.

Martyr Christi quæ pro-
    fanos
Deos sternis, ac paganos
  Fide vestis, et sic sanos
Mores facis hominum.
Tota manens speciosa,
Velut rubens fragrans rosa,
  Ad conflictum roborosa,
Minante Fabricio.

Vinculata carceraris,
In catasta cruciaris,
  Vultu cæsa flagellaris,
Omni carens vitio.
Gens perversa malæ spei
Quam dum doces verbum
    Dei,
  Lumen tuæ faciei
Conterit cum baculis.
Furens auget tormentales
Pœnas sævas et lethales,
  Dum mamillas virginales
Tuas cremat faculis.
Supplicamus : nos tuere
Et peccata fac timere,
  Martyr sancta, confer
    veræ
Tempus pœnitentiæ.
Virgo bona, crimen terge,

glad voices, led on by the organ's peal, proclaim her praise.

O noble and sinless hand-maid of Christ ! O bright lamp shining to the whole world ! O cup-bearer, that profferest us rich mystic wines !

Child of paradise, that payest evil with good, and givest to thine enemy roses and fragrant apples of heaven.

Thou leadest the life of an angel, and whilst in the flesh, livest not according to the flesh ; scorning to be spouse of man, because betrothed to Christ.

Thou art his martyr too, trampling on the pagan gods ; and, giving faith to infidels, convertest them from madness to wisdom.

Red fragrant rose ! nothing could impair thy beauty. Fabricius may threaten what he lists, thou hast a heart brave enough for all.

Chains and prisons, racks and buffets, thou sufferest all, yet innocent, deserving none.

Wicked men, whose hopes were bent on evil, beat thy beaming face, for that thou darest to teach them the word of God.

But they could increase their tortures, keen and deadly as they were ; furiously, then, they burn thy innocent breast.

O holy martyr ! we beseech thee, protect us, obtain for us a fear of sin, and pray that time be given us for true repentance.

Kind virgin ! pray for us

Victum dona, mores rege,
　Ne damnemur gravi lege
Causa negligentiæ.

that our sins be cleansed, our
souls be nourished with grace,
our lives well regulated, that
so we be not condemned for
negligence by God's dread law
of justice.

Sponsa Christi´Dorothea,
Tua nos virtute bea,
　Ut purgata mente rea,
Digni simus præmio.

O Dorothy, thou spouse of
Christ! may thy merits draw
down his blessing upon us;
and we be found worthy of the
reward that he gives to those
whose souls are free from sin.

Deum nobis fac placatum,
Ut post hujus incolatum,
　Sed et locum det optatum
In cœlesti gremio.
　Amen.

Render our Lord propitious
to us, and beseech him to give
us, after our sojourn here, the
longed-for place of rest in the
bosom of his heaven. Amen.

Thy promises, O Dorothy, are faithful as thyself.
In the garden of thy heavenly Spouse, thou forgettest not the exiles on earth. How fortunate
was Theophilus to have had one of thy promises!
He asked for fruits and flowers; he received them,
and with them the richer gifts of faith and perseverance, which we also would now ask thee to send
us. Thou knowest our wants. We want courage
to conquer the world and our passions; we want
the grace of conversion; we want the spirit of
penance, without which we can never reach that
heaven of our vocation, where we are to be thy
companions in bliss. Promise us thy prayers, and
we shall not fail. And on the grand day of Easter
for which we are preparing, our souls, having been
purified in the Blood of the Lamb, will be as
fragrant as the fruits and as fair as the flowers
thou didst send to a pagan, whose prayer was less
confident than ours.

FEBRUARY 7

SAINT ROMUALD, ABBOT

THE calendar's list of martyrs is interrupted for two days; the first of these is the feast of Romuald, the hero of penance, the saint of the forests of Camaldoli. He is a son of the great patriarch St. Benedict, and, like him, is the father of many children. The Benedictine family has a direct line from the commencement, even to this present time; but, from the trunk of this venerable tree there have issued four vigorous branches, to each of which the Holy Spirit has imparted the life and fruitfulness of the parent stem. These collateral branches of the Benedictine Order are: Camaldoli, founded by Romuald; Cluny, by Odo; Vallombrosa, by John Gualbert; and Citeaux, by Robert of Molesmes.

The saint of this seventh day of February is Romuald. The martyrs whom we meet with on our way to Lent, give us an important lesson by the contempt they had for this short life. But the teaching offered us by such holy penitents as the great abbot of Camaldoli is even more practical than that of the martyrs. 'They that are Christ's,' says the apostle, 'have crucified their flesh, with its vices and concupiscences';[1] and in these words he tells us what is the distinguishing character of every true Christian. We repeat it: what a powerful encouragement we have in these models of mortification, who have sanctified the deserts by their lives of heroic penance! How they make us ashamed of our own cowardice, which can scarcely bring itself to do the little that must be done to satisfy God's justice and merit His grace! Let us

[1] Gal. v. 24.

take the lesson to heart, cheerfully offer our offended Lord the tribute of our repentance, and purify our souls by works of mortification.

The Office for St. Romuald's feast gives us the following sketch of his life.

Romualdus Ravennæ, Sergio patre nobili genere natus, adolescens in propinquum monasterium Classense, pœnitentiæ causa secessit: ubi religiosi hominis sermone, ad pietatis studium vehementius incensus, viso etiam semel et iterum per noctem in ecclesia beato Apollinari, quod Dei servus illi futurum promiserat, monachus efficitur. Mox ad Marinum, vitæ sanctitate ac severiore disciplina in finibus Venetorum eo tempore celebrem, se contulit, ut ad arctam et sublimem perfectionis viam eo magistro ac duce uteretur.

Multis Satanæ insidiis, et hominum invidia oppugnatus, tanto humilior se assidue jejuniis et orationibus exercebat, et rerum cœlestium meditatione, vim lacrymarum profundens fruebatur : vultu tamen adeo læto semper erat, ut intuentes exhilararet. Magno apud principes et reges in honore fuit, multique ejus consilio, mundi illecebris abjectis, solitudinem

Romuald was the son of a nobleman, named Sergius. He was born at Ravenna, and while yet a boy, withdrew to the monastery of Classis, there to lead a life of penance. The conversation of one of the religious increased in his soul his already ardent love of piety ; and after being twice favoured with a vision of St. Apollinaris, who appeared to him, during the night, in the church which was dedicated to him, he entered the monastic state, agreeably to the promise made him by the holy martyr. A few years later on, he betook himself to a hermit named Marinus, who lived in the neighbourhood of Venice, and was famed for his holy and austere life, that, under such a master and guide, he might follow the narrow path of high perfection.

Many were the snares laid for him by Satan, and envious men molested him with their persecutions ; but these things only excited him to be more humble, and assiduous in fasting and prayer. In the heavenly contemplation wherewith he was favoured, he shed abundant tears. Yet such was the joy which ever beamed in his face, that it made all who looked at him cheerful. Princes and kings held him in great

petierunt. Martyrii quoque
cupiditate flagravit, cujus
causa dum in Pannoniam
proficiscitur, morbo quo af-
flictabatur cum progredere-
tur, levabatur cum recede-
ret, reverti cogitat.

In vita et post mortem
miraculis clarus, spiritu
etiam prophetiæ non caruit.
Scalam a terra cœlum per-
tingentem in similitudinem
Jacob patriarchæ, per quam
homines in veste candida
ascendebant et descende-
bant, per visum conspexit,
eoque Camaldulenses mo-
nachos, quorum instituti
auctor fuit, designari mirabiliter agnovit. Denique
cum annos centum et vi-
ginti ageret, et centum
ipsos in summa vitæ aspe-
ritate Deo servisset, ad eum
migravit anno salutis millesimo vigesimo septimo.
Ejus corpus quinquennio
postquam sepultum fuerat,
integrum repertum, Fabri-
ani in ecclesia sui ordinis
honorifice conditum est.

veneration, and his advice
induced many to leave the
world and its allurements, and
live in holy solitude. An
ardent desire for martyrdom
induced him to set out for
Pannonia ; but a malady,
which tormented him as often
as he went forward, and left
him when he turned back,
obliged him to abandon his
design.

He wrought many miracles
during his life, as also after
his death, and was endowed
with the gift of prophecy.
Like the patriarch Jacob, he
saw a ladder that reached from
earth to heaven, on which men,
clad in white robes, ascended
and descended. He inter-
preted this miraculous vision
as signifying the Camaldolese
monks, whose founder he was.
At length, having reached the
age of a hundred and twenty,
after having served his God
by a life of most austere
penance for a hundred years,
he went to his reward, in the
year of our Lord one thousand
and twenty-seven. His body
was found incorrupt after it had
been five years in the grave ;
and was then buried, with due
honour, in the church of his
Order at Fabriano.

Faithful servant and friend of God ! how different
was thy life from ours ! We love the world and
its distractions. We think we do wonders if we
give, each day, a passing thought to our Creator,
and make Him, at long intervals, the sole end of
some one of our occupations. Yet we know how
each hour is bringing us nearer to that moment,

when we must stand before the divine tribunal,
with our good and our evil works, to receive the
irrevocable sentence we shall have merited. Thou,
Romuald, didst not thus waste life away. It
seemed to thee as though there were but one
thought and one interest worth living for: how
best to serve thy God. Lest anything should
distract thee from this infinitely dear object, thou
didst flee into the desert. There, under the rule
of the great patriarch, St. Benedict, thou wagedst
war against the flesh and the devil; thy tears
washed away thy sins, though so light if compared
with what we have committed; thy soul, invigorated
by penance, was inflamed with the love of Jesus,
for whose sake thou wouldst fain have shed thy
blood. We love to recount these thy merits, for
they belong to us in virtue of that communion
which our Lord has so mercifully established
between saints and sinners. Assist us, therefore,
during the penitential season, which is soon to be
upon us. The justice of God will not despise our
feeble efforts, for He will see them beautified by
the union He allows them to have with such
glorious works as thine. When thou wast living in
the Eden of Camaldoli, thy amiable and sweet
charity for men was such, that all who came near
thee were filled with joy and consolation: what
may we not expect from thee, now that thou art face
to face with the God of love? Remember, too, the
Order thou hast founded; protect it, give it increase,
and make it ever, to those who become its children,
a ladder to lead them up to heaven.

FEBRUARY 8

SAINT JOHN OF MATHA, CONFESSOR

WE were celebrating, not many days ago, the memory of Peter Nolasco, who was inspired, by the holy Mother of God, to found an Order for the ransoming of Christian captives from the infidels: to-day, we have to honour the generous saint, to whom this sublime work was first revealed. He established, under the name of the most holy Trinity, a body of religious men, who bound themselves by vow to devote their energies, their privations, their liberty, nay, their very life, to the service of the poor slaves who were groaning under the Saracen yoke. The Order of the Trinitarians, and the Order of Mercy, though distinct, have the same end in view, and the result of their labours, during the six hundred years of their existence, has been the restoration to liberty and preservation from apostasy of upwards of a million slaves. John of Matha, assisted by his faithful co-operator, Felix of Valois (whose feast we shall keep at the close of the year), established the centre of his grand work at Meaux, in France. We are preparing for Lent, when one of our great duties will have to be that of charity towards our suffering brethren: what finer model could we have than John of Matha, and his whole Order, which was called into existence for no other object than that of delivering from the horrors of slavery brethren who were utter strangers to their deliverers, but were in suffering and in bondage. Can we imagine any almsgiving, let it be ever so generous, which can bear comparison with this devotedness of men, who bind themselves by their rule, not only to traverse every Christian land begging alms for the ransom of slaves, but to

change places with the poor captives, if their liberty cannot be otherwise obtained? Is it not, as far as human weakness permits, following to the very letter the example of the Son of God Himself, who came down from heaven that He might be our ransom and our Redeemer? We repeat it: with such models as these before us, we shall feel ourselves urged to follow the injunction we are shortly to receive from the Church, of exercising works of mercy towards our fellow-creatures, as being one of the essential elements of our lenten penance.

But it is time we should listen to the account given us by the liturgy of the virtues of this apostolic man, who has endeared himself, both to the Church and to mankind, by his heroism of charity.

Joannes de Matha, Ordinis sanctissimæ Trinitatis redemptionis captivorum institutor, Falcone in Provincia natus est, parentibus pietate et nobilitate conspicuis. Studiorum causa Aquas Sextias, mox Parisios profectus, confectoque theologiæ curriculo, magisterii lauream adeptus, doctrinæ, et virtutum splendore enituit : quibus motus Parisiensis Antistes, ad sacrum presbyteratus ordinem, præ humilitate reluctantem promovit, eo consilio, ut in ea civitate commorans, sapientia et moribus studiosæ juventuti præluceret. Cum autem in sacello ejusdem episcopi, ipso cum aliis adstante, primum Deo sacrum offerret, cœlesti favore meruit recreari. Nam angelus candida et fulgenti veste in-

John of Matha, the institutor of the Order of the most Holy Trinity for the ransom of captives, was born at Faucon, in Provence, of parents conspicuous for their nobility and virtue. He went through his studies first at Aix, and afterwards at Paris, where, after having completed his theological course, he received the degree of doctor. His eminent learning and virtues induced the bishop of Paris to promote him, in spite of his humble resistance, to the holy order of priesthood, that, during his sojourn in that city, he might be a bright example to young students by his talents and piety. While celebrating his first Mass in the bishop's chapel, in the presence of the prelate and several assistants, he was honoured by a signal favour

dutus, cui in pectore crux rubei et cærulei coloris assuta erat, brachiis cancellatis, et super duos captivos ad latera positos, Christianum unum, alterum Maurum, extensis apparuit. Qua visione in exstasim raptus, intellexit protinus vir Dei se ad redimendos ab infidelibus captivos destinari.

Quo vero maturius in re tanti momenti procederet, in solitudinem secessit ; ibique divino nutu factum est, ut Felicem Valesium in ipsa eremo jam multis annis degentem repererit. Cum quo inita societate, se per triennium in oratione et contemplatione, omniumque virtutum studio exercuit. Contigit autem, ut dum secum de rebus divinis prope fontem colloquerentur, cervus ad eos accesserit, crucem inter cornua gerens, rubei et cærulei coloris. Cumque Felix ob rei novitatem miraretur, narravit ei Joannes visionem in prima Missa habitam : et exinde ferventius orationi incumbentes, ter in somnis admoniti, Romam proficisci decreverunt, ut a summo Pontifice novi Ordinis pro redimendis captivis institutionem impetrarent. Electus fuerat eo tempore Innocentius tertius ; qui, illis benigne acceptis, dum secum de re proposita deliberaret, in festo sanctæ Agne-

from heaven. There appeared to him an angel clad in a white and brilliant robe ; he had on his breast a red and blue cross, and his arms were stretched out, crossed one above the other, over two captives, one a Christian, the other a Moor. Falling into an ecstasy at this sight, the man of God at once understood that he was called to ransom captives from the infidels.

But, that he might the more prudently carry out so important an undertaking, he withdrew into a solitude. There. by divine appointment, he met with Felix of Valois, who had been living many years in that same desert. They agreed to live together, and for three years did John devote himself to prayer and contemplation, and the practice of every virtue. It happened, that as they were one day seated near a fountain, conferring with each other on holy things, a stag came towards them, bearing a red and blue cross between his antlers. John, perceiving that Felix was surprised by so strange an occurrence, told him of the vision he had had in his first Mass. They gave themselves more fervently than ever to prayer, and having been thrice admonished in sleep, they resolved to set out for Rome, there to obtain permission from the sovereign Pontiff to found an Order for the ransom of captives. Innocent III., who had shortly before been elected Pope, re-

tis secundo, Laterani intra Missarum solemnia, ad sacræ Hostiæ elevationem, angelus ei candida veste, cruce bicolori, specie redimentis captivos apparuit. Quo viso, Pontifex institutum approbavit, et novum Ordinem sanctissimæ Trinitatis redemptionis captivorum vocari jussit, ejusque professoribus albas vestes, cum cruce rubei et cærulei coloris præbuit.

ceived them kindly, and while deliberating upon what they proposed, it happened that as he was celebrating Mass in the Lateran church, on the second feast of St. Agnes, there appeared to him, during the elevation of the sacred Host, an angel robed in white, bearing a two-coloured cross, and in the attitude of one that was rescuing captives. Whereupon, the Pontiff gave his approbation to the new institute, and would have it called the Order of the most Holy Trinity for the ransom of captives, bidding its members wear a white habit, with a red and blue cross.

Sic stabilito Ordine, sancti fundatores in Galliam redierunt; primoque cœnobio Cervi Frigidi in diœcesi Meldensi constructo, ad ejus regimen Felix remansit, et Joannes Romam cum aliquot sociis reversus est ubi Innocentius domum, ecclesiam, et hospitale sancti Thomæ de Formis in monte Cœlio eis donavit, cum multis redditibus, et possessionibus. Datis quoque litteris ad Miramolinum regem Marochii, opus redemptionis felici auspicio inchoatum fuit. Tum ad Hispanias, sub jugo Saracenorum, magna ex parte oppressas, Joannes profectus est, regumque, principum, atque aliorum fidelium animos ad captivorum et pauperum commiserationem commovit. Monasteria ædificavit, hospitalia erexit,

The Order being thus established, its holy founders returned to France, and erected their first monastery at Cerfroid, in the diocese of Meaux. Felix was left to govern it, and John returned, accompanied by a few of his brethren, to Rome. Innocent III. gave them the house, church, and hospital of St. Thomas *de Formis*, together with various revenues and possessions. He also gave them letters to Miramolin, king of Morocco, and thus was prosperously begun the work of ransom. John afterwards went into Spain, a great portion of which country was then under the Saracen yoke. He stirred up kings, princes, and others of the faithful, to compassion for the captives and the poor. He built monasteries, founded hospitals, and saved the souls of many

magnoque lucro animarum, plures captivos redemit. Romam tandem reversus, sanctisque operibus incumbens, assiduis laboribus attritus, et morbo confectus, ardentissimo Dei et proximi amore exæstuans, ad extremum devenit. Quare fratribus convocatis, eisque ad opus redemptionis cœlitus præmonstratum efficaciter cohortatis, obdormivit in Domino, sextodecimo kalendas Januarii, anno salutis millesimo ducentesimo decimo tertio, ejusque corpus in ipsa ecclesia Sancti Thomæ de Formis condigno honore tumulatum fuit.

captives by purchasing their freedom. Having, at length, returned to Rome, he spent his days in doing good. Worn out by incessant labour and sickness, and burning with a most ardent love of God and his neighbour, it was evident that his death was at hand. Wherefore, calling his brethren round him, he eloquently besought them to labour in the work of ransom, which heaven had entrusted to them, and then slept in the Lord, on the sixteenth of the Calends of January (December 17), in the year of grace 1213. His body was buried with the honour that was due to him in the same church of St. Thomas *de Formis*.

And now, generous-hearted saint, enjoy the fruits of thy devoted charity. Our blessed Redeemer recognizes thee as one of His most faithful imitators, and the whole court of heaven is witness of the recompense wherewith He loves to honour thy likeness to Himself. We must imitate thee; we must walk in thy footsteps; for we too hope to reach the same eternal resting-place. Fraternal charity will lead us to heaven, for the works it inspires us to do have the power of freeing the soul from sin, as our Lord assures us.[1] Thy charity was formed on the model of that which is in the heart of God, who loves our soul yet disdains not to provide for the wants of our body. Seeing so many souls in danger of apostasy, thou didst run to their aid, and men were taught to love a religion which can produce heroes of charity like thee. Thy heart bled at hearing of the bodily sufferings

[1] Ecclus. iii. 33.

of these captives, and thy hand broke the chains of
their galling slavery. Teach us the secret of ardent
charity. Is it possible that we can see a soul in
danger of being lost, and remain indifferent? Have
we forgotten the divine promise, told us by the
apostle: 'He that causeth a sinner to be converted
from the error of his way, shall save his soul from
death, and shall cover a multitude of his own sins'?[1]
Obtain for us, also, a tender compassion for such as
are in bodily suffering and poverty, that so we may
be generous in comforting them under these trials,
which are but too often an occasion of their blas-
pheming Providence. Dear friend and liberator of
slaves! pray, during this holy season, for those
who groan under the captivity of sin and Satan;
for those, especially, who, taken with the frenzy
of earthly pleasures, feel not the weight of their
chains, but sleep on peacefully through their
slavery. Ransom them by thy prayers, convert
them to the Lord their God, lead them back to the
land of freedom. Pray for France which was thy
country, and save her from infidelity. Protect the
venerable remnants of thy Order, that so it may
labour for the present wants of the Christian world,
since the object for which thou didst institute it
has ceased to require its devotedness.

FEBRUARY 9

SAINT APOLLONIA, VIRGIN AND MARTYR

THE holy virgin who this day claims the homage
of our devotion and praise, is offered to us by the
Church of Alexandria. Apollonia is a martyr of
Christ; her name is celebrated and honoured

[1] St. James v. 20.

throughout the whole world ; and she comes to us on this ninth day of February, to add her own example to that which we have so recently had from her sister saints, Agatha and Dorothy; like them, she bids us fight courageously for heaven. To her this present life was a thing of little value, and no sooner did she receive God's inspiration to sacrifice it, than she did what her would-be executioners intended doing : she threw herself into the flames prepared for her.   It is no unusual thing, nowadays, for men that are wearied of the trials, or afraid of the humiliations, of this world, to take away their own lives, and prefer suicide to the courageous performance of duty : but Apollonia's motive for hastening her death by a moment's anticipation, was to testify her horror of the apostasy that was proposed to her.   This is not the only instance we meet with, during times of persecution, of the holy Spirit's inspiring this lavish sacrifice to saintly virgins, who trembled for their faith or their virtue.   It is true, such examples are rare ; but they teach us, among other things, that our lives belong to God alone, and that we should be in readiness of mind to give them to Him, when and as He pleases to demand them of us.

There is one very striking circumstance in the martyrdom of St. Apollonia.   Her executioners, to punish the boldness wherewith she confessed our Lord Jesus Christ, beat out her teeth.   This has suggested to the faithful, when suffering the cruel pain of toothache, to have recourse to St. Apollonia; and their confidence is often rewarded, for God would have us seek the protection of His saints, not only in our spiritual, but even in our bodily sufferings and necessities.

The liturgy thus speaks the praises of our saint.

Apollonia, virgo Alexandrina, sub Decio imperato-	Apollonia was a virgin of Alexandria. In the persecu-

re, cum ingravescente jam
ætate ad idola sisteretur,
ut eis venerationem adhi-
beret, illis contemptis, Jesum Christum verum Deum
colendum esse prædicabat.
Quamobrem omnes ei con-
tusi sunt et evulsi dentes:
ac, nisi Christum detestata
deos coleret, accenso rogo
combusturos vivam minati
sunt impii carnifices. Quibus illa, se quamvis mor-
tem pro Jesu Christi fide
subituram respondit. Ita-
que comprehensa ut combu-
reretur, cum paulisper
quasi deliberans quid agen-
dum esset, stetisset, ex illorum manibus elapsa, alacris
in ignem sibi paratum, ma-
jori Spiritus sancti flamma
intus accensa, se injecit.
Unde brevi consumpto cor-
pore, purissimus spiritus in
cœlum ad sempiternam
martyrii coronam evolavit.

tion under the Emperor Decius,
when she was far advanced in
years, she was brought up
to trial, and ordered to pay
adoration to idols. She turned
from them with contempt, and
declared that worship ought to
be given to Jesus Christ, the
true God. Whereupon, the
impious executioners broke
and pulled out her teeth; then
lighting a pile of wood, they
threatened to burn her alive,
unless she would hate Christ,
and adore their gods. She replied, that she was ready to
suffer every kind of death for
the faith of Jesus Christ. Upon
this, they seized her, intending
to do as they said. She stood
for a moment, as though hesi-
tating what she should do;
then, snatching herself from
their hold, she suddenly threw
herself into the fire, for there
was within her the intenser
flame of the Holy Ghost. Her
body was soon consumed, and
her most pure soul took its
flight, and was graced with
the everlasting crown of martyrdom.

What energy was thine, Apollonia ! Thy persecutors threaten thee with fire; but far from fearing
it, thou art impatient for it, as though it were a
throne, and thou ambitious to be queen. Thy dread
of sin took away the fear of death, nor didst thou
wait for man to be thy executioner. This thy
courage surprises our cowardice; and yet, the burning pile into which thou didst throw thyself when
asked to apostatize, and which was a momentary
pain leading thy soul to eternal bliss, was nothing
when we compare it with that everlasting fire, to

which the sinner condemns himself almost every day of his life. He heeds not the flames of hell, and deems it no madness to purchase them at the price of some vile passing pleasure. And with all this, worldlings can be scandalized at the saints, and call them exaggerated, extravagant, imprudent; because they believed that there is but one thing necessary! Awaken in our hearts, Apollonia, the fear of sin ; for sin gnaws eternally the souls of them who die with its guilt upon them. If the fire, which had a charm for thee, seems to us the most frightful of tortures, let us turn our fear of suffering and death into a preservative against sin, which plunges men into that abyss, whence the smoke of their torments shall ascend for ever and ever,[1] as St. John tells us in his Revelation. Have pity on us, most brave and prudent martyr. Pray for sinners. Open their eyes to see the evils that threaten them. Procure for us the fear of God, that so we may merit His mercies, and may begin in good earnest to love Him.

FEBRUARY 10

SAINT SCHOLASTICA, VIRGIN

THE sister of the patriarch St. Benedict comes to us to-day, sweetly inviting us to follow her to heaven. Apollonia the martyr is succeeded by Scholastica, the fervent daughter of the cloister. Both of them are the brides of Jesus, both of them wear crowns, for both of them fought hard, and won the palm. Apollonia's battle was with cruel persecutors, and in those hard times when one had to die to conquer ; Scholastica's combat was the lifelong struggle, whose only truce is the soldier's

[1] Apoc. xiv. 11.

dying breath. The martyr and the nun are sisters now in the Heart of Him they both so bravely loved.

God, in His infinite wisdom, gave to St. Benedict a faithful co-operatrix, a sister of such angelic gentleness of character, that she would be a sort of counterpoise to the brother, whose vocation, as the legislator of monastic life, needed a certain dignity of grave and stern resolve. We continually meet with these contrasts in the lives of the saints; and they show us that there is a link, of which flesh and blood know nothing; a link which binds two souls together, gives them power, harmonizes their differences of character, and renders each complete. Thus it is in heaven with the several hierarchies of the angels; a mutual love, which is founded on God Himself, unites them together, and makes them live in the eternal happiness of the tenderest brotherly affection.

Scholastica's earthly pilgrimage was not a short one; and yet it has left us but the history of the dove, which told the brother, by its flight to heaven, that his sister had reached the eternal home before him. We have to thank St. Gregory the Great for even this much, which he tells us as a sequel to the holy dispute she had with Benedict, three days previous to her death. But how admirable is the portrait thus drawn in St. Gregory's best style! We seem to understand the whole character of Scholastica:—an earnest simplicity, and a child-like eagerness for what was worth desiring; an affectionate and unshaken confidence in God; a winning persuasiveness, where there was opposition to God's will, which, when it met such an opponent as Benedict, called on God to interpose, and gained its cause. The old poets tell us strange things about the swan, how sweetly it can sing when dying; how lovely must have been the last notes of the dove of

the Benedictine cloister, as she was soaring from
earth to heaven!

But how came Scholastica, the humble retiring
nun, by that energy, which could make her resist
the will of her brother, whom she revered as her
master and guide? What was it told her that her
prayer was not a rash one, and that what she asked
was a higher good than Benedict's unflinching
fidelity to the rule he had written, and which it was
his duty to teach by his own observance of it? Let
us hear St. Gregory's answer: 'It is not to be
wondered at, that the sister, who wished to prolong
her brother's stay, should have prevailed over him;
for, whereas St. John tells us that God is charity,
it happened, by a most just judgment, that she
that had the stronger love had the stronger power.'

Our season is appropriate for the beautiful lesson
taught us by St. Scholastica, fraternal charity.
Her example should excite us to the love of our
neighbour, that love for which God bids us labour,
now that we are intent on giving Him our undivided
service, and our complete conversion. The Easter
solemnity for which we are preparing, is to unite us
all in the grand banquet, where we are all to feast
on the one divine Victim of love. Let us have our
nuptial garment ready: for He that invites us
insists on our having union of heart when we dwell
in His house.[1]

The Church has inserted in her Office of this
feast the account given by St. Gregory of the last
interview between St. Scholastica and St. Benedict.
It is as follows:

Ex libro secundo Dialogo-rum sancti Gregorii Papæ.	From the second book of the Dialogues of St. Gregory, Pope.
Scholastica venerabilis patris Benedicti soror, omni-	Scholastica was the sister of the venerable father Bene-

[1] Ps. lxvii. 7.

potenti Domino ab ipso infantiæ tempore dedicata, ad eum semel per annum venire consueverat. Ad quam vir Dei non longe extra januam in possessione monasterii descendebat. Quadam vero die venit ex more, atque ad eam cum discipulis venerabilis ejus descendit frater ; qui totum diem in Dei laudibus, sacrisque colloquiis ducentes, incumbentibus jam noctis tenebris, simul acceperunt cibum. Cumque adhuc ad mensam sederent, et inter sacra colloquia tardior se hora protraheret, eadem sanctimonialis femina soror ejus eum rogavit dicens : Quæso te, ut ista nocte me non deseras, ut usque mane de cœlestis vitæ gaudiis loquamur. Cui ille respondit : Quid est quod loqueris, soror ? manere extra cellam nullatenus possum. Tanta vero erat cœli serenitas, ut nulla in aëre nubes appareret. Sanctimonialis autem femina, cum verba fratris negantis audivisset, insertas digitis manus super mensam posuit, et caput in manibus omnipotentem Dominum rogatura declinavit. Cumque levaret de mensa caput, tanta coruscationis et tonitrui virtus, tantaque inundatio pluviæ erupit, ut neque venerabilis Benedictus, neque fratres qui cum eo aderant, extra loci limen, quo consederant, pedem movere potuerint.

Sanctimonialis quippe fe-

dict. She had been consecrated to almighty God from her very infancy, and was accustomed to visit her brother once a year. The man of God came down to meet her at a house belonging to the monastery, not far from the gate. It was the day for the usual visit, and her venerable brother came down to her accompanied by some of his brethren. The whole day was spent in the praises of God and holy conversation, and at night - fall they took their repast together. While they were at table, and it grew late as they conferred with each other on sacred things, the holy nun thus spoke to her brother : ‘ I beseech thee, stay the night with me, and let us talk till morning on the joys of heaven.’ He replied : ‘ What is this thou sayest, sister ? On no account may I remain out of the monastery.’ The evening was so fair, that not a cloud could be seen in the sky. When, therefore, the holy nun heard her brother's refusal, she clasped her hands together, and resting them on the table, she hid her face in them, and made a prayer to the God of all power. As soon as she raised her head from the table, there came down so great a storm of thunder and lightning, and rain, that neither the venerable Benedict, nor the brethren who were with him, could set foot outside the place where they were sitting.

The holy virgin had shed a

mina caput in manibus
declinans, lacrymarum flu-
vium in mensam fuderat,
per quas serenitatem aëris
ad pluviam traxit. Nec paulo tardius post orationem
inundatio illa secuta est:
sed tanta fuit convenientia
orationis et inundationis,
ut de mensa caput jam cum
tonitruo levaret: quatenus
unum idemque esset mo-
mentum, et levare caput,
et pluviam deponere. Tunc
vir Dei inter coruscos, et
tonitruos, atque ingentis
pluviæ inundationem, vi-
dens se ad monasterium non
posse remeare, cœpit con-
queri contristatus, dicens:
Parcat tibi omnipotens Deus,
soror, quid est quod fecisti?
Cui illa respondit: Ecce rogavi te, et audire me no-
luisti; rogavi Deum meum,
et audivit me: modo ergo,
si potes, egredere, et me di-
missa, ad monasterium re-
cede. Ipse autem exire extra
tectum non valens, qui re-
manere sponte noluit, in loco
mansit invitus. Sicque factum est, ut totam noctem
pervigilem ducerent, atque
per sacra spiritalis vitæ colloquia, sese vicaria rela-
tione satiarent.

Cumque die altero eadem
venerabilis femina ad cellam propriam recessisset,
vir Dei ad monasterium re-
diit. Cum ecce post tri-
duum in cella consistens,
elevatis in aëra oculis, vidit
ejusdem sororis suæ ani-
mam de corpore egressam,
in columbæ specie cœli se-

flood of tears as she leaned
her head upon the table, and
the cloudless sky poured down
the wished-for rain The
prayer was said, the rain fell
in torrents; there was no interval; but so closely on each
other were prayer and rain,
that the storm came as she
raised her head. Then the man
of God, seeing that it was impossible to reach his monastery amidst all this lightning,
thunder, and rain, was sad,
and said complainingly: 'God
forgive thee, sister! What
hast thou done?' But she replied: 'I asked thee a favour,
and thou wouldst not hear
me; I asked it of my God,
and he granted it. Go now, if
thou canst, to the monastery,
and leave me here!' But it
was not in his power to stir
from the place; so that he
who would not stay willingly,
had to stay unwillingly, and
spend the whole night with his
sister, delighting each other
with their questions and answers about the secrets of
the spiritual life.

On the morrow, the holy
woman returned to her monastery, and the man of God to
his.   When lo! three days
after, he was in his cell; and
raising his eyes, he saw the
soul of his sister going up to
heaven, in the shape of a dove.
Full of joy at her being thus
glorified, he thanked his God

creta penetrare. Qui tantæ ejus gloriæ congaudens, omnipotenti Deo in hymnis et laudibus gratias reddidit, ejusque obitum fratribus denuntiavit. Quos etiam protinus misit, ut ejus corpus ad monasterium deferrent, atque in sepulchro, quod sibi ipsi paraverat, ponerent. Quo facto, contigit ut quorum mens una semper in Deo fuerat, eorum quoque corpora nec sepultura separaret.

in hymns of praise, and told the brethren of her death. He straightway bade them go and bring her body to the monastery ; which having done, he had it buried in the tomb he had prepared for himself. Thus it was that, as they had ever been one soul in God, their bodies were united in the same grave.

We select the following from the monastic Office for the feast of our saint :

RESPONSORIES AND ANTIPHONS

R. Alma Scholastica, sanctissimi patris Benedicti soror, * Ab ipso infantiæ tempore omnipotenti Domino dedicata, viam justitiæ non deseruit.
V. Laudate pueri Dominum, laudate nomen Domini. * Ab ipso infantiæ.

R. The venerable Scholastica, the sister of the most holy father Benedict, * Being from her very infancy consecrated to almighty God, never left the path of righteousness.
V. O ye children, praise the Lord; praise ye the name of the Lord. * Being.

R. Exemplo vitæ venerabilis, et verbo sanctæ prædicationis informari cupiens, ad eum semel in anno venire consueverat : * Et eam vir Dei doctrinis cœlestibus instruebat.
V. Beatus qui audit verba ipsius, et servat ea quæ scripta sunt. * Et eam.

R. Anxious to be trained by the saintly life and the words of his holy teaching, she used to visit him once a year : * And the man of God instructed her in heavenly doctrine.
V. Blessed is he that heareth Benedict's words, and keepeth those things which he hath written. * And.

R. Sancta virgo Scholastica, quasi hortus irriguus,* Gratiarum cœlestium jugi rore perfundebatur.

R. The holy virgin Scholastica, like a watered garden, * Was enriched with the ceaseless dew of heaven's graces.

V. Sicut fons aquarum, cujus non deficient aquæ. * Gratiarum.

V. Like a fountain of water whose stream shall not fail. * Was enriched.

R. Desiderium cordis ejus tribuit ei Dominus : * A quo obtinuit quod a fratre obtinere non potuit.
V. Bonus est Dominus omnibus sperantibus in eum, animæ quærenti illum. * A quo obtinuit.

R. The Lord granted her the desire of her heart : * And from him she obtained what her brother refused.
V. The Lord is good to all them that trust in him, to the soul that seeketh him. * And.

R. Moram faciente Sponso, ingemiscebat Scholastica dicens : * Quis dabit mihi pennas sicut columbæ, et volabo et requiescam ?
V. En dilectus meus loquitur mihi : Surge, amica mea, et veni. * Quis dabit.

R. The Bridegroom tarrying, Scholastica moaned, saying : * Who will give me the wings of a dove, and I will fly and take my rest ?
V. Lo ! my beloved speaketh unto me : Arise, my love, and come. * Who will.

R. In columbæ specie Scholasticæ anima visa est, fraterna mens lætata est hymnis et immensis laudibus : * Benedictus sit talis exitus, multo magis talis introitus !
V. Totus cœlesti gaudio perfusus remansit pater Benedictus. * Benedictus.

R. Scholastica's soul was seen in the form of a dove, and the brother's glad heart sang hymns and praises beyond measure : * Blessed be such a departure, and still more blessed such an entrance !
V. Father Benedict was filled with heavenly joy. * Blessed.

R. Anima Scholasticæ ex arca corporis instar columbæ egressa, portans ramum olivæ, signum pacis et gratiæ. * In cœlos evolavit.
V. Quæ cum non inveniret ubi requiesceret pes ejus. * In cœlos evolavit.

R. Scholastica's soul went forth, like a dove, from the ark of her body, bearing an olive branch, the sign of peace and grace. * She took her flight to heaven.
V. She found not whereon to rest her feet. * She took.

ANT. Exsultet omnium turba fidelium pro gloria virginis almæ Scholasticæ : lætentur præcipue catervæ

ANT. Let all the assembly of the faithful rejoice at the glory of the venerable virgin Scholastica ; but above the

virginum, celebrantes ejus solemnitatem, quæ fundens lacrymas, Dominum roga-vit, et ab eo plus potuit, quia plus amavit.

ANT. Hodie sacra virgo Scholastica in specie columbæ, ad æthera tota festiva perrexit: hodie cœlestis vitæ gaudiis cum fratre suo meretur perfrui in sempiternum.

rest, let the choirs of virgins be glad, as they celebrate the feast of her who besought her Lord with many tears, and had more power with him, because she had more love.

ANT. On this day, the holy virgin Scholastica took her flight, in the shape of a dove, all joyfully to heaven: on this day she is enjoying, with her brother, the eternal joys of the heavenly life she so well deserves.

The same Benedictine breviary gives us these two hymns for this feast:

HYMN

Te beata sponsa Christi,
Te columba virginum,
Siderum tollunt coloni
Laudibus, Scholastica:
Nostra te lætis salutant
Vocibus præcordia.

Sceptra mundi cum coro-nis
Docta quondam spernere,
Dogma fratris insecuta
Atque sanctæ regulæ,
Ex odore gratiarum,
Astra nosti quærere.

O potens virtus amoris !
O decus victoriæ !
Dum fluentis lacrymarum
Cogis imbres currere,
Ore Nursini parentis
Verba cœli suscipis.

Luce fulges expetita
In polorum vertice,
Clara flammis charitatis
Cum nitore gratiæ :

O Scholastica, blessed bride of Christ! O dove of the cloister! the citizens of heaven proclaim thy merits, and we, too, sing thy praises with joyful hymns and loving hearts.

Thou didst scorn the honours and glory of the world; thou didst follow the teaching of thy brother and his holy rule; and, rich in the fragrance of every grace, thou caredst for heaven alone.

Oh! what power was in thy love, and how glorious thy victory, when thy tears drew rain from the skies, and forced the patriarch of Nursia to tell thee what he knew of the land above!

And now thou shinest in heaven's longed-for light; thou art as a seraph in thy burning love, beautiful in thy

Juncta Sponso conquiescis
In decore gloriæ.

Nunc benigna pelle nubes
Cordibus fidelium,
Ut serena fronte splendens
Sol perennis luminis,
Sempiternæ claritatis
Impleat nos gaudiis.

Gloriam Patri canamus
Unicoque Filio ;
Par tributum proferamus
Inclyto Paraclito,
Nutibus cujus creantur,
Et reguntur sæcula.
   Amen.

bright grace ; and united with thy divine Spouse, thou art reposing in the splendour of glory.

Have pity on us the faithful of Christ, and drive from us the miseries which cloud our hearts ; that thus the Sun of light eternal may sweetly shine upon us, and fill us with the joys of his everlasting beams.

Let us sing a hymn of glory to the Father, and to his only Son ; let us give an equal homage of our praise to the blessed Paraclete : yea, to God, the Creator and Ruler of all, be glory without end.   Amen.

HYMN

Jam noctis umbræ concidunt,
Dies cupita nascitur,
Qua virgini Scholasticæ
Sponsus perennis jungitur.
   Brumæ recedit tædium,
Fugantur imbres nubibus,
Vernantque campi siderum
Æternitatis floribus.

   Amoris auctor evocat,
Dilecta pennas induit ;
Ardens ad oris oscula
Columba velox evolat.

   Quam pulchra gressum promoves,
O chara proles Principis !
Nursinus Abbas aspicit,
Grates rependit Numini.
   Amplexa Sponsi dextera,
Metit coronas debitas,

The shades of night are passing away : the longed-for day is come, when the virgin Scholastica is united to her God, her Spouse.

Winter's tedious gloom is over ; the rainy clouds are gone ; and the Spring of the starry land yields its eternal flowers.

The God of love bids his beloved come ; and she, taking the wings of a dove, flies swiftly to the embrace so ardently desired.

How beautiful is thy soaring, dear daughter of the King ! Thy brother, the abbot, sees thee, and fervently thanks his God.

Scholastica receives the embrace of her Spouse, and the

Immersa rivis gloriæ,
Deique pota gaudiis.

Te, Christe, flos conval-
lium,
Patremque cum Paraclito,
Cunctos per orbis cardines
Adoret omne sæculum.
Amen.

crown her works have won ;
inebriated with the torrent of
glory, she drinks of the joys
of her Lord.
May the world-wide crea-
tion of every age adore thee,
O Jesus, sweet Flower of the
vale, together with the Father
and the Holy Ghost. Amen.

Dear bride of the Lamb ! Innocent and simple
dove ! How rapid was thy flight to thy Jesus,
when called home from thine exile ! Thy brother's
eye followed thee for an instant, and then heaven
received thee, with a joyous welcome from the
choirs of the angels and saints. Thou art now at
the very source of that love, which here filled thy
soul, and gained thee everything thou askedst of
thy divine Master. Drink of this fount of life to
thy heart's eternal content. Satiate the ambition
taught thee by thy brother in his rule, when he
says that we must 'desire heaven with all the
might of our spirit.'[1] Feed on that sovereign
Beauty, who Himself feeds, as He tells us, among
the lilies.[2]

But forget not this lower world, which was to thee,
what it is to us, a place of trial for winning heavenly
honours. During thy sojourn here, thou wast the
dove in the clefts of the rock,[3] as the Canticle describes a soul like thine own ; there was nothing on
this earth which tempted thee to spread thy wings
in its pursuit, there was nothing worthy of the love
which God had put in thy heart. Timid before
men, and simple as innocence ever is, thou knewest
not that thou hadst wounded the Heart of the
Spouse.[4] Thy prayers were made to Him with all
the humility and confidence of a soul that had

[1] Ch. iv., Instrument 46.
[3] *Ibid.*, 14.
[2] Cant. ii. 16.
[4] *Ibid.*, iv. 9.

never been disloyal; and He granted thee thy petitions with the promptness of tender love : so that thy brother, the venerable saint, who was accustomed to see nature obedient to his command, was overcome by thee in that contest, wherein thy simplicity was more penetrating than his profound wisdom.

And who was it, O Scholastica, that gave thee this sublime knowledge, and made thee, on that day of thy last visit, wiser than the great patriarch, who was raised up in the Church to be the living rule of them that are called to perfection? It was the same God, who chose Benedict to be one of the pillars of the religious state, but who wished to show that a holy and pure and tender charity is dearer to Him than the most scrupulous fidelity to rules, which are only made for leading men to what thou hadst already attained. Benedict, himself such a lover of God, knew all this ; the subject so dear to thy heart was renewed, and brother and sister were soon lost in the contemplation of that infinite Beauty, who had just given such a proof that He would have thee neglect all else. Thou wast ripe for heaven, O Scholastica! Creatures could teach thee no more love of thy Creator; He would take thee to Himself. A few short hours more, and the divine Spouse would speak to thee those words of the ineffable Canticle, which the holy Spirit seems to have dictated for a soul like thine : ' Arise, make haste, my love, my dove, my beautiful one, and come! Show me thy face; let thy voice sound in mine ears; for thy voice is sweet, and comely is thy face.'[1]

Thou hast left us, O Scholastica! but do not forget us. Our souls have not the same beauty in the eyes of our God as thine, and yet they are called to the same heaven. It may be that years

[1] Cant. ii. 10, 14.

are still needed to fit them for the celestial abode, where we shall see thy grand glory. Thy prayer drew down a torrent of rain upon the earth; let it now be offered for us, and obtain for us tears of repentance. Thou couldst endure no conversation which had not eternity for its subject; give us a disgust for useless and dangerous talk, and a relish for hearing of God and of heaven. Thy heart had mastered the secret of fraternal charity, yea of that affectionate charity which is so well-pleasing to our Lord; soften our hearts to the love of our neighbour, banish from them all coldness and indifference, and make us love one another as God would have us love.

Dear dove of holy solitude! remember the tree, whose branches gave thee shelter here on earth. The Benedictine cloister venerates thee, not only as the sister, but also as the daughter of its sainted patriarch. Cast thine eye upon the remnants of that tree, which was once so vigorous in its beauty and its fruits, and under whose shadow the nations of the west found shelter for so many long ages. Alas! the hack and hew of impious persecutions have struck its root and branches. Every land of Europe, as well as our own, sits weeping over the ruins. And yet, root and branches, both must needs revive; for we know that it is the will of thy divine Spouse, O Scholastica, that the destinies of this venerable tree keep pace with those of the Church herself. Pray that its primitive vigour be soon restored; protect, with thy maternal care, the tender buds it is now giving forth; cover them from the storm; bless them; make them worthy of the confidence wherewith the Church deigns to honour them!

FEBRUARY 14

SAINT VALENTINE, PRIEST AND MARTYR

THE Church honours, on this fourteenth day of February, the memory of the holy priest Valentine, who suffered martyrdom towards the middle of the third century. The ravages of time have deprived us of the details of his life and sufferings; so that extremely little is known of our saint. This is the reason of there being no lessons of his life in the Roman liturgy. His name, however, has always been honoured throughout the whole Church, and it is our duty to revere him as one of our protectors during the season of Septuagesima. He is one of those many holy martyrs, who meet us at this period of our year, and encourage us to spare no sacrifice which can restore us to, or increase within us, the grace of God.

Pray, then, O holy martyr, for the faithful, who are so persevering in celebrating thy memory. The day of judgment will reveal to us all thy glorious merits: oh, intercede for us, that we may then be made thy companions at the right hand of the great Judge, and be united with thee eternally in heaven.

ANTIPHON

Iste sanctus pro lege Dei sui certavit usque ad mortem, et a verbis impiorum non timuit; fundatus enim erat supra firmam petram.

This saint fought even unto death, for the law of his God, and feared not the words of the wicked; for he was set upon a firm rock.

OREMUS.

Præsta, quæsumus, omnipotens Deus, ut qui beati Valentini martyris tui natalitia colimus, a cunctis ma-

LET US PRAY.

Grant, we beseech thee, O almighty God, that we who solemnize the festival of blessed Valentine, thy martyr, may, by

lis imminentibus ejus intercessione liberemur. Per
Christum Dominum no-
strum. Amen.

his intercession, be delivered
from all the evils that threaten
us. Through Christ our Lord.
Amen.

FEBRUARY 15

SAINTS FAUSTINUS AND JOVITA, MARTYRS

THE two brothers whom we are to honour to-day
suffered martyrdom in the beginning of the second
century, and their memory has ever been celebrated
in the Church. The glory of the great ones of this
world passes away, and men soon forget even their
very names. Historians have oftentimes a difficulty
in proving that such heroes ever existed, or, if they
did exist, that they flourished at such a period, or
achieved anything worth notice. Brescia, the
capital of one of the Italian provinces, can scarcely
mention the names of those who were its governors
or leading men in the second century; and yet here
are two of her citizens, whose names will be handed
down, with veneration and love, to the end of the
world, and the whole of Christendom is filled with
the praise of their glorious martyrdom. Glory,
then, to these sainted brothers, whose example so
eloquently preaches to us the great lesson of our
season, fidelity in God's service.

The sufferings which merited for them the crown
of immortality, are thus recorded in the liturgy:

Faustinus et Jovita fratres
nobiles Brixiani, in multis
Italiæ urbibus quo vincti,
sæviente Trajani persecu-
tione, ducebantur, acerbis-
sima supplicia perpessi,
fortes in christianæ fidei confessione perstiterunt. Nam
Brixiæ diu vinculis con-

The two brothers, Faustinus
and Jovita, were born of a
noble family in Brescia. During the persecution under
Trajan, they were led captives
through various cities of Italy,
in each of which they were
made to endure most cruel
sufferings, by reason of their

stricti, feris etiam objecti in ignemque conjecti, et a bestiis et flamma integri et incolumes servati sunt; inde vero iisdem catenis colligati Mediolanum venerunt, ubi eorum fides tentata exquisitissimis tormentis, tanquam igne aurum, in cruciatibus magis enituit. Postea Romam missi, ab Evaristo Pontifice confirmati, ibi quoque crudelissime torquentur. Denique perducti Neapolim, in ea etiam urbe varie cruciati, vinctis manibus pedibusque in mare demerguntur: unde per angelos mirabiliter erepti sunt. Quare multos et constantia in tormentis, et miraculorum virtute ad Christi fidem converterunt. Postremo reducti Brixiam, initio suscepti ab Adriano imperii, securi percussi, illustrem martyrii coronam acceperunt.

brave confession of the Christian faith, which nothing could induce them to deny. At Brescia, they were for a long time confined in chains; then were exposed to wild beasts, and cast into fire, from neither of which tortures did they receive hurt or harm. From Brescia they were sent to Milan, still fettered with the same chains: and there their faith was put to the test of every torment that cruelty could devise; but, like gold that is tried by fire, their faith shone the brighter by these sufferings. After this, they were sent to Rome, where they received encouragement from Pope Evaristus; but there, also, they were made to endure most cruel pains. At length they were taken to Naples, and there, again, put to sundry tortures; after which, they were bound hand and foot, and cast into the sea; but were miraculously delivered by angels. Many persons were converted to the true faith, by seeing their courage in suffering, and the miracles they wrought. Finally, they were led back to Brescia, at the commencement of the reign of the Emperor Adrian; there they were beheaded, and received the crown of a glorious martyrdom.

When we compare our trials with yours, noble martyrs of Christ, and our combats with those that you had to fight, how grateful ought we to be to our Lord for having so mercifully taken our weakness into account! Should we have been able to endure the tortures, wherewith you had to purchase heaven, we that are so easily led to break the law of God, so tardy in our conversion, so weak in faith and charity? And yet, we are made for that same heaven which you now possess. God holds out a crown to us also, and we are not at liberty to refuse it. Rouse up our courage, brave martyrs! Obtain for us a spirit of resistance against the world and our evil inclinations; that thus we may confess our Lord Jesus Christ, not only with our lips, but with our works too, and testify, by our conduct, that we are Christians.

FEBRUARY 18

SAINT SIMEON, BISHOP AND MARTYR

How venerable our saint of to-day, with his hundred and twenty years, and his episcopal dignity, and his martyr-crown! He succeeded the apostle St. James in the see of Jerusalem; he had known Jesus, and had been His disciple; he was related to Jesus, for he was of the house of David; his father was Cleophas, and his mother that Mary, whom the tie of kindred united so closely to the blessed Mother of God that she has been called her sister. What grand titles these of Simeon who comes with all our other martyrs of Septuagesima, to inspirit us to penance! Such a veteran, who had been a contemporary of the Saviour of the world, and was a pastor who could repeat to his flock the very lessons Jesus had given him, could never rejoin his divine Master save by the path of martyr-dom, and that martyrdom must be the cross. Like Jesus, then, he dies on a cross; and his death, which happened in the year 106, closes the first period of the Christian era, or, as it is called, the

apostolic age.   Let us honour this venerable pontiff,
whose name awakens within us the recollection of all
that is dear to our faith.   Let us ask him to extend
to us that fatherly love, which nursed the Church
of Jerusalem for so many long years.   He will
bless us from that throne which he won by the
cross, and will obtain for us the grace we so much
need, the grace of conversion.

The following is the lesson given on St. Simeon:

Simeon, filius Cleophæ, post Jacobum proximus Hierosolymis ordinatus episcopus, Trajano imperatore, apud Atticum consularem est accusatus, quod christianus esset, et Christi propinquus.   Comprehendebantur enim omnes eo tempore, quicumque ex genere David orti essent.   Quare multis cruciatus tormentis, eodem passionis genere, quod Salvator noster subierat, afficitur, mirantibus omnibus, quod homo ætate confectus (erat enim centum et viginti annorum) acerbissimos crucis dolores fortiter constanterque pateretur.

Simeon, the son of Cleophas, was ordained bishop of Jerusalem, and was Saint James's immediate successor in that see.   In the reign of the Emperor Trajan, he was accused to the Consul Atticus of being a Christian and a relation of Christ; for, at this time, all they that were of the house of David were seized.   After having endured various tortures, Simeon was put to death by the same punishment which our Saviour suffered, and all the beholders were filled with astonishment to see how, at his age (for he was a hundred and twenty years old), he could go through the intense pains of crucifixion, without showing a sign of fear or irresolution.

Receive, most venerable saint, the humble
homage of our devotion.   What is all human glory
compared with thine?   Thou wast of the family of
Christ; thy teaching was that which His divine
lips had given thee; thy charity for men was
formed on the model of His sacred Heart; and thy
death was the closest representation of His.   We
may not claim the honour thou hadst, of calling
ourselves brothers of the Lord Jesus: but pray for

us, that we may be of those of whom He thus
speaks : 'Whosoever shall do the will of My Father
that is in heaven, he is My brother, and sister, and
mother.'[1] We have not, like thee, received the
doctrine of salvation from the very lips of Jesus ;
but we have it in all its purity, by means of holy
tradition, of which thou art one of the earliest links ;
oh, obtain for us a docility to this word of God,
and pardon for our past disobedience. We have
not to be nailed to a cross, as thou wast ; but the
world is thickly set with trials, to which our Lord
Himself gives the name of the cross. These we
must bear with patience, if we would have part with
Jesus in His glory. Pray for us, O Simeon, that
henceforth we may be more faithful ; that we may
never more become rebels to our duty ; and that
we may repair the faults we have so often committed
by infringing the law of our God.

February 22

SAINT PETER'S CHAIR AT ANTIOCH

We are called upon, a second time, to honour
St. Peter's chair : first, it was his pontificate in
Rome ; to-day, it is his episcopate at Antioch.
The seven years spent by the prince of the apostles
in the second of these cities, were the grandest glory
she ever had ; and they are too important a portion
of the life of St. Peter to be passed by without
being noticed in the Christian cycle.

Three years had elapsed since our Lord's Ascension. The Church had already been made fruitful
by martyrdom, and from Jerusalem she had spread
into distant countries. Antioch, the first of the
cities of Asia, had received the Gospel ; and it was

[1] St. Matt. xii. 50.

there that those who professed the faith of Jesus
were first called Christians. Jerusalem was doomed
to destruction for having not only refused to
acknowledge, but even crucified, the Messias : it
was time for Peter, in whom resided the supreme
power, to deprive the faithless city of the honour
she had heretofore enjoyed, of possessing within her
walls the chair of the apostolate. It was towards
the Gentiles that the Holy Spirit drove those clouds,
which were shown to Isaias as the symbol of the
holy apostles.[1] Accordingly, it is in Antioch, the
third capital of the Roman Empire, that Peter
first places the august throne, on which, as vice-
gerent of Christ, he presides over the universal
Church.

But the progress of the apostles was so rapid ; the
conquests they made, in spite of every opposition,
were so extensive, that the vicar of Christ was inspired to leave Antioch, after he had honoured it
with the chair during the space of seven years.
Alexandria, the second city of the empire, is also to
be made a see of Peter ; and Rome, the capital of
the world, awaits the grand privilege for which
God has long been preparing her. Onwards, then,
does the prince advance, bearing with him the
destinies of the Church ; where he fixes his last
abode, and where he dies, there will he have his
successor in his sublime dignity of vicar of Christ.
He leaves Antioch, making one of his disciples,
Evodius, its bishop. Evodius succeeds Peter as
bishop of Antioch ; but that see is not to inherit the
headship of the Church, which goes whithersoever
Peter goes. He sends Mark, another of his disciples,
to take possession, in his name, of Alexandria ; and
this Church he would have to be the second in the
world, and though he has not ruled it in person, he
raises it above that of Antioch. This done, he

[1] Isa. lx. 8.

goes to Rome, where he permanently establishes that chair, on which he will live, and teach, and rule, in his successors, to the end of time.

And here we have the origin of the three great patriarchal sees, which were the object of so much veneration in the early ages : the first is Rome, invested with all the prerogatives of the prince of the apostles, which, when dying, he transmitted to her ; the second is Alexandria, which owes her pre-eminence to Peter's adopting her as his second see ; the third is Antioch, whither he repaired in person, when he left Jerusalem to bring to the Gentiles the grace of adoption. If, therefore, Antioch is below Alexandria in rank, Alexandria never enjoyed the honour granted to Antioch, of having been governed, in person, by him whom Christ appointed to be the supreme pastor of His Church. Nothing, then, could be more just, than that Antioch should be honoured, as having, for seven years, had the privilege of being the centre of Christendom ; and this is the object of to-day's feast.

The children of the Church have a right to feel a special interest in every solemnity that is kept in memory of St. Peter. The father's feast is a feast for the whole family ; for to him it owes its very life. If there be but one fold, it is because there is but one Shepherd. Let us, then, honour Peter's divine prerogative, to which Christianity owes its preservation ; and let us often reflect upon the obligations we are under to the apostolic see. On the feast of the chair at Rome, we saw how faith is taught, and maintained, and propagated by the mother-Church, which has inherited the promises made to Peter. To-day, let us consider the apostolic see as the sole source of the legitimate power, whereby mankind is ruled and governed in all that concerns eternal salvation.

Our Saviour said to Peter: 'To thee will I give the keys of the kingdom of heaven,'[1] that is to say, of the Church. He said to him on another occasion : 'Feed My lambs, feed My sheep.'[2] So that Peter is prince; for, in the language of the sacred Scriptures, keys denote princely power: he is also pastor, and universal pastor ; for the whole flock is comprised under the two terms, lambs and sheep. And yet there are other pastors in every portion of the Christian world. The bishops, whom the Holy Ghost hath placed to rule the Church of God,[3] govern, in his name, their respective dioceses, and are also pastors. How comes it that the keys, which were given to Peter, are found in other hands than his? The Catholic Church explains the difficulty to us by her tradition. She says to us, by Tertullian: 'Christ gave the keys to Peter, and through him to the Church.'[4] By St. Optatus of Milevis: 'For the sake of unity, Peter was made the first among all the apostles, and he alone received the keys, that he might give them to the rest.'[5] By St. Gregory of Nyssa: 'It is through Peter that Christ gave to bishops the keys of their heavenly prerogative.'[6] By St. Leo the Great: 'If our Lord willed that there should be something common to Peter and the rest of the princes of His Church, it was only on this condition, that whatsoever He gave to the rest, He gave it to them through Peter.'[7]

Yes, the episcopate is most sacred, for it comes from the hands of Jesus Christ through Peter and his successors. Such is the unanimous teaching of Catholic tradition, which is in keeping with the language used by the Roman pontiffs, from the

[1] St. Matt. xvi. 19.
[2] St. John xxi. 15, 17.
[3] Acts xx. 28.
[4] *Scorpiac.*, cap. x.
[5] *Contra Parmenianum*, lib. vii.
[6] *Opp.*, tom. iii.
[7] *In Anniv. assumpt.*, serm. iv.

earliest ages, who have always spoken of the dignity
of bishops as consisting in their being 'called to a
share of their own solicitude.' Hence St. Cyprian
does not hesitate to say that 'our Saviour, wishing
to establish the episcopal dignity and constitute
His Church, says to Peter: "To thee will I give the
keys of the kingdom of heaven"; and here we
have both the institution of bishops, and the con-
stitution of the Church.'[1] This same doctrine is
clearly stated in a letter written to Pope St. Sym-
machus by St. Cesarius of Arles, who lived in the
fifth century: 'The episcopate flows from the
blessed apostle Peter; and consequently, it belongs
to your holiness to prescribe to the several Churches
the rules which they are to follow.'[2] This fundamental principle, which St. Leo the Great has so
ably and eloquently developed (as we have seen on
the feast of the chair at Rome, January 18), this
principle, which is taught us by universal tradition,
is laid down with all possible precision in the
magnificent letters, still extant, of Pope St. Innocent I., who preceded St. Leo by several years.
Thus he writes to the Council of Carthage, that
'the episcopate, with all its authority, emanates
from the apostolic see';[3] to the Council of Milevis,
that 'bishops must look upon Peter as the source
whence both their name and their dignity are
derived';[4] to St. Victricius, bishop of Rouen, that
'the apostolate and the episcopate both owe their
origin to Peter.'[5]

Controversy is not our object. All we aim at by
giving these quotations from the fathers on the
prerogatives of Peter's chair, is to excite the faithful to be devoted to it and venerate it. This we
have endeavoured to do, by showing them that this
chair is the source of the spiritual authority, which,

---

[1] Epist. xxxiii.   [2] *Ibid.*, x.   [3] *Ibid.*, xxix.
[4] *Ibid.*, xxx.   [5] *Ibid.*, ii.

in its several degrees, rules and sanctifies them. All spiritual authority comes from Peter; all comes from the bishop of Rome, in whom Peter will continue to govern the Church to the end of time. Jesus Christ is the founder of the episcopate; it is the Holy Ghost who establishes bishops to rule the Church; but the mission and the institution, which assign the pastor his flock, and the flock its pastor, these are given by Jesus Christ and the Holy Ghost through the ministry of Peter and his successors.

How sacred, how divine, is this authority of the keys, which is first given by heaven itself to the Roman Pontiff; then is delegated by him to the prelates of the Church; and thus guides and blesses the whole Christian world! The apostolic see has varied its mode of transmitting such an authority according to the circumstances of the several ages; but the one source of the whole power was always the same, the chair of Peter. We have already seen how, at the commencement, there were three chairs: Rome, Alexandria, and Antioch; and all three were sources of the canonical institution of the bishops of their respective provinces; but they were all three chairs of Peter, for they were founded by him that they might preside over their patriarchates, as St. Leo,[1] St. Gelasius,[2] and St. Gregory the Great,[3] expressly teach. But of these three chairs, the Pontiff of Rome had his authority and his institution from heaven; whereas, the two other patriarchs could not exercise their rights, until they were recognized and confirmed by him who was Peter's successor, as vicar of Christ. Later on, two other sees were added to these first three: but it was only by the consent of the Roman Pontiff that

---

[1] Epist. civ. *Ad Anatolium.*

[2] *Concil. Romanum.* Labb., tom. **iv.**

[3] Epist. *Ad Eulogium.*

Constantinople and Jerusalem obtained such an honour. Let us notice, too, the difference there is between the accidental honours conferred on four of these Churches, and the divine prerogative of the Church of Rome. By God's permission, the sees of Alexandria, Antioch, Constantinople, and Jerusalem, were defiled by heresy; they became chairs of pestilence;[1] and having corrupted the faith they received from Rome, they could not transmit to others the mission they themselves had forfeited. Sad indeed was the ruin of such pillars as these! Peter's hand had placed them in the Church. They had merited the love and veneration of men; but they fell; and their fall gave one more proof of the solidity of that edifice, which Christ Himself had built on Peter. The unity of the Church was made more visible. Obliged by the treachery of her own favoured children to deprive them of the privileges they had received from her, Rome was, more evidently than ever, the sole source of pastoral power.

We, then, both priests and people, have a right to know whence our pastors have received their power. From whose hand have they received the keys? If their mission come from the apostolic see, let us honour and obey them, for they are sent to us by Jesus Christ, who has invested them, through Peter, with His own authority. If they claim our obedience without having been sent by the bishop of Rome, we must refuse to receive them, for they are not acknowledged by Christ as His ministers. The holy anointing may have conferred on them the sacred character of the episcopate: it matters not; they must be as aliens to us, for they have not been sent, they are not pastors.

Thus it is that the divine Founder of the Church,

[1] Ps. i. 1.

who willed that she should be a city seated on a mountain,[1] gave her visibility; it was an essential requisite; for since all were called to enter her pale, all must be able to see her. But He was not satisfied with this.. He moreover willed that the spiritual power exercised by her pastors should come from a visible source, so that the faithful might have a sure means of verifying the claims of those who were to guide them in His name. Our Lord (we say it reverently) owed this to us; for, on the last day, He will not receive us as His children, unless we shall have been members of His Church, and have lived in union with Him by the ministry of pastors lawfully constituted. Honour, then, and submission to Jesus in His vicar! honour and submission to the vicar of Christ in the pastors he sends!

As a tribute of our devotion to the prince of the apostles, let us recite, in his honour, the following hymn, composed by St. Peter Damian:

HYMN

Senatus apostolici
Princeps, et præco Domini:
Pastor prime fidelium,
Custodi gregem creditum.

O prince of the apostolic senate! Herald of our Lord! First pastor of the faithful! watch over the flock entrusted to thee.

Per pascua virentia,
Nos verbi fruge recrea:
Refectas oves prævius
Caulis infer cœlestibus.

Lead us through verdant pastures, feeding us with the nourishment of the word; and lead us, thus fed, into the heavenly fold, whither thou hast already gone.

Supernæ claves januæ
Tibi, Petre, sunt traditæ:
Tuisque patent legibus
Terrena cum cœlestibus.

To thee, Peter, have been delivered the keys of heaven's gate; and all things, both in heaven and on earth, acknowledge thy authority.

---

[1] St. Matt. v. 14.

Tu petram veræ fidei, Tu basim ædificii Fundas, in qua Catholica Fixa surgit Ecclesia.	'Tis thou that choosest the city where is to be established the rock of the true faith, the foundation of the building, on which the Catholic Church stands immovable.
Umbra tua, dum graderis, Fit medicina languidis ; Textrinis usa vestium Sprevit Tabitha feretrum.	Thy shadow, as thou passest by, heals the sick ; and Tabitha, that made garments for the poor, was raised to life at thy bidding.
Catena vinctum gemina, Virtus solvit angelica ; Veste sumpta cum caligis, Patescunt fores carceris.	Bound with two chains, thou wast set free by an angel's power ; he bids thee put on thy garments and thy sandals, and lo ! the prison-door is opened.
Sit Patri laus ingenito, Sit decus Unigenito, Sit utriusque parili Majestas summa Flamini. Amen.	To the Father unbegotten, and to the only-begotten Son, and to the coequal Spirit of them both, be praise and kingly highest power. Amen.

Glory be to thee, O prince of the apostles, on thy chair at Antioch, where thou didst for seven years preside over the universal Church ! How magnificent are the stations of thy apostolate ! Jerusalem, Antioch, Alexandria (by thy disciple Mark), and Rome, these are the cities which have been honoured by thy august chair. After Rome, Antioch was the longest graced by its presence : justly, therefore, do we honour this Church, which was thus made, by thee, the mother and mistress of all other Churches. Alas ! all her beauty has now left her ; her faith is dead ; she is in bondage to the Saracen. Save her, take her once more under thy power, bring her into allegiance to Rome, where thou hast thy chair, not for seven years only, but for all ages. The gates of hell have let loose the fury of every tempest upon thee, firm rock of the Church ! and we ourselves have seen the immortal chair banished for a time from Rome. The words of St. Ambrose then came to our minds : ' Where Peter is, there is the Church.' How could we despair? Did we not know, that it was God's inspiration which made thee choose Rome for the fixed resting-place of thy throne? No human will can put asunder what God has united; the bishop of Rome must ever be the vicar of Christ; and the vicar of Christ, let sacrilege and persecution banish him as they will, must ever be the bishop of Rome. Holy apostle! calm the wildness of the tempest, lest the weak should take scandal. Beseech our Lord that He permit not the residence of thy successor to be disturbed in that holy city, which has been chosen for so great an honour. If it be that her inhabitants deserve punishment for their offences, spare them for the sake of their brethren of the rest of the world; and pray for them, that their faith may once more become what it was when St. Paul praised it, and said to them: ' Your faith is spoken of in the whole world.'[1]

FEBRUARY 23

SAINT PETER DAMIAN, CARDINAL AND DOCTOR OF THE CHURCH

IT is the feast of the austere reformer of the eleventh century, Peter Damian, the precursor of the holy pontiff Gregory VII., that we are called upon to celebrate to-day. To him is due in part that glorious regeneration, which was effected at that troubled period when judgment had to begin at the house of God.[2] The life he had led under the monastic rule had fitted him for the great contest. So zealously did he withstand the disorders and abuses of his times, that we may attribute to him, at least in great measure, the ardent faith of

---

[1] Rom. i. 8.   [2] 1 St. Peter iv. 17.

the two centuries which followed the scandals of
the tenth. The Church ranks him among her
doctors, on account of his admirable writings : and
his penitential life ought to excite us to be fervent
in the work we have in hand, the work of our
conversion.

The following lessons, read by the Church, on
this feast, give us a sketch of our saint's life :

Petrus, Ravennæ honestis
parentibus natus, adhuc
lactens a matre numerosæ
prolis pertæsa abjicitur, sed
domesticæ mulieris opera
semivivus exceptus ac re-
creatus, genitrici ad humanitatis sensum revocatæ
redditur. Utroque orbatus
parente, tamquam vile man-
cipium sub aspera fratris
tutela duram servitutem
exercuit. Religionis in Deum
ac pietatis erga patrem egre-
gium tunc specimen dedit;
inventum siquidem forte
nummum non propriæ ine-
diæ sublevandæ, sed sacer-
doti qui divinum sacrifi-
cium ad illius expiationem
offerret, erogavit. A Damia-
no fratre, a quo, uti fertur,
cognomentum accepit, be-
nigne receptus, ejus cura
litteris eruditur, in quibus
brevi tantum profecit, ut
magistris admirationi esset.
Quum autem liberalibus
scientiis floreret et nomine,
eas cum laude docuit. In-
terim ut corpus rationi sub-
deret, sub mollibus vestibus
cilicium adhibuit, jejuniis,
vigiliis, et orationibus soler-
ter insistens. Calente ju-
venta, dum carnis stimulis

Peter was born at Ravenna,
of respectable parents. His
mother, wearied with the care
of a large family, abandoned
him when a babe ; but one of
her female servants found him
in an almost dying state, and
took care of him, until such
time as the mother, repenting
of her unnatural conduct, con-
sented to treat him as her
child. After the death of his
parents, one of his brothers, a
most harsh man, took him as
a servant, or more truly as his
slave. It was about this period
of his life that he performed
an action, which evinced his
virtue and his filial piety.
He happened to find a sum
of money : but instead of
using it for his own wants, he
gave it to a priest, begging
him to offer up the holy sacrifice for the repose of his
father's soul. Another of his
brothers, called Damian (after
whom, it is said, he was named),
had him educated ; and so
rapid and so great was the
progress he made in his studies,
that he was the admiration
of his masters. He became
such a proficient in the liberal
sciences, that he was made to
teach them in the public

acriter urgeretur, insultan-
tium libidinum faces rigen-
tibus fluvii mersus aquis
noctu extinguebat : tum
venerabilia quæque loca
obire, totumque psalterium
recitare consueverat. Ope
assidua pauperes levabat,
quibus frequenter pastis
convivio, propriis ipse manibus ministrabat.

Perficiendæ magis vitæ
causa, in Avellanensi Eugu-
binæ diœcesis cœnobio,
Ordini monachorum sanc-
tæ Crucis Fontis Avellanæ,
a beato Ludulpho sancti
Romualdi discipulo fundato,
nomen dedit. Non ita multo
post in monasterium Pom-
posianum, mox in cœnobium
Sancti Vincentii Petræ Per-
tusæ ab abbate suo missus,
utrumque asceterium verbo
sacro, præclaris institutioni-
bus et moribus excoluit.
Ad suos revocatus, post
præsidis obitum Avellani-
tarum familiæ præficitur,
quam novis variis in locis
extructis domiciliis, et sanctissimis institutis ita auxit,
ut alter ejus Ordinis parens

schools, which he did with
great success. During all this
time, it was his study to bring
his body into subjection to the
spirit; and to this end, he wore
a hair-shirt under an outwardly comfortable dress, and
practised frequent fasting,
watching, and prayer. Being
in the very ardour of youth,
and being cruelly buffeted by
the sting of the flesh, he, during the night, would go and
plunge himself into a frozen
pool of water, that he might
quench the impure flame
which tormented him; or he
would make pilgrimages to
holy sanctuaries, and recite
the entire psalter. His charities
to the poor were unceasing,
and when he provided them
with a meal, which was frequently, he would wait upon
them himself.

Out of a desire to lead a still
more perfect life, he became
a religious in the monastery
of Avellino, in the diocese of
Gubbio, of the Order of the
monks of holy Cross of Fon-
tavellana, which was founded
by the blessed Ludolphus, a
disciple of St. Romuald. Being
sent by his abbot, not very
long after, first to the monastery of Pomposia, and then to
that of Saint Vincent of Pietra-
Pertusa, he edified both
houses by his preaching, admirable teaching, and holy
life. At the death of the
abbot of Avellino, he was recalled to that monastery, and
was made its superior. The
institute was so benefited by
his government, not only by

ac præcipuum ornamentum jure sit habitus. Salutarem Petri sollicitudinem alia quoque diversi instituti cœnobia, canonicorum conventus, et populi sunt experti. Urbinati diœcesi non uno nomine profuit: Theuzoni episcopo in causa gravissima assedit, ipsumque in recte administrando episcopatu consilio et opera juvit. Divinorum contemplatione, corporis macerationibus, cæterisque spectatæ sanctimoniæ exemplis excelluit. His motus Stephanus Nonus, Pontifex maximus, eum licet invitum et reluctantem sanctæ Romanæ Ecclesiæ Cardinalem creavit, et Ostiensem episcopum. Quas Petrus dignitates splendidissimis virtutibus, et consentaneis episcopali ministerio operibus gessit.

Difficillimo tempore Romanæ Ecclesiæ summisque Pontificibus doctrina, legationibus, aliisque susceptis laboribus mirifice adfuit. Adversus Nicolaitarum et Simoniacam hæreses ad mortem usque strenue decertavit. Hujusmodi depulsis malis, Mediolanensem Ecclesiæ Romanæ conciliavit. Benedicto, et Cadaloo, falsis Pontificibus,

the new monasteries which he founded in several places, but also by the very saintly regulations he drew up, that he was justly looked upon as the second founder of the Order, and its brightest ornament. Houses of other Orders, canons, yea, entire congregations of the faithful, were benefited by Peter's enlightened zeal. He was a benefactor, in more ways than one, to the diocese of Urbino: he aided the bishop Theuzo in a most important suit, and assisted him, both by advice and work, in the right administration of his diocese. His spirit of holy contemplation, his corporal austerities, and the saintly tenor of his whole conduct, gained for him so high a reputation, that Pope Stephen IX., in spite of Peter's extreme reluctance, created him Cardinal of the holy Roman Church and bishop of Ostia. The saint proved himself worthy of these honours by the exercise of the most eminent virtues, and by the faithful discharge of his episcopal office.

It would be impossible to describe the services he rendered to the Church and the sovereign Pontiffs, during those most trying times, by his learning, his prudence as legate, and his untiring zeal. His life was one continued struggle against simony, and the heresy of the Nicolaites. He purged the Church of Milan of these disorders, and brought her into subjection

fortiter restitit. Henricum quartum Germaniæ regem ab iniquo uxoris divortio deterruit : Ravennates ad debita Romano Pontifici obsequia revocatos sacris restituit. Canonicos Veliternos ad sanctioris vitæ leges composuit. In provincia præsertim Urbinate vix ulla fuit episcopalis ecclesia, de qua Petrus non sit bene meritus : Eugubinam, quam aliquando creditam habuit, multis levavit incommodis : alias alibi, quando oportuit, perinde curavit, ac si suæ essent tutelæ commissæ. Cardinalatu, et episcopali dignitate depositis, nihil de pristina juvandi proximos sedulitate remisit. Jejunium sextæ feriæ in honorem sanctæ crucis Jesu Christi, horarias beatæ Dei Genitricis preces, ejusque die Sabbato cultum propagavit. Inferendæ quoque sibi verberationis morem ad patratorum scelerum expiationem provexit. Demum sanctitate, doctrina, miraculis, et præclare actis illustris, dum e Ravennate legatione rediret, Faventiæ octavo Kalendas Martii migravit ad Christum. Ejus corpus ibidem apud Cistercienses multis miraculis clarum frequenti populorum veneratione colitur. Ipsum Faventini non semel in præsenti discrimine propitium experti, patronum apud Deum delegerunt : Leo vero duodecimus, Pontifex maximus, Officium Missamque in ejus

to the Holy See. He courageously resisted the anti-popes Benedict and Cadalous. He deterred Henry IV., king of Germany, from an unjust divorce of his wife. He restored the people of Ravenna to their allegiance to the Roman Pontiff, and absolved them from interdict. He reformed the abuses which had crept in among the canons of Velletri. There was scarcely a single cathedral church in the province of Urbino that had not experienced the beneficial effects of Peter's holy zeal : thus, that of Gubbio, which was for some time under his care, was relieved by him of many evils ; and other churches, that needed his help, found him as earnest for their welfare as though he were their own bishop. When he obtained permission to resign his dignity as Cardinal and his bishopric, he relented nothing of his former charity, but was equally ready in doing good to all. He was instrumental in propagating many devout practices ; among these may be mentioned, fasting on Fridays in honour of the holy cross ; the reciting the Little Office of our Lady ; the keeping the Saturday as a day especially devoted to Mary ; the taking of the discipline in expiation of past sins. At length, after a life which had edified the world by holiness, learning, miracles, and glorious works, on his return from Ravenna, whither he had been sent as legate,

honorem tamquam confes- soris pontificis, quæ aliqui- bus in diœcesibus, atque in Ordine Camaldulensium jam celebrabantur, ex Sacrorum Rituum Congregationis con- sulto, addita doctoris quali- tate, ad universam extendit Ecclesiam.

he slept in Christ, on the eighth of the Calends of March (February 23), at Faënza. His relics, which are kept in the Cistercian church of that town, are devoutly honoured by the faithful, and many miracles are wrought at the holy shrine. The inhabitants of Faënza have chosen him as the patron of their city, having several times experi- enced his protection when threatened by danger. His Mass and Office, which were kept under the rite of con- fessor and bishop, had been long observed in several dio- ceses, and by the Camaldolese Order; but they were extend- ed to the whole Church by a decree of the Congregation of Sacred Rites, which was approved by Pope Leo XII., who also added to the name of the saint the title of Doctor.

Thy soul was inflamed by the zeal of God's house, O Peter! God gave thee to His Church in those sad times when the wickedness of the world had robbed her of well-nigh all her beauty. Thou hadst the spirit of an Elias within thee, and it gave thee courage to waken the servants of the Lord: they had slept, and while they were asleep, the enemy came, and the field was oversown with tares.[1] Then did better days dawn for the bride of Christ; the promises made by our Lord were fulfilled; but who was the friend of the bridegroom?[2] Who was the chief instrument used by God to bring back to His house its ancient beauty? A saint who bore the glorious name of Peter Damian! In those days, the

[1] St. Matt. xiii. 25.   [2] St. John iii. 29.

sanctuary was degraded by secular interference.
The princes of the earth said: 'Let us possess the
sanctuary of God for an inheritance.'[1]   The Church,
which God intended to be free, was but a slave, in
the power of the rulers of this world; and the vices,
which are inherent to human weakness, defiled the
temple.   But God had pity on the bride of Christ, and
for her deliverance He would use human agency:
He chose thee, Peter, as His principal co-operator
in restoring order.   Thy example and thy labours
prepared the way for Gregory, the faithful and
dauntless Hildebrand, into whose hands the keys
were no sooner placed, than the work of regeneration was completed.   Thou hast fought the good
fight; thou art now in thy rest; but thy love of
the Church, and thy power to help, are greater than
ever.   Watch, then, over her interests.   Obtain for
her pastors that apostolic energy and courage,
which alone can cope with enemies so determined
as hers are.   Obtain for her priests the holiness
which God demands from them that are the salt of
the earth.[2]   Obtain for the faithful the respect and
obedience they owe to those who direct them in the
path of salvation.   Thou wast not only the apostle,
thou wast moreover the model, of penance in the
midst of a corrupt age; pray for us, that we may
be eager to atone for our sins by works of mortification.   Excite within our souls the remembrance
of the sufferings of our Redeemer, that so His
Passion may urge us to repentance and hope.
Increase our confidence in Mary, the refuge of
sinners, and make us, like thyself, full of filial
affection towards her, and of zeal that she may be
honoured and loved by those who are around us.

[1] Ps. lxxxii. 13.   [2] St. Matt. v. 13.

FEBRUARY 24

SAINT MATHIAS, APOSTLE

*In leap-year, the feast of St. Mathias is kept on
February 25*

AN apostle of Jesus Christ, St. Mathias, is one of
the blessed choir which the Church would have
us honour during the season of Septuagesima.
Mathias was one of the first to follow our Saviour ;
and he was an eye-witness of all His divine actions
up to the very day of the Ascension. He was one
of the seventy-two disciples ; but our Lord had not
conferred upon him the dignity of an apostle.
And yet, he was to have this great glory, for it was
of him that David spoke, when he prophesied that
another should take the bishopric[1] left vacant by
the apostasy of Judas the traitor. In the interval
between Jesus' Ascension and the descent of the
Holy Ghost, the apostolic college had to complete
the mystic number fixed by our Lord Himself, so
that there might be the twelve on that solemn day,
when the Church, filled with the Holy Ghost, was
to manifest herself to the Synagogue. The lot fell
on Mathias ;[2] he shared with his brother-apostles
the persecution in Jerusalem, and, when the time
came for the ambassadors of Christ to separate, he
set out for the countries allotted to him. Tradition
tells us that these were Cappadocia and the provinces bordering on the Caspian Sea.

The virtues, labours, and sufferings of St. Mathias
have not been handed down to us : this explains the
lack of proper lessons on his life, such as we have
for the feasts of the rest of the apostles. Clement
of Alexandria records in his writings several sayings

---

[1] Ps. cviii. 8; Acts i. 20.   [2] Acts i. 26.

of our holy apostle.   One of these is so very appropriate to the spirit of the present season, that we consider it a duty to quote it.   'It behoves us to combat the flesh, and make use of it, without pampering it by unlawful gratifications.   As to the soul, we must develop her power by faith and knowledge.'[1]   How profound is the teaching contained in these few words!   Sin has deranged the order which the Creator had established.   It gave the outward man such a tendency to grovel in things which degrade him, that the only means left us for the restoration of the image and likeness of God unto which we were created, is the forcible subjection of the body to the spirit.   But the spirit itself, that is, the soul, was also impaired by original sin, and her inclinations were made prone to evil; what is to be her protection?   Faith and knowledge. Faith humbles her, and then exalts and rewards her; and the reward is knowledge.   Here we have a summary of what the Church teaches us during the two seasons of Septuagesima and Lent.   Let us thank the holy apostle, on this his feast, for leaving us such a lesson of spiritual wisdom and fortitude. The same traditions, which give us some slight information regarding the holy life of St. Mathias, tell us that his apostolic labours were rewarded with the palm of martyrdom.   Let us celebrate his triumph by the following stanzas, which are taken from the Menæa of the Greeks.

HYMN

(Die IX. Augusti)

Mathia beate, Eden spiritualis, fontibus divinis ut fluvius inundans scaturisti, et mysticis terram irrigasti rivulis, et illam fructiferam

O blessed Mathias! spiritual Eden! thou didst flow, like a full river, from the divine fountain; thou didst water the earth with thy mystic

---

[1] *Stromat.*, lib. iii., cap. iv.

reddidisti ; ideo deprecare Dominum ut animabus nostris pacem concedat et magnam misericordiam.

Mathia apostole, divinum replevisti collegium ex quo Judas ceciderat, et divinis sapientum sermonum tuorum fulgoribus tenebras fugasti idololatriæ, virtute Spiritus sancti ; et nunc deprecare Dominum, ut mentibus nostris concedat pacem et magnam misericordiam.

Ut multifrugiferum palmitem te Vitis vera direxit, colentem uvam quæ salutis vinum profundit ; illud bibentes qui detinebantur ignorantia, erroris temulentiam rejecerunt.

Erroris axes, iniquitatis currus, verbi Dei ipse currus factus, gloriose, in perpetuum contrivisti ; et idololatras, et columnas et templa radicitus divina virtute destruxisti, Trinitatis vero templa ædificasti clamantia : Populi, superexaltate Christum in sæcula.

Ut spirituale cœlum apparuisti, enarrans gloriam unigeniti Filii Dei ineffabilem, Mathia venerabilis ; fulgur Spiritus sancti, piscator errantium, lumen divinæ claritatis, mysteriorum doctor ; ipsum in lætitia unanimi voce celebremus.

rivulets, and make it fruitful. Do thou, therefore, beseech the Lord that he grant peace and much mercy to our souls.

O apostle Mathias ! thou didst complete the sacred college, from which Judas had fallen ; and by the power of the Holy Ghost, thou didst put to flight the darkness of idolatry by the admirable lightnings of thy wise words. Do thou now beseech the Lord that he grant peace and much mercy to our souls.

He that is the true Vine sent thee, a fruitful branch, bearing the grapes that give out the wine of salvation. When they drank it that before were slaves to ignorance, they turned from the drunkenness of error.

Being made, O glorious Mathias, the chariot of God's word, thou didst break for ever the wheels of error, and the chariots of iniquity. By the divine power, thou didst defeat the idolaters, and destroy the pillars and the temples ; but thou didst build up to the Trinity other temples, which echoed with these words : All ye people, praise Christ above all for ever !

O venerable Mathias ! thou, like a spiritual firmament, didst proclaim the glory of the only-begotten Son of God. Let us with one glad voice celebrate the praise of this apostle, who was effulgent with the Holy Ghost ; he was the fisher of them that had gone astray, the light that reflected the divine brightness, the teacher of the mysteries.

Amicum te dixit Salvator, suis obtemperantem mandatis, beate apostole, et ipsius regni hæredem, et cum ipso sedentem in throno in futura terribili die, sapientissime Mathia, collegii duodenarii apostolorum complementum.

Crucis velamine instructus, vitæ sæviens mare trajecisti, beate, et ad requiei portum pervenisti; et nunc lætus cum apostolorum choro judicum altissimo adstare digneris, Dominum pro nobis exorans misericordem.

Lampas aureo nitore fulgens, Spiritus sancti ellychnio ardens, lingua tua apparuit, extranea comburens dogmata, extraneum extinguens ignem, o sapiens Mathia, lucem fulgurans sedentibus in tenebris ignorantiæ.

O blessed apostle! the Saviour called thee his friend, because thou didst keep his commandments. Thou art heir to his kingdom, and thou art to sit with him, on a throne, at the last terrible day, O most wise Mathias, who didst complete the number of the apostolic college.

Guided by the sail of the cross, thou, O blessed one, didst pass over the troubled sea of life, and didst reach the haven of rest. Do thou now vouchsafe to join the glad choir of the apostles, and beseech the infinite Judge, that he would show himself a merciful Lord unto us.

Thy tongue was a bright lamp of glittering gold, burning with the flame of the Holy Ghost. Thou didst consume all strange doctrines, thou didst quench all fire that was profane, and to them that sat in the darkness of ignorance, thou, O wise Mathias, didst show a brilliant light.

FEBRUARY 26

SAINT MARGARET OF CORTONA, PENITENT

CLOSE to the faithful virgins, who form the court of Jesus, there stand those holy women, whose repentance has merited for them a prominent place in the calendar of the Church. They are the bright trophies of God's mercy. They expiated their sins by a life of penance; the tears of their compunction

wiped away their guilt; He that is purity itself has
found them worthy of His love, and, when pharisees
affect to be shocked at His allowing them to be near
Him, He warmly defends them. Foremost among
these is Mary Magdalene, to whom much was forgiven, because she loved much;[1] but there are two
on the list of penitent saints whose names shine
most brightly on the calendar of this portion of the
year; and who were, like Mary Magdalene, ardent
in their love of the divine Master, whom they had
once offended: these are, Mary of Egypt, and
Margaret of Cortona. It is the second of these who
to-day tells us the consoling truth that if sin
separate us from God, penance has the power not
only of disarming His anger, but of forming
between God and the sinner that ineffable bond of
love, which the apostle alludes to when he says:
'Where sin hath abounded, grace hath more
abounded.'[2]

Let us study the virtues of the illustrious penitent
of the thirteenth century. They are thus summed
up by the Church in the lessons of to-day's feast.

Margarita, a loco dormitionis Cortonensis appellata,
Laviani in Tuscia ortum
habuit. Primis adolescentiæ
suæ annis mundi volupta-
tibus capta, in Montis Poli-
tiani civitate, vanam et
lubricam vitam duxit: sed
cum amasium ab hostibus
fœde transfossum, indicio
canis in fovea sub strue lignorum tumulatum fortuito
reperisset, illico facta est
manus Domini super eam,
quæ magno culparum su-
arum mœrore tacta, exiit
foras et flevit amare. Itaque

Margaret of Cortona (so
called from the town where
she died), was born at Alviano
in Tuscany. In her early
youth she was a slave to the
pleasures of this world, and
led a vain and sinful life in
the city of Montepulciano.
Her attention was, one day,
attracted by a dog, which
seemed to wish her to follow
it. She did so, and it led her to
a pile of wood which covered
a large hole. Looking in,
she saw the body of her lover,
whose enemies had murdered
him, and thrown his mangled

---

[1] St. Luke vii. 47. [2] Rom. v. 20.

Lavianum reversa, crine detonso, neglecto capite, pullaque veste contecta, erroribus suis mundique illecebris nuntium misit; inque ædibus Deo sacris fune ad collum alligato, humi procumbens, ab omnibus quos antea moribus suis palam offenderat, veniam exoravit. Mox Cortonam profecta, in cinere et cilicio ab se læsam Dei majestatem placare studuit, donec post triennale virtutum experimentum a Fratribus Minoribus spiritualis vitæ ducibus, Tertii Ordinis habitum impetravit. Uberes exinde lacrymæ ei familiares fuerunt, atque ima suspiria tanta animi contritione ducta, ut diu elinguis consisteret. Lectulus nuda humus, cervical lapis aut lignum porrexit; atque ita noctes insomnes in cœlestium meditatione trahere consuevit, nullum amplius pravum desiderium perpessa, dum bonus spiritus promptior infirmam carnem ad subeundos labores erigebat.

corpse into that place. She suddenly felt that the hand of God was upon her, and being overwhelmed with intense sorrow for her sins, she went forth, and wept bitterly. She returned to Alviano, cut off her hair, laid aside her trinkets, and, putting on a dark-coloured dress, she abandoned her evil ways and the pleasures of the world. She was to be found in the churches, with a rope tied round her neck, prostrate on the ground, and imploring pardon of all whom she had scandalized by her past life. She shortly afterwards set out for Cortona, and there, in sackcloth and ashes, she sought how she might appease the divine anger. For three years did she try herself in the practice of every virtue: and at the end of that time, she obtained permission from the Friars Minors (under whose spiritual guidance she had placed herself), to receive the habit of the Third Order. From that time forward, her tears were almost incessant; and the sighs which deep contrition wrung from her heart were such as to leave her speechless for hours. Her bed was the naked ground; and her pillow, a stone or piece of wood: so that she frequently passed whole nights in heavenly contemplation. Evil desires no longer tormented her, for her fervent spirit was so prompt, that the weak flesh was made to labour and obey.

A dæmone insidiis, funestisque conatibus lacessita, mulier fortis hostem, ex verbis detectum, semel atque iterum invicta repulit. Ad eludendum vanæ gloriæ lenocinium, quo a malo spiritu petebatur, præteritos mores suos per vicos et plateas alta voce accusare non destitit, omni supplicio se ream inclamans; nec, nisi a confessario deterrita, in speciosam faciem, olim impuri amoris causam, sævire abstinuit, ægre ferens suam formam longa carnis maceratione non aboleri. Quibus aliisque magnæ pœnitentiæ argumentis, suorum criminum labe expiata, atque ita de se triumphatrix, ut sensus plane omnes a mundi illecebris custodiret, digna facta est quæ sæpe Domini consuetudine frueretur. Ejusdem quoque Christi et Virginis Matris dolorum, quod ipsa ardenter expetierat, particeps facta, cunctis sensibus destituta, et vere mortua interdum visa est. Ad eam proinde veluti ad perfectionis magistram, ex dissitis etiam regionibus plurimi conveniebant : ipsa vero cœlesti, quo erat perfusa, lumine, cordium secreta, conscientias hominum, imo et peccata in remotis licet partibus Deum offendentium cum dolore et lacrymis detegens, summaque in Deum et proximum charitate fervens, ingentem animarum fructum operata

The devil spared neither snares nor violent assaults, whereby to lead her from her holy purpose : but she, like a strong woman, detected him by his words, and drove him from her. This wicked spirit having tempted her to vain glory, she went into the streets, and cried out with a loud voice, that she had been a great sinner, and deserved the worst of punishments. It was obedience to her confessor that alone prevented her from disfiguring her features, which had been the cause of much sin : for the long and severe penance she had imposed on herself had not impaired her beauty. By these and such like exercises of a mortified life, she cleansed her soul from the stains of her sins, and gained such a victory over herself, that the allurements of the world had not the slightest effect upon her, and our Lord rewarded her by frequently visiting her. She also received the grace she so ardently desired, of being allowed to have a share in the sufferings of Jesus and Mary; so much so, indeed, that, at times, she lay perfectly unconscious, as though she were really dead. All this made her be looked up to as a guide in the path of perfection, and persons would come to her, even from distant countries, in order to seek her counsel. By the heavenly light granted her, she could read the hearts and consciences of others, and could see the sins committed

est. Ægris ad se venienti-
bus salutem, obsessis a
dæmone liberationem im-
petravit. Puerum defun-
ctum, lugente matre, ad vitam reduxit. Imminentes
bellorum tumultus assiduis
orationibus sedavit. Denique summæ pietatis operi-
bus vivos et mortuos sibi
demeruit.

Tot sanctis operibus occu-
pata, de rigore, quo assidue corpus suum exercebat,
nihil remisit, neque a studio
cœlestia meditandi se avelli
passa est, in utroque vitæ
genere plane admiranda,
utramque sororem, Magda-
lenam et Martham, refe-
rens. Tandem pro se Do-
minum orans, ut ex hac valle
lacrymarum sursum in cœ-
lestem patriam evocaretur,
exaudita est oratio ejus, die
atque hora dormitionis ei
patefactis. Meritis itaque
et laboribus plena, ac cœlestibus donis cumulata, cœpit
corporis viribus destitui,
perque dies decem et septem
nullo cibo, sed divinis tantum colloquiis refecta est :
tum sanctissimis Ecclesiæ
sacramentis rite susceptis,
vultu hilari, atque oculis in
cœlum conversis, octavo Ka-

against our Lord in various
parts of the world, for which
she would offer up, in atonement, her own sorrow and
tears. Great indeed was the
good she effected by the ardent
charity she bore to God and
her neighbour. She healed
the sick who came to her,
and drove out the devil from
such as were possessed. A
mother besought her, with
many tears, to restore her
child to life, which she did.
Her prayers more than once
averted war, when on the
point of being declared. In
a word, both the living and
the dead experienced the effects of her unbounded
charity.

While engaged in these
manifold holy works, she relented not in the severity of
her bodily mortifications, or
in her contemplation of heavenly things. The two lives
of Mary and Martha were
admirably blended together
in her; and rich in the merits
of each, she besought our Lord
to take her from this vale of
tears, and give her to enter
the heavenly country. Her
prayer was heard, and the day
and the hour of her death were
revealed to her. Laden with
meritorious works and divine
favours, her bodily strength
began to fail. For the last
seventeen days of her life her
only food was that of conversation with her Creator. At
length, after receiving the
most holy Sacraments of the
Church, with a face beaming
with joy, and her eyes raised

lendas Martias, anno ætatis quinquagesimo, suæ conversionis vigesimo tertio, humanæ vero salutis millesimo ducentesimo nonagesimo septimo, felix migravit ad Sponsum. Corpus in hanc usque diem vegetum, incorruptum, illæsum et suaviter olens, summa religione colitur in ecclesia fratrum Minorum, quæ jam ab eadem Margarita appellatur. Miraculis continuo floruit; quibus permoti Romani Pontifices, ad augendum ejus cultum plurima liberaliter indulserunt. Benedictus vero decimus tertius, in festo Pentecostes, die sexta decima Maii) anni millesimi septingentesimi vigesimi octavi, solemnem ejus canonizationem religiosissime celebravit.

up to heaven, her happy soul fled to its divine Spouse, on the eighth of the Calends of March (February 22), in the fiftieth year of her age, the twenty-third of her conversion, and in the year of our Lord one thousand two hundred and ninety-seven. Her body, which, even to this day, is fresh, incorrupt, and unaltered, and sheds a sweet fragrance, is devoutly honoured in the church (called after her *Saint Margaret's*) belonging to the Friars Minor. The many miracles which have been wrought at her shrine, have induced the Sovereign Pontiffs to promote devotion to Saint Margaret by the grant of many spiritual favours. She was canonized, with great solemnity, by Pope Benedict XIII., on May 16, which was the feast of Pentecost, in the year 1728.

If the angels of God rejoiced on the day of thy conversion, when Margaret the sinner became the heroic and saintly penitent, what a grand feast must they have kept when thy soul left this world, and they led thee to the eternal nuptials with the Lamb! Thou art one of the brightest trophies of divine mercy, and when we think of the saint of Cortona, our hearts glow with hope. We are sinners; we have deserved hell; and yet, when we hear thy name, heaven and mercy seem so near to us, yea, even to us. Margaret of Cortona! see how like we are to thee in thy weakness, and thy wanderings from the fold; but thou forcest us to hope that we may, like thee, be converted, do penance, and reach heaven at last. The instrument

of thy conversion was death; and is not death busy
enough around us? The sight of that corpse taught
thee, and with an irresistible eloquence, that sin is
madness, for it exposes the soul to fall into infinite
misery; how comes it that death is almost daily
telling us that life is uncertain, and that our eternal
lot may be decided at any hour, and yet the lesson
is so lost upon us? We are hard-hearted sinners,
and we need thy prayers, O fervent lover of Jesus!
The Church will soon preach to us the great
Memento; she will tell us that we are but dust, and
into dust must speedily return. Oh that this
warning might detach us from the world and ourselves, and man us to the resolution of penance,
that port of salvation for them that have suffered
shipwreck! Oh that it might excite within us the
desire of returning to that God, who knows not how
to resist the poor soul who comes to Him after all
her sins, throws herself into the bosom of His
mercy, and asks Him to forgive! Thy example
proves that we may hope for every grace. Pray for
us, and exercise in our favour that maternal charity
which filled thy heart even when thou wast living
here below.

MARCH 4

SAINT CASIMIR, CONFESSOR

It is from a court that we are to be taught to-day
the most heroic virtues. Casimir is a prince; he is
surrounded by all the allurements of youth and
luxury; and yet he passes through the snares of
the world with as much safety and prudence, as
though he were an angel in human form. His
example shows us what we may do. The world has
not smiled on us as it did on Casimir; but how

20

much we have loved it! If we have gone so far as to make it our idol, we must now break what we have adored, and give our service to the sovereign Lord, who alone has a right to it. When we read the lives of the saints, and find that persons who were in the ordinary walks of life practised extraordinary virtues, we are inclined to think that they were not exposed to great temptations, or that the misfortunes they met with in the world made them give themselves up unreservedly to God's service. Such interpretations of the actions of the saints are shallow and false, for they ignore this great fact, that there is no condition or state, however humble, in which man has not to combat the evil inclinations of his heart, and that corrupt nature alone is strong enough to lead him to sin. But in such a saint as Casimir we have no difficulty in recognizing that all his Christian energy was from God, and not from any natural source ; and we rightly conclude that we, who have the same good God, may well hope that this season of spiritual regeneration will change and better us. Casimir preferred death to sin. But is not every Christian bound to be thus minded every hour of the day? And yet, such is the infatuation produced by the pleasures or advantages of this present life, that we every day see men plunging themselves into sin, which is the death of the soul; and this, not for the sake of saving the life of the body, but for a vile and transient gratification, which is oftentimes contrary to their temporal interests. What stronger proof could there be than this, of the sad effects produced in us by original sin? The examples of the saints are given us as a light to lead us in the right path, let us follow it, and we shall be saved. Besides, we have a powerful aid in their merits and intercession: let us take courage at the thought that these friends of God have a most affectionate compassion for us their brethren, who are surrounded by so many and great dangers.

The Church, in her liturgy, thus describes to us the virtues of our young prince:

Casimirus, patre Casimiro, matre Elisabetha Austriaca, Poloniæ regibus ortus, a pueritia sub optimis magistris pietate, et bonis artibus instructus, juveniles artus aspero domabat cilicio, et assiduis extenuabat jejuniis. Regii spreta lecti mollitie, dura cubabat humo, et clam intempesta nocte, præ foribus templorum pronus in terra divinam exorabat clementiam. In Christi contemplanda Passione assiduus, Missarum solemniis adeo erecta in Deum mente solebat adesse, ut extra se rapi videretur.

Casimir was the son of Casimir, king of Poland, and of Elizabeth of Austria. He was put, when quite a boy, under the care of the best masters, who trained him to piety and learning. He brought his body into subjection by wearing a hair-shirt, and by frequent fasting. He could not endure the soft bed which is given to kings, but lay on the hard floor, and during the night, he used privately to steal from his room, and go to the church, where, prostrate before the door, he besought God to have mercy on him. The Passion of Christ was his favourite subject of meditation; and when he assisted at Mass, his mind was so fixed on God, that he seemed to be in one long ecstasy.

Catholicam promovere fidem summopere studuit, et Ruthenorum schisma abolere; quapropter Casimirum patrem induxit, ut legem ferret, ne schismatici nova templa construerent, nec vetera collabentia restaurarent. Erga pauperes et calamitatibus oppressos beneficus et misericors, patris et defensoris egenorum nomen obtinuit. Virginitatem, quam ab incunabulis servavit illæsam, sub extremo vitæ termino fortiter asseruit, dum gravi pressus infirmitate.

Great was his zeal for the propagation of the Catholic faith, and the suppression of the Russian schism. He persuaded the king, his father, to pass a law, forbidding the schismatics to build new churches, or to repair those which had fallen to ruin. Such was his charity for the poor and all sufferers, that he went under the name of the father and defender of the poor. During his last illness, he nobly evinced his love of purity, which virtue he had maintained unsullied during

mori potius, quam castitatis jacturam ex medicorum consilio subire, constanter decrevit.

Consummatus in brevi, virtutibus et meritis plenus, prænuntiato mortis die, inter sacerdotum, et religiosorum choros spiritum Deo reddidit, anno ætatis vigesimo quinto. Corpus Vilnam delatum multis claret miraculis. Etenim, præterquam quod puella defuncta vitam, cæci visum, claudi gressum, et varii infirmi sanitatem ad ejus sepulchrum recuperarunt. Lithuanis exiguo numero ad potentissimi hostis insperatam irruptionem trepidantibus in aere apparens, insignem tribuit victoriam. Quibus permotus Leo decimus, eumdem sanctorum catalogo adscripsit.

his whole life. He was suffering a cruel malady; but he courageously preferred to die, rather than suffer the loss of his chastity, whereby his physicians advised him to purchase his cure.

Being made perfect in a short space of time, and rich in virtue and merit, after having foretold the day of his death, he breathed forth his soul into the hands of his God, in the twenty-fifth year of his age, surrounded by priests and religious. His body was taken to Vilna, and was honoured by many miracles. A young girl was raised to life at his shrine; the blind recovered their sight, the lame the use of their limbs, and the sick their health. He appeared to a small army of Lithuanians, who were unexpectedly attacked by a large force, and gave them the victory over the enemy. Leo X. was induced by all these miracles to enrol him among the saints.

Enjoy thy well-earned rest in heaven, O Casimir! Neither the world with all its riches, nor the court with all its pleasures, could distract thy heart from the eternal joys it alone coveted and loved. Thy life was short, but full of merit. The remembrance of heaven made thee forget the earth. God yielded to the impatience of thy desire to be with Him, and took thee speedily from among men. Thy life, though most innocent, was one of penance, for knowing the evil tendencies of corrupt nature, thou hadst a dread of a life of comfort. When shall we be made to understand that penance is a debt we owe to God, a debt of expiation for the sins we have

committed against Him? Thou didst prefer death
to sin; obtain for us a fear of sin, that greatest of
all the evils that can befall us, because it is an evil
which strikes at God Himself. Pray for us during
this holy season, which is intended as a preparation
for penance; impress our minds with the truths
now put before us. The Christian world is honouring thee to-day; repay its homage by thy blessing.
Poland, thy fatherland, once the bulwark of the
Church, which kept back the invasion of schism,
heresy, and infidelity, beseeches thy prayers.

MARCH 6

SAINTS PERPETUA AND FELICITAS, MARTYRS

THE real feast of these two illustrious heroines of
the faith is to-morrow, which is the anniversary
of their martyrdom and triumph; but the memory
of the angel of the schools, St. Thomas of Aquin,
shines so brightly on the seventh of March, that
it almost eclipses the two glorious stars of Africa.
In consequence of this, the Holy See orders the
Church to anticipate their feast, and keep it to-day.
We at once offer to the Christian reader the
glorious spectacle of which Carthage was the scene
in the year 203. Nothing could give us a clearer
idea of that spirit of the Gospel, according to
which we are now studying to conform our whole
life. Here are two women, two mothers; God
asks great sacrifices from them; He asks them

to give Him their lives, nay, more than their lives; and they obey with that simplicity and devotedness which made Abraham merit to be the father of believers.

Their two names, as St. Augustine observes, are a presage of what awaits them in heaven: a perpetual felicity. The example they set of Christian fortitude, is, of itself, a victory, which secures to the true faith a triumph in the land of Africa. St. Cyprian will soon follow them, with his bold and eloquent appeal to the African Christians, inspiring them to die for their faith: but his words, grand as they are, are less touching than the few pages written by the hand of the brave Perpetua, who, though only twenty-two years of age, relates, with all the self-possession of an angel, the trials she had to go through for God; and when she has to hurry off to the amphitheatre, she puts her pen into another's hand, bidding him go on where she leaves off, and write the rest of the battle. As we read these charming pages, we seem to be in the company of the martyrs; the power of divine grace, which could produce such heroism amidst a people demoralized by paganism, appears so great that even we grow courageous; and the very fact that the instruments employed by God for the destruction of the pagan world were frequently women, induces us to say with St. John Chrysostom: 'I feel an indescribable pleasure in reading the "Acts of the Martyrs"; but when the martyr is a woman, my enthusiasm is doubled. For the frailer the instrument, the greater is the grace, the brighter the trophy, the grander the victory; and this, not because of her weakness, but because the devil is conquered by her, by whom he once conquered us. He conquered by a woman, and now a woman conquers him. She that was once his weapon, is now his destroyer, brave and invincible. That first one sinned, and died; this one died that she might not sin. Eve was flushed by a lying promise, and broke the law of God; our heroine disdained to live, when her living was to depend on her breaking her faith to Him who was her dearest Lord. What excuse, after this, for men, if they be soft and cowards? Can they hope for pardon, when women fought the holy battle with such brave, and manly, and generous hearts?'[1]

The lessons appointed to be read on this feast will be found in the Supplement. The following passage from the account written by Perpetua herself, which used to be read at Matins, will make some readers long to read the whole of what she has left us. They will find it in our first volume of the 'Acts of the Martyrs.'

Severo imperatore, apprehensi sunt in Africa adolescentes catechumeni, Revocatus et Felicitas conserva ejus, Saturninus et Secundulus: inter quos et Vivia Perpetua, honeste nata, liberaliter instituta, matronaliter nupta, habens filium ad ubera. Erat autem ipsa annorum circiter viginti duorum. Hæc ordinem martyrii sui conscriptum manu sua reliquit. Quum adhuc, inquit, cum persecutoribus essemus, et me pater avertere, pro sua affectione, perseveraret: Pater, inquio, aliud me dicere non possum, nisi quod sum Christiana. Tunc pater, motus in hoc verbo, misit se in me, ut oculos mihi erueret. Sed vexavit

During the reign of the Emperor Severus, several catechumens were apprehended at Carthage, in Africa. Among these were Revocatus and his fellow-servant Felicitas, Saturninus and Secundulus, and Vivia Perpetua, a lady by birth and education, who was married to a man of wealth. Perpetua was about twenty-two years of age, and was suckling an infant. She has left us the following particulars of her martyrdom. 'As soon as our persecutors had apprehended us, my father came to me, and out of his great love for me, he tried to make me change my resolution. I said to him: "Father, I cannot consent to call myself other than what I am,

---

tantum; et profectus est
victus cum argumentis diaboli. In spatio paucorum
dierum baptizati sumus:
mihi autem Spiritus dictavit
nihil aliud petendum in
aqua, nisi sufferentiam carnis. Post paucos dies, reci-
pimur in carcerem : et ex-
pavi, quia nunquam exper-
ta eram tales tenebras. Mox
rumor cucurrit ut audiremur.
Supervenit autem et de civitate pater meus, consum-
ptus tædio ; et ascendit ad
me, ut me dejiceret, dicens:
Miserere, filia, canis meis ;
miserere patri, si dignus
sum a te pater vocari. A-
spice ad fratres tuos, aspice
ad matrem tuam : aspice ad
filium tuum, qui post te vi-
vere non poterit. Depone
animos, ne universos nos
extermines. Hæc dicebat
pater pro sua pietate : se ad
pedes meos jactans, et lacrymis non filiam, sed domi-
nam me vocabat. Et ego
dolebam canos patris mei :
quod solus de passione mea
gavisurus non esset de toto
genere meo. Et confortavi
eum, dicens : Hoc fiet quod
Deus voluerit. Scito enim
nos non in nostra potestate
esse constitutos, sed in Dei.
Et recessit a me contristatus.

a Christian." At these words,
he rushed at me threatening to
tear out my eyes. But he only
struck me, and then he left me,
when he found that the arguments suggested to him by the
devil, were of no avail. A few
days after this, we were baptized ; and the Holy Ghost inspired me to look on this Baptism as a preparation for bodily
suffering. A few more days
elapsed, and we were sent to
prison. I was terrified, for I
was not accustomed to such
darkness. The report soon
spread that we were to be
brought to trial. ' My father
left the city, for he was heart-
broken, and he came to me,
hoping to shake my purpose.
These were his words to me :
" My child, have pity on my
old age. Have pity on thy
father, if I deserve to be called
father. Think of thy brothers,
think of thy mother, think of
thy son, who cannot live when
thou art gone. Give up this
mad purpose, or thou wilt bring
misery upon thy family."
Whilst saying this, which he
did out of love for me, he threw
himself at my feet, and wept
bitterly, and said he besought
this of me not as his child, but
as his lady. I was moved to
tears to see my aged parent in
this grief, for I knew that he
was the only one of my family
that would not rejoice at my
being a martyr. I tried to console him, and said : " I will do
whatsoever God shall ordain.
Thou knowest that we belong to
God, and not to ourselves." He
then left me, and was very sad.

Alio die, quum pranderemus, subito rapti sumus ut audiremur : et pervenimus ad forum. Ascendimus in catasta. Interrogati cæteri confessi sunt. Ventum est et ad me. Et apparuit pater illico cum filio meo : et extraxit me de gradu, et dixit supplicans : Miserere infanti. Et Hilarianus procurator : Parce, inquit, canis patris tui, parce infantiæ pueri : fac sacrum pro salute imperatorum. Et ego respondi : Non facio : christiana sum. Tunc nos universos pronuntiat et damnat ad bestias : et hilares descendimus ad carcerem. Sed quia consueverat a me infans mammas accipere, et mecum in carcere manere, statim mitto ad patrem, postulans infantem. Sed pater dare noluit : et, quomodo Deus voluit, neque ille amplius mammas desideravit, neque mihi fervorem fecerunt. Atque hoc scripsit beata Perpetua usque in pridie certaminis. Felicitas vero, quæ prægnans octo jam mensium fuerat apprehensa, instante spectaculi die, in magno erat luctu, ne propter ventrem differretur. Sed et commartyres ejus graviter contristabantur, ne tam bonam sociam in via ejusdem spei relinquerent. Conjuncto itaque gemitu, ad Dominum orationem fuderunt ante tertium diem muneris. Statim post orationem dolores eam invaserunt. Et quum in par-

'On the following day, as we were taking our repast, they came upon us suddenly, and summoned us to trial. We reached the forum. We were made to mount a platform. My companions were questioned, and they confessed the faith. My turn came next, and I immediately saw my father approaching towards me, holding my infant son. He drew me from the platform, and besought me, saying : "Have pity on thy babe!" Hilarian, too, the governor, said to me : "Have pity on thy aged father, have pity on thy babe! Offer up sacrifice for the emperors." I answered him : "I cannot ; I am a Christian." Whereupon, he sentences all of us to be devoured by the wild beasts ; and we, full of joy, return to our prison. But as I had hitherto always had my child with me in prison, and fed him at my breasts, I immediately sent word to my father, beseeching him to let him come to me. He refused ; and from that moment, neither the babe asked for the breast, nor did I suffer inconvenience ; for God thus willed it.' All this is taken from the written account left us by the blessed Perpetua, and it brings us to the day before she was put to death. As regards Felicitas, she was in the eighth month of her pregnancy, when she was apprehended. The day of the public shows was near at hand, and the fear that her martyrdom would be deferred on account of her being with child,

tu laborans doleret, ait illi quidam ex ministris : Quæ sic modo doles, quid facies objecta bestiis, quas contempsisti quum sacrificare noluisti? Et illa respondit : Modo ego patior quod patior : illic autem alius erit in me qui patietur pro me ; quia et ego pro illo passura sum. Ita enixa est puellam, quam sibi quædam soror in filiam educavit.

made her very sad. Her fellow-martys, too, felt much for her, for they could not bear the thought of seeing so worthy a companion disappointed in the hope, she had in common with themselves, of so soon reaching heaven. Uniting, therefore, in prayer, they with tears besought God in her behalf. It was but three days before the public shows. No sooner was their prayer ended, than Felicitas was seized with pain. One of the gaolers, who overheard her moaning, cried out : ‘If this pain seem to thee so great, what wilt thou do when thou art being devoured by the wild beasts, which thou pretendedst to heed not when thou wast told to offer sacrifice.’ She answered : ‘What I am suffering now, it is indeed I that suffer ; but there, there will be another in me, who will suffer for me, because I shall be suffering for him.’ She was delivered of a daughter, and one of our sisters adopted the infant as her own.

Illuxit dies victoriæ illorum : et processerunt de carcere in amphitheatrum, quasi in cœlum, hilares, vultu decori: si forte, gaudio paventes, non timore. Sequebatur Perpetua placido vultu, et pedum incessu ut matrona Christi dilecta : vigorem oculorum suorum dejiciens ab omnium conspectu. Item Felicitas, salvam se peperisse gaudens, ut ad bestias pugnaret. Illis ferocissimam vaccam diabolus præpa-

The day of their victory dawned. They left their prison for the amphitheatre, cheerful, and with faces beaming with joy, as though they were going to heaven. They were excited, but it was from delight, not from fear. The last in the group was Perpetua. Her placid look, her noble gait, betrayed the Christian matron. She passed through the crowd and saw no one, for her beautiful eyes were fixed upon the ground. By her side was Felicitas, rejoicing that her

ravit. Itaque reticulis indutæ producuntur. Induritur prior Perpetua. Jactata est et concidit in lumbos : et ut conspexit tunicam a latere discissam ad velamentum femorum adduxit, pudoris potius memor quam doloris. Dehinc requisita et dispersos capillos infibulavit. Non enim decebat martyrem dispersis capillis pati : ne in sua gloria plangere videretur. Ita surrexit ; et elisam Felicitatem quum vidisset, accessit et manum ei tradidit, et sublevavit illam. Et ambæ pariter steterunt : et populi duritia devicta, revocatæ sunt in portam Sanavivariam. Illic Perpetua, quasi a somno expergita, adeo in spiritu et extasi fuerat, circumspicere cœpit : et stupentibus omnibus, ait : Quando producimur ad vaccam illam, nescio. Et quum audisset quod jam evenerat ; non prius credidit, nisi quasdam notas vexationis in corpore et habitu suo recognovisset. Exinde accersitum fratrem suum, et catechumenum Rusticum nomine, allocuta est eos, dicens : In fide state, et invicem omnes diligite ; et passionibus nostris ne scandalizemini.

Secundulum Deus maturiore exitu de sæculo adhuc

safe delivery enabled her to encounter the wild beasts. The devil had prepared a savage cow for them. They were put into a net. Perpetua was brought forward the first. She was tossed into the air, and fell upon her back. Observing that one side of her dress was torn, she adjusted it, heedless of her pain, because thoughtful for modesty. Having recovered from the fall, she put up her hair which was dishevelled by the shock, for it was not seemly that a martyr should win her palm and have the appearance of one distracted by grief. This done, she stood up. Seeing Felicitas thrown down she went to her, and giving her hand to her, raised her from the ground. Both were now ready for a fresh attack ; but the people were moved to pity, and the martyrs were led to the gate called Sana - Vivaria. There Perpetua, like one that is roused from sleep, awoke from the deep ecstasy of her spirit. She looked around her, and said to the astonished multitude : 'When will the cow attack us ?' They told her that it had already attacked them. She could not believe it, until her wounds and torn dress reminded her of what had happened. Then beckoning to her brother, and to a catechumen named Rusticus, she thus spoke to them : 'Be stanch in the faith, and love one another, and be not shocked at our sufferings.'

God had already taken Secundulus from this world ;

in carcere evocaverat. Saturninus et Revocatus leopardum experti, etiam ab
urso vexati sunt. Saturus
apro oblatus est ; deinde ad
ursum tractus, qui de cavea
prodire noluit : itaque bis
illæsus revocatur. In fine
spectaculi, leopardo objectus, de uno morsu ejus tanto
perfusus est sanguine, ut
populus revertenti illi secundi Baptismatis testimonium reclamaverit : Salvum
lotum, salvum lotum. Exinde jam exanimis, prosternitur cum cæteris ad jugulationem solito loco. Et quum
populus illos in medium
postularet, ut gladio penetrante in eorem corpore,
oculos suos comites homicidii adjungeret ; ultro surrexerunt, et se quo volebat
populus transtulerunt : ante
jam osculati invicem, ut
martyrium per solemnia pacis consummarent. Cæteri
quidem immobiles et cum
silentio ferrum receperunt :
multo magis Saturus, qui
prior reddidit spiritum. Perpetua autem, ut aliquid doloris gustaret, inter costas
puncta exululavit ; et errantem dexteram tirunculi gladiatoris ipsa in jugulum
suum posuit. Fortasse tanta
femina aliter non potuisset
occidi, quia ab immundo
spiritu timebatur, nisi ipsa
voluisset.

for he died while he was in the
prison. Saturninus and Revocatus were exposed first to a
leopard, and then to a bear.
Saturus was exposed to a boar,
and then to a bear, which would
not come out of its den ; thus
was he twice left uninjured;
but at the close of the games,
he was thrown to a leopard,
which bit him so severely, that
he was all covered with blood,
and as he was taken from the
amphitheatre, the people jeered
at him for this second Baptism,
and said : 'Saved, washed !
Saved, washed !' He was then
carried off, dying as he was, to
the appointed place, there to be
dispatched by the sword, with
the rest. But the people demanded that they should be
led back to the middle of the
amphitheatre, that their eyes
might feast on the sight, and
watch the sword as it pierced
them. The martyrs hearing
their request, cheerfully stood
up, and marched to the place
where the people would have
them go ; but first they embraced one another, that the
sacrifice of their martyrdom
might be consummated with
the solemn kiss of peace. They
all received the fatal stroke
without a movement or a
moan; Saturus being the first
to expire. Perpetua was permitted to feel more than the
rest. Her executioner, who was
a novice in his work, thrust
his sword through her ribs:
she slightly moaned, then took
his right hand, and pointing his sword towards her
throat, told him that that was

the place to strike.   Perhaps it
was that such a woman could
not be otherwise slain than by
her own consent, for the un-
clean spirit feared her.

The Holy See has approved of the three following
hymns composed in honour of our two martyrs.
We unite them under one conclusion.

HYMN

Christi sponsa piis laudi-
   bus efferat
Binas impavido pectore fe-
   minas :
In sexu fragili corda virilia
   Hymnis pangat ovanti-
   bus.
   Ad lucem genitæ sole sub
   Africo,
Nunc ambæ pugiles actibus
   inclytis
In toto radiant orbe : mi-
   cantibus
   Fulgent tempora laureis.
   Exornat generis Perpetu-
   am decus ;
Sponso connubiis juncta re-
   centibus
Clarescit ; sed honor hanc
   trahit altior :
   Christi fœdera prætulit.
   Se Regis famulam libera
   profitens,
Dum servile jugum Felicitas
   subit :
Ad luctam properans gres-
   sibus æmulis,
   Palmas ad similes volat.
   Frustra Perpetuam fleti-
   bus et minis
Impugnat genitor : quæ si-
   mul angitur,

Let the Church, the bride of
Christ, celebrate in holy praise,
the two dauntless women ; and
sing, in joyous hymns, how the
weaker sex had here two manly
hearts.

Both were born in Afric's
sunny land ; and now both
shine throughout the whole
world as the two glorious combatants, wearing bright laurels
on their brows.

Perpetua is honoured by her
fellow-citizens as being of high
birth, and had but recently
contracted an honourable marriage.   But there was an honour
far higher, in her eyes, the love
and service of Christ.
   Felicitas, though she served
an earthly master, was free in
this, that she was a servant of
the great King.   Like Perpetua,
she thirsts for battle ; and like
her, she culls a palm.

In vain did Perpetua's father
strive, by tears and threats, to
make her deny her faith.   She,
on her side was full of grief,

Errantem miserans. Oscula
   filio
Lactenti dedit ultima.

Terris Eva parens quæ
   mala contulit,
Horum sentit onus Felicitas
   grave ;
Nunc et passa sibi partu-
   riens gemit,
Mox passura Deo libens.

Cœli Perpetuæ panditur
   ostium ;
Inspectare datur : jam sibi
   prælia
Exortura videt ; sed requiem
   Deus
   Post certamina conferet.
Tangit scala domos aurea
   cœlitum :
Ast utrumque latus cuspi-
   dibus riget ;
Lapsos terribilis faucibus
   excipit
   Hanc infra recubans
   draco.

Ascendas, mulier, nec
   draco terreat ;
Contritumque caput sit tibi
   pro gradu,
Per quem sidereos incipias
   pede
   Orbes scandere concito.
Hortus deliciis jam patet
   affluens,
In quo mulget oves pastor
   amabilis :
Huc optata venis, filia : sic
   ait,
   Hanc dulci recreans cibo.

In circum rapitur : fœdus
   et horrida
Occurrit specie vir gladium
   vibrans :

and pity at seeing him a victim of error. Her babe was taken from her; she kissed him and was content.

Felicitas begins her sufferings by those cruel pangs which Eve, our mother, brought upon the earth. Now, in child-birth, she suffers for herself, and she moans; but, in her martyrdom, she suffers for her God, and she rejoices.

The gate of heaven is thrown open to Perpetua, and she is permitted to look within. She there learns that a contest awaits her, but that, after the battle, God will grant her repose.

She sees a golden ladder reaching to the palace of heaven; but both its sides are armed with spikes, and at its foot lies an angry dragon, which devours them that fall.

Ascend, Perpetua! fear not the dragon. Trample on his head, and make it a stepping-stone, whereby thou mayst quickly mount to the starry land above.

There shalt thou find a paradise of delights, where the loving shepherd caresses his sheep. 'Thou art welcome here, my daughter!' Thus did he address the martyr, and then gave her to eat of sweetest food.

In another vision, she thought she was hurried to the amphitheatre. There she was met by a man, whose face was

Dejectus teritur femineo
    pede.
Victrix, suscipe præmia.

Luxit clara dies, vincere
    qua datur
Athletis Domini. Pergite
    martyres:
Omnis Perpetuam curia
    cœlitum,
Et te, Felicitas, cupit.
Quassat Perpetuæ mem-
    bra tenerrima,
Elidit sociam bellua. Te
    soror
Stans. o Felicitas, ad nova
    prælia
Erectam reparat manu.
E cœlo pugilum respiciens
    Deus
Certamen, geminas ad bra-
    vium vocat.
Effuso properet sanguine
    spiritus,
In Christi remeans sinum.
Optatus penetrat corpora
    martyrum
Lictoris gladius: sed tre-
    pidam manum
Fortis Perpetuæ dextera di-
    rigit,
Præbens guttura cuspidi.
Nunc, o magnanimæ,
    gaudia quæ manent
In Sponsi thalamo carpite
    jugiter.
Vos exempla dedit: præsi-
    dium potens
Vestris ferte clientibus.
Laus æterna Patri, laus
    quoque Filio;
Par individuo gloria Fla-
    mini;

swarth and terrible to look at.
He brandished his sword. She
encountered him, threw him
on the ground, and trampled
on his head. A cry was heard:
'Thou hast conquered! Come,
take the prize!'

But at length came the glorious day of victory for the
soldiers of Christ. On, martyrs, to the field! Perpetua
and Felicitas! the court of
heaven is longing to receive
you!

The wild beast rushes upon
them, tossing, tearing, and
wounding their tender limbs.
See, Felicitas! thy sister's
hand emboldens thee to renew
the fight.

God looks down from heaven
on the two brave combatants,
and calls them to the prize.
Their blood streams from the
wounds, and their spirits speed
their way to the bosom of
Christ.

The sword, the welcome
sword, is thrust; the martyrs
die, all save Perpetua; bravely
she takes the trembling lictor's
hand, and offering him her
neck, tells him his surest aim
is there.

Go now, brave-hearted ones,
to him who is your Spouse,
and there eternally enjoy the
bliss he has in store for you.
He gave you to us as models;
Oh, show your power, and help
us your clients.

Eternal glory be to the
Father, and to the Son, and
to the coequal Spirit! And
let every choir in Christian

In cunctis resonet Christia-
    dum choris
  Virtus martyribus data.
    Amen.

lands sound forth its praise
to the grace bestowed on the
martyrs. Amen.

Perpetua! Felicitas! O glorious and prophetic
names, which come like two bright stars of March,
pouring out upon us your rays of light and life!
You are heard in the songs of the angels; and we
poor sinners, as we echo them on earth, are told to
love and hope. You remind us of that brave
woman, who, as the Scripture says, kept up the
battle begun by men: The valiant men ceased:
who will follow them? A mother in Israel.[1] Glory
be to that almighty power, which loves to choose
the weak things of the world that it may confound
the strong![2] Glory to the Church of Africa, the
daughter of the Church of Rome; and glory to the
Church of Carthage, which had not then heard the
preachings of her Cyprian, and yet could produce
two such noble hearts!

As to thee, Perpetua, thou art held in veneration
by the whole Christian world. Thy name is mentioned by God's priests in the holy Mass, and thus
thy memory is associated with the sacrifice of the
Man-God, for love of whom thou didst lay down
thy life. And those pages written by thine own
hand, how they reveal to us the generous character
of thy soul! How they comment those words of
the Canticle: Love is strong as death![3] It was
thy love of God that made thee suffer, and die, and
conquer. Even before the water of Baptism had
touched thee, thou wast enrolled among the martyrs.
When the hard trial came of resisting a father, who
wished thee to lay down the palm of martyrdom,
how bravely didst thou triumph over thy filial affection, in order to save that which is due to our
Father who is in heaven! Nay, when the hardest

[1] Judges v. 7.   [2] 1 Cor. i. 27.   [3] Cant. viii. 6.

test came, when the babe that fed at thy breast was taken from thee in thy prison, even then thy love was strong enough for the sacrifice, as was Abraham's, when he had to immolate his Isaac.

Thy fellow-martyrs deserve our admiration; they are so grand in their courage; but thou, dear saint, surpassest them all. Thy love makes thee more than brave in thy sufferings, it makes thee forget them. 'Where wast thou,' we would ask thee in the words of St. Augustine, 'where wast thou, that thou didst not feel the goading of that furious beast, asking when it was to be, as though it had not been? Where wast thou? What didst thou see, that made thee see not this? On what wast thou feasting, that made thee dead to sense? What was the love that absorbed, what was the sight that distracted, what was the chalice that inebriated thee? And yet the ties of flesh were still holding thee, the claims of death were still upon thee, the corruptible body was still weighing thee down!'[1] But our Lord had prepared thee for the final struggle, by asking sacrifice at thy hands. This made thy life wholly spiritual, and gave thy soul to dwell, by love, with Him, who had asked thee for all and received it; and thus living in union with Jesus, thy spirit was all but a stranger to the body it animated.

It was impatient to be wholly with its sovereign Good. Thy eager hand directs the sword that is to set thee free; and as the executioner severs the last tie that holds thee, how voluntary was thy sacrifice, how hearty thy welcome of death! Truly, thou wast the valiant, the strong woman,[2] that conqueredst the wicked serpent! Thy greatness of soul has merited for thee a high place among the heroines of our holy faith, and for sixteen hundred

[1] Sermon for the feast of SS. Perpetua and Felicitas.
[2] Prov. xxxi. 10.

years thou hast been honoured by the enthusiastic devotion and love of the servants of God.

And thou, too, Felicitas! receive the homage of our veneration, for thou wast found worthy to be a fellow-martyr with Perpetua. Though she was a rich matron of Carthage, and thou a servant, yet Baptism and martyrdom made you companions and sisters. The lady and the slave embraced, for martyrdom made you equal; and as the spectators saw you hand in hand together, they must have felt that there was a power in the religion they persecuted, which would put an end to slavery. The power and grace of Jesus triumphed in thee, as it did in Perpetua; and thus was fulfilled thy sublime answer to the pagan, who dared to jeer thee: that when the hour of trial came, it would not be thou that wouldst suffer, but Christ who would suffer in thee. Heaven is now the reward of thy sacrifice; well didst thou merit it. And that babe, that was born in thy prison, what a happy child to have for its mother a martyr in heaven! How wouldst thou bless both it and the mother who adopted it! Oh, what fitness, in such a soul as thine, for the kingdom of God![1] Not once looking back, but ever bravely speeding onwards to Him that called thee. Thy felicity is perpetual in heaven; thy glory on earth shall never cease.

And now, dear saints, Perpetua and Felicitas, intercede for us during this season of grace. Go, with your palms in your hands, to the throne of God, and beseech Him to pour down His mercy upon us. It is true, the days of paganism are gone by; and there are no persecutors clamouring for our blood. You, and countless other martyrs, have won victory for faith; and that faith is now ours; we are Christians. But there is a second paganism, which has taken deep root among us. It is the

[1] St. Luke ix. 62.

source of that corruption which now pervades every rank of society, and its own two sources are indifference, which chills the heart, and sensuality, which induces cowardice. Holy martyrs! pray for us that we may profit by the example of your virtues, and that the thought of your heroic devotedness may urge us to be courageous in the sacrifices which God claims at our hands. Pray, too, for the Churches which are now being established on that very spot of Africa, which was the scene of your glorious martyrdom : bless them, and obtain for them, by your powerful intercession, firmness of faith and purity of morals.

MARCH 7

SAINT THOMAS OF AQUIN, DOCTOR OF THE CHURCH

THE saint we are to honour to-day is one of the sublimest and most lucid interpreters of divine truth. He rose up in the Church many centuries after the apostolic age, nay, long after the four great Latin doctors, Ambrose, Augustine, Jerome, and Gregory. The Church, the ever young and joyful mother, is justly proud of her Thomas, and has honoured him with the splendid title of the angelical doctor, on account of the extraordinary gift of understanding wherewith God had blessed him ; just as his contemporary and friend, St. Bonaventure, has been called the seraphic doctor, on account of the wonderful unction which abounds in the writings of this worthy disciple of St. Francis. Thomas of Aquin is an honour to mankind, for perhaps there never existed a man whose intellect surpassed his. He is one of the brightest ornaments of the Church, for not one of her doctors has equalled him in the

clearness and precision wherewith he has explained
her doctrines. He received the thanks of Christ
Himself, for having well written of Him and His
mysteries. How welcome ought this feast of such
a saint to be to us during this season of the year,
when our main study is our return and conversion to God ! What greater blessing could we have
than to come to the knowledge of God ? Has
not our ignorance of God, of His claims, and of
His perfections, been the greatest misery of our
past lives ? Here we have a saint whose prayers
are most efficacious in procuring for us that knowledge, which is unspotted, and converteth souls,
and giveth wisdom to little ones, and gladdeneth
the heart, and enlighteneth the eyes.[1] Happy we
if this spiritual wisdom be granted us ! We shall
then see the vanity of everything that is not eternal,
the righteousness of the divine commandments,
the malice of sin, and the infinite goodness wherewith God treats us when we repent.

Let us learn from the Church the claims of the
angelical doctor to our admiration and confidence.

Præclarum Christiani or-
bis decus et Ecclesiæ lumen,
beatissimus vir Thomas,
Landulpho Comite Aquinate
et Theodora Neapolitana,
nobilibus parentibus natus,
futuræ in Deiparam devo-
tionis affectum adhuc infan-
tulus ostendit. Nam char-
tulam ab eo inventam, in
qua salutatio angelica scripta erat, frustra adnitente
nutrice, compressa manu
valide retinuit, et a matre
per vim abreptam, ploratu
et gestu repetiit, ac mox
redditam deglutivit. Quin-

The distinguished ornament
of the Christian world and light
of the Church, the most blessed
man Thomas, was born of noble
parents, his father being Land-
ulph, Count of Aquino, and his
mother a rich Neapolitan lady,
by name Theodora. While yet
an infant he gave proof of his
future devotion towards the
Mother of God ; for having
found a leaflet on which was
written the angelical salutation,
he clenched it so fast that the
nurse tried in vain to take it
from his hand. His mother,
however, having forced it from

---

[1] Ps. xviii. 8, 9.

tum annum agens, monachis sancti Benedicti Cassinatibus custodiendus traditur. Inde Neapolim studiorum causa missus, jam adolescens Fratrum Prædicatorum Ordinem suscepit. Sed matre ac fratribus id indigne ferentibus, Lutetiam Parisiorum mittitur. Quem fratres in itinere per vim raptum in arcem castri Sancti Joannis perducunt, ubi varie exagitatus, ut sanctum propositum mutaret, mulierem etiam, quæ ad labefactandam ejus constantiam introducta fuerat, titione fugavit. Mox beatus juvenis, flexis genibus ante signum crucis orans, ibique somno correptus, per quietem sentire visus est sibi ab angelis constringi lumbos : quo ex tempore omni postea libidinis sensu caruit. Sororibus, quæ, ut eum a pio consilio removerent, in castrum venerant, persuasit ut, contemptis curis sæcularibus, ad exercitationem cœlestis vitæ se conferrent.

Emissus e castro per fenestram, Neapolim reducitur : unde Romam, postea

him, the child succeeded by tears and signs, in recovering the paper, which he immediately swallowed. When he was five years old he was sent to Monte Cassino, that he might receive from the Benedictine monks his first training. Thence he was sent to Naples, where he went through a course of studies, and, young as he was, joined the Order of Friars Preachers. This step caused great displeasure to his mother and brothers, and it was therefore deemed advisable to send him to Paris. He was waylaid by his brothers, who seized him, and imprisoned him in the castle of Saint John. After having made several unsuccessful attempts to induce him to abandon the holy life he had chosen, they assailed his purity, by sending to him a wicked woman : but he drove her from his chamber with a firebrand. The young saint then threw himself on his knees before a crucifix. Having prayed some time, he fell asleep, and it seemed to him that two angels approached him, and tightly girded his loins. From that time forward, he never suffered the slightest feeling against purity. His sisters also had come to the castle, and tried to make him change his mind ; but he, on the contrary, persuaded them to despise the world, and devote themselves to the exercise of a holy life.

It was contrived that he should escape through a window of the castle, and return

Parisium a fratre Joanne Theutonico, Ordinis Prædicatorum generali magistro, ductus, Alberto Magno doctore, philosophiæ ac theologiæ operam dedit. Viginti quinque annos natus, magister est appellatus, publiceque philosophos ac theologos summa cum laude est interpretatus. Nunquam se lectioni aut scriptioni dedit, nisi post orationem. In difficultatibus locorum sacræ Scripturæ, ad orationem jejunium adhibebat. Quin etiam sodali suo fratri Reginaldo dicere solebat, quidquid sciret non tam studio aut labore suo peperisse, quam divinitus traditum accepisse. Neapoli, cum ad imaginem Crucifixi vehementius oraret, hanc vocem audivit : Bene scripsisti de me, Thoma : quam ergo mercedem accipies ? Cui ille : Non aliam, Domine, nisi teipsum. Collationes patrum assidue pervolutabat ; et nullum fuit scriptorum genus in quo non esset diligentissime versatus. Scripta ejus et multitudine, et varietate et facilitate explicandi res difficiles adeo excellunt, ut uberrima atque incorrupta illius doctrina, cum revelatis veritatibus mire consentiens, aptissima sit ad omnium temporum errores pervincendos.

to Naples. He was thence taken by John the Teutonic, the General of the Dominican Order, first to Rome and then to Paris, in which latter city he was taught philosophy and theology by Albert the Great. At the age of twenty-five, he received the title of doctor, and explained in the public schools, and in a manner that made him the object of universal admiration, the writings of philosophers and theologians. He always applied himself to prayer, before reading or writing anything. When he met with any difficult passage in the sacred Scriptures, he both fasted and prayed. He used often to say to his companion, brother Reginald, that if he knew anything, it was more a gift from God, than the fruit of his own study and labour. One day, when at Naples, as he was praying with more than his usual fervour, before a crucifix, he heard these words: 'Well hast thou written of me, Thomas ! What reward wouldst thou have me give thee ?' He answered : 'None other, Lord, than thyself.' His favourite spiritual book was the *Conferences of the Fathers*, and there was not a book which he had not most carefully read. His writings are so extraordinary, not only for their number and variety, but also for their clearness in explaining difficult points of doctrine, that his copious and sound teaching, so wonderfully consonant with revealed truth, is most apt for utterly refuting the errors of all ages.

A summo Pontifice Urbano quarto Romam vocatus, ejus jussu ecclesiasticum lucubravit Officium in Corporis Christi solemnitate celebrandum ; oblatos vero honores, et Neapolitanum archiepiscopatum etiam deferente Clemente quarto recusavit. A prædicatione divini verbi non desistebat; quod cum faceret per octavam Paschæ in basilica sancti Petri, mulierem, quæ ejus fimbriam tetigerat, a fluxu sanguinis liberavit. Missus a beato Gregorio decimo ad Concilium Lugdunense, in monasterio Fossæ Novæ in morbum incidit, ubi ægrotus Cantica canticorum explanavit. Ibidem obiit, quinquagenarius, anno salutis millesimo ducentesimo septuagesimo quarto, Nonis Martii. Miraculis etiam mortuus claruit; quibus probatis, a Joanne vigesimo secundo in sanctorum numerum relatus est, anno millesimo trecentesimo vigesimo tertio; translato postea ejus corpore Tolosam, ex mandato beati Urbani quinti. Cum sanctis angelicis spiritibus non minus innocentia quam ingenio comparatus, doctoris angelici nomen jure est adeptus, eidem auctoritate sancti Pii quinti confirmatum. Leo autem decimus tertius, libentissime excipiens postulationes et vota omnium pene sacrorum antistitum orbis Catholici, ad tot præcipue philosophicorum systema-

Being called to Rome by Pope Urban IV., he composed, at his command, the ecclesiastical Office for the solemnity of Corpus Christi ; but he refused to accept any honours, as likewise the archbishopric of Naples offered to him by Pope Clement IV. He was most zealous in preaching the word of God. On one occasion, during Easter week, as he was preaching in the church of St. Peter, a woman touched the hem of his habit, and was cured of an issue of blood. He was sent by Gregory X. to the Council of Lyons ; but having reached Fossa Nova, he fell sick, and was received as a guest in the monastery of that place, where he wrote a commentary on the Canticle of Canticles. There he died in the fiftieth year of his age, in the year of our Lord 1274 on the Nones of March (March 7). His sanctity was made manifest after his death, by miracles : which being proved, he was canonized by Pope John XXII. in the year 1323. His body was translated to Toulouse by command of blessed Urban V. Being comparable to the angels, no less by his innocence than by his genius, he has received the title of angelical doctor, confirmed to him by the authority of St. Pius V. Pope Leo XIII. joyfully acceding to the "desires and petitions of the bishops of the Catholic world, by a decree of the sacred Congregation of rites and by letters apostolic, ordained and declared him the

tum a veritate aberrantium luem propulsandam, ad incrementa scientiarum, et communem humani generis utilitatem, eum ex sacrorum rituum Congregationis consulto, per apostolicas litteras cœlestem patronum scholarum omnium Catholicarum declaravit et instituit.

heavenly patron of all Catholic schools; and this especially for the purpose of repelling the evil of so many philosophical systems abandoned to error, for the increase of knowledge, and for the common utility of mankind.

The Dominican Order, of which St. Thomas is one of the greatest ornaments, has inserted the three following hymns in its liturgy of his feast:

HYMN

Exsultet mentis jubilo
Laudans turba fidelium,
Errorum pulso nubilo
Per novi solis radium.

Let the assembly of the faithful exult in spiritual joy, and give praise to God, who has made a new sun to shine in our world, and disperse the clouds of error.

Thomas in mundi vespere,
Fudit thesauros gratiæ:
Donis plenus ex æthere
Morum et sapientiæ.

It was in the evening of the world that Thomas shed his treasures of heavenly light. Heaven had enriched him with gifts of virtue and wisdom:

De cujus fonte luminis,
Verbi coruscant faculæ,
Scripturæ sacræ Numinis,
Et veritatis regulæ.

From this fountain of light we have derived a brighter knowledge of the Word, the understanding of the divine Scriptures and the rules of truth.

Fulgens doctrinæ radiis,
Clarus vitæ munditia,
Splendens miris prodigiis,
Dat toti mundo gaudia.

The effulgent rays of his wisdom, the light of his spotless life, and the splendour of his miracles, have filled the universe with joy.

Laus Patri sit, ac Genito
Simulque sancto Flamini,
Qui sancti Thomæ merito
Nos cœli jungat agmini.
Amen.

Praise, then, be to the Father, and to the Son, and to the Holy Ghost. And may our God, by the intercession and merits of his saint, admit us into the choir of the blessed in heaven. Amen.

HYMN

Thomas insignis genere,
Claram ducone originem,
Subit ætatis teneræ
Prædicatorum Ordinem.
　Typum gessit luciferi,
Splendens in cœtu nubium,
Plusquam doctores cæteri
Purgans dogma Gentilium.

Profunda scrutans flumi-
　　num,
In lucem pandit abdita,
Dum supra sensus homi-
　　num
Obscura facit cognita.
　Fit paradisi fluvius,
Quadripartite pervius :
Fit Gedeonis gladius,
Tuba, lagena, radius.

Laus Patri sit, ac Genito
Simulque sancto Flamini,
Qui sancti Thomæ merito,
Nos cœli jungat agmini.
　　Amen.

Noble by birth and parent-
age, Thomas, while in the
bloom of youth, embraced the
Order of Preachers.
　Like to the star of morn,
brightly does he shine amidst
the luminaries of earth, and,
more than any doctor of the
Church, refutes the doctrines of
the Gentiles.
　He explores the depth of
mysteries, and brings to light
the hidden gems of truth, for
he teaches us what the mind
of man had else never understood.
　God gives him to the Church
as a fountain of wisdom, like
to that four-branched river of
paradise. He made him to be
her Gedeon's sword, her trumpet, her vase, her torch.
　Praise, then, be to the Father,
and to the Son, and to the
Holy Ghost. And may our
God, by the intercession and
merits of his saint, admit us
into the choir of the blessed in
heaven. Amen.

HYMN

Lauda, mater Ecclesia,
Thomæ felicem exitum,
Qui pervenit ad gaudia
Per Verbi vitæ meritum.

Fossa Nova tunc suscipit
Thecam thesauri gratiæ,
Cum Christus Thomam effi-
　　cit
Hæredem regni gloriæ.

Dear Church, our mother !
the happy death of thy Thomas
deserves a hymn of praise. By
the merits of him that is the
Word of life, he is now in endless joy.
　It was at Fossa Nova that
the rich treasury of grace was
welcomed as a guest. It was
there that he received from
Christ the inheritance of eternal
glory.

Manens doctrinæ veritas,
Et funeris integritas,
Mira fragrans suavitas,
Ægris collata sanitas.

Monstrat hunc dignum
    laudibus
Terræ, ponto, et superis ;
Nos juvet suis precibus,
Deo commendet meritis.

Laus Patri sit ac Genito,
Simulque sancto Flamini,
Qui sancti Thomæ merito
Nos cœli jungat agmini.
    Amen.

He has left us the fruits of truth ; he has left us his glorious relics which breathe forth a heavenly fragrance, and work cures for the suffering sick.

Right well, then, is honour his due : earth, and sea, and heaven, all may give him praise. May his prayers and merits intercede for us with God.

Praise, then, be to the Father, and to the Son, and to the Holy Ghost. And may our God, by the intercession and merits of his saint, admit us into the choir of the blessed in heaven. Amen.

How shall we worthily praise thee, most holy Doctor ! How shall we thank thee for what thou hast taught us ? The rays of the divine Sun of justice beamed strongly upon thee, and thou hast reflected them upon us. When we picture thee contemplating truth, we think of those words of our Lord : ' Blessed are the clean of heart, for they shall see God.'[1] Thy victory over the concupiscence of the flesh merited for thee the highest spiritual delights ; and our Redeemer chose thee, because of the purity of thy angelic soul, to compose for His Church the Office whereby she should celebrate the divine Sacrament of His love. Learning did not impair thy humility. Prayer was ever thy guide in thy search after truth ; and there was but one reward for which, after all thy labours, thou wast ambitious, the possession of God.

Thy life, alas ! was short. The very masterpiece of thy angelical writings was left unfinished. But thou hast not lost thy power of working for the Church. Aid her in her combats against error. She holds thy teachings in the highest estimation,

[1] St. Matt. v. 8.

because she feels that none of her saints has ever known so well as thou, the secrets and mysteries of her divine Spouse. Now, perhaps more than in any other age, truths are decayed among the children of men;[1] strengthen us in our faith, procure us light. Check the conceit of those shallow self-constituted philosophers, who dare to sit in judgment on the actions and decisions of the Church, and to force their contemptible theories upon a generation that is too ill-instructed to detect their fallacies. The atmosphere around us is gloomy with ignorance; loose principles, and truths spoilt by cowardly compromise, are the fashion of our times; pray for us; bring us back to that bold and simple acceptance of truth, which gives life to the intellect and joy to the heart.

Pray, too, for the grand Order which loves thee so devoutly, and honours thee as one of the most illustrious of its many glorious children. Draw down upon the family of thy patriarch St. Dominic the choicest blessings, for it is one of the most powerful auxiliaries of God's Church.

We are on the eve of the holy season of Lent, preparing for the great work of earnest conversion of our lives. Thy prayers must gain for us the knowledge both of the God we have offended by our sins, and of the wretched state of a soul that is at enmity with its Maker. Knowing this, we shall hate our sins; we shall desire to purify our souls in the Blood of the spotless Lamb; we shall generously atone for our faults by works of penance.

[1] Ps. xi. 2.

MARCH 8

SAINT JOHN OF GOD, CONFESSOR

THIS day month we were keeping the feast of
St. John of Matha, whose characteristic virtue was
charity; our saint of to-day was like him: love for
his neighbour led him to devote himself to the
service of them that most needed help. Both are
examples to us of what is a principal duty of this
present season : they are models of fraternal charity.
They teach us this great lesson, that our love of
God is false if our hearts are not disposed to show
mercy to our neighbour, and help him in his necessities and troubles. It is the same lesson as that
which the beloved disciple gives us, when he says:
' He that hath the substance of this world, and shall
see his brother in need, and shall put up his mercy
from him, how doth the charity of God abide in him?'[1]
But if there can be no love of God where there
is none for our neighbour, the love of our neighbour
itself is not genuine unless it be accompanied by a
love of our Creator and Redeemer. The charity
which the world has set up, which it calls philanthropy, and which it exercises not in the name of
God, but solely for the sake of man, is a mere
delusion ; it is incapable of producing love between
those who give and those who receive, and its
results must necessarily be unsatisfactory. There
is but one tie which can make men love one another:
that tie is God, who created them all, and commands them all to be one in Him. To serve mankind for its own sake, is to make a god of it ; and
even viewing the workings of the two systems in
this single point of view—the relief they afford to
temporal suffering—what comparison is there be-

<hr>

[1] 1 St. John iii. 17

tween mere philanthropy, and that supernatural charity of the humble disciples of Christ, who make Him the very motive and end of all they do for their afflicted brethren? The saint we honour to-day, was called John of God, because the name of God was ever on his lips. His heroic acts of charity had no other motive than that of pleasing God; God alone was the inspirer of the tender love he had for his suffering fellow-creatures. Let us imitate his example, for our Lord assures us that He considers as done to Himself whatsoever we do even for the least of His disciples.

The liturgy thus portrays the virtues of our saint:

Joannes de Deo, ex Catholicis piisque parentibus in oppido Montis-Majoris, junioris regni Lusitaniæ natus, quam sublimiter in sortem Domini fuerit electus, insuetus splendor super ejus domo refulgens, sonitusque æris campani sua sponte emissus, ab ipso ejus nativitatis tempore non obscure prænuntiarunt. A laxioris vivendi ratione, divina operante virtute, revocatus, magnæ sanctitatis exhibere specimen cœpit, et ob auditam prædicationem verbi Dei sic ad meliora se excitatum sensit, ut jam ab ipso sanctioris vitæ rudimento consummatum aliquid, perfectumque visus sit attigisse. Bonis omnibus in pauperes carceribus inclusos erogatis, admirabilis pœnitentiæ, suique ipsius contemptus cuncto populo spectaculum factus, a plerisque ceu demens graviter affli-

John of God was born of Catholic and virtuous parents, in Portugal, in the town of Montemor. At his birth, a bright light shone upon the house, and the church bell was heard to ring of itself; God thus evincing to what great things he destined this his servant. For some time he fell into a lax way of living; but was reclaimed by God's grace, and led a very holy life. His conversion was effected by his hearing a sermon, and so fervently did he practise the exercises of a devout life, that, from the very first, he seemed to have attained the height of perfection. He gave whatsoever he possessed to the poor who were in prison. Extraordinary were the penances he inflicted on himself; and the contempt he had for himself induced him to do certain things, which led some people to accuse him of madness, so that he was for some time confined in a madhouse.

ctus, in carcerem amentibus
destinatum conjicitur. At
Joannes cœlesti charitate
magis incensus, gemino atque amplo valetudinario ex
piorum eleemosynis in civitate Granatensi exstructo,
jactoque novi Ordinis fun-
damento, Ecclesiam nova
prole fœcundavit, Fratrum
hospitalitatis, infirmis præ-
claro animarum corporum-
que profectu inservientium,
et longe lateque per orbem
diffusorum.

Pauperibus ægrotis, quos
propriis quandoque humeris
domum deferebat, nulla re
ad animæ corporisque salutem proficua deerat. Effusa
quoque extra nosocomium
charitate, indigentibus mulieribus viduis, et præcipue
virginibus periclitantibus,
clam alimenta subministra-
bat, curamque indefessam
adhibebat ut carnis concu-
piscentiam a proximis hu-
jusmodi vitio inquinatis ex-
terminaret. Cum autem
maximum in regio Grana-
tensi valetudinario exci-
tatum fuisset incendium,
Joannes impavidus prosiliit
in ignem, huc illuc discur-
rens, quousque tum infirmos
humeris exportatos, tum
lectulos e fenestris projectos
ab igne vindicavit, ac per
dimidiam horam inter flam-
mas jam in immensum suc-
crescentes versatus, exinde
divinitus incolumis, universis civibus admirantibus,
exivit, in schola charitatis
edocens, segniorem in eum
fuisse ignem qui foris us-

His charity only increased by
such treatment. He collected
alms sufficient to build two
large hospitals in the city of
Granada, where also he began
the new Order, wherewith he
enriched the Church. This
Order was called the Institute
of Friars Hospitallers. Its object was to assist the sick, both
in their spiritual and corporal
wants. Its success was very
great, and it had houses in
almost all parts of the world.

The saint often carried the
sick poor on his own shoulders
to the hospital, and there he
provided them with everything
they could want, whether for
soul or body. His charity was
not confined within the limits
of his hospitals. He secretly
provided food for indigent
widows, and girls whose virtue
was exposed to danger. Nothing
could exceed the zeal wherewith he laboured to reclaim
such as had fallen into sins of
impurity. On occasion of an
immense fire breaking out in
the royal hospital of Granada,
John fearlessly threw himself
into the midst of the flames.
He went through the several
wards, taking the sick upon his
shoulders, and throwing the
beds through the windows, so
that all were saved. He remained half an hour amidst
the flames, which raged with
wildest fury in every part of
the building. He was miraculously preserved from the
slightest injury, and came forth
to the astonishment of the
whole city, teaching the people,

serat, quam qui intus accenderat.

Multiplici asperitatum genere, demississima obedientia, extrema paupertate, orandi studio, rerum divinarum contemplatione, ac in beatam Virginem pietate mirifice excelluit, et lacrymarum dono enituit. Denique gravi morbo correptus, omnibus Ecclesiæ sacramentis rite sancteque refectus, viribus licet destitutus, propriis indutus vestibus e lectulo surgens, ac provolutus in genua, manu et corde Christum Dominum e cruce pendentem perstringens : octavo Idus Martii, anno millesimo quingentesimo quinquagesimo, obiit in osculo Domini : quem etiam mortuus tenuit nec dimisit, et in eadem corporis constitutione sex circiter horas, quousque inde dimotus fuisset, tota civitate inspectante, mirabiliter permansit, odorem mire fragrantem diffundens. Quem ante et post obitum plurimis miraculis clarum Alexander octavus, Pontifex maximus, in sanctorum numerum retulit; et Leo decimus tertius, ex sacrorum catholici orbis antistitum voto, ac rituum congregationis consulto, cœlestem omnium hospitalium et infirmorum ubique degentium patronum declaravit, ipsiusque nomen in agonizantium litaniis invocari præcepit.

who had witnessed what had happened, that the disciples of charity have a fire within their hearts more active than any which could burn the body.

Among the virtues wherein he wonderfully excelled, may be mentioned his many practices of bodily mortification, profound obedience, extreme poverty, love of prayer, contemplation, and devotion to the blessed Virgin. He also possessed, in an extraordinary degree, the gift of tears. At length, falling seriously ill, he fervently received the last Sacraments. Though reduced to a state of utter weakness, he dressed himself, rose from his bed, fell on his knees, devoutly took the crucifix into his hands, pressed it to his heart, and kissing it, died on the eighth of the Ides of March (March 8) in the year 1550. He remained in this same attitude with the crucifix still in his hand, for about six hours after his death. The entire city came to see the holy corpse, which gave forth a heavenly fragrance. The body was then removed, in order that it might be buried. God honoured his servant by many miracles, both before and after his death, and he was canonized by Pope Alexander VIII. Leo XIII., at the desire of the bishops of the Catholic world, and having consulted the sacred congregation of rites, declared him the heavenly patron of all hospitals and of the sick in all places, and ordered his name to be inserted in the litany for the dying.

What a glorious life was thine, O John of God!
It was one of charity, and of miracles wrought by
charity. Like Vincent of Paul thou wast poor, and,
in thy early life, a shepherd-boy like him; but the
charity which filled thy heart gave thee a power to
do what worldly influence and riches never can.
Thy name and memory are dear to the Church;
they deserve to be held in benediction by all mankind, for thou didst spend thy life in serving thy
fellow-creatures, for God's sake. That motive gave
thee a devotedness to the poor, which is an im-
possibility for those who befriend them from mere
natural sympathy. Philanthropy may be generous,
and its workings may be admirable for ingenuity
and order; but it never can look upon the poor man
as a sacred object, because it refuses to see God in
him. Pray for the men of this generation, that they
may at length desist from perverting charity into a
mere mechanism of relief. The poor are the repre-
sentatives of Christ, for He Himself has willed that
they be such; and if the world refuse to accept
them in this their exalted character, if it deny their
resemblance to our Redeemer, it may succeed in
degrading the poor, but by this very degradation it
will make them its enemies. Thy predilection, O
John of God, was for the sick; have pity, therefore,
on our times, which are ambitious to eliminate the
supernatural, and exclude God from the world by
what is called secularization of society. Pray for
us, that we may see how evil a thing it is to have
changed the Christian for the worldly spirit. Enkindle holy charity within our hearts, that during
these days, when we are striving to draw down the
mercy of God upon ourselves, we also may show
mercy. May we, as thou didst, imitate the example
of our blessed Redeemer, who gave Himself to us
His enemies, and deigned to adopt us as His
brethren. Protect also the Order thou didst insti-

tute, which has inherited thy spirit; that it may prosper, and spread in every place the sweet odour of that charity, which is its very name.

MARCH 9

SAINT FRANCES OF ROME, WIDOW

THE period intervening between the Purification of our blessed Lady and Ash Wednesday (when it occurs at its latest date), gives us thirty-six days; and these offer us feasts of every order of saint. The apostles have given us St. Mathias, and St. Peter's Chair at Antioch; the martyrs have sent us, from their countless choir, Simeon, Lucius, Blase, Valentine, Faustinus and Jovita, Perpetua and Felicitas, and the forty soldiers of Sebaste, whose feast is kept to-morrow; the holy pontiffs have been represented by Titus, Andrew Corsini, and also by Cyril of Alexandria and Peter Damian, who, like Thomas of Aquin, are doctors of the Church; the confessors have produced Romuald of Camaldoli, John of Matha, John of God, the Seven Founders of the Servites, and the angelic prince Casimir; the virgins have gladdened us with the presence of Agatha, Dorothy, Apollonia, and Scholastica, three wreathed with the red roses of martyrdom, and the fourth with the fair lilies of the enclosed garden[1] of her Spouse; and lastly, we have had a penitent saint, Margaret of Cortona. The state of Christian marriage is the only one that has not yet deputed a saint during this season, which is less rich in feasts than most of the year. The deficiency is supplied to-day by the admirable Frances of Rome.

Having, for forty years, led a most saintly life in the married state, upon which she entered when but twelve years of age, Frances retired from the

---

[1] Cant. iv. 12.

world, where she had endured every sort of tribulation. But she had given her heart to her God long before she withdrew to the cloister. Her whole life had been spent in the exercise of the highest Christian perfection, and she had ever received from our Lord the sublimest spiritual favours. Her amiable disposition had won for her the love and admiration of her husband and children: the rich venerated her as their model, the poor respected her as their devoted benefactress and mother.

God recompensed her angelic virtues by these two special graces: the almost uninterrupted sight of her guardian angel, and the most sublime revelations. But there is one trait of her life, which is particularly striking, and reminds us forcibly of St. Elizabeth of Hungary, and of St. Jane Frances Chantal: her austere practices of penance. Such an innocent, and yet such a mortified, life is full of instruction for us. How can we think of murmuring against the obligation of mortification, when we find a saint like this practising it during her whole life? True, we are not bound to imitate her in the manner of her penance; but penance we must do, if we would confidently approach that God who readily pardons the sinner when he repents, but whose justice requires atonement and satisfaction.

The Church thus describes the life, virtues, and miracles of St. Frances.

Francisca, nobilis matrona romana, ab ineunte ætate illustria dedit virtutum exempla : etenim pueriles ludos, et illecebras mundi respuens, solitudine, et oratione magnopere delectabatur. Undecim annos nata virginitatem suam Deo consecrare, et monasterium ingredi proposuit. Parentum

Frances, a noble lady of Rome, led a most virtuous life, even in her earliest years. She despised all childish amusements, and worldly pleasures, her only delight being solitude and prayer. When eleven years old, she resolved on consecrating her virginity to God, and seeking admission into a monastery. But she humbly

tamen voluntati humiliter obtemperans, Laurentio de Pontianis, juveni æque diviti ac nobili nupsit. In matrimonio arctioris vitæ propositum, quantum licuit, semper retinuit: a spectaculis, conviviis, aliisque hujusmodi oblectamentis abhorrens, lanea ac vulgari veste utens, et quidquid a domesticis curis supererat temporis, orationi, aut proximorum utilitati tribuens, in id vero maxima sollicitudine incumbens, ut matronas romanas a pompis sæculi, et ornatus vanitate revocaret. Quapropter domum Oblatarum, sub regula sancti Benedicti, Congregationis Montis Oliveti, adhuc viro alligata, in Urbe instituit. Viri exilium, bonorum jacturam, ac universæ domus mœrorem non modo constantissime toleravit, sed gratias agens cum beato Job, illud frequenter usurpabat: Dominus dedit, Dominus abstulit: sit nomen Domini benedictum.

Viro defuncto, ad prædictam Oblatarum domum convolans, nudis pedibus, fune ad collum alligato, humi prostrata, multis cum lacrymis, earum numero adscribi suppliciter postulavit. Voti compos facta, licet esset omnium mater, non alio tamen quam ancillæ, vilissimæque

yielded to the wishes of her parents, and married a young and rich nobleman, by name Lorenzo Ponziani. As far as it was possible, she observed, in the married state, the austerities of the most perfect life to which she had aspired. She carefully shunned theatrical entertainments, banquets, and other such amusements. Her dress was of serge, and extremely plain. Whatever time remained after she had fulfilled her domestic duties was spent in prayer and works of charity. But her zeal was mainly exercised in endeavouring to persuade the ladies of Rome, to shun the world, and vanity in dress. It was with a view to this that she founded during her husband's life, the house of Oblates of the Congregation of Monte - Oliveto, under the rule of Saint Benedict. She bore her husband's banishment, the loss of all her goods, and the trouble which befell her whole family, not only with heroic patience, but was frequently heard to give thanks, saying with holy Job: 'The Lord hath given, and the Lord hath taken away: blessed be the name of the Lord.'

At the death of her husband, she fled to the aforesaid house of Oblates, and there, barefooted, with a rope tied round her neck, and prostrate on the ground, she humbly, and with many tears, begged admission. Her petition being granted, she, though mother of the whole community, gloried

feminæ, et immunditiæ vasculi titulo gloriabatur. Quam vilem sui existimationem, et verbo declaravit, et exemplo. Sæpe enim e suburbana vinea revertens, et lignorum fascem proprio capiti impositum deferens, vel eisdem onustum agens per Urbem asellum, pauperibus subveniebat, in quos etiam largas eleemosynas erogabat ; ægrotantesque in xenodochiis visitans, non corporali tantum cibo, sed salutaribus monitis recreabat. Corpus suum vigiliis, jejuniis, cilicio, ferreo cingulo, crebrisque flagellis, in servitutem redigere jugiter satagebat. Cibum illi semel in die, herbæ et legumina : aqua potum præbuit. Hos tamen corporis cruciatus aliquando confessarii mandato, a cujus ore nutuque pendebat, modice temperavit.

Divina mysteria, præsertim vero Christi Domini Passionem, tanto mentis ardore, tantaque lacrymarum vi contemplabatur, ut præ doloris magnitudine pene confici videretur. Sæpe etiam cum oraret, maxime sumpto sanctissimæ Eucharistiæ sacramento, spiritu in Deum elevata, ac cœlestium contemplatione rapta, immobilis permanebat. Quapropter humani generis

in calling herself everyone's servant, and a worthless woman, and a vessel of dishonour. She evinced the contempt she had for herself by her conduct, as well as by her expressions. Thus, when returning from a vineyard in the suburbs, she would go through the city, sometimes carrying faggots on her head, sometimes driving an ass laden with them. She looked after, and bestowed abundant alms upon the poor. She visited the sick in the hospitals. and consoled them, not only with corporal food, but with spiritual advice. She was untiring in her endeavours to bring her body into subjection, by watchings, fasting, wearing a hair-shirt and an iron girdle, and by frequent disciplines. Her food, which she took but once in the day, consisted of herbs and pulse, and her only drink was water. But she would somewhat relent in these corporal austerities, as often as she was requested to do so by her confessor, whom she obeyed with the utmost exactitude.

Her contemplation of the divine mysteries, and especially of the Passion, was made with such intense fervour and abundance of tears, that she seemed as though she would die with grief. Frequently, too, when she was praying, and above all after holy Communion, she would remain motionless, with her soul fixed on God, and rapt in heavenly contemplation. The enemy of mankind seeing this, endea-

hostis variis eam contume- liis ac verberibus a proposito dimovere conabatur: quem tamen illa imperterrita sem- per elusit, angeli præsertim præsidio, cujus familiari consuetudine gloriosum de eo triumphum reportavit. Gratia curationum, et pro- phetiæ dono eñituit, quo et futura prædixit, et cordium secreta penetravit. Non se- mel aquæ, vel per rivum decurrentes, vel e cœlo laben- tes, intactam prorsus, dum Deo vacaret, reliquerunt. Modica panis fragmenta, quæ vix tribus sororibus re- ficiendis fuissent satis, sic ejus precibus Dominus mul- tiplicavit, ut quindecim inde exsaturatis, tantum super- fuerit, ut canistrum imple- verit: et aliquando, earum- dem sororum extra Urbem mense Januario ligna paran- tium, sitim recentis uvæ racemis ex vite in arbore pendentibus mirabiliter ob- tentis, abunde expleverit. Denique meritis, et mira- culis clara, migravit ad Dominum, anno ætatis suæ quinquagesimo sexto, quam Paulus quintus, Pontifex maximus, in sanctarum nu- merum retulit.

voured to frighten her out of so holy a life, by insults and blows; but she feared him not, invariably baffled his attempts, and, by the assistance of her angel guardian, whose visible presence was granted to her, she gained a glorious victory. God favoured her with the gift of healing the sick, as also with that of prophecy, whereby she foretold future events, and could read the secrets of hearts. More than once, when she was intent on prayer, either in the bed of a torrent, or during a storm of rain, she was not touched by the water. On one occasion, when all the bread they had was scarcely enough to provide a meal for three of the sisters, she besought our Lord, and he multiplied the bread; so that after fifteen persons had eaten as much as they needed, there was suffi- cient left to fill a basket. At another time, when the sisters were gathering wood outside the city walls, in the month of January, she amply quenched their thirst by offering them bunches of fresh grapes, which she miraculously obtained from a vine hanging on a tree. Her virtues and miracles procured for her the greatest veneration from all. Our Lord called her to himself in the fifty-sixth year of her age, and she was canonized by Pope Paul the fifth.

O Frances, sublime model of every virtue! thou wast the glory of Christian Rome, and the ornament of thy sex. How insignificant are the pagan heroines

of old compared with thee! Thy fidelity to the
duties of thy state, and all thy saintly actions, had
God for their one single end and motive. The
world looked on thee with amazement, as though
heaven had lent one of its angels to this earth.
Humility and penance put such energy into thy
soul, that every trial was met and mastered. Thy
love for those whom God Himself had given thee,
thy calm resignation and interior joy under tribulation, thy simple and generous charity, to every
neighbour—all was evidence of God's dwelling
within thy soul. Thy seeing and conversing with
thy angel guardian, and the wonderful revelations
granted thee of the secrets of the other world, how
much these favours tell us of thy merits! Nature
suspended her laws at thy bidding; she was sub-
servient to thee, as to one that was already face to
face with the sovereign Master, and had the power
to command. We admire these privileges and gifts
granted thee by our Lord; and now beseech thee to
have pity on us, who are so far from being in that
path, in which thou didst so perseveringly walk.
Pray for us, that we may be Christians, practically
and earnestly; that we may cease to love the world
and its vanities; that we may courageously take up
the yoke of our Lord, and do penance; that we
may give up our pride; that we may be patient and
firm under temptation. Such was thy influence
with our heavenly Father, that thou hadst but to
pray, and a vine produced the richest clusters of
fruit, even in the midst of winter. Our Jesus calls
Himself the true Vine; ask Him to give us of the
wine of His divine love, which His cross has so
richly prepared for us. When we remember how
frequently thou didst ask Him to let thee suffer,
and accept thy sufferings for poor sinners, we feel
encouraged to ask thee to offer thy merits to Him
for us. Pray, too, for Rome, thy native city, that

her people may be stanch to the faith, edifying by holiness of life, and loyal to the Church. May thy powerful intercession bring blessings on the faithful throughout the world, add to their number, and make them fervent as were our fathers of old.

MARCH 10

THE FORTY MARTYRS

WE know the mystery of the number forty. This tenth of March brings it before us. Forty new advocates! Forty encouraging us to enter bravely on our career of penance! On the frozen pool, which was their field of battle, these martyrs reminded one another that Jesus had fasted for forty days, and that they themselves were forty in number! Let us, in our turn, compare their sufferings with the lenten exercises which the Church imposes upon us; and humble ourselves on seeing our cowardice; or, if we begin with fervour, let us remember that the grand thing is to be faithful to the end, and bring to the Easter solemnity the crown of our perseverance. Our forty martyrs patiently endured the cruellest tortures; the fear of God, and their deep-rooted conviction that He had an infinite claim to their fidelity, gave them the victory. How many times we have sinned, and had not such severe temptations as theirs to palliate our fall! How can we sufficiently bless that divine mercy, which spared us, instead of abandoning us as it did that poor apostate, who turned coward and was lost! But, on what condition did God spare us? That we should not spare ourselves, but do penance. He put into our hands the rights of His own justice; justice, then, must be satisfied, and we must exercise it against ourselves. The lives of the

saints will be of great help to us in this, for they
will teach us how we are to look upon sin, how to
avoid it, and how strictly we are bound to do
penance for it after having committed it.

The Church, in her liturgy, thus relates to us the
martyrdom of the soldiers of Sebaste.

Licinio imperatore, et
Agricolao præside, ad Se-
basten Armeniæ urbem,
quadraginta militum fides
in Jesum Christum, et fortitudo in cruciatibus perfe-
rendis enituit. Qui sæpius
in horribilem carcerem
detrusi, vinculisque con-
stricti, cum ora ipsorum
lapidibus contusa fuissent,
hiemis tempore frigidissimo,
nudi sub aperto aere supra
stagnum rigens pernoctare
jussi sunt, ut frigore con-
gelati necarentur. Una
autem erat omnium oratio :
Quadraginta in stadium in-
gressi sumus, quadraginta
item, Domine, corona done-
mur ; ne una quidem huic
numero desit. Est in honore
hic numerus, quem tu qua-
draginta dierum jejunio de-
corasti, per quem divina lex
ingressa est in orbem terrarum. Elias quadraginta dierum jejunio Deum quærens,
ejus visionem consecutus
est. Et hæc quidem illorum
erat oratio.

Cæteris autem custodibus
somno deditis, solus vigila-
bat janitor, qui et illos oran-
tes, et luce circumfusos, et
quosdam e cœlo descenden-

During the reign of the
Emperor Licinius, and under
the presidency of Agricolaus,
the city of Sebaste in Armenia
was honoured by being made
the scene of the martyrdom of
forty soldiers, whose faith in
the Lord Jesus Christ, and
patience in bearing tortures,
were so glorious. After having
been frequently confined in a
horrid dungeon, shackled with
chains, and having had their
faces beaten with stones, they
were condemned to pass a
most bitter winter night in
the open air, and on a frozen
pool, that they might be
frozen to death. When there,
they united in this prayer :
' Forty have we entered on the
battle ; let us, O Lord, receive
forty crowns, and suffer not our
number to be broken. The
number is an honoured one,
for thou didst fast for forty
days, and the divine law was
given to the world after the
same number of days was observed. Elias, too, sought God
by a forty days' fast, and was
permitted to see him.' Thus
did they pray.

All the guards, except one,
were asleep. He overheard
their prayer, and saw them
encircled with light, and angels
coming down from heaven, like

tes angelos tanquam a Rege missos, qui coronas triginta novem militibus distribuerent, intuens, ita secum loquebatur: Quadraginta hi sunt ; quadragesimi corona ubi est ? Quæ dum cogitaret, unus ex illo numero, cui animus ad frigus ferendum defecerat in proximum tepefactum balneum desiliens, sanctos illos summo dolore affecit. Verum Deus illorum preces irritas esse non est passus ; nam rei eventum admiratus janitor, mox custodibus e somno excitatis, detractisque sibi vestibus, ac se christianum esse clara voce professus, martyribus se adjunxit. Cum vero præsidis satellites janitorem quoque christianum esse cognovissent, bacillis comminuta omnium eorum crura fregerunt.

In eo supplicio mortui sunt omnes præter Melithonem, natu minimum. Quem cum præsens mater ejus fractis cruribus adhuc viventem vidisset, sic cohortata est: Fili, paulisper sustine, ecce Christus ad januam stat adjuvans te. Cum vero reliquorum corpora plaustris imponi cerneret, ut in rogum inferrentur, ac filium suum relinqui, quod speraret impia turba, puerum, si vixisset, ad idolorum cultum revocari posse ; ipso in humeros sublato, sancta mater vehicula mar-

messengers sent by a King, who distributed crowns to thirty-nine of the soldiers. Whereupon, he thus said to himself: 'There are forty men; where is the fortieth crown ?' While he was thus pondering, one of the number lost his courage ; he could bear the cold no longer, and threw himself into a warm bath, which had been placed near at hand. His saintly companions were exceedingly grieved at this. But God would not suffer their prayer to be void. The sentinel, astonished at what he had witnessed, went immediately and awoke the guards ; then, taking off his garments, he cried out, with a loud voice, that he was a Christian, and associated himself with the martyrs. No sooner did the governor's guards perceive that the sentinel had also declared himself to be a Christian, than they approached the martyrs, and broke their legs with clubs.

All died under this torture except Melithon, who was the youngest of the forty. His mother, who was present, seeing that he was still living after his legs were broken, thus encouraged him : 'My son, be patient yet a while. Lo ! Christ is at the door, helping thee.' But, as soon as she saw the other bodies being placed on carts, that they might be thrown on the pile, and her son left behind (for the impious men hoped that, if the boy survived, he might be induced to worship the idols), she lifted him up into her

tyrum corporibus onusta strenue prosequebatur; in cujus amplexu Melithon spiritum Deo reddidit, ejusque corpus in eumdem illum cæterorum martyrum rogum pia mater injecit: ut qui fide et virtute conjunctissimi fuerant, funeris etiam societate copulati, una in cœlum pervenirent. Combustis illis, eorum reliquiæ projectæ in profluentem, cum mirabiliter in unum confluxissent locum, salvæ et integræ repertæ, honorifico sepulchro conditæ sunt.

arms, and, summing up all her strength, ran after the waggons, on which the martyrs' bodies were being carried. Melithon died in his mother's arms, and the holy woman threw his body on the pile, where the other martyrs were, that as he had been so united with them in faith and courage, he might be one with them in burial, and go to heaven in their company. As soon as the bodies were burnt, the pagans threw what remained into a river. The relics miraculously flowed to one and the same place, just as they were when they were taken from the pile. The Christians took them, and respectfully buried them.

That we may the more worthily celebrate the memory of the forty martyrs, we borrow a few stanzas from the hymn in which the Greek liturgy so enthusiastically sings their praises.

HYMN

(*Die IX. Martii*)

Generose præsentia sufferentes, in præmiis quæ sperabant gaudentes, sancti martyres ad invicem dicebant: Non vestimentum exuimus, sed veterem hominem deponimus; rigida est hiems, sed dulcis paradisus; molesta est glacies, sed jucunda requies. Non ergo recedamus, O commilitones: paulum sustineamus, ut victoriæ coronas obtineamus a Christo Domino et Salvatore animarum nostrarum.

The holy martyrs, generously suffering present evils, and rejoicing in the hope of reward, said to each other: 'It is not our raiment, but the old man that we have put off. The winter is cold; but paradise is sweet. The ice is a torture; but the repose is pleasant. Fellow-soldiers! let us not retreat. Let us suffer for a while, that we may obtain our crowns of victory from Christ our Lord, the Saviour of our souls.'

Fortissima mente marty-
rium sustinentes, athletæ
admirandi, per ignem et
aquam transivistis, et inde
ad salutis latitudinem per-
venistis, in hæreditatem
accipientes regnum cœlo-
rum, in quo divinas pro
nobis preces facite, sapientes
quadraginta martyres.

Attonitus stetit quadra-
ginta martyrum custos co-
ronas aspiciens, et amore
hujus vitæ contempto, desiderio gloriæ tuæ, Domine,
quæ illi apparuerat, suble-
vatus est, et cum martyribus cecinit : Benedictus es,
Deus patrum nostrorum.

Vitæ amator miles ad la-
vacrum currens pestiferum
mortuus est ; Christi autem
amicus egregius raptor co-
ronarum quæ apparuerant,
velut in lavacro immortali-
tatis, cum martyribus cane-
bat : Benedictus es, Deus
patrum nostrorum.

Virili prædita pectore,
mater Deo amica, super
humeros tollens quem ge-
nuerat fructum pietatis,
martyrem cum martyribus
victimam adducit, patris
Abrahæ imitatrix. O fili,
ad perenniter manentem
vitam velocius currens carpe
viam, Christi amica mater
ad puerum clamabat. Non
fero te secundum ad Deum
præmia largientem perve-
nire.

Venite, fratres, martyrum
laudibus celebremus pha-

O admirable combatants !
you suffered martyrdom with
most brave hearts. You passed
through fire and water, and
thence you came to the spacious
land of salvation, receiving the
kingdom of heaven as your
inheritance. There, O prudent
forty martyrs, offer up your
holy prayers for us.

The gaoler of the forty
martyrs stood in astonishment
as he beheld the crowns.
Despising this present life,
and ambitious to enjoy thy
glory, O Lord, which had been
shown him in vision, he joined
the martyrs in this hymn :
'Blessed art thou, O God of
our fathers !'

The soldier that loved this
life, ran to the cursed bath,
and there he met with death :
but the friend of Christ, he
that nobly seized the crown
which was offered him, as it
were laved in immortality,
sang with the martyrs : 'Blessed
art thou, the God of our
fathers !'

The mother, whose manly
spirit made her dear to God,
taking on her shoulders the
beloved fruit of her womb,
brings him to the martyrs
that he may be a martyred
victim with them. Thus does
she imitate our father Abraham. This mother, dear to
Christ, cried out to her child :
' O my son ; quickly run the
path that leads to life eternal.
I cannot brook thy being
second to any in coming to the
God, who rewards us.'

Come, brethren, let us sing
the praises of the troop of

langem, frigore incensam, et erroris frigus ardenti zelo incendentem ; generosissimum exercitum, sacratissimum agmen, consertis pugnans clypeis, infractum et invictum, defensores fidei et custodes, martyres quadraginta, divinam choream, legatos Ecclesiæ, potenter Christum deprecantes ut pacem animis nostris concedat et magnam misericordiam.

martyrs, who were burnt with frost, and whose ardent zeal set fire to the frosty cold of error. Most heroic army ; most holy legion, that fought with shields close knit together ; unbroken and unconquered troop ; defenders and guardians of the faith ; the forty martyrs, the sacred choir, the legates of the Church : their powerful prayers to Christ draw down upon our souls his peace and rich mercy.

Valiant soldiers of Christ, who meet us, with your mysterious number, at this commencement of our forty days' fast, receive the homage of our devotion. Your memory is venerated throughout the whole Church, and your glory is great in heaven. Though engaged in the service of an earthly prince, you were the soldiers of the eternal King: to Him were you faithful, and from Him did you receive your crown of eternal glory. We, also, are His soldiers ; we are fighting for the kingdom of heaven. Our enemies are many and powerful ; but, like you, we can conquer them, if, like you, we use the arms which God has put in our hands. Faith in God's word, hope in His assistance, humility, and prudence, with these we are sure of victory. Pray for us, O holy martyrs, that we may avoid all compromise with our enemies ; for our defeat is certain, if we try to serve two masters. During these forty days, we must put our arms in order, repair our lost strength, and renew our engagements ; come to our assistance, and get us a share in your brave spirit. A crown is also prepared for us : it is to be won on easier terms than yours ; and yet we shall lose it, unless we keep up within us an esteem for our vocation. How many times, in our past lives, have we forfeited that glorious crown ! But God,

in His mercy, has offered it to us again, and we are
resolved on winning it. Oh, for the glory of our
common Lord and Master, make intercession for us.

Our work of preparation is over : we are ready to
obey our mother's call to Lent. During the three
past weeks, we have studied the fall of our first
parents, and the miseries it brought upon man ; the
necessity of a Saviour ; the justice of God, against
which the human race dared to rebel ; the terrible
chastisement of the deluge, wherewith that revolt
was punished ; and finally, the covenant made by
God, through Abraham, with those who are faithful to Him, and shun the maxims of a perverse and
guilty world.

Now we are to see the accomplishment of the
great mysteries, whereby the wounds of our fall
were healed, the divine justice was disarmed, and
God's grace was poured out upon us, delivering us
from the yoke of Satan and the world.

The Man-God, whose sweet presence has been less
sensible during this Septuagesima season, is now
about to show Himself to us again, but this time it
is on His way to Calvary, where He is to be immolated for our redemption. The dolorous Passion,
which our sins have imposed upon Him, is about
to be brought before us : the greatest of anniversaries will soon be upon us.

Let us be all attention to the mysteries : let us be
fervent in the great work of our own purification.
Let us walk on courageously in the path of penance,
so that each day the burden of our sins may be
lightened, and after we have partaken, by heartfelt
compassion, of the cup of our Redeemer's Passion,
our lips will be once more permitted to sing the
songs of joy, and our hearts will thrill at Easter
with the loud burst of the Church's *Alleluia!*

THE SEVEN PENITENTIAL PSALMS

I

DAVID, struck down by sickness, asks pardon of God, and beseeches Him to heal the wounds of his soul.

PSALM 6

Domine, ne in furore tuo arguas me : * neque in ira tua corripias me.

Miserere mei, Domine, quoniam infirmus sum : * sana me Domine, quoniam conturbata sunt ossa mea.

Et anima mea turbata est valde : * sed tu Domine usquequo ?

Convertere, Domine, et eripe animam meam : * salvum me fac propter misericordiam tuam.

Quoniam non est in morte qui memor sit tui : * in inferno autem quis confitebitur tibi ?

Laboravi in gemitu meo, lavabo per singulas noctes lectum meum : * lacrymis meis stratum meum rigabo.

Turbatus est a furore oculus meus : * inveteravi inter omnes inimicos meos.

Discedite a me, omnes qui operamini iniquitatem : * quoniam exaudivit Dominus vocem fletus mei.

Exaudivit Dominus deprecationem meam : * Dominus orationem meam suscepit.

O Lord, rebuke me not in thy indignation, nor chastise me in thy wrath.

Have mercy on me, O Lord, for I am weak ; heal me, O Lord, for my bones are troubled.

And my soul is troubled exceedingly : but thou, O Lord, how long ?

Turn to me, O Lord, and deliver my soul : O save me, for thy mercy's sake.

For there is no one in death that is mindful of thee: and who shall confess to thee in hell ?

I have laboured in my groanings, every night I will wash my bed : I will water my couch with my tears.

My eye is troubled through indignation : I have grown old among all mine enemies.

Depart from me, all ye workers of iniquity : for the Lord hath heard the voice of my weeping.

The Lord hath heard my supplication : the Lord hath received my prayer.

Erubescant et conturben-
tur vehementer omnes ini-
mici mei : * convertantur et
erubescant valde velociter.

Let all mine enemies be
ashamed and be very much
troubled : let them be turned
back, and be ashamed very
speedily.

II

David experiences the happiness felt by a soul
whose sins have been forgiven her by God; he expresses his feelings, by comparing himself to a sick
man, who was at the point of death, and is restored
to health.

PSALM 31

Beati, quorum remissæ
sunt iniquitates : * et quorum tecta sunt peccata.

Beatus vir, cui non impu-
tavit Dominus peccatum : *
nec est in spiritu ejus dolus.

Quoniam tacui, invetera-
verunt ossa mea : * dum
clamarem tota die.

Quoniam die ac nocte
gravata est super me manus
tua : * conversus sum in
ærumna mea, dum configi-
tur spina.

Delictum meum cognitum
tibi feci : * et injustitiam
meam non abscondi.

Dixi Confitebor adver-
sum me injustitiam meam
Domino : * et tu remisisti
impietatem peccati mei.

Pro hac orabit ad te
omnis sanctus : * in tempore
opportuno.

Verumtamen in diluvio
aquarum multarum : * ad
eum non approximabunt.

Tu es refugium meum a
tribulatione, quæ circum-

Blessed are they whose iniquities are forgiven : and whose
sins are covered.

Blessed is the man, to whom
the Lord hath not imputed sin :
and in whose spirit there is no
guile.

Because I was silent, my
bones grew old : whilst I cried
out all the day long.

For day and night thy hand
was heavy upon me : I am
turned in my anguish, whilst
the thorn is fastened.

I have acknowledged my sin
to thee : and my injustice I
have not concealed.

I said, I will confess against
myself my injustice to the
Lord : and thou hast forgiven
the wickedness of my sin.

For this shall every one that
is holy pray to thee, in a season-
able time.

And yet, in a flood of many
waters they shall not come nigh
unto him.

Thou art my refuge from
the trouble which hath encom-

dedit me : * exsultatio mea,
erue me a circumdantibus
me.

Intellectum tibi dabo, et
instruam te in via hac qua
gradieris : * firmabo super
te oculos meos.

Nolite fieri sicut equus et
mulus : * quibus non est
intellectus.

In camo et freno maxillas
eorum constringe : * qui
non approximant ad te.

Multa flagella peccato-
ris : * sperantem autem in
Domino misericordia cir-
cumdabit.

Lætamini in Domino, et
exsultate justi : * et gloriamini omnes recti corde.

passed me : my joy ! deliver
me from them that surround
me.

Thou hast said to me : I
will give thee understanding,
and I will instruct thee in this
way in which thou shalt go : I
will fix mine eyes upon thee.

Do not become like the horse
and the mule, who have no
understanding.

With bit and bridle bind fast
their jaws, who come not near
unto thee.

Many are the scourges of
the sinner : but mercy shall
encompass him that hopeth in
the Lord.

Be glad in the Lord, and
rejoice ye just : and glory, all
ye right of heart.

III

The royal prophet feels the consequences left in
him by his past sins, and he begs God to have pity
on him.

PSALM 37

Domine, ne in furore tuo
arguas me : * neque in ira
tua corripias me.

Quoniam sagittæ tuæ in-
fixæ sunt mihi : * et confir-
masti super me manum
tuam.

Non est sanitas in carne
mea a facie iræ tuæ : * non
est pax ossibus meis a facie
peccatorum meorum.

Quoniam iniquitates meæ
supergressæ sunt caput
meum : * et sicut onus
grave gravatæ sunt super
me.

Rebuke me not, O Lord, in
thy indignation : nor chastise
me in thy wrath.

For thine arrows are fastened
in me : and thy hand hath been
strong upon me.

There is no health in my
flesh, because of thy wrath :
there is no peace in my bones,
because of my sins.

For my iniquities are gone
over my head : and as a heavy
burden, are become heavy upon
me.

Putruerunt, et corruptæ sunt cicatrices meæ, * a facie insipientiæ meæ.

Miser factus sum, et curvatus sum usque in finem : * tota die contristatus ingrediebar.

Quoniam lumbi mei impleti sunt illusionibus : * et non est sanitas in carne mea.

Afflictus sum et humiliatus sum nimis : * rugiebam a gemitu cordis mei.

Domine, ante te omne desiderium meum : * et gemitus meus a te non est absconditus.

Cor meum conturbatum est, dereliquit me virtus mea : * et lumen oculorum meorum, et ipsum non est mecum.

Amici mei et proximi mei : * adversum me appropinquaverunt et steterunt.

Et qui juxta me erant, de longe steterunt : * et vim faciebant qui quærebant animam meam.

Et qui inquirebant mala mihi, locuti sunt vanitates : * et dolos tota die meditabantur.

Ego autem tanquam surdus non audiebam : * et sicut mutus non aperiens os suum.

Et factus sum sicut homo non audiens : * et non habens in ore suo redargutiones.

Quoniam in te, Domine, speravi : * tu exaudies me, Domine Deus meus.

Quia dixi : Nequando supergaudeant mihi inimici

My sores are putrefied and corrupted, because of my foolishness.

I am become miserable and am bowed down even to the end : I walked sorrowful all the day long.

For my loins are filled with illusions : and there is no health in my flesh.

I am afflicted and humbled exceedingly : I roared with the groaning of my heart.

O Lord, all my desire is before thee : and my groaning is not hidden from thee.

My heart is troubled, my strength hath left me : and the light of mine eyes itself is not with me.

My friends and my neighbours have drawn near, and stood against me.

And they that were near me, stood afar off : and they that sought my soul, used violence.

And they that sought evils to me, spoke vain things : and studied deceits all the day long.

But I as a deaf man heard not : and as a dumb man not opening his mouth.

And i became as a man that heareth not : and that hath no reproofs in his mouth.

For in thee, O Lord, have I hoped : thou wilt hear me, O Lord my God.

For I said : Lest at any time mine enemies rejoice over me :

mei : * et dum commoventur pedes mei, super me magna locuti sunt.

Quoniam ego in flagella paratus sum: * et dolor meus in conspectu meo semper.

Quoniam iniquitatem meam annuntiabo : * et cogitabo pro peccato meo.

Inimici autem mei vivunt, et confirmati sunt super me : * et multiplicati sunt qui oderunt me inique.

Qui retribuunt mala pro bonis, detrahebant mihi: * quoniam sequebar bonitatem.

Ne derelinquas me, Domine Deus meus : * ne discesseris a me.

Intende in adjutorium meum : * Domine, Deus salutis meæ.

and whilst my feet are moved, they speak great things against me.

For I am ready for scourges : and my sorrow is continually before me.

For I will declare my iniquity : and I will think for my sin.

But mine enemies live, and are stronger than I : and they that hate me wrongfully, are multiplied.

They that render evil for good have detracted me : because I followed goodness.

Forsake me not, O Lord my God : do not thou depart from me.

Attend unto my help, O Lord the God of my salvation.

IV

The grief and prayer of David, when the prophet Nathan was sent, by God, to reproach him for the twofold crime he had committed by his sin with Bethsabee, are the subject of this psalm.

PSALM 50

Miserere mei Deus : * secundum magnam misericordiam tuam.

Et secundum multitudinem miserationum tuarum : * dele iniquitatem meam.

Amplius lava me ab iniquitate mea : * et a peccato meo munda me.

Quoniam iniquitatem meam ego cognosco : * et peccatum meum contra me est semper.

Have mercy on me, O God, according to thy great mercy.

And according to the multitude of thy tender mercies, blot out my iniquity.

Wash me yet more from my iniquity, and cleanse me from my sin.

For I know my iniquity, and my sin is always before me.

Tibi soli peccavi, et malum coram te feci : * ut justificeris in sermonibus tuis et vincas cum judicaris.

Ecce enim in iniquitatibus conceptus sum : * et in peccatis concepit me mater mea.

Ecce enim veritatem dilexisti : * incerta et occulta sapientiæ tuæ manifestasti mihi.

Asperges me hyssopo, et mundabor : * lavabis me, et super nivem dealbabor.

Auditui meo dabis gaudium et lætitiam : * et exsultabunt ossa humiliata.

Averte faciem tuam a peccatis meis : * et omnes iniquitates meas dele.

Cor mundum crea in me Deus : * et spiritum rectum innova in visceribus meis.

Ne projicias me a facie tua : * et Spiritum sanctum tuum ne auferas a me.

Redde mihi lætitiam salutaris tui : * et spiritu principali confirma me.

Docebo iniquos vias tuas : * et impii ad te convertentur.

Libera me de sanguinibus, Deus, Deus salutis meæ : * et exsultabit lingua mea justitiam tuam.

Domine, labia mea aperies : * et os meum annuntiabit laudem tuam.

Quoniam si voluisses sacrificium, dedissem uti-

To thee only have I sinned, and have done evil before thee : that thou mayst be justified in thy words, and mayst overcome when thou art judged.

For behold ! I was conceived in iniquities, and in sins did my mother conceive me.

For behold ! thou hast loved truth : the uncertain and hidden things of thy wisdom thou hast made manifest to me.

Thou shalt sprinkle me with hyssop, and I shall be cleansed : thou shalt wash me, and I shall be made whiter than snow.

To my hearing thou shalt give joy and gladness : and the bones that have been humbled, shall rejoice.

Turn away thy face from my sins : and blot out all my iniquities.

Create a clean heart in me, O God : and renew a right spirit within my bowels.

Cast me not away from thy face : and take not thy holy Spirit from me.

Restore unto me the joy of thy salvation : and strengthen me with a perfect spirit.

I will teach the unjust thy ways : and the wicked shall be converted to thee.

Deliver me from blood, O God, thou God of my salvation ! and my tongue shall extol thy justice.

O Lord, thou wilt open my lips : and my mouth shall declare thy praise.

For if thou hadst desired sacrifice, I would indeed have

que : * holocaustis non delectaberis.

given it: with burnt offerings thou wilt not be delighted.

Sacrificium Deo spiritus contribulatus : * cor contritum et humiliatum, Deus, non despicies.

A sacrifice to God is an afflicted spirit : a contrite and humbled heart, O God, thou wilt not despise.

Benigne fac, Domine, in bona voluntate tua Sion : * ut ædificentur muri Jerusalem.

Deal favourably, O Lord, in thy good-will with Sion; that the walls of Jerusalem may be built up.

Tunc acceptabis sacrificium justitiæ, oblationes, et holocausta : * tunc imponent super altare tuum vitulos.

Then shalt thou accept the sacrifice of justice, oblations, and whole-burnt offerings : then shall they lay calves upon thine altar.

V

David laments over the captivity of God's people in Babylon, and prays for the restoration of Sion. His words are appropriate for the soul, who grieves over her sins, and implores to be regenerated by grace.

PSALM 101

Domine, exaudi orationem meam : * et clamor meus ad te veniat.

Hear, O Lord, my prayer : and let my cry come unto thee.

Non avertas faciem tuam a me : * in quacumque die tribulor, inclina ad me aurem tuam.

Turn not away thy face from me : in the day when I am in trouble, incline thine ear to me.

In quacumque die invocavero te : * velociter exaudi me.

In what day soever I shall call upon thee, hear me speedily.

Quia defecerunt sicut fumus dies mei : * et ossa mea sicut cremium aruerunt.

For my days are vanished like smoke : and my bones are grown dry like fuel for the fire.

Percussus sum ut fœnum, et aruit cor meum : * quia oblitus sum comedere panem meum.

I am smitten as grass, and my heart is withered : because I forgot to eat my bread.

A voce gemitus mei · *

Through the voice of my

adhæsit os meum carni meæ.

Similis factus sum pellicano solitudinis : * factus sum sicut nycticorax in domicilio.

Vigilavi : * et factus sum sicut passer solitarius in tecto.

Tota die exprobrabant mihi inimici mei : * et qui laudabant me adversum me jurabant.

Quia cinerem tamquam panem manducabam : * et potum meum cum fletu miscebam.

A facie iræ et indignationis tuæ : * quia elevans allisisti me.

Dies mei sicut umbra declinaverunt : * et ego sicut fœnum arui.

Tu autem, Domine, in æternum permanes : * et memoriale tuum in generationem et generationem.

Tu exsurgens misereberis Sion : * quia tempus miserendi ejus, quia venit tempus.

Quoniam placuerunt servis tuis lapides ejus : * et terræ ejus miserebuntur.

Et timebunt gentes nomen tuum, Domine : * et omnes reges terræ gloriam tuam.

Quia ædificavit Dominus Sion : * et videbitur in gloria sua.

Respexit in orationem humilium : * et non sprevit precem eorum.

groaning, my bone hath cleaved to my flesh.

I am become like to a pelican of the wilderness : I am like a night-raven in the house.

I have watched, and am become as a sparrow all alone on the housetop.

All the day long mine enemies reproached me : and they that praised me, did swear against me.

For I did eat ashes like bread : and mingled my drink with weeping.

Because of thy anger and indignation : for having lifted me up, thou hast thrown me down.

My days have declined like a shadow : and I am withered like grass.

But thou, O Lord, endurest for ever : and thy memorial to all generations.

Thou shalt arise and have mercy on Sion : for it is time to have mercy on it, for the time is come.

For the stones thereof have pleased thy servants : and they shall have pity on the earth thereof.

And the Gentiles shall fear thy name, O Lord : and all the kings of the earth thy glory.

For the Lord hath built up Sion : and he shall be seen in his glory.

He hath had regard to the prayer of the humble : and he hath not despised their petition.

Scribantur hæc in gene-
ratione altera : * et populus
qui creabitur laudabit Dominum.

Quia prospexit de excelso
sancto suo : * Dominus de
cœlo in terram aspexit.

Ut audiret gemitus com-
peditorum : * ut solveret
filios interemptorum.

Ut annuntient in Sion
nomen Domini : * et lau-
dem ejus in Jerusalem.

In conveniendo populos
in unum : * et reges, ut ser-
viant Domino.

Respondit ei in via virtutis suæ : * paucitatem dierum meorum nuntia mihi.

Ne revoces me in dimidio
dierum meorum : * in generationem et generationem
anni tui.

Initio tu, Domine, terram
fundasti : * et opera manuum tuarum sunt cœli.

Ipsi peribunt, tu autem
permanes : * et omnes sicut
vestimentum veterascent.

Et sicut opertorium muta-
bis eos, et mutabuntur : *
tu autem idem ipse es, et
anni tui non deficient.

Filii servorum tuorum ha-
bitabunt : * et semen eorum
in sæculum dirigetur.

Let these things be written
unto another generation : and
the people that shall be created,
shall praise the Lord.

Because he hath looked forth
from his high sanctuary : from
heaven, the Lord hath looked
upon the earth.

That he might hear the
groans of them that are in
fetters : that he might release
the children of the slain.

That they may declare the
name of the Lord in Sion, and
his praise in Jerusalem.

When the people assembled
together, and kings to serve the
Lord.

He (*the royal prophet*),
*longing to see these glorious
things,* answered him *though
still* in the way of his strength :
Declare unto me the fewness
of my days ;

Call me not away in the
midst of my days : thy years
are unto generation and generation.

In the beginning, O Lord,
thou foundedst the earth : and
the heavens are the works of
thy hands.

They shall perish, but thou
remainest : and all of them
shall grow old, like a garment.

And as a vesture thou shalt
change them, and they shall
be changed : but thou art
always the self-same, and thy
years shall not fail.

The children of thy servants
shall continue : and their seed
shall be directed for ever.

VI

The sinner seeing the *depths* of the abyss into which sin has led him, can hope for help from none but his God, whose mercy is infinite.

PSALM 129

De profundis clamavi ad te, Domine : * Domine, exaudi vocem meam.

Fiant aures tuæ intendentes : * in vocem deprecationis meæ.

Si iniquitates observaveris Domine : * Domine, quis sustinebit ?

Quia apud te propitiatio est : * et propter legem tuam sustinui te, Domine.

Sustinuit anima mea in verbo ejus : * speravit anima mea in Domino.

A custodia matutina usque ad noctem : * speret Israël in Domino.

Quia apud Dominum misericordia : * et copiosa apud eum redemptio.

Et ipse redimet Israël : * ex omnibus iniquitatibus ejus.

Out of the depths I have cried to thee, O Lord : Lord, hear my voice.

Let thine ears be attentive to the voice of my supplication.

If thou, O Lord, wilt mark iniquities : Lord, who shall stand it ?

For with thee there is merciful forgiveness : and by reason of thy law, I have waited for thee, O Lord.

My soul hath relied on his word : my soul hath hoped in the Lord.

From the morning watch even until night, let Israel hope in the Lord.

Because with the Lord there is mercy : and with him, plentiful redemption.

And he shall redeem Israel from all his iniquities.

VII

David, who had taken refuge in a cave, sees himself surrounded by the army of Saul ; he beseeches God not to deal with him according to the rigour of His just judgments, but to show him a way whereby to escape the danger that threatens him. The sinner implores God to deliver him from the sins and temptations which beset him.

PSALM 142

Domine, exaudi oratio-
nem meam, auribus percipe
obsecrationem meam in
veritate tua : * exaudi me
in tua justitia.

Et non intres in judicium
cum servo tuo : * quia non
justificabitur in conspectu
tuo omnis vivens.

Quia persecutus est inimicus animam meam : * hu-
miliavit in terra vitam
meam.

Collocavit me in obscuris
sicut mortuos sæculi : et
anxiatus est super me spiritus meus : * in me turbatum
est cor meum.

Memor fui dierum anti-
quorum, meditatus sum in
omnibus operibus tuis : * in
factis manuum tuarum me-
ditabar.

Expandi manus meas ad
te : * anima mea sicut terra
sine aqua tibi.

Velociter exaudi me, Do-
mine : * defecit spiritus
meus.

Non avertas faciem tuam
a me : * et similis ero des-
cendentibus in lacum.

Auditam fac mihi mane
misericordiam tuam : * quia
in te speravi.

Notam fac mihi viam in
qua ambulem : * quia ad te
levavi animam meam.

Eripe me de inimicis meis,
Domine, ad te confugi : *
doce me facere voluntatem
tuam, quia Deus meus es tu.

Spiritus tuus bonus dedu-
cet me in terram rectam : *

Hear, O Lord, my prayer;
give ear to my supplication in
thy truth : hear me in thy
justice.

And enter not into judg-
ment with thy servant: for in
thy sight no man living shall
be justified.

For the enemy hath perse-
cuted my soul : he hath
brought down my life to the
earth.

He hath made me to dwell
in darkness, as those that have
been dead of old ; and my spirit
is in anguish within me : my
heart within me is troubled.

I remembered the days of
old, I meditated on all thy
works : I meditated upon the
works of thy hands.

I stretched forth my hands
to thee : my soul is as earth
without water, unto thee.

Hear me speedily, O Lord :
my spirit hath fainted away.

Turn not away thy face from
me : lest I be like unto them
that go down into the pit.

Cause me to hear thy mercy
in the morning : for in thee
have I hoped.

Make the way known to me,
wherein I should walk : for I
have lifted up my soul to
thee.

Deliver me from mine ene-
mies, O Lord; to thee have I
fled : teach me to do thy will,
for thou art my God.

Thy good Spirit shall lead
me into the right land : for

propter nomen tuum, Domine, vivificabis me in æquitate tua.

Educes de tribulatione animam meam : * et in misericordia tua disperdes inimicos meos.

Et perdes omnes qui tribulant animam meam : * quoniam ego servus tuus sum.

ANT. Ne reminiscaris, Domine, delicta nostra, vel parentum nostrorum, neque vindictam sumas de peccatis nostris.

thy name's sake, O Lord, thou wilt quicken me in thy justice.

Thou wilt bring my soul out of trouble : and in thy mercy, thou wilt destroy mine enemies.

And thou wilt cut off all them that afflict my soul : for I am thy servant.

ANT. Remember not, O Lord, our offences, nor those of our parents, and take not revenge on our sins.

THE DEVOTIONS FOR THE FORTY HOURS

HYMN

Pange, lingua, gloriosi
Corporis mysterium,
Sanguinisque pretiosi,
Quem in mundi pretium,
Fructus ventris generosi,
Rex effudit gentium.

Sing, O my tongue, the mystery of the glorious Body, and precious Blood which was shed as the world's ransom, by him who is the fruit of Mary's glorious womb, him the King of nations.

Nobis datus, nobis natus
Ex intacta Virgine,
Et in mundo conversatus,
Sparso verbi semine,
Sui moras incolatus
Miro clausit ordine.

Given unto us, and born for us from the purest of Virgins, he lived in this our world, casting the seed of the word; and closed the days of his sojourn here, by a way full of marvel.

In supremæ nocte cœnæ
Recumbens cum fratribus,
Observata lege plene
Cibis in legalibus,
Cibum turbæ duodenæ
Se dat suis manibus.

On the night of the last Supper, he sat at table with his brethren; and having fully observed the Law as to its legal repast, he gave himself, with his own hands, as food to the assembled twelve.

Verbum caro, panem verum
Verbo carnem efficit :
Fitque sanguis Christi merum :
Et si sensus deficit,
Ad firmandum cor sincerum
Sola fides sufficit.

The Word made Flesh, makes, by a word, true bread become Flesh, and wine the Blood of Christ ; and though our sense may fail, faith of itself is enough to assure an upright heart.

Tantum ergo Sacramentum
Veneremur cernui :
Et antiquum documentum
Novo cedat ritui :
Præstet fides supplementum
Sensuum defectui.

Then let us, prostrate, adore so great a Sacrament : and let the ancient law give place to the new rite : let faith supply the senses' deficiency.

Genitori, Genitoque
Laus et jubilatio,
Salus, honor, virtus quoque
Sit et benedictio :
Procedenti ab utroque
Compar sit laudatio.
  Amen.

To the Father and the Son,
be praise and jubilation, salvation, honour, power and benediction · to him that proceedeth
from both, be equal praise !
  Amen.

THE LITANY OF THE SAINTS

Kyrie, eleison.

Christe, eleison.

Kyrie, eleison.

Christe, audi nos.

Christe, exaudi nos.

Pater de cœlis, Deus, miserere nobis.

Fili, Redemptor mundi, Deus, miserere nobis.

Spiritus sancte, Deus, miserere nobis.

Sancta Trinitas, unus Deus, miserere nobis.

Sancta Maria, ora pro nobis.

Sancta Dei Genitrix,   ora.

Sancta Virgo virginum, ora.

Sancte Michael,   ora.

Sancte Gabriel,   ora.

Sancte Raphael,   ora.

Omnes sancti angeli et archangeli,   orate.

Omnes sancti beatorum spirituum ordines, orate.

Sancte Joannes Baptista,   ora.

Sancte Joseph,   ora.

Omnes sancti patriarchæ et prophetæ,   orate.

Sancte Petre,   ora.

Sancte Paule,   ora.

Sancte Andrea,   ora.

Sancte Jacobe,   ora.

Sancte Joannes,   ora.

Lord, have mercy on us.

Christ, have mercy on us.

Lord, have mercy on us.

Christ, hear us.

Christ, graciously hear us.

God the Father of heaven, have mercy on us.

God the Son, Redeemer of the world, have mercy on us.

God the Holy Ghost, have mercy on us.

Holy Trinity, one God, have mercy on us.

Holy Mary, pray for us.

Holy Mother of God, pray for us.

Holy Virgin of virgins, pray for us.

Saint Michael, pray for us.

Saint Gabriel,

Saint Raphael,

All ye holy angels and archangels,

All ye holy orders of blessed spirits,

Saint John Baptist,

Saint Joseph,

All ye holy patriarchs and prophets,

Saint Peter,

Saint Paul,

Saint Andrew,

Saint James,

Saint John,

Sancte Thoma,	ora.	Saint Thomas,
Sancte Jacobe,	ora.	Saint James,
Sancte Philippe,	ora.	Saint Philip,
Sancte Bartholomæe,	ora.	Saint Bartholomew,
Sancte Matthæe,	ora.	Saint Matthew,
Sancte Simon,	ora.	Saint Simon,
Sancte Thaddæe,	ora.	Saint Thaddeus,
Sancte Mathia,	ora.	Saint Mathias,
Sancte Barnaba,	ora.	Saint Barnaby,
Sancte Luca,	ora.	Saint Luke,
Sancte Marce,	ora.	Saint Mark,
Omnes sancti apostoli et evangelistæ, orate.		All ye holy apostles and evangelists,
Omnes sancti discipuli Domini, orate.		All ye holy disciples of our Lord,
Omnes sancti Innocentes, orate.		All ye holy Innocents,
Sancte Stephane,	ora.	Saint Stephen,
Sancte Laurenti,	ora.	Saint Laurence,
Sancte Vincenti,	ora.	Saint Vincent,
Sancti Fabiane et Sebastiane, orate.		Saints Fabian and Sebastian,
Sancti Joannes et Paule, orate.		Saints John and Paul,
Sancti Cosma et Damiane, orate.		Saints Cosmas and Damian,
Sancti Gervasi et Protasi, orate.		Saints Gervasius and Protasius,
Omnes sancti martyres, orate.		All ye holy martyrs,
Sancte Sylvester,	ora.	Saint Sylvester,
Sancte Gregori,	ora.	Saint Gregory,
Sancte Ambrosi,	ora.	Saint Ambrose,
Sancte Augustine,	ora.	Saint Augustine,
Sancte Hieronyme,	ora.	Saint Jerome,
Sancte Martine,	ora.	Saint Martin,
Sancte Nicolae,	ora.	Saint Nicholas,
Omnes sancti pontifices et confessores, orate.		All ye holy bishops and confessors,
Omnes sancti doctores, orate.		All ye holy doctors,
Sancte Antoni,	ora.	Saint Antony,
Sancte Benedicte,	ora.	Saint Benedict,
Sancte Bernarde,	ora.	Saint Bernard,
Sancte Dominice,	ora.	Saint Dominic,
Sancte Francisce,	ora.	Saint Francis,

Omnes sancti sacerdotes et levitæ, orate.

All ye holy priests and levites,

Omnes sancti monachi et eremitæ, orate.

All ye holy monks and hermits,

Sancta Maria Magdalena, ora.

Saint Mary Magdalene,

Sancta Agatha, ora.

Saint Agatha,

Sancta Lucia, ora.

Saint Lucy,

Sancta Agnes, ora.

Saint Agnes,

Sancta Cæcilia, ora.

Saint Cecily,

Sancta Catharina, ora.

Saint Catharine,

Sancta Anastasia, ora.

Saint Anastasia,

Omnes sanctæ virgines et viduæ, orate.

All ye holy virgins and widows,

Omnes sancti et sanctæ Dei, intercedite pro nobis.

All ye saints of God, make intercession for us.

Propitius esto, parce nobis, Domine.

Be merciful to us, spare us, O Lord.

Propitius esto, exaudi nos, Domine

Be merciful to us, graciously hear us, O Lord.

Ab omni malo, libera nos, Domine.

From all evil, deliver us, O Lord.

Ab omni peccato, libera nos, Domine.

From all sin, deliver us, O Lord.

Ab ira tua, libera.

From thy wrath,

Ab imminentibus periculis, libera.

From all dangers that threaten us,

A flagello terræmotus, libera.

From the scourge of earthquakes,

A peste, fame, et bello, libera.

From plague, famine, and war,

A subitanea et improvisa morte, libera.

From sudden and unprovided death,

Ab insidiis diaboli, libera.

From the snares of the devil,

Ab ira, et odio, et omni mala voluntate, libera.

From anger, hatred, and all ill-will,

A spiritu fornicationis, libera.

From the spirit of fornication,

A fulgure et tempestate, libera.

From lightning and tempest,

A morte perpetua, libera.

From everlasting death,

Per mysterium sanctæ Incarnationis tuæ, libera.

Through the mystery of thy holy Incarnation,

Per adventum tuum, libera.

Through thy coming,

Per nativitatem tuam, libera.

Through thy nativity,

Per baptismum et sanctum jejunium tuum, libera.

Per crucem et Passionem tuam, libera.

Per mortem et sepulturam tuam, libera.

Per sanctam Resurrectionem tuam, libera.

Per admirabilem Ascensionem tuam, libera.

Per adventum Spiritus sancti Paracliti, libera.

In die judicii, libera.

Peccatores,
te rogamus, audi nos.

Ut nobis parcas,
te rogamus, audi nos.

Ut nobis indulgeas, te, etc.

Ut ad veram pœnitentiam nos perducere digneris,
te rogamus.

Ut Ecclesiam tuam sanctam regere et conservare digneris, te rogamus.

Ut Domnum apostolicum, et omnes ecclesiasticos ordines, in sancta religione conservare digneris,
te rogamus.

Ut inimicos sanctæ Ecclesiæ humiliare digneris,
te rogamus.

Ut Turcarum et hæreticorum conatus reprimere, et ad nihilum redigere digneris,
te rogamus.

Ut regibus et principibus Christianis pacem et veram concordiam donare digneris, te rogamus.

Ut omnes errantes ad unitatem Ecclesiæ revocare, et infideles universos ad Evangelii lumen perducere digneris,
te rogamus.

Through thy baptism and holy fasting,

Through thy cross and Passion,

Through thy death and burial,

Through thy holy Resurrection,

Through thy admirable Ascension,

Through the coming of the Holy Ghost the Comforter,

In the day of judgment,

We sinners, beseech thee, hear us.

That thou spare us, we beseech thee, hear us.

That thou pardon us,

That thou vouchsafe to bring us to true penance,

That thou vouchsafe to govern and preserve thy holy Church,

That thou vouchsafe to preserve our apostolic lord, and all ecclesiastical orders, in holy religion,

That thou vouchsafe to humble the enemies of thy holy Church,

That thou vouchsafe to defeat the attempts of Turks and heretics, and bring them to nought,

That thou vouchsafe to give peace and true concord to Christian kings and princes,

That thou vouchsafe to recall all wanderers to the unity of the Church, and to lead all unbelievers to the light of the Gospel,

Ut cuncto populo Christiano pacem et unitatem largiri digneris, te rogamus.

That thou vouchsafe to grant peace and unity to all Christian people,

Ut nosmetipsos in tuo sancto servitio confortare et conservare digneris,
          te rogamus.

That thou vouchsafe to strengthen and preserve us in thy holy service.

Ut mentes nostras ad cœlestia desideria erigas,
          te rogamus.

That thou lift up our minds to heavenly desires,

Ut omnibus benefactoribus nostris sempiterna bona retribuas,   te rogamus.

That thou render eternal good things to all our benefactors,

Ut animas nostras, fratrum, propinquorum, et benefactorum nostrorum ab æterna damnatione eripias,
          te rogamus.

That thou deliver our souls, and those of our brethren, kinsfolk and benefactors, from eternal damnation,

Ut fructus terræ dare et conservare digneris,
          te rogamus.

That thou vouchsafe to give and preserve the fruits of the earth,

Ut omnibus fidelibus defunctis requiem æternam donare digneris,
          te rogamus.

That thou vouchsafe to give eternal rest to all the faithful departed,

Ut nos exaudire digneris,
          te rogamus.

That thou vouchsafe graciously to hear us.

Fili Dei,   te rogamus.

Son of God, we beseech thee, hear us.

Agnus Dei, qui tollis peccata mundi,
          parce nobis, Domine.

Lamb of God, who takest away the sins of the world, spare us, O Lord,

Agnus Dei, qui tollis peccata mundi,
          exaudi nos, Domine.

Lamb of God, who takest away the sins of the world, graciously hear us, O Lord,

Agnus Dei, qui tollis peccata mundi, miserere nobis.

Lamb of God, who takest away the sins of the world, have mercy on us.

Christe, audi nos.

Christ, hear us.

Christe, exaudi nos.

Christ, graciously hear us.

Kyrie, eleison.

Lord, have mercy on us.

Christe, eleison.

Christ, have mercy on us.

Kyrie, eleison.

Lord, have mercy on us.

Pater noster. (*Secreto.*)

Our Father. (*In secret.*)

V. Et ne nos inducas in tentationem.

V. And lead us not into temptation.

R. Sed libera nos a malo.

R. But deliver us from evil.

PSALM 69

Deus, in adjutorium meum intende : * Domine, ad adjuvandum me festina.

O God, come to my assistance : O Lord, make haste to help me.

Confundantur et revereantur : * qui quærunt animam meam.

Let them be confounded and ashamed that seek my soul.

Avertantur retrorsum et erubescant : * qui volunt mihi mala.

Let them be turned backward, and blush for shame, that desire evils to me.

Avertantur statim erubescentes : * qui dicunt mihi, Euge, euge.

Let them be presently turned away blushing for shame, that say to me : 'Tis well, 'tis well.

Exsultent et lætentur in te omnes qui quærunt te : * et dicant semper, magnificetur Dominus qui diligunt salutare tuum.

Let all that seek thee rejoice and be glad in thee : and let such as love thy salvation, say always, the Lord be magnified.

Ego vero egenus et pauper sum : * Deus adjuva me.

But I am needy and poor : O God, help me.

Adjutor meus et liberator meus es tu : * Domine, ne moreris.

Thou art my helper and my deliverer : O Lord, make no delay.

Gloria Patri, et Filio, * et Spiritui sancto.

Glory be to the Father, and to the Son, and to the Holy Ghost.

Sicut erat in principio, et nunc, et semper : * et in sæcula sæculorum, Amen.

As it was in the beginning, is now, and ever shall be, world without end. Amen.

V. Salvos fac servos tuos.

V. Save thy servants.

R. Deus meus sperantes in te.

R. Trusting in thee, O my God.

V. Esto nobis, Domine, turris fortitudinis.

V. Be unto us, O Lord, a tower of strength.

R. A facie inimici.

R. From the face of the enemy.

V. Nihil proficiat inimicus in nobis.

V. Let not the enemy prevail against us.

R. Et filius iniquitatis non apponat nocere nobis.

R. Nor the son of iniquity have any power to hurt us.

V. Domine, non secundum peccata nostra facias nobis.

V. O Lord, deal not with us according to our sins.

R. Neque secundum iniquitates nostras retribuas nobis.

R. Nor reward us according to our iniquities.

V. Oremus pro Pontifice nostro N.

R. Dominus conservet eum, et vivificet eum, et beatum faciat eum in terra, et non tradat eum in animam inimicorum ejus.

V. Oremus pro benefactoribus nostris.

R. Retribuere dignare, Domine, omnibus nobis bona facientibus, propter nomen tuum, vitam æternam. Amen.

V. Oremus pro fidelibus defunctis.

R. Requiem æternam dona eis, Domine, et lux perpetua luceat eis.

V. Requiescant in pace.

R. Amen.

V. Pro fratribus nostris absentibus.

R. Salvos fac servos tuos, Deus meus, sperantes in te.

V. Mitte eis, Domine, auxilium de sancto.

R. Et de Sion tuere eos.

V. Domine, exaudi orationem meam.

R. Et clamor meus ad te veniat.

V. Dominus vobiscum.

R. Et cum spiritu tuo.

OREMUS.

Deus, qui nobis, sub Sacramento mirabili, Passionis tuæ memoriam reliquisti: tribue, quæsumus, ita nos Corporis et Sanguinis tui sacra mysteria venerari, ut Redemptionis tuæ fructum in nobis jugiter sentiamus.

V. Let us pray for our chief Bishop N.

R. May our Lord preserve him, and give him life, and make him blessed upon earth, and deliver him not to the will of his enemies.

V. Let us pray for our benefactors.

R. Vouchsafe, O Lord, for thy name's sake, to reward, with eternal life, all them that have done us good. Amen.

V. Let us pray for the faithful departed.

R. Eternal rest give to them, O Lord, and let perpetual light shine upon them.

V. May they rest in peace.

R. Amen.

V. For our absent brethren.

R. O my God, save thy servants trusting in thee.

V. Send them help, O Lord, from thy holy place.

R. And from Sion protect them.

V. O Lord, hear my prayer.

R. And let my cry come unto thee.

V. The Lord be with you.

R. And with thy spirit.

LET US PRAY.

O God, who, in this wonderful Sacrament, hast left us a perpetual memorial of thy Passion: grant us, we beseech thee, so to reverence the sacred mysteries of thy Body and Blood, that in our souls we may always be sensible of the fruit of the Redemption thou hast purchased for us.

[1] Concede nos famulos tuos, quæsumus, Domine Deus, perpetua mentis et corporis sanitate gaudere : et gloriosa beatæ Mariæ sem per Virginis intercessione, a præsenti liberari tristitia, et æterna perfrui lætitia.

Omnipotens sempiterne Deus, miserere famulo tuo Pontifici nostro N., et dirige eum, secundum tuam clementiam, in viam salutis æternæ ; ut, te donante, tibi placita cupiat, et tota virtute perficiat.

Deus refugium nostrum et virtus, adesto piis Ecclesiæ tuæ precibus, auctor ipse pietatis, et præsta ; ut quod fideliter petimus, efficaciter consequamur.

Omnipotens sempiterne Deus, in cujus manu sunt omnium potestates, et omnia jura regnorum, respice in auxilium Christianorum ; ut gentes paganorum et hæreticorum, quæ in sua feritate et fraude confidunt, dexteræ tuæ potentia conterantur.

Omnipotens sempiterne Deus, qui vivorum dominaris simul et mortuorum, omniumque misereris, quos tuos fide et opere futuros esse prænoscis ; te supplices exoramus ; ut pro quibus

[1] Grant, O Lord, we beseech thee, that we thy servants may enjoy constant health of body and mind : and by the glorious intercession of blessed Mary, ever a Virgin, be delivered from all present affliction, and come to that joy which is eternal.

O almighty and eternal God, have mercy on thy servant N., our chief Bishop, and direct him, according to thy clemency, in the way of everlasting salvation ; that, by thy grace, he may desire those things that are agreeable to thee, and perform them with all his strength.

O God, our refuge and strength, fountain of all goodness, mercifully give ear to the fervent prayers of thy Church, and grant, that what we ask with faith, we may effectually obtain.

O almighty and eternal God, in whose hand are all the powers and all the rights of kingdoms, come to the assistance of thy Christian people ; that all pagan and heretical nations, who trust in their own violence and craft, may be broken by the might of thy right hand.

O almighty and eternal God, who hast dominion over the living and the dead, and art merciful to all, who thou foreknowest shall be thine by faith and good works ; we humbly beseech thee, that

---

[1] This Collect varies in Advent, and at Christmas. See the Collects for these times, page 371.

effundere preces decrevimus, quosque vel præsens sæculum adhuc in carne retinet, vel futurum jam exutos corpore suscepit, intercedentibus omnibus sanctis tuis, pietatis tuæ clementia, omnium delictorum suorum veniam consequantur. Per Dominum nostrum Jesum Christum Filium tuum, qui tecum vivit et regnat, in unitate Spiritus sancti, Deus, per omnia sæcula sæculorum.

R. Amen.

V. Domine exaudi orationem meam.

R. Et clamor meus ad te veniat.

V. Exaudiat nos omnipotens et misericors Dominus.

R. Et custodiat nos semper, Amen.

V. Fidelium animæ, per misericordiam Dei, requiescant in pace.

R. Amen.

they, for whom we have determined to offer up our prayers, whether this present world still detain them in the flesh, or the world to come hath already received them out of their bodies, may, by the clemency of thy goodness, all thy saints interceding for them, obtain pardon and full remission of all their sins. Through our Lord Jesus Christ, thy Son, who liveth and reigneth, one God with thee and the holy Ghost, world without end.

R. Amen.

V. O Lord hear my prayer.

R. And let my cry come unto thee.

V. May the almighty and most merciful Lord graciously hear us.

R. And may he ever graciously preserve us, Amen.

V. May the souls of the faithful, through the mercy of God, rest in peace.

R. Amen.

The second of these six Collects is thus varied:

From Advent to Christmas Day.

Deus, qui de beatæ Mariæ Virginis utero, Verbum tuum, angelo nuntiante, carnem suscipere voluisti: præsta supplicibus tuis, ut qui vere eam Genitricem Dei credimus, ejus apud te intercessionibus adjuvemur.

O God, who wast pleased that thy Word, at the message of an angel, should take flesh in the womb of the blessed Virgin Mary: grant to us thy humble servants, that we, who believe her to be truly the Mother of God, may be assisted by her intercessions with thee.

From Christmas Day to the Purification.

Deus, qui salutis æternæ, beatæ Mariæ virginitate fœcunda, humano generi præmia præstitisti: tribue quæsumus, ut ipsam pro nobis intercedere sentiamus, per quam meruimus auctorem vitæ suscipere, Dominum nostrum Jesum Christum Filium tuum.

O God, who by the fruitful virginity of blessed Mary, hast given to mankind the rewards of eternal salvation: grant, we beseech thee, that we may experience her intercession, by whom we received the Author of life, our Lord Jesus Christ thy Son.

END OF SEPTUAGESIMA

APPENDIX

ST. TITUS, BISHOP AND CONFESSOR

WE are to celebrate, to-day, the Feast of a holy Bishop of the Apostolic Age—a Disciple of the Apostle St. Paul. Little is known of his life; but, by addressing to him one of his inspired Epistles, the Apostle of the Gentiles has immortalised his memory. Wheresoever the Faith of Christ has been or shall be preached, Titus' name has been venerated by the Faithful; and as long as the world lasts, the holy Church will read to her children this Epistle, which was written, indeed, to a simple Bishop of the Isle of Crete, but was dictated by the Holy Ghost, and therefore destined to be a part of those Sacred Scriptures, which contain the Word of God. The counsels and directions given in this admirable Letter, were the rule of the holy Bishop, for whom St. Paul entertained a very strong affection. St. Titus had the honour of establishing the Christian Religion in that famous Island, which was one of the strongholds of Paganism. He survived his master, who was put to death by Nero. Like St. John, he sweetly slept in Christ at a very advanced age, respected and loved by the Church he had founded. As we have already observed, his life left but few traces behind it; but these few are sufficient to prove him to have been one of those wonderful men whom God chose as the directors of His infant Church.

Titum Cretensium Episcopum vix Pauli Apostoli verbo christianæ fidei sacramentis, mysteriisque excultum, ea sanctitatis luce

Titus, Bishop of Crete, was initiated into the mysteries of the Christian faith by Paul the Apostle; and being prepared by the sacraments, he shed so

Ecclesiæ tunc vagienti effulsisse compertum est, ut inter ejusdem Doctoris Gentium discipulos meruerit cooptari. Adscitus in partem oneris prædicationis adeo evangelizandi ardore et fidelitate Paulo exstitit carus, ut ipse cum venisset Troadem propter Evangelium Christi testatus sit, non habuisse requiem spiritui sue, eo quod Titum fratrem suum ibi non invenerit. Et paulo post Macedoniam petens, rursus suam in eum charitatem ita exprimit: Sed qui consolatur humiles, consolatus est nos Deus in adventu Titi.

Quamobrem Corinthum ab Apostolo missus, ea sapientia et lenitate legationis hujus munere functus est, quæ præsertim de fidelium pietate eleemosynas colligendas ad sublevandam Ecclesiæ Hebræorum inopiam spectabat, ut Corinthios non solum in Christi fide continuerit, sed etiam desiderium, fletum, æmulationem inter eos pro Paulo qui illos primum instituit, excitaverit. Ad effundendum interim inter gentes linguis, locisque distinctas, divini verbi semen, pluribus terra, marique itineribus relectis, magnaque animi firmitate pro Crucis trophæo curis laboribusque exantlatis, una cum duce Paulo Cretæ insulam appulit. Cum porro

bright a light of sanctity on the infant Church, that he merited to be chosen as one of the Disciples of the Doctor of the Gentiles. Being called to bear the burden of preaching the Gospel, so ardent and persevering was he in the discharge of that duty, that he endeared himself to St. Paul so much, as to make the Apostle say in one of his Epistles, that being come to Troas, to preach the faith in that city, he found no rest for his heart, because he found not there his brother Titus. And having, a short time after this, gone to Macedonia, he thus expresses his affection for his disciple in these terms: *But God who comforteth the humble, comforted us by the coming of Titus.*

Being sent to Corinth by the Apostle, he acquitted himself in this mission (which mainly consisted in collecting the alms given by the piety of the faithful towards alleviating the distress of the Hebrew Church) with so much prudence and patience, that he not only confirmed the Corinthians in the faith of Christ, but made them so desirous of a visit from Paul, who had been their first teacher in the faith, that they shed tears of long affection. After having undertaken several journeys, both by sea and land, in order to sow the seed of the divine word among people of various tongues and countries; and after having supported, with great firmness

huic Ecclesiæ Episcopus ab ipso Apostolo delectus esset, dubitandum non est, quin in eo munere ita versatus sit, ut juxta ipsius Pauli præceptoris monita, seipsum præbuerit exemplum bonorum operum in doctrina, in integritate, in gravitate.

Itaque tamquam lucerna inter eos qui in idololatriæ et mendaciorum tenebris, veluti in umbra mortis, sedebant, religionis jubar diffudit. Traditur eum inter Dalmatas, ut Crucis vexillum explicaret, strenue consudasse. Tandem meritorum et dierum plenus quarto supra nonagesimum anno, pridie Nonas Januarii, pretiosa justorum morte obdormivit in Domino, et sepultus est in Ecclesia, ubi ab Apostolo Minister fuerat constitutus. Hujus nomen a sancto Joanne Chrysostomo et a sancto Hieronymo præcipue commendatum, Martyrologio Romano eadem die inscriptum legitur; ejus autem festum summus Pontifex Pius Nonus ab universa Ecclesia celebrari præcepit.

of soul, countless anxieties and fatigues, in order to plant the standard of the Cross;— he landed at the island of Crete in company with his master St. Paul. The Apostle made him Bishop of the Church which he had founded in that island; and it is not to be doubted but that Titus so discharged his duty as that he became a model to the Faithful, according to the advice given to him by his master, *in good works, in doctrine, in integrity, in gravity.*

Thus did he become a shining light, pouring forth the rays of Christian faith on them that were sitting in the darkness of idolatry and lies, as in the shadow of death. Tradition tells us that he passed into Dalmatia, where he laboured with extraordinary zeal to enlist that people under the banner of the Cross. At length, full of days and merit, in the ninety-fourth year of his age, he slept in the Lord the death of the just, on the vigil of the nones of January (January 4), and was buried in the Church in which the Apostle had appointed him Minister of the word. St. John Chrysostom and St. Jerome pass great eulogium upon this holy Bishop, and his name is inscribed in the Roman Martyrology on the day above mentioned; but the sovereign Pontiff Pius the Ninth ordered his Feast to be kept by the Universal Church.

Favoured Disciple of the great Apostle! the holy Church has decreed that one of the days of the ecclesiastical year should be spent in celebrating thy virtues, and offering thee our prayers. Look down with love upon the Faithful who glorify the Holy Spirit that gave thee thy rich graces. Thou didst discharge thy pastoral duties with untiring zeal. Every quality enumerated in the Epistle addressed to thee by St. Paul, as required in a Bishop, was possessed by thee; and thou shinest in the crown of Jesus, the Prince of Pastors, as one of the brightest of its gems. Forget not the Church militant, of which thou wast one of the first guides. Eighteen hundred years have passed away since thou wast taken from her. During this long period, she has had sufferings and trials without end; but she has triumphed over every obstacle, and she continues her glorious path, saving souls and offering them to her heavenly Spouse; and this will she persevere doing, until her Jesus comes to stop the course of time, and open the gates of eternity. Meanwhile, O glorious Saint! she counts on the aid of thy prayers, in the great work of the salvation of souls. Ask of Jesus, that He send us Pastors like unto thee. Pray for that Island, which thou didst convert to the true faith, but which is now buried in the darkness of infidelity and schism. Pray, too, for the Greek Church, that it may regain its ancient glory by union with the See of Peter. Hear, O Titus! the prayers of the Pontiff, who has made thy name be venerated in the Liturgy throughout the world, in order that he might draw down peace and mercy upon the world, by thy powerful intercession.

FEBRUARY 9

ST. CYRIL OF ALEXANDRIA,
BISHOP AND DOCTOR OF THE CHURCH

' I will put enmities between thee and the woman, and thy
seed and her seed : she shall crush thy head, and thou shalt
lie in wait for her heel.'[1]

THESE words, addressed to the serpent in the days
which the Church now seeks to bring before the
minds of her children, have dominated the world's
history.   The woman, who was the first to fall
victim to Satan's deceits, was, in Mary, the first to
rise.   In her Immaculate Conception, in her virginal
motherhood, in her offering of the new Adam to
God on the mount of expiation, the new Eve made
the enemy of mankind feel the power of her victorious foot ; and so the rebel angel, who by man's
complicity has become the prince of this world, has
never ceased to direct against the woman who has
triumphed over him the united forces of his double
empire, over the legions of hell and the children of
darkness.   Mary in heaven continues the conflict
she began on earth.   As queen of the blessed
spirits and of the children of light she leads to
battle as one army the heavenly hosts and the
battalions of the Church Militant.   The triumph of
these faithful soldiers is that of their sovereign
lady—it is a continual crushing of the head of the
father of lies by the defeat of error and the exaltation of truth, the victory of the Divine Word, who
is both Son of Mary and Son of God.

But the connection between the victory of the

---

[1] Gen. iii. 15.

Divine Word and the triumph of his glorious Mother
has never been more manifest than in the combats
sustained by the Pontiff whom we are to honour to-
day. Cyril of Alexandria is the Doctor of the Divine
Maternity as his predecessor Athanasius was that
of the Consubstantiality of the Word. The dogma
of the Incarnation is founded upon these two ineffable mysteries, which they confessed and defended
in two succeeding centuries. As Son of God Christ
must be consubstantial with the Father, for the
infinite simplicity of the divine essence excludes all
idea of division. To deny the unity of substance
and principle in Jesus, the Divine Word, was to
deny His divinity. As Son of Man, as well as true
God of true God, Jesus was to be born on earth of
a daughter of Adam, and yet in His humanity be
still one Person with the Word which is consubstantial with the Father. To deny the personal
union of the two natures in Christ was again
equivalent to denying His divinity; it was also
equivalent to declaring that the Blessed Virgin, who
until then had been honoured as having given birth
to God in the nature which He assumed for our
salvation, was only the mother of a man.

Three centuries of persecution had not been able
to wring from the Church a denial of the divinity
of her Spouse. But hardly had the world witnessed
the triumph of the Incarnate Word, when the enemy
turned the victory to his own advantage. Profiting
by the new position of Christianity and its security
from public violence, he sought to win in the domain
of false science the denial which had been refused
him on the field of martyrdom. Apostasy did less
to serve the hostile influence of the serpent and
foster the growth of his accursed race than the
bitter zeal of heretics for the reform of the Church's
faith.

Arius was the first of these teachers of the

doctrines of hell—a worthy first in his pride.   He carried his questionings into the very depths of the divine essence, and rejected consubstantiality on the evidence of texts which he misunderstood.   Upheld principally by the powers of this world, Arianism fell at the end of a century, having no root but in recently converted nations who had not had to shed their blood for the divinity of the Son of God.

It was then that Satan produced Nestorius, crowned with a fictitious halo of sanctity and knowledge.   This man, who was to give the clearest expression to the hatred of the serpent for the woman, was enthroned in the Chair of Constantinople amid the applause of the whole East, which hoped to see in him a second Chrysostom.   The joy of the good was of short duration.   In the very year of his exaltation, on Christmas Day 428, Nestorius, taking advantage of the immense concourse which had assembled in honour of the Virgin Mother and her Child, pronounced from the episcopal pulpit the blasphemous words : ‘ Mary did not bring forth God ; her Son was only a man, the instrument of the Divinity.’   The multitude shuddered with horror.   Eusebius, a simple layman, rose to give expression to the general indignation, and protested against this impiety.   Soon a more explicit protest was drawn up and disseminated in the name of the members of this grief-stricken Church, launching an anathema against anyone who should dare to say : ‘ The Only-begotten Son of the Father and the Son of Mary are different persons.’   This generous attitude was the safeguard of Byzantium, and won the praise of Popes and Councils.   When the shepherd becomes a wolf, the first duty of the flock is to defend itself.   It is usual and regular, no doubt, for doctrine to descend from the bishops to the faithful, and those who are subject

in the faith are not to judge their superiors. But
in the treasure of revelation there are essential
doctrines which all Christians, by the very fact of
their title as such, are bound to know and defend.
The principle is the same whether it be a question
of belief or conduct, dogma or morals. Treachery
like that of Nestorius is rare in the Church, but it
may happen that some pastors keep silence for one
reason or another in circumstances when religion
itself is at stake. The true children of Holy Church
at such times are those who walk by the light of
their baptism, not the cowardly souls who, under
the specious pretext of submission to the powers
that be, delay their opposition to the enemy in the
hope of receiving instructions which are neither
necessary nor desirable.

The emotion produced by the blasphemy of
Nestorius spread through the East and soon reached
Alexandria. Cyril was then ruling the see which
had been founded by Mark in the name of Peter
and raised to the second place by the Head of the
Church. The union of Athanasius and the Roman
Pontiffs had overcome Arianism in the previous
century, and now Rome and Alexandria were once
more to unite in crushing heresy. But the enemy
had learnt by experience and acted with infernal
foresight. When the future champion of the
Mother of God was raised to the Chair of St.
Athanasius, this formidable alliance was a thing of
the past. Theophilus, the late Patriarch, who was
the principal author of the condemnation of St.
John Chrysostom at the Pseudo-council ' of the
Oak,' had refused to subscribe to the rehabilitation
of his victim by the Holy See, and Rome had been
obliged to break with her eldest daughter. Cyril
was the nephew of Theophilus. He knew nothing
of the secret motives by which his uncle had been
governed. He had been brought up to honour him

as his superior, his benefactor, and his master in sacred science, and when, in his turn, he became Patriarch, he had no thought of reversing the decisions of one whom he had always regarded as a father.   Alexandria remained separated from the Church of Rome.   Like the serpent, whose venom poisons all that it touches, Satan turned the most noble sentiments against the cause of God, but our Lady, who loves an upright heart, did not abandon her champion.   After a few years of mishaps, which taught him to know men, the young Patriarch had his eyes opened to the truth by a holy monk named Isidore of Pelusium.   Once convinced, he did not hesitate to restore the name of John Chrysostom to the sacred diptychs.   The schemes of hell came to naught.   Rome found a new Athanasius on the banks of the Nile to assist her in her new combats for the faith.

Cyril, restored to Christian unity by a monk, showed as great a devotion to the holy solitaries as his predecessor had done.   He confided to them his grief at the first news of Nestorius' impiety. The letter in which he appeals to their faith and warns them of the danger which threatens the Church has become celebrated.   'Those,' he says, 'who have embraced in Christ the noble and enviable lot which is yours, ought to shine most brilliantly with the light of a perfect and unhesitating faith, and add to this light the special radiance of virtue.   Then they ought to employ their wealth in increasing in themselves the knowledge of the mysteries of Christ, and striving to understand them perfectly.   This,' says the holy Doctor, 'is what I think St. Paul means when he speaks of the development of the perfect man,[1] the way to arrive at the measure and the fullness of Christ.'[2]

[1] Eph. iv. 13.   [2] Cyr. Al. Ep. 1 ad monach.

The Patriarch of Alexandria could not rest content with opening his heart to those of whose sympathy he was assured. He strove to win back Nestorius by letters, in which his personal meekness is only rivalled by the vigour and breadth of his doctrine. But Nestorius was obdurate. Having no arguments at his command, he complained of the Patriarch's interference. As it always happens, there were pacifists who, though not sharing Nestorius' errors, thought it would be best not to answer him for fear of embittering him, increasing the scandal, and wounding charity. Cyril thus answers that singular virtue which fears the affirmations of the Christian faith more than the audacity of heresy : ' What ! Nestorius dares to suffer men to say in public and in his presence that he who calls Mary the Mother of God is to be anathema ! He hurls his anathema, through his partisans, at us, at the other Bishops of the Universal Church and the ancient Fathers, who in all ages and all places with one accord have acknowledged and honoured the holy Mother of God ! And have we not the right to repay him in his own coin and say, " If anyone denies that Mary is the Mother of God let him be anathema "? Nevertheless, out of regard for him, I have not yet uttered these words.'[1]

Men of another type, also represented in all ages, revealed the true motive of their hesitation when, after insisting on the advantages of peace and their ancient friendship with Nestorius, they suggested timidly that it would be dangerous to oppose so powerful an adversary. ' Could I but satisfy the Bishop of Constantinople and heal the wounded spirit of my brother by suffering the loss of all my possessions !' was Cyril's reply. ' But the faith is at stake. The scandal has spread through the

[1] Ep viii. al. vi.

Church, and all men are inquiring about the new doctrine. If we, who have received from God the office of teacher, fail to remedy such great evils, will there be flames enough for us at the Day of Judgment? I have already been struck by insult and calumny—let it pass. If only the faith be safe, I will yield to none in my love of Nestorius. But if the faith suffers through the deeds of some —let there be no doubt about it—I will not risk my soul even if instant death threaten me. If the fear of some disturbance is stronger than our zeal for God's glory and prevents us from speaking the truth, how shall we dare in the presence of the Christian people to celebrate the holy martyrs, whose glory lies in the very fact that they carried out in their lives the words[1] : " Even unto death fight for justice " ?'[2]

When the combat became inevitable, he organized the forces of the Church, and summoned monks and Bishops to his side. He did not attempt to conceal the holy enthusiasm which filled his heart. ' As far as I am concerned,' he writes to the clerics who represent him in the imperial city, 'my greatest desire is to suffer, live and die for the faith of Jesus Christ. As it is written : " If I shall give sleep to my eyes, or slumber to my eyelids, or rest to my temples "[3] until I have fought the battle which is necessary for the well-being of all. Therefore let your hearts be full of the same spirit and do manfully. Watch the enemy and inform us of his slightest movements. As soon as I can, I will send you some Bishops and monks, pious and prudent men, chosen out of many. I am already preparing my letters. I have resolved to labour without truce for the faith of Christ and to suffer

[1] Ecclus. iv. 33.   [2] Cyr. Al. Ep. ix. al. vii.
[3] Ps. cxxxi. 4, 5.

all torments, yea death itself, which in such a cause would be sweet to me.'[1]

Informed of these troubles by the Patriarch of Alexandria, Pope St. Celestine I. condemned the new heresy, and commissioned Cyril to depose the Bishop of Constantinople in the name of the Roman Pontiff. But Nestorius prolonged the contest by his intrigues. At this point there appears at the side of Cyril the figure of a saintly woman who for forty years was the terror of hell, and who twice crushed the head of the hateful serpent in the name of the Queen of heaven. Pulcheria had assumed the reins of government at the age of fifteen. It was a time of disasters, but she arrested interior disturbances by her prudence and energy, and in union with her sisters, virgins like herself, held back the barbarian hordes by the might of divine Psalmody. While the West was in its last agony, the East, thanks to its gifted empress, was enjoying once more the prosperity of its best days. The sight of a granddaughter of Theodosius the Great, who employed her private wealth in multiplying churches in honour of our Lady, taught Byzantium that devotion to Mary which was her safeguard in evil days, and which obtained for her from Mary's Son a thousand years of mercy and incomprehensible patience. General Councils have hailed St. Pulcheria as the guardian of faith and the bulwark of unity.[2] St. Leo says that the greatest share in the defence of divine truth was hers.[3] 'A double palm is in her hands,' says this great Pope, 'a double crown on her head, for the Church owes to her a double victory over impiety in the persons of Nestorius and Eutyches, who from different sides tended towards the same

---

[1] Cyr. Al. Ep. x. al. viii. [2] Labbe, Conc. iv. 464.
[3] Leo. Ep. xxxi. al. xxvii.

point—the denial of the Incarnation of the Son of God and of the share of the Virgin Mother in the salvation of mankind.'[1]

But we must not overstep our limits. The summary of the life of this great Pontiff read by the Church at Matins will give us some idea of those glorious combats witnessed by the city of Ephesus when Cyril, supported by Rome and upheld by Pulcheria, established for ever our Lady's title to the most noble diadem that a mere creature can ever wear:

Cyrillus Alexandrinus, cujus præconia non unius tantum vel alterius sunt comprobata testimonio, sed etiam œcumenicorum Conciliorum Ephesini et Chalcedonensis actis celebrata, claris ortus parentibus, ac Theophili episcopi Alexandrini nepos, adhuc adolescens præcellentis ingenii clara specimina dedit. Litteris ac scientiis egregie imbutus, ad Joannem episcopum Hierosolymitanum se contulit, ut in christiana fide perficeretur. Alexandriam deinde cum rediisset, Theophilo vita functo, ad illius sedem evectus est: quo in munere ita optimi pastoris formam ab Apostolo definitam constanter præ se tulit, ut sanctissimi præsulis gloriam merito sit adeptus.

Salutis animarum zelo incensus curas omnes intendit, ut sibi commissum gregem

The praises of Cyril of Alexandria not only have been celebrated by individual writers, but are even registered in the acts of the Œcumenical Councils of Ephesus and Chalcedon. He was born of noble parents, and was the nephew of Theophilus, Patriarch of Alexandria. While still young he gave proofs of an excellent understanding, and after having profoundly studied literature and science, he betook himself to John, Bishop of Jerusalem, to be perfected in the Christian faith. After his return to Alexandria and the death of Theophilus, he was raised to that see. In this office he kept ever before his eyes the type of the shepherd of souls described by the Apostle, and by adhering faithfully to it, earned the glory of a holy Bishop

He burnt with zeal for the salvation of souls, and took all care to keep the flock

---

[1] Leo. Ep. xxxi. al. xxvii. and Ep. lxxix. al. lix.

in fidei et morum integritate servaret, atque a venenatis infidelium et hæreticorum pascuis defenderet. Hinc tum Novati asseclas e civitate expelli, tum Judæos qui furore acti in cædem Christianorum conspiraverant, juxta leges puniri sategit. Singulare vero Cyrilli pro catholicæ fidei incolumitate enituit studium contra Nestorium Constantinopolitanum episcopum, asserentem Jesum Christum ex Maria Virgine hominem tantum et non Deum natum, eique divinitatem pro meritis esse collatam ; cujus emendationem cum frustra tentasset, eum sancto Cælestino Pontifici Maximo denuntiavit.

Cælestini delegata auctoritate, Concilio Ephesino præfuit, in quo hæresis Nestoriana penitus proscripta est, damnatus Nestorius et a sua sede dejectus, ac dogma catholicum de una in Christo, eaque divina persona, et divina gloriosæ Virginis Mariæ maternitate assertum ; plaudente populo universo, qui incredibili gaudio gestiens, collucentibus facibus domum deduxit episcopos. Sed hac de causa Cyrillus calumniis, injuriis et persecutionibus plurimis a Nestorio ejusque fautoribus impetitus fuit ; quas ipse patientissime tulit, ita ut de sola fide sollicitus, quid-

entrusted to him in purity of faith and life, and to guard them from the poisonous pastures of heresy and infidelity. Hence, in accordance with the laws. he caused the followers of Novatus to be expelled from the city, and procured the punishment of the Jews whose hatred had led them to plan a massacre of the Christians. His eminent care for the preservation of the Catholic faith shone forth especially in his conflict with Nestorius, Bishop of Constantinople, who declared that Jesus Christ had been born of the Virgin Mary as man only, and that the divinity had been bestowed upon him because of his merits. Cyril first attempted to convert Nestorius, but when he found the task hopeless, he denounced him to Pope St. Celestine.

As delegate of Pope Celestine, he presided over the Council of Ephesus where the Nestorian heresy was condemned, Nestorius deprived of his see, and the Catholic doctrine as to the unity of Person in Christ and the divine maternity of the glorious Virgin Mary was laid down amid the rejoicings of all the people, who escorted the bishops to their lodgings with a torchlight procession. Nestorius and his followers made Cyril the object of slanders, insults, and persecutions, which he bore with great patience, for he cared only for the purity of the

quid adversus sum effutiebant ac moliebantur hæretici, pro nihilo haberet. Tandem pro Ecclesia Dei maximis perfunctus laboribus, plurimisque scriptis editis tum ad ethnicos et hæreticos confutandos, tum ad sacras scripturas et catholica explananda dogmata, sancto fine quievit anno quadringentesimo quadragesimo quarto, episcopatus trigesimo secundo. Leo decimus tertius Pontifex Maximus Officium et Missam præclarissimi hujus fidei catholicæ propugnatoris et Orientalis Ecclesiæ luminis, Ecclesiam universam extendit.

faith, and took no heed of what the heretics might say or do against him. At length, after having performed great labours for the Church of God, and having composed numerous works, both in refutation of paganism and heresy and in explanation of the Catholic faith, he died a holy death in the year 444, the thirty-second year of his episcopal consecration. The supreme Pontiff Leo XIII. extended to the Universal Church the Office and Mass of this most eminent champion of the Catholic faith and light of the Eastern Church.

O holy Pontiff, the heavens rejoice and the earth is glad at the thought of that conflict in which the Queen of heaven and earth chose thee as the instrument of her triumph. The East has ever honoured thee as her light; the West has long hailed thee as champion of the Mother of God, and now seeks to give stronger expression to her gratitude. A new flower has appeared in our day in Mary's crown, and it springs from the very soil cultivated by thee. When thou didst proclaim the divine maternity in the name of Peter and Celestine thou wast preparing for our Lady another triumph, which was to be the consequence of the first. The Mother of God must be immaculate. The definition of Pius IX. completes the work done by Celestine and thee. The two days—June 22, 431, and December 8, 1854—are equally glorious in heaven, and were celebrated with like manifestations of joy and love on earth. And so, O Cyril, the whole Church turns to thee after fourteen centuries and proclaims thee Doctor. She sees that thy work is complete, and will have nothing lacking in the homage rendered to thee on earth. Devotion to thee has found its fullest expression at the same time as devotion to the Mother of God. Thy glory is an extension of her glory.

We understand that the greatest honour we can pay to thee is to sing the praises of thy sovereign Lady. We therefore repeat the burning words which the Holy Ghost put upon thy lips on that day of triumph at Ephesus: 'We hail thee, O Mary, Mother of God, as the bright gem of the whole creation; the lamp whose light shall never be put out, the crown of virginity, the sceptre of orthodox faith, the indestructible temple and shrine of the Infinite, through whom we have received Him whom the Gospels call Blessed, Him who comes in the name of the Lord. Hail Mary, whose spotless and virginal womb bore that Infinite One, by whom the Trinity is glorified and the precious Cross honoured and adored throughout the earth. Hail Mary, joy of heaven, peace of angels and archangels, terror of demons. Through thee the tempter fell from heaven, through thee the fallen are raised up to heaven. The world was held captive in idolatrous folly, and thou hast opened its eyes to the truth. To thee the faithful owe their baptism, to thee they owe the oil of gladness. Throughout all the earth thou foundest churches and leadest the nations to penance. What shall I say more? It was through thee that the only-begotten Son of God shone forth as the light of those who sat in darkness and in the shadow of death; through thee that the prophets foretold things to come; through thee that the Apostles preached salvation to the nations; through thee that the dead rise again; through thee that kings reign by the grace of the Holy Trinity. What man could ever adequately praise Mary, who is worthy of all praise?'[1]

[1] Cyr. al. Hom. iv. Ephesi habita ad St. Mariam.

If then, O Cyril, the dignity of the Mother of God surpasses all praise, beseech her to raise up among us men capable of praising her as thou didst. May the power with which she armed thee against her foes descend to those who in our days have to carry on the age-long combat between the woman and the serpent. The adversary has grown bolder. This age has surpassed in its denial of Jesus not only Nestorius, but also the apostate Emperor Julian, against whom thou didst defend the divinity of the Son of the Virgin Mother. Thou didst rain terrible blows upon error. Teach our Doctors how to conquer ; teach them to lean upon Peter, to interest themselves in all that concerns the Church, to look upon her foes as their personal enemies, and the only real enemies they have. Our pastors will draw from thy sublime writings that true knowledge of sacred Scripture without which their zeal would be powerless. Christians will learn from thee that they cannot grow in virtue without first increasing their faith and their know-ledge of the mysteries of the Incarnate Word. Many souls in these times content themselves with vague ideas. Let them learn from thee that it is the love of truth which leads us to life.[1] The approach of Lent reminds us of these Paschal Letters which at this season carried to all the announcement of the Feast of Feasts and an ex-hortation to penance. Our souls have grown soft. Obtain for us a sense of the seriousness of the Christian life, so that we may enter valiantly upon the holy campaign which is to win back our peace with God through the triumph of the spirit over the flesh.

[1] Cyr. Al. Hom., div. 1.

February 11

OUR LADY OF LOURDES

'My bow shall appear in the clouds and I will remember My covenant with you.'[1]

The lessons at Matins on February 11, 1854 (Thursday in Sexagesima week) recalled these words, and the world soon learned that on this very day Mary had appeared, more fair than the sign of hope which typified her at the time of the deluge.

Portents, the realization of which we see in these days, were being multiplied. Mankind had grown old, and seemed about to perish in a deluge more dreadful than the former one. 'I am the Immaculate Conception,' said the Mother of divine grace to the humble child whom she chose at such a time to bear her message to the captain of the Ark of salvation. She pierced the gathering darkness with the light of that sublime privilege which the supreme pilot, to his eternal glory, had declared three years before to be dogma.

Indeed, if, as the beloved disciple says, it is our faith to which victory on earth is promised,[2] and if faith is nourished by light—what individual dogma is there which so presupposes and recalls all other dogmatic truths, and at the same time throws such light upon them? It is a royal crown on the brow of the victorious queen, resplendent like the rainbow which breaks through the clouds with all the glories of heaven.

But perchance it was still necessary to open the eyes of the blind to these splendours, to inspire courage into hearts saddened by hell's denials, and to infuse strength to make an act of faith into so many understandings weakened by the education

[1] Gen. ix. 14-15.   [2] 1 John v. 4.

of these days. The Immaculate Virgin summoned the multitudes to the scene of her blessed visit, and both sweetly and strongly succoured the weakness of souls by healing bodies. She smiled upon publicity, welcomed investigation, and confirmed by the authority of miracles her own words and the definition of the Vicar of Christ.

The Psalmist said that the works of God tell His praises in all tongues,[1] and St. Paul taxes with folly and impiety those who will not accept this testimony.[2] So, too, we may say that the men of these times have no excuse if they do not recognize the blessed Virgin in her works. May she extend the field of her beneficence and take pity on that worst of diseases—that weakness of soul which refuses to see out of a secret fear of the conclusions to be drawn from the evidence, and struggles against the truth until the mind is filled with contradictions and the heart with darkness, so that it seems as though the reason itself were given over to that reprobate sense[3] which St. Paul describes as striking the pagans in their flesh.

The things that take place at Lourdes are as famous as any events of contemporary history. Let us listen to the short account which the Church has enshrined in the Liturgy :

Anno quarto a dogmatica definitione de immaculato beatæ Virginis Conceptu, ad Gavi fluminis oram prope oppidum Lourdes Diœcesis Tarbiensis in Gallia, ipsa Virgo in rupis sinu super specum Massabielle puellæ cuidam, vernacula lingua Bernadette nuncupatæ, pauperrimæ quidem, sed ingenuæ ac piæ, pluries se conspiciendam obtulit. Immaculata

In the fourth year after the definition of the dogma of the Immaculate Conception, the blessed Virgin vouchsafed to appear on several occasions to a poor but pious and innocent child named Bernadette, in a rocky cavern overlooking the grotto of Massabielle on the banks of the Gave near the town of Lourdes in the diocese of Tarbes in France. She

---

[1] Ps. xviii. 2-5.   [2] Rom. i. 18-22.   [3] *Ibid.* i. 28.

Virgo juvenili ac benigno videbatur aspectu, nivea veste niveoque pallio contecta, ac zona cærulea succincta : nudos pedes aurea rosa ornabat. Primo apparitionis die, qui fuit undecimus Februarii anno millesimo octingentesimo quinquagesimo octavo, puellam signum crucis rite pieque faciendum edocuit, atque ad sacri rosarii recitationem, exemplo suo, coronam, quæ prius ex brachio demissa pendebat, manu advolens, excitavit : quod in ceteris etiam apparitionibus præstitit. Altera autem apparitionis die, puella in simplicitate cordis sui, diabolicam fraudem timens, lustralem aquam in Virginem effudit : sed beata Virgo, leniter arridens, benigniorem illi vultum ostendit. Cum vero tertio apparuisset, puellam ad specum per quindecim dies invitavit. Exinde eam sæpius est alloquuta, ac pro peccatoribus orare, terram deosculari, pœnitentiamque agere est hortata : deinde imperavit ut sacerdotibus ediceret, ædificandum ibi esse sacellum, solemnisque supplicationis more illo accedendum. Mandavit insuper ut e fonte, qui sub arena adhuc latebat sed mox erat erupturus, aquam biberet eaque se abstergeret. Denique die festo Annuntiationis, percontanti enixe puellæ illius nomen, cujus aspectu toties dignata fuerat, Virgo admotis pectori manibus elatisque in cælum oculis, respondit : Immaculata Conceptio ego sum.

showed herself as a young and gracious figure, robed in white, with a white veil and blue girdle, and golden roses on her bare feet. At the first apparition on February 11, 1858, she taught the child to make the sign of the Cross correctly and devoutly, and, taking a chaplet from her own arm, encouraged her by example to say her rosary. This was repeated at subsequent apparitions. On the second day, Bernadette, who feared an illusion of the devil, in all simplicity cast holy water at the apparition, who smiled more graciously than before. At the third apparition Bernadette was invited to repeat her visits to the grotto for fifteen days, during which the blessed Virgin conversed with her, exhorted her to pray for sinners, kiss the ground and do penance, and finally commanded her to tell the priests that a chapel was to be built in the place and processions held. She was also bidden drink and wash in the water, and a spring, until then invisible, gushed out of the ground. On the feast of the Annunciation, the child earnestly begged the Lady who had so often visited her to reveal her name, and the blessed Virgin, joining her hands and raising her eyes to heaven, said : 'I am the Immaculate Conception.'

Percrebrescente fama beneficiorum, quæ in sacro specu recepisse fideles dicebantur, augebatur in dies hominum concursus, quos loci religio ad specum advocabat. Itaque prodigiorum fama puellæque candore motus Tarbiensis episcopus, quarto ab enarratis anno, post juridicam factorum inquisitionem, supernaturales esse apparitionis notas sua sententia probavit, cultumque Virginis Immaculatæ in eodem specu permisit. Mox ædificatum sacellum: ex illa die pene innumeræ fidelium turbæ, voti ac supplicationis causa, ex Gallia, Belgio, Italia, Hispania, ceterisque Europæ provinciis necnon ex longinquis Americæ regionibus quovis anno illuc adveniunt, nomenque Immaculatæ de Lourdes ubique terrarum inclarescit. Fontis aqua in cunctas orbis partes delata, ægris sanitatem restituit. Orbis vero catholicus tantorum memor benefactorum, ædes sacras mirabili opere ibi exstruxit. Vexilla innumera, acceptorum beneficiorum veluti monumenta, illuc a civitatibus ac gentibus missa, ædem Virginis miro ornatu decorant. In hac sua veluti sede Immaculata Virgo jugiter colitur; interdiu quidem precibus, religioso cantu solemnibusque aliis cæremoniis; noctu vero sacris illis supplicationibus, quibus infinitæ propemodum peregrinantium turbæ cereis facibusque accensis procedunt et laudes beatæ Virginis concinunt.

Rumours of favours received at the holy grotto spread rapidly, and the crowds of devout visitors increased daily, so that the Bishop of Tarbes, who had been impressed by the candour of Bernadette, found it advisable to hold a judicial enquiry into the facts. In the course of the fourth year he gave sentence, recognizing the supernatural character of the apparition, and permitting devotions to our Lady under the title of the Immaculate Conception to be held in the grotto. A chapel was soon built, and since then every year has witnessed innumerable pilgrimages from France, Belgium, Italy, Spain, and all parts of Europe and America. The name of Our Lady of Lourdes has become famous all over the world, and cures are obtained everywhere by use of the water. Lourdes has been enriched by a grateful world with splendidly decorated churches, where countless banners bear witness to the favours received and to the desire of peoples and cities to adorn the house of the blessed Virgin, who is honoured there as in her own palace. The days are filled with prayers, hymns and solemn ceremonies, and the nights are sanctified by the pious supplications of countless people who walk in procession carrying torches, and singing the praises of the blessed Virgin Mary.

Peregrinationes hujusmodi fidem frigescente sæculo excitasse, animum ad christianam legem profitendam addidisse, cultumque Virginis immaculatæ mirum in modum auxisse, omnibus compertum est. In qua mirabili fidei professione Christianus populus sacerdotes veluti duces habet, qui illuc suas plebes adducunt. Ipsi etiam sacrorum Antistites sanctum locum frequenter adeunt, peregrinationibus præsunt, solemnioribusque festis intersunt. Nec adeo rarum est ipsos Romanæ Ecclesiæ Purpuratos Patres humili peregrinorum more accedentes conspicere. Ipsi quoque Romani Pontifices, pro sua erga Immaculatam de Lourdes pietate, sacram ædem donis nobilissimis cumularunt. Pius nonus, sacris indulgentiis, Archiconfraternitatis privilegio ac minoris Basilicæ titulo ipsam insignivit ; ac Deiparæ imaginem ibidem cultam, solemni ritu per Legatum suum Apostolicum in Gallia diademate distinctam voluit. Leo vero decimus tertius innumera etiam contulit beneficia, indulgentias ad modum Jubilæi vigesimo quinto Apparitionis anno vertente concessit, peregrinationes sua auctoritate verboque provexit, ac solemnem Ecclesiæ sub titulo Rosarii dedicationem suo nomine peragi curavit. Quorum beneficiorum amplitudinem cumulavit, cum plurium Episcoporum rogatu,

All men know how, in spite of the coldness of the world, these pilgrimages have revived faith, restored the observance of the Christian religion, and increased devotion to the Immaculate Virgin. The Faithful are led by their priests in this marvellous development of faith and devotion. The Bishops make frequent visits to the holy spot, lead pilgrimages, and take part in the ceremonies, and the Cardinals of Holy Church are often seen in the humble quality of pilgrims. The Roman Pontiffs have shown their devotion to our Lady of Lourdes, and have bestowed remarkable favours on her sanctuary. Pius IX. enriched it with indulgences, gave it the privilege of an Archconfraternity and the title of minor basilica, and delegated the Apostolic Nuncio in France to crown in his name the statue of the Mother of God. Leo XIII. also granted many favours, including the jubilee of the twenty-fifth anniversary of the Apparition. He encouraged pilgrimages, and ordained that the consecration of the Rosary Church should be performed in his name. Moreover, he crowned all these favours by conceding, at the request of many bishops, the celebration of a solemn feast under the title of the Apparition of Our Lady Immaculate, with a proper Office and Mass. Finally, Pius X., out of devotion to the

solemne festum sub titulo Apparitionis beatæ Mariæ Virginis Immaculatæ proprio Officio et propria Missa celebrandum benigne concessit. Tandem Pius decimus Pontifex Maximus pro sua erga Deiparam pietate, ac plurimorum votis annuens sacrorum Antistitum, idem festum ad Ecclesiam universam extendit.

Mother of God, granted the petition of many prelates that this feast should be extended to the Universal Church.

' O Mary, conceived without sin, pray for us who have recourse to thee!' Thou didst teach us this prayer in 1830 as a safeguard against the dangers of the future. In 1846 the two shepherds of La Salette reminded us of thy tears and exhortations: ' Pray for poor sinners, pray for the world which is so disturbed.' To-day the little seer of the grotto of Massabielle brings us thy message: ' Penitence! Penitence! Penitence!'

We desire to obey thee, O blessed Virgin, to combat in ourselves and all around us that enemy of mankind who is our only real enemy, and sin, that supreme evil which is the source of all others. Praise be to the Almighty, who saved thee from all stain of sin, and thus inaugurated in thee the full restoration of our fallen race. Praise be to thee, who, having no debts of thy own, didst pay our debts with the Blood of thy Son and the tears of His Mother, thus reconciling heaven and earth and crushing the head of the serpent.

Prayer, expiation—the Church from apostolic times has ever urged these thoughts upon us during the days which immediately precede Lent. Dear Mother in heaven, we bless thee for having thus united thy voice to that of our Mother on earth. The world no longer desired, no longer understood, the infallible but indispensable remedy offered by the justice and mercy of God to the misery of man.

Men seemed to have forgotten the words: 'Except you do penance, you shall all perish.'[1] Thy pity wakes us from this fatal stupor, O Mary. Thou knowest our weakness, and hast mingled sweetness in the bitter draught. Thou lavishest temporal favours upon man in order that he may ask of thee eternal blessings. We will not be like those children who welcome their mother's caresses, but neglect her admonitions and the corrections which her tenderness sought to make acceptable. We will pray and suffer in union with Jesus and thee. By thine assistance during this Lent we will be converted and do penance.

FEBRUARY 12

THE SEVEN HOLY FOUNDERS OF THE ORDER OF SERVITES, CONFESSORS

CLOUDS are gathering over Holy Church. We are reminded on every side of the approach of those days when our Emmanuel will show Himself to us in the pitiable state to which our sins have brought Him. Bethlehem is so soon followed by Calvary. We shall find the Mother of divine grace at the foot of the Cross as we found her at Ephrata. She brought forth her firstborn in joy, but now in tears she is to bring forth those brothers of His whose birth cost her so much. We have shared her joy, and we shall not refuse to weep and suffer with her.

Let us take for our models the saints whom the Church honours to-day. They passed their lives in the contemplation of our Lady's sorrows, and the Order which they founded has the special mission to spread this devotion. St. Francis of Assisi raised the standard of the Cross anew in a world grown

[1] Luke xiii. 5.

cold. The work of redemption seemed to be taken up afresh, and, as on the great Friday Jesus would not manifest Himself without Mary, the Servites completed the work of the Founder of the Friars Minor. Men regained confidence as they meditated on the Passion of the Son and the Compassion of the Mother.

The two feasts consecrated to the Dolours of our Lady will teach us in due course what place her compassion had in the economy of the Redemption. The Queen of heaven herself showed her predilection for the Order which made itself her apostle, in the striking outpouring of holiness which marked its origin. The simultaneous blooming of seven lilies, gathered on earth to-day by the angels, was a sight new even to heaven. Peter of Verona had a vision of them when they were implanting themselves on Monte Senario ; and the future martyr saw the blessed Virgin smile as she gazed on that mountain where countless other flowers sprang up to perfume holy Church. Florence, the city of flowers, had never before given such blooms to God. Hell multiplied its attacks against the noble city, but could not prevail against Mary within its walls. We shall be reminded of these things by the feasts of St. Juliana Falconieri and St. Philip Benizi, which were established before the one we are keeping to-day. Let us unite our gratitude to that which the Church feels for the Religious family of the Servites. The world owes to them the grace of a new development in the knowledge and love of the Mother of God, who became our Mother at the price of unparalleled sufferings.

The lessons read by the Church on this day speak of the merits of our Saints and the favours with which our Lady rewarded their fidelity. February 11, the day first chosen as their common feast, is not the anniversary of the death of any one of them, but the day on which, in the year 1304, after passing through many vicissitudes, their Order obtained the definitive approbation of the Church.

Sæculo tertio decimo, cum Friderici secundi diro schismate, cruentisque factionibus cultiores Italiæ populi scinderentur, providens Dei misericordia præter alios sanctitate illustres, septem e Florentina nobilitate viros suscitavit, qui in caritate conjuncti, præclarum fraternæ dilectionis præberent exemplum. Hi, nimirum, Bonfilius Monaldius, Bonajuncta Manettus, Manettus Antelensis, Amedeus de Amideis, Uguccio Uguccionum, Sostenus de Sosteneis et Alexius Falconerius, cum anno trigesimo tertio ejus sæculi, die sacra cælo Virgini receptæ, in quodam piorum hominum conventu, Laudantium nuncupato, ferventius orarent; ab eadem Deipara singulis apparente sunt admoniti, ut sanctius perfectiusque vitæ genus amplecterentur. Re itaque prius cum Florentino præsule collata, hi septem viri, generis nobilitate divitiisque posthabitis, sub vilissimis detritisque vestibus cilicio induti, octava die Septembris in ruralem quamdam ædiculam secessere, ut ea die primordia vitæ sanctioris auspicarentur, qua ipsa Dei Genitrix mortalibus orta sanctissimam vitam inceperat.

Hoc vitæ institutum quam

When in the thirteenth century the most cultured peoples of Italy were divided by factions, and the schism fostered by Frederic II, the merciful providence of God raised up many persons remarkable for their holiness, among whom were seven noble Florentines whose union of spirit gave to the world a striking example of fraternal love. They were Bonfilius Monaldi, Bonagiunta Manetti, Manettus dell' Antella, Amadeus de Amadei, Hugo Lippi, Gerard Sostegni, and Alexis Falconieri. The Mother of God appeared to each of them on the feast of her Assumption, 1233, when they were praying fervently in the Chapel of the pious Confraternity of the Laudesi, and exhorted them to embrace a more perfect life. They took counsel with the Bishop of Florence, and at once bade farewell to their wealth and rank, clothing themselves in hair cloth and old and ragged garments. On September 8 they established themselves in a humble retreat outside the city, desiring to begin their new life on the day when the Mother of God began her own most holy life upon earth.

God showed by a miracle

sibi foret acceptum Deus miraculo ostendit. Nam cum paulo deinceps hi septem viri per Florentinam urbem ostiatim eleemosynam emendicarent, accidit, ut repente infantium voce, quos inter fuit sanctus Philippus Benitius quintum ætatis mensem vix ingressus, beatæ Mariæ Servi acclamarentur : quo deinde nomine semper appellati sunt. Quare, vitandi populi occursus ac solitudinis amore ducti in Senarii montis recessu omnes convenere, ibique cæleste quoddam vitæ genus aggressi sunt. Victitabant enim in speluncis, sola aqua herbisque contenti : vigiliis aliisque asperitatibus corpus attenebant : Christi passionem ac mœstissimæ ejusdem Genitricis dolores assidue meditantes. Quod quum olim sacra Parasceves die impensius exsequerentur, ipsa beata Virgo illis iterato apparens, lugubrem vestem quam induerent, ostendit, sibique acceptissimum fore significavit, ut novum in Ecclesia regularem Ordinem excitarent, qui jugem recoleret ac promoveret memoriam dolorum, quos ipsa pertulit sub cruce Domini. Hæc sanctus Petrus, inclytus Ordinis Prædicatorum martyr, ex familiari cum sanctis illis viris consuetudine ac peculiari etiam Deiparæ visione quum didicisset ; iis auctor fuit ut Ordinem Regularem sub appellatione Servorum beatæ Virginis instituerent ; qui postea ab Innocentio quarto

that their resolution was pleasing to him. One day shortly afterwards, when all seven were begging from door to door in Florence, they were hailed by the voices of children, among whom was St. Philip Benizi, then only five months old, as the "Servants of Mary," which was for the future to be their title. This prodigy and their love of solitude led them to choose Monte Senario as a place of retreat, that thus they might avoid great concourse of people. Their life was truly heavenly. They lived in caves, took no food but herbs and water, and subdued their bodies by vigils and penances. The Passion of Christ and the Dolours of his afflicted Mother were the subject of their continual meditations. One Good Friday, when they were absorbed in fervent prayer, the blessed Virgin appeared to them all in person a second time, showed them the sombre habit they were to adopt, and told them that she wished them to found a new Order of Religious, whose mission was to cultivate and spread devotion to the sorrows which she endured at the foot of the Cross. They were aided in this work by Peter, an illustrious Friar Preacher, who died the death of a martyr. He was their intimate friend, and had been instructed about the new Order in a vision by the blessed Virgin herself. The Order received the name of

Pontifice Maximo approbatus fuit.

Porro sancti illi viri, quum plures sibi socios adjunxissent, Italiæ civitates atque oppida, præsertim Etruriæ, excurrere cœperunt, prædicantes ubique Christum crucifixum, civiles discordias compescentes, et innumeros fere devios ad virtutis semitam revocantes. Neque Italiam modo, sed et Galliam, Germaniam ac Poloniam suis evangelicis laboribus excoluerunt. Denique quum bonum Christi odorem longe lateque diffudissent, portentorum quoque gloria illustres, migrarunt ad Dominum. Sed quos unus veræ fraternitatis ac religionis amor in vita sociaverat, unum pariter demortuos contexit sepulchrum, unaque populi veneratio prosecuta est. Quapropter Clemens undecimus et Benedictus decimus tertius Pontifices Maximi delatum iisdem a pluribus sæculis individuum cultum confirmarunt : ac Leo decimus tertius, approbatis antea miraculis, post indultam venerationem ad collectivam earumdem invocationem a Deo patratis, eosdem anno quinquagesimo sacerdotii sui Sanctorum honoribus cumulavit eorumque memoriam Officio ac Missa in universa Ecclesia quotannis recolendam instituit.

Servites, or Servants of the blessed Virgin Mary, and was approved by Innocent IV. The holy Founders were soon joined by many disciples, and began to preach Christ Crucified in the towns and cities of Italy, especially in Tuscany. They brought civil feuds to an end, and recalled numbers of sinners to the paths of virtue. Not only Italy, but France, Germany, and Poland benefited by their apostolic labours, and their miracles made them famous. Finally, after having carried the good odour of Christ into distant lands, they went to God. In life they were one in their love of religion and of the brotherhood, in death they were united in one tomb and in the veneration of the people. Popes Clement XI. and Benedict XIII. confirmed the cultus which had been paid to them unitedly for many centuries. Leo XIII., having approved this devotion, and recognized the miracles wrought by God in answer to this collective invocation, proceeded to their formal canonization in the fiftieth year of his priesthood, and ordered that their Office and Mass should be said every year throughout the Church.

You made the sorrows of Mary your own, and now she shares her eternal joys with you. The vine with its miraculously ripening grapes, which prefigured your fruitfulness in a frozen world, still yields a sweet odour in this land of exile, and the faithful still appreciate its fruit. Philip and Juliana have long been honoured as branches of this blessed vine, and to-day we pay our homage to the seven-fold root from which they sprang. You rejoiced in the obscurity which covered the life upon earth of the Queen of saints herself, but to-day the glory of Mary pierces all clouds, and no shadow can withdraw the servants from the radiance which surrounds the Mistress. May your glory be increased by the favours you bestow upon men! Teach an aged world to seek warmth at the fire whence you draw a love strong enough to triumph over the world and sacrifice self for God.

O Heart of Mary, pierced by the sword of sorrow, furnace of love which throughout all eternity feeds the fires of the very Seraphim, be our model, our refuge, and our consolation until the dawn of that blissful day which is to be the end of our exile in this vale of tears.

MARCH 4

COMMEMORATION OF ST. LUCIUS, POPE AND MARTYR

ON this day a commemoration is made of St. Lucius, Pope and Martyr. He was a Roman by birth, and succeeded Pope Cornelius in 252. Shortly after his accession he was sent into exile by the Emperor Gallus, but was soon recalled, to the great joy of the Roman people. St. Cyprian quotes decrees issued by him against the Novatians. He died after a very short pontificate on March 4, 253. His relics were translated to the church of St. Cecilia, where they are exposed to the veneration of the Faithful.

26

ANTIPHON

Qui odit animam suam in hoc mundo, in vitam æternam custodit eam.

He that hateth his life in this world keepeth it unto life eternal.

OREMUS.

Deus qui nos beati Lucii Martyris tui atque Pontificis annua solemnitate lætificas : concede propit:us ; ut, cujus natalitia colimus, de ejusdem etiam protectione gaudeamus. Per Dominum.

LET US PRAY.

O God, who dost year by year give us joy in the feast of blessed Lucius, Thy Martyr and Pontiff, mercifully grant that, as we celebrate his birthday unto life eternal, so we may also rejoice in his protection.

Through our Lord.

March 6

SS. PERPETUA AND FELICITAS, MARTYRS

At the recent revision of the Breviary the office of this feast was changed, and the following lessons were appointed to be read at Matins :

Perpetua et Felicitas, in persecutione Severi imperatoris, in Africa, una cum Revocato, Saturnino et Se cundulo comprehensæ sunt, et in tenebricosum carcerem detrusæ, quibus ultra adjunctus est Satyrus. Erant adhuc catechumenæ, sed paulo post baptizatæ sunt. Paucis diebus interjectis, e carcere ad forum deductæ cum sociis, post gloriosam confessionem, ab Hilarione procuratore damnantur ad bestias. Inde hilares descendunt ad carcerem, ubi variis

Perpetua and Felicitas were arrested during the persecution of the Emperor Severus, in Africa, together with Revocatus, Saturninus, and Secundulus, and were cast into a darksome dungeon, where Satyrus was added to their company. They were as yet catechumens, but a short while after they were baptized. After a few days, they, with their companions, were led forth from their prison to the court, and, after a glorious confession, were condemned by the procurator

visionibus recreantur, et ad martyrii palmam accenduntur. Perpetuam, nec patris senio pene confecti iteratæ preces et lacrymæ, nec erga filium infantem pendentem ad ubera maternus amor, nec supplicii atrocitas, a Christi fide dimovere unquam potuerunt.

Hilarion to be thrown to the beasts. Thereupon they went down to their prison rejoicing, and while there were refreshed with divers visions, and fired with a longing for the martyr's palm. Neither the repeated prayers and tears of Perpetua's father, a man almost decrepit with old age, nor her motherly love for her baby son, still at the breast, nor the horror of the penalty, could avail at all to shake her faith in Christ.

Felicitas vero, instante spectaculi die, cum octo jam menses prægnans esset in magno erat luctu, ne differetur; leges quippe vetebant prægnantes supplicio affici. At precibus commartyrum accelerato partu, enixa est filiam. Cumque in partu laborans doleret, ait illi quidam de custodibus: Quæ sic modo doles, quid facies, objecta bestiis? Cui illa: Modo ego patior, illic autem alius erit in me, qui patietur pro me, quia et ego pro illo passura sum.

But Felicitas, when the day of the spectacle drew nigh, was in great grief lest it should be put off, seeing that she was eight months with child: for the law ordained that no woman with child should be put to the torture. But at the prayer of her fellow-martyrs her delivery was hastened, and she gave birth to a daughter. While she was groaning amid the pains of childbirth, one of the gaolers said to her: 'What wilt thou do when thou art thrown to the beasts, if thou groanest thus now?' She replied: 'Now it is I who suffer, but then Another will be within me who will suffer on my behalf, seeing that it is for Him that I am to suffer.'

In amphitheatrum, toto inspectante populo, producuntur tandem generosæ mulieres, Nonis Martii, ac primum flagellis cæduntur. Tunc a ferocissima vacca aliquamdiu jactatæ, plagis concisæ et in terram elisæ

At length the noble-hearted women were brought into the amphitheatre, in the sight of all the people, on the Nones of March (March 7). They were first beaten with scourges. Then they were tossed for some time by a

APPENDIX

sunt : demum cum sociis, qui a variis bestiis vexati fuerant, gladiorum ictibus conficiuntur. Harum sanctarum Martyrum festum Pius Decimus Pontifex Maximus ad ritum duplicem pro universa Ecclesia evexit, ac diei sextæ Martii adsignari mandavit.

ferocious cow, torn with wounds, and dragged on the ground ; and lastly, together with their companions, who had been attacked by divers wild beasts, they were slain by the sword. Pope Pius X. raised the feast of these holy martyrs to the rank of a double for the Universal Church, and ordered it to be kept on March 6.